C0-ASP-590

CAMBRIDGE LATIN AMERICAN STUDIES

62

A TROPICAL *BELLE EPOQUE*

CAMBRIDGE LATIN AMERICAN STUDIES

3 Peter Calvert. *The Mexican Revolution in 1910–1914: The Diplomacy of Anglo-American Conflict*
8 Celso Furtado. *Economic Development of Latin America: Historical Background and Contemporary Problems* (second edition)
10 D. A. Brading. *Miners and Merchants in Bourbon Mexico, 1763–1810*
15 P. J. Bakewell. *Silver Mining and Society in Colonial Mexico, Zacatecas 1564–1700*
22 James Lockhart and Enrique Otte. *Letters and People of the Spanish Indies: The Sixteenth Century*
31 Charles F. Nunn. *Foreign Immigrants in Early Bourbon Mexico, 1700–1760*
32 D. A. Brading. *Haciendas and Ranchos in the Mexican Bajio*
34 David Nicholls. *From Dessalines to Duvalier: Race, Colour and National Independence in Haiti*
38 D. A. Brading. *Caudillo and Peasant in the Mexican Revolution*
39 Joe Foweraker. *The Struggle for Land: A Political Economy of the Pioneer Frontier in Brazil from 1930 to the Present Day*
40 George Philip. *Oil and Politics in Latin America: Nationalist Movements and State Companies*
41 Noble David Cook. *Demographic Collapse: Indian Peru, 1520–1620*
42 Gilbert Joseph. *Revolution from Without: Yucatan, and the United States, 1880–1924*
43 B. S. McBeth. *Juan Vicente Gomez and the Oil Companies in Venezuela, 1908–1935*
44 J. A. Offner. *Law and Politics in Aztec Texcoco*
45 Thomas J. Trebat. *Brazil's State-Owned Enterprises: A Case Study of the State as Entrepreneur*
46 James Lockhart and Stuart B. Schwartz. *Early Latin America: A History of Colonial Spanish America and Brazil*
47 Adolfo Figueroa. *Capitalist Development and the Peasant Economy in Peru*
48 Norman Long and Bryan Roberts. *Miners, Peasants and Entrepreneurs: Regional Development in the Central Highlands of Peru*
49 Ian Roxborough. *Unions and Politics in Mexico: The Case of the Automobile Industry*
50 Alan Gilbert and Peter Ward. *Housing, the State and the Poor: Policy and Practice in Three Latin American Cities*
51 Jean Stubbs. *Tobacco on the Periphery: A Case Study in Cuban Labour History, 1860–1958*
52 Stuart B. Schwartz. *Sugar Plantations in the Formation of Brazilian Society: Bahia, 1550–1835*
53 Richard J. Walter. *The Province of Buenos Aires and Argentine Politics, 1912–1945*
54 Alan Knight. *The Mexican Revolution, vol. 1: Porfirians, Liberals and Peasants*
55 Alan Knight. *The Mexican Revolution, vol. 2: Counter-revolution and Reconstruction*
56 P. Michael McKinley. *Pre-revolutionary Caracas: Politics, Economy and Society*
57 Adriaan C. van Oss. *Catholic Colonialism: A Parish History of Guatemala, 1524–1821*
58 Leon Zamosc. *The Agrarian Question and the Peasant Movement in Colombia: Struggles of the National Peasant Association, 1967–1981*
59 Brian R. Hamnett. *Roots of Insurgency: Mexican Regions 1750–1824*
60 Manuel Caballero. *Latin America and the Comintern, 1919–1943*
61 Inga Clendinnen. *Ambivalent Conquests. Maya and Spaniard in Yucatan 1517–1570*

A TROPICAL *BELLE EPOQUE*

Elite culture and society in turn-of-the-century Rio de Janeiro

JEFFREY D. NEEDELL
Department of History, University of Florida

CAMBRIDGE UNIVERSITY PRESS
Cambridge
New York New Rochelle Melbourne Sydney

Published by the Press Syndicate of the University of Cambridge
The Pitt Building, Trumpington Street, Cambridge CB2 1RP
32 East 57th Street, New York, NY 10022, USA
10 Stamford Road, Oakleigh, Melbourne 3166, Australia

First published 1987

Printed in Great Britain at the University Press, Cambridge

British Library cataloguing in publication data

Needell, Jeffrey D.
A tropical belle époque: elite culture and society in turn-of-the-century
Rio de Janeiro. – (Cambridge Latin American studies).
1. Elite (Social sciences) – Brazil – Rio de Janeiro
I. Title
305.5′2′098153 HN190.Z9E4

Library of Congress cataloguing in publication data

Needell, Jeffrey D.
A tropical belle époque.
(Cambridge Latin American studies; 62)
Bibliography.
Includes index.
1. Elite (Social sciences) – Brazil – Rio de Janeiro – History – 19th century.
2. Rio de Janeiro (Brazil) – Social life and customs.
I. Title. II. Series.
HN290.Z9E4543 1987 305.5′2′098153 87-9399

ISBN 0 521 33374 1

CE

For my mother, Novella C. Belden

For many years, I planned to dedicate my first book to you.
Now I bring you this work; with whatever shortcomings it may have, it is the first, and it should be yours. You taught me the most important things.

". . . science has nothing to do with the usefulness or perversity of institutions. The social side of things is not proper to it, only the mechanical. Moreover, there is a principle of solidarity that links all the institutions of a country, the lottery and engineering."

Machado de Assis, "Balas de Estalo"

"Everything that is of the same time bears a resemblance; the artists who illustrate the poems of an epoch are the same whom the finance corporations employ."

Proust, *A l'ombre des jeunes filles en fleurs*

". . . attempt to capture the portrait of history in the most insignificent representations of reality, its scraps, as it were."

Benjamin, *Briefe*, II

Contents

Illustrations

Maps

Figures

Photographs

All photographs are published here by courtesy of the Oliveira Lima Library of the Catholic University of America in Washington, D.C., and are drawn from the contemporary reviews, *Kósmos* and *Renascença*, personal mementos, and rare books of the collection there.

Preface

Brazil cut her formal bonds to the Portuguese empire in 1822, only to continue in an informal economic colonialism long established with Britain. This neo-colonial economic status, increasingly strengthened over the course of the nineteenth century, was but one of a number of bonds to the global economic and political center ringing the North Atlantic. My concern is with the place of culture in this neo-colonial context.

The purpose of this study is to analyze the role of culture of European derivation in the social and economic structure of what was then Brazil's capital, Rio de Janeiro. I will focus on the group most involved with such culture, the Carioca elite, and on the period in which that culture enjoyed its florescence, 1898–1914 – the *belle époque*. The argument to be made is that elite culture and society served to maintain and promote the interests and vision of the elite, and that cultural paradigms of aristocratic European derivation were adapted in the Carioca milieu to those ends.

The present study, while focussing on the *belle époque*, will also encompass a study of elite socio-cultural trends over the nineteenth century, with emphasis on the Second Reign (1840–89), as the necessary historical context within which bases of *belle-époque* culture and society developed. In many ways, this is a history of institutions, both formal and informal, which were part and parcel of enduring tendencies in Brazilian society.

I undertook this work to explore two problems: one concerns culture and colonialism; the other, urban culture. As a student of colonialism in Latin America and Africa, I had come to see a common pattern in the relations between the colonized and the colonizers' culture that played out in three steps: conflict, adaptation, and rejection. The first represents the clash of cultures during the phase of conquest and colonial establishment; the second, the phase in which the colonized accept the colonists' hegemony and seek to rise by playing within the new rules of the game; the third, the phase when, after reaching the limits imposed by colonialism, the colonized react in frustration and disappointment, and, using elements of the hegemonic culture and remnants of their own, seek to remake their world, usually by way of anticolonial struggle and a self-consciously nationalist culture.

Such general notions describe only in the roughest terms the process in French and British Africa, say, or British India; in Latin America, they are only suggestive. Matters in this hemisphere are complicated by Latin America's distinct experience of colonialism, which ended sooner, and neo-colonialism, which actually paralleled the historical development of European high imperialism, coming to fruition in the period 1880–1914. Thus, what one has in this study is an attempt to analyze a "neo"-colonial culture going through the second phase of cultural colonialism described above. Culturally speaking, the differences seemed less important than the similarities to which the era was witness. I wanted to explore the nature and impact that such acceptance and adaptation of metropolitan culture would have at its high point. And I wanted to do so not from the surface, where so many of us have talked about "copying," and "cultural dependency," but from the inside, where foreign elements must commingle and join in a vital way with native ones.

The urban cultural impulse came from an idea in José Luis Romero's study of Latin American urban history,[1] in which he pointed out the ideological purpose of the urban metamorphosis that changed the cityscape of so many Latin American cities in the period 1870–1914. I was struck with his idea that a city might be remade to make an ideological point and to emphasize certain cultural values. Rio de Janeiro, along with Buenos Aires and Mexico City, is one of the cities that best illustrates Romero's point. I was interested in seeing how and analyzing why. The importance and meaning of such a shift, in the context of this truly crucial era of Latin American history, seemed compelling.

These starting points are the origins of the work to follow – they brought me to the general argument noted in the first three paragraphs above and they help to explain the organization of this study. I attempt to move from the most obvious material and institutional aspects of the elite's world to the more intimate and then the more intellectual. Given the cultural argument made, one will not be surprised to find the impact of metropolitan culture strongest at the more formal ends of the cultural spectrum (architecture and urban planning on the one hand, and literature and literary life on the other) and most elusive and complicated in the more informal, more "anthropological" region in between (the domestic ways of the elite). I have emphasized individuals' lives and experiences throughout, as the best way in to this past and, in the case of certain people, as unifying aspects to the disparate matters addressed. If something like a full sense of what the elite's world was emerges, and how and why it was, I shall be content. The theoretical points will have necessarily been made on the way.

Acknowledgments

By its nature, work of this sort is labor essentially carried out alone. However, although the choices, research, and style are one's own, one is aided in all of it by many others – if one is fortunate. I have been very fortunate. It is a pleasant obligation to acknowledge here those who have helped me on my way.

I first thought of this study in a graduate seminar taught by Richard M. Morse at Yale. Since the day I proposed the idea to him, Dr. Morse has steadfastly supported me in my endeavors to realize it with encouragement, criticism, introductions, suggestions, and good, hard questions. Indeed, some of the most personally satisfying parts of the pages that follow were written in answer to questions he raised. I am grateful for the pleasure of learning with him.

Other colleagues spurred me on: Richard Halpern and Dana Brand at Yale; Larry Jensen and Wylann Solomon at Yale and Stanford. Harold Mah has been a good listener, as has Richard Silver. Dain Borges has me in debt for good talk about theoretical and historical problems; Daniel Donaghy for searching methodological questions on my arrival in Rio. Samuel Adamo's research and commitment during our year in the archives were an inspiration.

Such an inquiry as this cannot succeed without the generosity and interest of people in the host country. I was particularly fortunate to be an *afilhado* of the Centro de Estudos Históricos of the Casa de Rui Barbosa in Rio. This favor I owe to Américo Jacobina Lacombe. Once there, I was welcomed and helped immeasurably by the Centro's director, Francisco de Assis Barbosa, who always found time to advise me and made possible most of the interviews so important to my work. Both in 1979–80 and in 1983, I was made to feel *à vontade* by staff and colleagues alike, among them José Murilo de Carvaho, Rosa Maria Barboza de Araújo, and Sérgio Pechman.

Others opened doors for me, as well. Isac Volchau, Tito Urbano da

Silveira, Maria Lêda de Moraes Chini, Diomar Silva Ramos, and especially, Esmeralda Peçanha de Paiva Coelho welcomed me to the Colégio Pedro II; Irmã Carmem Maria welcomed me in the Collège de Sion; and Hilda Alves de Souza did me the honors at the Automóvel Club do Brasil. José Honório Rodrigues introduced me to the Academia Brasileira de Letras; Janice Monte-Mór, Esther Bertoletti, and their staff made the Biblioteca Nacional and its periodicals accessible to me; Raul Lima introduced me to the Arquivo Nacional and Celina Moreira Franco to the Centro de Pesquisas e Documentação, at the Fundação Getúlio Vargas. At various times I also benefited from the advice and criticism of Plínio Doyle, José Gabriel Calmon da Costa Pinto, Alexandre Eulálio Pimenta da Cunha, Eulália Maria Lahmeyer Lobo, Antônio Dimas, Walnice Nogueira Galvão, Florestan Fernandes, Roberto Schwarz, Otávio Velho, and Gentil Luíz Faria. In 1983, I relied on the good graces and collegial support of the staff of the Museu da República, especially Lauryston Guerra and Izabel Salles Serzedello.

Certain staff people were indispensable for my success, especially in the Biblioteca Nacional, the Arquivo Nacional, the Arquivo Geral da Cidade do Rio de Janeiro, and the Real Gabinete Português de Leitura. Often, I never learned their names, as in the Biblioteca's Seção de Manuscritos, where the staff of 1979–80 was graciously professional. In the Biblioteca's Seção de Periódicos, I can at least thank two by their given names, Maria Lúcia and Lineo. In the Arquivo Nacional, I remain grateful to Ana and Eliseu Araújo Lima; in the Biblioteca of the Casa de Rui Barbosa, I am thankful to Maria Celina do Amarante; and in the U.S. Consulate in Rio, I was often indebted to Ilsa Viegas.

My debt to the fourteen people whom I interviewed is especially marked. Their grace and hospitality as they welcomed me into their homes and allowed me to ask about their families, their friends, their city, and their impressions compel my profound gratitude. Each, a survivor of the era of which I wrote, gave me more than facts and impressions of the vanished city – they gave me something of its nuance. Their names are listed as they should be, as formal sources at the end of the book. I grieve that some of them are no longer here to read my gratitude. To all of these people, who consented to interviews with an unknown foreigner, I am very thankful and appreciative. I cannot expect that they would have agreed with all of my conclusions, but I know that they would have respected the thought and care with which I have arrived at them.

Since my return and through the years of writing and revision, I have profited immensely from the interested and critical reading of John

Wirth, Paul Robinson, Carl Degler, Efraín Kristal, Walnice Nogueira Galvão, Thomas Hart, and Juan Armando Épple. I am especially thankful to Joseph Love, whose sympathetic criticism encouraged me to make substantial and useful additions to the original manuscript. Finally, I would like to express my gratitude to my copyeditor, Margaret Jull Costa, for making what was often obscure and awkward, clear and graceful.

I also wish to record my thanks to those who made the technical preparation of this work possible: Phillip Fletcher, the consultants and staff at Stanford's Center for Information Technology, Enid Scofield, Kit Larson, John Nichols, and the staff at the Smithsonian's Office of Information Resource Management. I especially want to mention the help of Allan Needell in this regard; his patience and expertise staved off panic and disaster more than once.

Such research and writing as this depend on the financial and institutional generosity of others. I am grateful to be able to write of the support of those who sustained me and, more recently, my wife, and thus gave me the opportunity to pursue and complete this study. I enjoyed a "Mini-Grant" for summer research in Rio (1978) from the Council for Latin American Studies at Yale. My year abroad (1979–80) was made possible by a Full Grant from the Fulbright-Hays Commission and a Dissertation Fellowship from the Social Science Research Council. The SSRC also made my attendance possible at a conference on Latin American social history in New York (May 1980) and extended write-up support to me on my return to Stanford. It is a special pleasure to mention the support of the Danforth Foundation, whose flexibility with my Fellowship made my last two years of graduate work relatively free for research and writing. I am indebted to Stanford's Department of History and Center for Latin American Studies for technical expenses, to the Center for a congenial place to work, and to the generosity of the Mary McLeod Lewis Memorial Fund for a year of write-up support. Last, I thank the University of Oregon's Graduate School for a Summer Faculty Research Award, which facilitated travel to Rio in 1983.

In concluding, I have families to thank. My mother, brother, and two sisters stood by me with faith and love through all these years, despite my constant absences and time-consuming preoccupations. I would like to state again how much their confidence in me and their affection have meant to me over the years of work away from them. I hope that, when they read this study, something of the pleasure it has offered me will be shared.

My other family is the gift of my wife, Maria de Fátima Lima Maia de Needell. Her brothers and sisters and their families have taught me much about Brazil, and have shown me its greatest treasures – the warmth and generosity of its people, and their sensitivity to the difficulties and pleasures of life. Their acceptance and affection continue to quicken my attachment to their country and my abiding desire to return. I would hope that some day something born of my time with them in Rio will appear in Portuguese. Nothing could please me more than to share with them something that they helped me to create.

Most women enjoy courtship, their wedding, and their first years of marriage alone with their husbands and families. My wife, Fátima, has had this study along with us as an awkward guest since the day we met. She has welcomed it with grace and understanding, made me happy, and supported my efforts with untiring faith, patience, and, in desperate circumstances, her skill, strength, and resolve. She has done all of this while enduring exile from her own country and the absence of her family and friends, and while undertaking the successful conquest of a new language and culture. I write this not to say that I am grateful – that must continue to be shown in better ways – but to bear witness to her part in what I have been able to do in the pages that follow.

Washington, 1987 JEFFREY D. NEEDELL

A note on Brazilian Portuguese orthography and usage

I follow standard scholarly usage here by employing modern Brazilian Portuguese spelling, except in citations, where the original orthography is respected. This will result in considerable variation, both in letters and diacritical marks. Regarding names, I follow Brazilian usage in referring to persons by the names by which they are generally known after my initial reference, in which I generally try to give all of their names, bracketing those left aside in normal use. In the citations, the first citation of a work will have all of the author's names and the full title (but no subtitle) of the work; thereafter, I employ only the author's last family name(s), except in the case where several authors with the same family names require that initials be used to distinguish between authors. The bibliography at the end of the book is organized according to the author's last family name, except in those cases where another family name is commonly cited instead (e.g., Nabuco [de Araújo] is used there instead of Araújo, in the case of Joaquim [Aureliano Barreto] Nabuco [de Araújo]). In the cases where the author's given names are generally used instead of his family names, I will cite by the last family name, since this is what is generally used in the library catalogues (e.g., Sousa is used here instead of Cândido, in the case of Antônio Cândido [de Melo e Sousa]).

1

Rio de Janeiro: Capital of the Brazilian nineteenth century

The *belle époque* in Rio can be dealt with as both the culmination of specific long-term trends and as a new phenomenon, signaling a unique phase of Brazilian cultural history. The present study will discuss the period in both senses. Still, I have found that the discussion and analysis of any aspect of the *belle époque* touches on matters that have long, matted roots in the general Carioca past. It seems important, then, to begin by introducing the historical and urban context which will inform so much of what follows. As elite social and cultural history in Rio will be the stuff of the latter, I take the opportunity here to sketch the national and urban realities with which the Carioca grappled.

1. The Empire: change and challenge (1868–88)

The institutions of the Empire of Brazil had been elaborated in the second quarter of the nineteenth century; by the end of the third, realities were obviously quite different. Independent Brazil's first political edifice conformed to terrain shaped by a planter society, mainly confined to a thin, coastal strip of port cities and their immediate hinterlands, with the vast interior barely known or populated. It was a society divided between masters and slaves, plantations and ports, a society defined by two strata. One, big with wealth and power, made up of white planters and merchants; the other, big in numbers, made up of black and mulatto slaves and freedmen and their descendants: plantation workers, house servants, artisans, plantation "hands," urban workers, impoverished sharecroppers and small farmers. These strata made up the two great weights that pressed between them a thin, generally urban-based stratum of middle sectors: liberal professionals, petty bureaucrats, clerical workers, and small shopkeepers.[1]

From the decadent gold and diamond works of Minas Gerais and the old sugar region of the Northeastern provinces, the center of export dynamism had moved to the South-central coffee plantations in the provinces of Rio de Janeiro, São Paulo and Minas Gerais. But this was more a shift in the location of the predominant socio-economic structures, not in their nature. Changes in the pace of work, in the level of technology, and in the degree and complexity of entrepreneurial activity might occur, but the old social order of a small agro-export elite, a servile mass of workers, and a thin stratum of middle sectors, an order derived from a plantation society producing a crop for the international market, remained.[2]

The Brazil that emerged from the war with Paraguay (1865–70) was already different. Three changes were fundamental. First, the urban entrepots had grown as population, cultural, and infrastructural centers – which made them political centers in a new way. Now they were no longer primarily the meeting places of a rural-based elite and its commercial allies. They were also much more the bailiwicks of urban-based liberal professionals, bureaucrats, entrepreneurs, shop-keepers, and students, people with readier access to European thought and examples, free of the direct influence of the great landowners who ruled the countryside and who had thus far imposed their will on the nation. The political challenge nascent in the towns from late colonial times, with their urban conspiracies and revolts and their taste for European models for change, was taking on greater weight.[3]

Second, slavery, identified with Brazil since its beginning, was doomed. The end of the transatlantic slave trade between 1850 and 1852 and the inability of the slave population to reproduce itself sufficiently assured the planters that slavery must inevitably die. Yet, as only the expanding South-central coffee region was in dire need of labor, and the internal slave trade from the decadent Northeast seemed adequate for the time being, the immediate danger was seen to loom elsewhere. From the 1860s on, the political threat of abolition flickered with increasing insistence, a fundamental challenge to the old order.[4]

Third, while the monarchy's established political organization and circles continued to serve the old elites of the Northeast and the hinterlands of Rio de Janeiro, the appetites of newer elites went unattended. São Paulo shouldered more of the burden of the State as its phenomenal westward coffee expansion generated increasing tax revenues. Though the plantation areas tied to Rio began their decline in coffee production in the 1880s, the Province of São Paulo would, by that time, begin the climb to leadership. But, while they observed the growth of their relative economic strength and share of the tax burden, *paulista* planters also knew their political power remained small. They chafed at the disproportionate advantages, favors, and spoils going to the once-great provinces, while the hand of the Crown in their affairs seemed mostly to grasp and interfere.[5]

Another source of dissatisfaction among the newer elites derived from State recruitment. The two traditional parties, Liberal and Conservative, as well as the Empire's upper bureaucracy, had traditionally been dominated by men from Portugal, the old Northeastern provinces, and the more recent elites in the coffee region first established in Rio de Janeiro and the edges of São Paulo and Minas. The older generation, important up to and beyond the mid-nineteenth century, were trained in Coimbra or among the first classes of the newly established law faculties of Recife and São Paulo. The younger generation were men trained exclusively at the Brazilian faculties. The group as a whole tended to be interrelated within and across the generations, and such nepotism naturally blocked the advance of an increasing number of eligible *bacharéis* at a time when the absolute number of places grew very slowly.

The region whose sons were most likely to suffer from this was São Paulo, where the number of families newly able to support sons through the local faculty was bound to be disporportionately large, and where the number of fathers and uncles able to pull the proper strings was bound to be disproportionately small. Moreover, the locale likely to focus this *bacharel* frustration most severely was the urban one. There, the sons of planters who no longer could, or no longer would, try to maintain their traditional status on the land sought to make a way for themselves in the bureaucracy. This gave an edge to the political partisan struggles over places and to the increasingly bitter attacks on the entrenched establishment of the monarchy. In either case, this particular elite interest in successful promotion within the imperial hierarchy, left unattended, had dangerous results. It added fire to the dissatisfaction of the new *paulista* elite and the growing number of urban-based *bacharéis*.[6]

It was against these broad changes, then, that the institutions of the monarchy were pitted after 1868. The challenge was to be formulated in two political movements: Republicanism and Abolitionism.

The date traditionally associated with the beginning of the end, 1868, derives from a political crisis originating in the debilitating circumstances of the Paraguayan War. The Emperor, forced to choose between supporting the general on whom his hopes of victory rested and the president of the current ministry, chose to back the general. The latter, Luís Alves de Lima e Silva, Marquis, and later Duke, de

Caxias, long the favorite of the monarch, was a stalwart Conservative. He led the Emperor to believe that he would resign his command if he had to continue in obedience to the Progressive Liberal ministry in power, a ministry whose confidence in himself he doubted. The leader of the ministry, seeing the direction of Pedro's nod, found a way to resign that made the contradictions of the monarchy's constitutional powers dramatically clear. He left when the Emperor, in consultation with the Conservative-dominated Council of State, chose to exercise his usual right to select from among the usual three proposed senatorial candidates for a vacant seat in an unusual, and quite provocative, manner. The Emperor picked as senator the candidate who had neither the plurality of the provincial vote nor the approval of the Progressive Liberal ministry.

The Chamber expected that the Emperor would follow the usual custom after the ministry's resignation, and summon another Progressive Liberal chieftain to organize the next ministry, in conformity with the party represented by the Chamber's majority. Instead, the Emperor, seeking to ensure the happy conclusion of the war, broke with the usage. He called a Conservative to the palace, hoping to secure a ministry which would enjoy solid relations with Caxias. The Chamber, naturally, voted no confidence in the new ministry; the Emperor then followed through, dissolving the Chamber and allowing the ministry to "arrange" the next election and the inevitable return of a loyal, Conservative majority. The Progressive Liberals were indignant, termed the maneuver a *coup d'état*, and, in a rage, attacked the basic institutions of the regime.[7]

This event galvanized all Liberal factions; over the next ten years of exile from ministerial power many bound themselves together and attacked the Conservatives and the Emperor. One faction, though, went further. While most Liberals drew the line at reformist proposals for limitations on the Emperor's constitutional powers and championship of the new cause of Abolition, this faction issued a Republican Manifesto (1870) calling for an end to the monarchy. Later (1873), *paulista* republicans organized a party apparatus for their province. That the Manifesto and the *paulista* organization did not embrace Abolition and that the *paulistas* quickly organized their province is suggestive of two crucial characteristics of Republicanism. First, its leadership, largely divided between Rio and São Paulo, was interested in the success of its political goals and, to reach them, eschewed divisive socio-economic ones. Second, only one of the two poles of the new movement was based on a well-organized party with province-wide membership. While the

Rio ideologues were largely urban-based until the late 1880s, the *paulista* Republicans had early support among the rural-based elite.[8]

Men drawn from the new planter elite of São Paulo saw in the Republic a redistribution of power more amenable to their regional interests. They envisioned a decentralized federation, with each unit enjoying its respective revenues and ruled by its local elite-elected representatives. The weight of such men among the party's founders probably accounts for the opportune evasion of the Abolition issue.[9]

The other basis for Republicanism was quite distinct. It was that pool of urban-based men caught up in a passion for a new Brazil, one opposed to the agrarian realities with which the *paulista* elite was quite content. This concept of a new Brazil varied among its proponents, but a common hope involved the nation's regeneration according to political models provided by the US and French republicans. Even more common were proponents of a Brazil impelled forward by the same engines of modernity proven in the industrializing countries of the North Atlantic. Such men would count among their numbers place-seeking *bacharéis*; students in the law faculties, medical schools, and the Carioca military and polytechnic schools; graduates of such places who had found positions in the State apparatus or in professional careers; and many of the entrepreneurs who started emerging in the century's third quarter. All of these resented the restrictions traditionally imposed on business, industry, and mobility by a conservative, agriculturally-minded political establishment.[10]

If the *paulista* group provided the weight of men of substance, its link to elements in the nation's agro-export elite, the second provided many of the ideologues and conspirators, located in the strategic urban center of the nation. Thus, the impetus among the Republicans often came from Rio during the conspiratorial and revolutionary phase of the movement, but the Republic itself would see São Paulo move inevitably to take command. Only the *paulista* Republicans possessed the links to the preponderant class strength represented by the elite, a socio-economic base for power the urban-based middle-sector elements in the movement necessarily lacked.

The movement for Abolition, though preceded by precursors as early as the Independence period, and both awakened and temporarily contained by limited imperial reforms (1871), really began its career in the last decade of the Empire. The movement for the Republic was one which joined urban middle-sector and both rural and urban-based elite elements against the relatively recent institution of the monarchy. Abolition was quite different. It attracted, until the last moments (and then for the most blatantly opportunistic reasons), almost exclusively urban elements (from all strata, though primarily from the same middle sort), because it struck at something much more deeply rooted than the monarchy. It struck at the very basis of the centuries-old rural structure over which the planter elite, new and old alike, presided.[11]

The Abolitionists of the 1880s, after seeing their hopes of parliamentary success apparently blocked, organized into what were effectively two distinct, complementary wings. One sought reform through propaganda, going outside the Chamber to the theaters and the streets, appealing to the urban middle sectors and masses. The other coupled propaganda with illegal activity, from putting together an underground railroad to calls for slave resistance and rebellion. But even the legal wing, in its rhetoric at mass meetings, its court actions, and its radical socio-economic analyses calling for electoral, social, and land reform, threatened the established order. French constitutionalist Eclecticism of the Second Reign, which had served elite consensus by smothering the ideological fervor of the First Reign and the Regency with decorous drapery, now wore thin. It shriveled with the Romantic fire of the journalists and poets of Abolition. It crumbled before the materialist arguments of critics reared in the newest European thought at the law faculties or in the charged intellectual milieu of the schools and periodicals of the Côrte.

By the latter part of the 1880s, Abolition loomed, the triumph of a galvanized urban movement over increasingly splintered planter elites. Elite division derived from varying regional circumstances. The older coffee areas in Rio de Janeiro and Minas, with their soil exhausted, their coffee quality inferior, and their financial situation ominous, were headed by staunchly pro-slavery elites, desiring to protect their living collateral and unable to finance a shift to free labor. The planters of the Northeast, the North, and the province of São Paulo were less single-minded, albeit for varying reasons.

The Northeast, with its depressed economy, generally depended less on a thriving slave supply and could count on holding what labor it might need in other forms of bondage after abolition. Indeed, the area had been selling its slaves south for some time. Except for Bahia (whose elite still defended large investments in slaves, the legacy of a relatively recent prosperity), the movement for Abolition made great inroads there. The North was considerably more divided. Amazonas, never greatly dependent on African slavery for its economy of extraction, was least threatened. The Indian dependants who brought their *patrões* forest products would remain in local forms of bondage, after all; the elite could afford idealistic gestures. In Maranhão and Pará, however, fierce opposition reflected the entrenched interests of an elite whose precarious rural investments were identified with slavery. Yet again, in Ceará, poverty and sales had reduced slavery to negligible importance and it, like Amazonas, would lead the Abolitionist trend. Finally, São Paulo, riding a cresting wave of coffee expansion, drove its slaves hard and fought Abolition until the last year or so, the firm ally of the powerful "slavocratic" forces of Rio de Janeiro, Bahia, and Minas. However, when the militant actions of radical Abolitionists succeeded in reaching the plantations themselves, the *paulistas* began to shift tactics desperately. The traditional fear of social upheaval was always wonderfully persuasive.

Free immigrant labor, disdained since the failure of mid-century experiments, suddenly became palatable as slaves began to abandon the fields and talk of revolts and an attack on *latifundia* began to gain force. Pressed to the wall, the *paulistas* abandoned the *fluminense* and *mineiro* slavocrats, and turned Abolitionist. They apparently hoped to contain the movement's revolutionary potential by acceding to its most prominent demand, which was, in any case, increasingly a *fait accompli*. Some hoped to retain many of their former slaves by granting manumission *en masse*, others struggled indignantly for abolition with compensation. Most called for State subsidization of immigration.

It was this pattern of elite division and surrender in an ambience electric with the threat of social upheaval and charged by the throne's undisguised pro-abolitionist sympathies that made Abolition possible in 1888. But it was only a partial victory. The next step contemplated by many, that of larger socio-economic reforms, would be another matter. Reformers would find that elite landholdings, political domination, and agro-export orientation were much more strongly defended.

2. The Republic: the coup (1889)[12]

The Brazilian army, relatively weak before the Paraguayan War, was thrust by the conflict into bloody sacrifice and a new strength and national prominence. Afterwards, the officers were reluctant to resign themselves to their service's previous insignificance. They feared the Army's being neglected, and not without reason. Years of mismanaged, bloody grinding away at the Paraguayan military machine had instilled resentment and contempt for the representatives of the elite in Parliament. Veterans felt strongly that they had paid dearly for the indifference and incompetence of a self-satisfied, corrupt civilian elite. They blamed that elite for Brazil's material "backwardness" and its consequent military weakness.[13] Such veterans occupied the higher ranks by the 1880s. The lower ranks were even more restless, for they were made up of officers recently graduated from noted centers of socio-political criticism: the military schools of Rio.

Children of the urban-based middle strata or the rural small proprietors generally had only two ways to secure a superior degree and the prestige and position generally consequent upon it. They might enter the seminary (more common in the century's earlier years) or the Army's technical schools (a common choice in the century's later years).[14] The Escola Militar, founded by João VI in 1808, divided into two schools in 1858 – the Escola Militar and the Escola Central (which was renamed the Escola Politécnica in 1874) – both of which continued to teach the sciences integral to both military needs and material progress. Indeed, many of the students were probably more interested in such studies than military service; they were the medium for anyone seeking a degree in engineering or in other fields integral to the new opportunities made plain in the advances of Europe and the United States. The schools were the training ground for many of the most ambitious, committed, urban-based "modernizers."[15]

These students, whether under the direct influence of such positivists as Benjamin Constant [de Botelho Magalhães] (1837–91) or not, absorbed the scientism diffuse in contemporary European thought and commonly saw themselves as scientifically trained servants of their nation's future – selfless, embattled agents for the *pátria*'s "modernization." They often perceived the established ruling class as their natural opposition: a force holding Brazil back and keeping it weak merely to continue promoting elite agro-export interests and providing sinecures for elite members and their creatures. It seems superfluous to say that such officers were generally Republicans. The Monarchy, bastion of the old order, had no place in their hopes for a "modern" Brazil.

Though prestigious senior officers, such as [Manuel] Deodoro da Fonseca (1827–92) or Floriano [Vieira] Peixoto (1839–95) were of older generations, they did share a sense of antagonism toward the established elite's political representatives. This, as suggested above, sprang from their devotion to the Army, which Paraguay had shaped and tempered with a sharp resentment and suspicion of politicians. This would be the key to their politicization. After 1883, the so-called Military Question arose, unifying the generations as officers, despite disciplining, repeatedly asserted their right to take public positions or question the judgment of their civilian superiors. They organized into Military

Clubs, put Deodoro at their head, protested, and took a belligerent stand against the Emperor's ministers. It would take the Republican ideologues of Rio, however, to hurl them against the Emperor himself.[16]

Though Republican moderates had discarded the idea of an alliance with the Army initially, both radicals and moderates soon embraced it. At first, they only increased the tensions, playing on the officers' sense that their honor was impugned, their rights scorned, and the like. Then, however, thinking beyond the mere creation of problems for the regime, they began, in conjunction with Republicans among the younger officers, to consider a military coup.[17]

The time was propitious. The planter elites, by the end of the 1880s, had seen slavery eliminated under the auspices of the throne and the Conservative Party (which had held the ministry presiding over Abolition in 1888). They had also long come to see both of the old imperial parties, the Crown, indeed, the constitution itself, as abused, abusing, and generally discredited.

I have noted how members of the most dynamic force among the elites, the *paulistas*, had begun to see the centralized monarchy as an institution favoring older regions; by the late 1880s, they also viewed it as a parasite which strengthened the established Rio-based financial interests which were successfully exploiting the expanding *paulista* economy. In addition, the most conservative force in support of the Crown, the older regions' planters, was now terribly weakened. They had not only lost their slaves and, thus, collateral, but, as mentioned earlier, did so in the midst of the marked decline of their coffee. Moreover, even to such people, the future of their anomalous American monarchy, headed by a sick old man and to be taken up by a reformist heiress and her unpopular foreign consort, seemed dubious. Finally, new political reforms and the explicit threat of further socio-economic reforms, possibly under Crown patronage itself, were far from dubious.[18]

Thus, precisely at the time the Army completed its swing into opposition and the radical younger officers and civilians began to plan a Republican coup, the natural support of the Monarchy was vitiated. When the last ministry attempted to disarm the Republican movement by embracing many of its reforms, it was too late to co-opt the radicals and too early to win over the reactionaries. The Chamber voted no confidence and was in turn dissolved by the ministry.

In brief order, the Military Question erupted, the Republicans exploited it, rumors of blows against the Army and its leader, Deodoro, were spread, and the latter was finally won over to a Republican conspiracy. In a confused series of events on 15 November 1889, the ministry and, then, the throne were toppled. A Provisional Government headed by Deodoro and noted Republicans was quickly formed, and the imperial family shipped to Europe.

Some few monarchists cast about futilely to make a counterrevolution or waited vainly for the signal. Many soon went into exile, political seclusion, or useless conspiracy. But most in the traditional elites adhered to the new order and bided their time. For the moment, power in the capital had passed from their hands and into those of the Army and the radical Republicans, who had joined together to make a new Brazil.[19]

3. The Republic: the challenge of the radicals (1890–4)

Beneath the confusion of the next several years, a revolutionary struggle was fought. New urban-based groups tried to wrest away direction of the State from the regional planter elites and their allies. Simultaneously, elements of those elites began building new local political machines and a new national consensus which would respond to changed decentralized regional circumstances and still ensure their national domination.

The record suggests the violence resulting from such crossed purposes. In 1889, a Provisional Government was proclaimed after the military coup. In 1891, a Constituent Assembly created a federal constitution and obediently elected Deodoro and Floriano President and Vice-President. Later that year, Deodoro, attempting a coup against the first Congress, was foiled in a counter-coup by Floriano, who took over the presidency. In 1893, a civil war in Rio Grande do Sul was followed by a naval revolt in Rio's harbor, two struggles whose leaders allied and fought the Republic bitterly until 1895. In 1896, a local rebellion in the Bahian backlands, blown up by repeated Republican defeats into a major threat, required the best efforts of the Army to be put down, finally, in 1897. In that same year, the first civilian president narrowly escaped assassination by a petty officer. And, from beginning to end, all these events were marked by the debilitating impact of a tremendous economic "boom and bust" cycle, initiated by a period of inflation, investment, and speculation known as the *Encilhamento*.

Rio, Brazil's financial center, had known such oscillations before. The *praça* had seen a new surge of credit and capitalization in banks, infrastructure, and manufacturing in the mid-1850s; a crisis in credit resulting in bank failures in 1864; and another such crisis in 1873–8. All of these events were conditioned by Brazil's position in the world economy. As a peripheral agricultural producer exporting to the North Atlantic center, the health of Brazil's economy was established by good harvests and the prices to be had for her crops. The nature of the cycle for investment, planting, and marketing created a need for credit, which reinforced dependency on the center, the ultimate source of most credit. Other, peculiar circumstances derived from planters' debts being secured by collateral in human flesh, so that when abolition threatened, the planters' ability to command credit weakened. Finally, its meager industrial development forced Brazil to exchange export-earned capital for foreign manufactured and luxury goods – the most traditional colonial exchange. The results were a financial system typically short on capital and credit, subject to exchange-rate speculation, and very sensitive to the accidents of crop failure or disease, a fall in prices, reluctance in the center's money market, the threat of abolition, and the slow decline born of soil exhaustion.[20]

By 1888 all of these factors were bearing down, especially in the former mainstay of the coffee economy, the Paraíba Valley of the provinces of Rio de Janeiro and São Paulo. To salvage the situation, the last imperial ministries had combined a large foreign loan and increased emissions through an unprecedented, government-sponsored, newly consolidated banking structure. The hope was to provide easy credit to planters to get the economy (and monarchy) through the crisis.[21]

The results were unexpected, complicated by the hesitation of foreign capital occasioned by the 1889 coup. The initial imperial phase had already led to inflation and speculation, born of new, easy credit. Now, however, the foreign credit necessary to sustain the basis for emission dried up. Minister of Finance Rui Barbosa apparently decided the solution was continued emissions, based on bonds issued, again, by centralized banks linked to the State by privileges and guarantees and empowered to act as entrepreneurial agents in the expanding market for investment and credit such policies ensured. His policies went beyond protecting the fragile financial position of the State in the Republic's first year;[22] he also saw such policies as central to re-shaping the country.

The economic assumption dominating the imperial ruling class had been that Brazil was a natural producer of agricultural exports in the international division of labor. There had been no policy of industrial support. With the new access to power of urban-based groups and military radicals, many of whom were quite removed from established agro-export interests and firmly committed to Brazil's metamorphosis along North Atlantic lines, change was to be expected.[23]

Industrialization had heretofore found its way into the urban milieu through nooks and crannies provided by import taxes (designed for revenue, but yielding protection), periods of devaluation (making imports dear), and the odd years of more plentiful investment capital (such as the period following the end of the slave trade in 1850–2). By 1890, however, the situation in Rio had become more amenable to industrialization. The Carioca population was nearing half a million, the domestic market was improving with expansion in the native and immigrant wage-earning sector, the comparative risk of investment in agriculture had increased, the value of the currency against imports had declined, and cheap labor was arriving from the rural areas, Portugal, and Italy.[24] Rui felt the time was ripe. The new minister threw his considerable political weight behind an enormous expansion of credit and liberalization of business regulation, with the State heavily committed at every step of the way.[25]

The results were a boom of stock market activity, the foundation of numerous new companies and banks, and pervasive speculation and corruption. Expansion lasted until 1892. It was followed by a ruinous crash, worsened by the military expenditure in the 1893–5 revolts. Difficulties were exacerbated by exchange speculation in which the bankers, especially the foreign representatives, made large profits.[26]

The word *Encilhamento* suggests how the epoch was perceived. The name, in common use almost immediately, was borrowed from race-course jargon for the saddling-up before the starting gun.[27] And, for the entrepreneurs, financiers, and speculators in the *praça* and the bureaucrats and go-betweens on the inside, it was a race well run. *Nouveaux riches* popped up in a milieu of unprecedented luxury consumption. But the aftertaste for many of the traditional elite was bitter. Many of them lost heavily, and the arrival of others was resented. The *Encilhamento* passed into elite memory, and thence to that of the general public, as an epoch of chimerical development and frenzied speculation in enterprises of dubious integrity, undertaken by dupes and charlatans.[28]

That the foundation for a growing secondary sector was laid in banking, transportation, textiles, insurance, etc., was ignored or unknown, as was the imperial origin of the *Encilhamento*.[29] Instead, the boom and crash served to taint the early Republic's financial policy as one of incompetence and corruption. Further, it helped to divide the Republican leadership and increase the volatile tensions in the urban masses and middle sectors (whose employment and cost of living suffered most)[30] and, thus, undercut the efforts of the urban-based radicals and their allies to consolidate. This was the era when Deodoro slid into his struggle with other men and forces crucial to the Republic, and it was in the shambles of the collapse that Floriano was left the desperate task of the Republic's defense.[31]

Floriano, however, identified with the purifying, "modernizing" values of his younger military colleagues, reached out to similarly-minded civilians with a singular success. His followers were called both *jacobinos* (after the French Revolution's *jacobins*) and *florianistas*. They were junior officers, military cadets, petty bureaucrats and government workers, students, liberal professionals, clerical workers, journalists, and the like.

These sorts of people, along with all urban wage-earners, had suffered terribly over the last third of the century, and had not lacked for spokesmen to show them why. The rising cost of living, the lack of opportunity or job security, rampant nepotism and unemployment, onerous taxes, and economic backwardness – all of these were inflicted by the political representatives of the planters and the big merchants, or so they were told. It was from these city-dwellers that Abolition and the Republic, as ideals of national redemption and progress, had found their firmest supporters during the 1880s, and it was among them that the Republic now found its shock troops and zealots as it was challenged by rebellions that quickly took on, or were given, a monarchist color.[32] To this was added the popular hatred of the Portuguese, perennial urban shopkeeper and entrepreneur, whom the Cariocas commonly perceived as a parasite and an obstacle to Brazilian economic and political aspirations.[33]

Lusophobia and hatred of the *ancien régime* were aspects of a movement which also embraced the ideal of an authoritarian, inclusionary, industrial, modern Brazil, enjoying economic expansion and social melioration.[34] A decade of increasingly militant urban demogoguery, a keen nose for putative monarchist plotting, and the very real danger posed by a monarchist fleet bombarding the city had all rallied such urban elements. They were ready for resistance and reprisal, and were characterized by a sensitive, paranoid kind of patriotism, in which Brazil, Republic, and the radicals' struggle for political power and socio-economic change were identified as one.[35]

The *jacobinos* were encouraged in this identification by Floriano himself. This still-mysterious figure, who dominated the contemporary political imagination, kept his own counsel and moved decisively to protect his regime. Martial law, civilian volunteer battalions, acceptance of *jacobino* street violence, the denial of rights traditionally accorded political opposition – Floriano used them all to resist rebels, crush internal opposition, and consolidate the threatened Republic, with coffers left bled nearly dry by several successive finance ministers.[36]

In the end, Floriano's successes gained him the sobriquet "Iron Marshal" and idolization among urban middle sectors and military circles, as well as in the positivist ranks of the newly established state government of Rio Grande do Sul, allied to Floriano in the struggle against the common enemies that had taken up their rebel stand in that state.[37] But, among Republican and traditional elite opponents, these same successes stimulated a visceral loathing. Floriano was reviled by these elements as a bloody dictator, as merciless, cold, and cunning, a brutal soldier demagogue, foreign to the genteel parliamentary tradition of the Côrte.[38] Ironically, it was the desperate struggle of 1891–4, out of which fervent popular republicanism and the legend of Floriano emerged, that made possible the emergence of a newly powerful coalition among elements of the traditional and emergent elite. And this coalition would preside over a Republic quite different from that of which many ideologues and devotees had dreamt.

4. The Republic: the planters' return to power (1889–1902)

That the Republicans of São Paulo should be more conservative and accommodating has much to do with class interests. A substantial portion of the party and its leadership were planters, and the others, even urban residents, were dominated by agro-export concerns because all economic and political interests in the province were closely dependent on coffee planting and export. Thus, most *paulista* Republicans represented not so much a break with the old elite as the most liberal of its wings. Their fundamental interest in the Republic settled on desires for São Paulo's economic autonomy and political hegemony.

Thus, it is not a surprise to find such Republicans were able to take over the old province without much resistance and admit erstwhile monarchists of the highest rank into the ruling councils. Where most other traditional provincial elites maneuvered through the hypocrisies of eleventh-hour or post-facto conversion to the Republic to remain in, or regain, power, and Rio Grande do Sul was plunged into a ferocious civil war between two elite-run factions vying for control, São Paulo's elite had an easier time of it. They merely accepted the new prominence of one of their factions, which, in turn, incorporated the others. Their fundamental interests, after all, were the same.[39]

Among these interests, once federal autonomy was assured, were national stability and the projection of São Paulo's concerns into national policy (especially the reestablishment of foreign credit to sustain and promote the agro-export complex). To secure these, the *paulistas* apparently decided on cautious cooperation with, and insertion into, the national administrations of the early 1890s. Their most prestigious leaders, both Republican and ex-monarchist, went to Rio and took up portfolios in the ministries of the era, attempting to shore up the new regime, even under Floriano, while awaiting the opportunity to capture it. Among the more important were [Manuel Ferraz de] Campos Sales, Prudente [José] de Morais [e Barros], and [Francisco de Paula] Rodrigues Alves (all of whom were subsequently presidents), as well as Bernardino de Campos and Francisco Glicério [de Cerqueira Leite], crucial party men in the early struggles of the Republic.[40] Their historic Republican credentials even made Campos Sales and Prudente candidates for the presidency and vice-presidency as early as 1891. But that was still too early; the Constituent Assembly, overawed by the Army, elected Deodoro and Floriano, as noted.

By 1893–4, however, the nation's desperate situation forced São Paulo's preeminence as the price of the Republic's survival. By then, that state, with its solidly organized elite, its superior economy, and its own armed forces, was clearly preponderant – the crisis made it indispensable. Floriano, fearing an invasion from the rebels in Rio Grande, needed the shield of São Paulo between him and the southern thrust. In exchange, he apparently agreed to the "election" of Prudente de Morais. Despite rumors of a *florianista* coup, the planter took office in 1894. Shortly thereafter, in 1895, Floriano died, along with the rebellion in the south, and the process of national conciliation and consolidation under a reorganized, traditionally-oriented elite seemed to be emerging.[41]

Prudente's administration represents the retreat from the revolutionary charge sounded during Floriano's. Prudente was the choice of what had been newly organized during Floriano's regime as the official party of the Republic, and he was firmly allied to its chief, a *paulista*, Francisco Glicério. But the party reflected the still inchoate nature of the Republic, in which the passion of emergent urban forces without political skill or decisive strength was matched against the still reorganizing forces of the various regional elites. Political conflict soon erupted between the more conservative pro-administration forces and the *jacobinos*, who mounted a strident campaign against a regime they felt was betraying Floriano's Republic.[42]

The struggle was played out in four acts. First, the 1895 peace Prudente made in Rio Grande alienated both the Carioca *jacobinos* and the *gaúcho* (i.e. from Rio Grande do Sul) Republicans, who felt the enemies of the Republic were too easily readmitted into the polity. Second, unexpectedly ill, Prudente had to leave his office to his Vice-President, Manuel Vitorino [Pereira], who took up with the vigorous radical faction of the party, thus dividing the Republicans still further. Third, when Prudente returned to power, he knew that his Vice-President was betraying him and that Glicério, who enjoyed enormous *jacobino* prestige, was the Vice-President's ally and a threat, in any case, to Prudente's independence. Prudente's return was, in effect, a coup aimed at the near-successful resumption of power by the *jacobinos*. The party split between many of the historical Republican stalwarts, *jacobinos*, and *gaúchos*, now in formal opposition to Prudente, and Prudente's backers, comprising those beholden to the administration, as well as the representatives of the politically reorganized elite in Congress and in the various state party machines.

In the fourth act, the volatile partisan struggle that ensued was fired by what many Republicans, especially the *jacobinos*, felt was another monarchist ploy – the *guerrilha* at Canudos (1896–7). Canudos was the settlement in the Bahian hinterland of the followers of Antônio *Conselheiro* ("Counselor"), a mystic who had led his backcountry supporters in a messianic revolt, apparently in reaction to the local impositions of the Republican regime. The revolt exploded into a major confrontation because of the rebels' initial military successes and the charge, made by *florianista* military officers and journalists, that the revolt was sponsored by monarchists.[43] Prudente was accused of being, at best, a lukewarm Republican and poor patriot who had become the tool of reaction and a dangerous incompetent or, at worst, a traitor, betraying Floriano's legacy to its secret and proclaimed enemies.

The *dénouement* was violent. Prudente, on hand to greet the army returning victorious from Canudos, was attacked by a soldier from the waiting crowd. The President escaped, but his Minister of War and two other officers were wounded, the minister fatally. The assassination was the work of a small band of the more well-known *jacobinos*, infamous for their part in the era's street violence. Prudente quickly seized advantage of the event. He staged a massive funeral for the martyred minister, while successfully appealing for the proclamation of a state of seige. He then coordinated press, police, congress, and courts in the immediate aftermath of horror and sympathy the foiled attack inevitably brought. He crushed the opposition by tainting his principal enemies with formal charges of complicity, and disrupted any possibility of there being a truly contested election to choose his successor.[44]

The economic situation of the country was in ruins, the Republicans divided and bitter, and the blood of civil war, rebellions, and street violence still drying but, after reaching the abyss, Prudente had leapt it. He had dealt a mortal blow to the radicals and secured the peaceful transition of power to another civilian *paulista*, Campos Sales. The Republic had been wrested from the radicals and placed securely in the hands of another planter.

Campos Sales' administration (1898–1902) consolidated the reestablishment of elite agro-export interests at the expense of the emergent urban-based groups.[45] Two aspects of his policies are central to the Republic that now emerged. First, the emphasis placed on economic stability through financial conservatism and strong foreign credit relations; second, a political *modus operandi* securing the states' support for the government's financial policies in exchange for federal policies benefiting various local, established elites. The elite consensus was that the country's natural agrarian foundations had been irresponsibly shaken, impoverished by corrupt and unnatural State economic interventionism, and threatened by ugly civil struggles. It was time to stabilize the economy and the polity with *laissez-faire* economics, acceptable presidential authority, and the reestablishment of elite hegemony.

Brazil's economic plight was such that Campos Sales sought financial solutions even before assuming office. He went to London to reach an understanding with the City financiers whose role had been axiomatic in Brazil's capital-poor economy since 1822. At onerous cost, a funding loan was arranged with Lord Rothschild to keep Brazil from bankruptcy and defaults. In return, Campos Sales made numerous guarantees and, upon assuming the presidency, embarked on a number of policies to deflate the economy and raise revenues. The deflation and the recession that resulted affected various urban groups in different ways – some urban workers lost employment, but food prices and some wages improved, and others among the poor and the middle sectors enjoyed the effects of a stronger currency. However, there is little debate about the harsh impact on the people dependent on the newly emergent industries and capital market of the *Encilhamento* – a rash of bankruptcies and bank failures marked the century's turn. Just as under the old regime, it was the urban population and the urban-oriented entrepreneurs who paid for financial policies benefiting agriculture. Later, under both Campos Sales and his successors, various elements of the planter elite would secure concessions and financial support from the State, aid earlier denied the "artificial" urban-based industries and banks. It was a discriminating kind of *laissez-faire*.

After 1897, the purge of the *jacobinos* proceeded rapidly. Under Prudente, both his and the opposition party had, as their formal *raison d'être*, the schism between Prudente and Glicério. Campos Sales had, in exchange for not joining the opposition, won the support of Prudente for his election, without Campos Sales in turn having agreed to active support of Prudente. As a result, Campos Sales came to the presidency free of obligations to either party. The latter, furthermore, were inherently weakened by personalism. In the one case, Prudente's retirement from politics and, in the other, Glicério's discredit and his confederates' sudden disarray, tore out the central pivot of each new political machine, and both soon sputtered to a halt. Instead, politics began to spin around the two poles of greatest strength – that of the federal government and increasingly powerful presidency, and that of the states, in the form of the reemergent, local, elite-run political machines. Under this new dispensation, the urban middle-sector and army radicals, as well as the urban sector in general, lost their leverage. The radicals had found their formal institutional base, after Floriano's regime, in Republican party activism, articulated through a strong national Congress. Now, however, Congress was reduced to the brokerage house of the president and the state elites.

This was done piecemeal, in the shambles of the two earlier parties. The President, whose domination of the State and its favors naturally made him the supreme patron, began to seek an understanding with the state oligarchies. He had the support of São Paulo, of course. With the support that he soon won with Minas and Bahia, he had the votes necessary for dominance in Congress. He strengthened this by instituting a screening device for deputies. Campos Sales and friendly deputies agreed that the validation of newly-elected deputies' credentials would be the responsibility of a committee under the president's thumb. Campos Sales made it clear that only those candidates given the nod of their state governor (*ipso facto* head of the state oligarchy's machine) would be acceptable. In this way, the president destroyed the potential for independent action from Congress, cut away the possibility of any but a few radicals obtaining political position, and strengthened the articulation of the most powerful state oligarchies' interests while giving himself the stable support he needed to execute his policies. The states which emerged strongest were those with the best political organization and the largest number of deputies – São Paulo, Minas Gerais, and Rio Grande do Sul.

The name given the new arrangements had the virtue of clarity – *política dos governadores*. It bespeaks the consensus of the great local elites to support a government of compromise favorable to themselves and inherently inimical to the centralizing, reformist, urban-oriented Republic of Floriano. The elites repossessed the State. An order favoring the traditional social structure and economic direction of Brazil had been reimposed, taking on a new political formulation. The new urban and middle-sector groups, whose strength had been growing since at least the socio-economic changes of mid-century, had gone down in bitter defeat.

5. The Carioca elite and the birth of the *belle époque*

In 1898, with Campos Sales' assumption of power and the reassertion of a calm dominated by the regional elites, the Carioca *belle époque* begins. That year there was a noticeable change in the air which soon affected the cultural and social milieu. The revolutionary days were over. The time for stability and an urbane life of elegance was at hand again. In May 1898, the editor of a fashionable weekly announced,

We have order in progress and the [social] orders prosper.
The phantoms that frightened the bourgeois have disappeared.
No one is concerned any more with assassinations, now the theatrical companies offer so many temptations . . .
There's no more passionate talk about *habeus corpus* except, perhaps, with regard to the proper legislative bodies or to those of the coveted actresses, true *corpi delicti* (or delightful) . . .
Brazil drifts, serene and elegant, in a sea of roses, in complete calm . . . Thanks to the firm hand of the present rulers, all is peace in the interior. The last roots of conspiracies, real or imaginary, have been extirpated . . .
With our vigorous patriotism our credit will rise . . .
There is some talk of a financial crisis here, but this is no more than a rumor and, to prove it, there's a new craze for that expensive luxury, the bicycle.[46]

The same weekly made its point more seriously in welcoming Campos Sales back from his trip to the Rothschilds:

The ministry now said to have been organized by His Excellency is a symptom of what we have announced. His Excellency has chosen notable men known for their circumspection, intelligence, and morality. His government will obey, then, those noble dictates. The exclusion of the *jacobino* element and of those who were partisans of the tragic farces of 1893 and 1894 is also a sign that the future president wants to found his administration on the conservative classes, the only ones who can benefit the country, making it great, opening up new horizons in the fields of industry, commerce, and agriculture.

The politics of factions, which Sr. Dr. Prudente de Moraes so reasonably attempted to repress, must be extinguished completely. In young nations like ours, weighed down with such grave burdens, the interference of illiterate tyrants, subject to persecution mania and the falsest ideas about patriotism, and trying, above all, to satisfy their least confessable appetites, is intolerable. It is necessary for us to place ourselves at the height of contemporary civilization. We have faith in the administration of Sr. Campos Sales and feel sure it will be oriented by truth, law, humanity, and peace.[47]

Certain characteristic aspects of the Carioca *belle époque* would emerge later with the financial and political basis Campos Sales put together for four years and then bequeathed his successor. Here, we will focus not only on such new aspects of the era, but on those enduring ones which, just as basic to the *belle époque*, were now reemerging with the Campos Sales regime.

For 1898 in Rio, as in Brazil, marks not only a new beginning, but, as has been shown, the reemergence of old forces. The revolutionary period of 1880–97, which saw the rise and defeat of urban-based reformism and revolution, marks the failure of a shift away from traditionally-oriented elite rule. It was a shift that amounted to an important interregnum, one sufficient to affect the nature and the course of Abolition and the Republic without destroying the fundamental reasons for the power of the planter elites and their allies, or preventing a government structured to suit the desires of the most powerful of those groups. The year 1898 saw these people settling themselves firmly on top of the familiar socio-economic hierarchy, triumphant over radical political challenges. The end of the century marks the continuing vitality, indeed, the triumph, of patterns apparent throughout it.

For the understanding of the culture and the society of the Carioca elite, this is crucial. In neither Rio nor Brazil as a whole, however, is continuity suggested to mean the absence of change, so much as its containment. As we shall see, the elite in Rio, the center of so many of Brazil's nineteenth-century shifts, perforce experienced and resolved obvious contradictions – the elite was sorely tested.

Rio, after all, was the beachhead for all of the political tides that ran. It was in Rio that the Conservative Party, whose strength and sinew were planters in the city's hinterland, took form, to proclaim Rio's hegemony over the consolidating Empire at mid-century. The city was the focus of the movements and events that freed the slaves and snuffed out the monarchy. And, no matter how many of the Old Republic's threads were spun in the States, it was in Rio that they were woven together, in conspiracy, in revolt, in politicking.

Like the *paulista* elite, however, caught up in a particular metamorphosis of its own, the Carioca elite reconciled ubiquitous change with the maintenance of a social hierarchy. The result was an evolution under elite auspices: change contained by, and strengthening, the hierarchy. And, when change threatened to get out of hand and upset the social order, the Carioca elite, like the *paulista*, retreated to the wings and waited it out. The Carioca elite, as will be shown, contained Republicans and Abolitionists, liberal professionals and entrepreneurs, but it contained no *jacobinos*.

It is this tenacious, adaptive nature of the elite which will inform much of the study that follows. The Brazilian nineteenth century was a period in which, despite numerous challenges, the new, changing nation was consolidated and its course continually reaffirmed as colonial, under the concomitant direction of representatives of the country's elites – the planters, the merchants, the financiers, and other entrepreneurs of the agro-export complex. The growth of Rio as the Côrte and the main port made it both the socio-political and the economic center of the new Empire. It also made it, during the century's second half, the focal point of a potentially disturbing set of challenges. The growth of the urban population, the continued impact of European ideologies and models of behavior, the emergence of new possibilities, interests, and enterprises, and greater independence from the traditional, rural-based elite, all thread their way through the lives of the men and women to be studied here.

Yet, in the city as well as in the nation, the enduring, characteristic trends imposed by the colonial economic reality and its traditional corollary, an economically vulnerable, status-minded hierarchy, proved the limiting factors, the shaping forces in change, as well as its brakes. High culture and high society figured actively in this essential socio-economic heritage. As we shall see, even those members of the elite who best represented the changes in Rio's economic and political functions under the Republic recreated an aristocratic milieu. Change occurred, but not to the point where the yoked phenomena of elite control and elite socio-cultural expression were radically altered.

Rather, elite culture and society in the capital continued to maintain and promote the on-going interests of the elite by helping to provide a sense of aristocratic continuity, exclusive meeting places for contacts and alliances, shared values and assumptions, and, perhaps most profoundly, a sense of legitimization – all in the face of economic, social, and political metamorphoses. In the pages that follow, then, it will be seen that the Carioca *belle époque* is closely identified with the

Brazil that reemerged under Campos Sales. There was certainly change involved, but the reassertion of enduring structures, adapted to changing circumstances, is perhaps the more important point.

The ways in which the *belle époque* represented both colonial continuity and the new era's potential for change is best introduced in the story of the capital itself. Rio's history gives one the setting of the elite's evolution and the clearest expression of the Carioca *belle époque.* In the frenchifying of this tropical port by the Paris-trained son of a coffee planter, many of the themes to follow in other chapters are manifest.

6. The Rio de Janeiro of 1836–68: an enduring colonial tradition

The dates of the central figure here provide useful reference points. Francisco Pereira Passos was born in 1836, when Brazilian integration into North-Atlantic commerce and culture had already begun the phase of neo-colonialism. He died in 1913, just before the Great War and its dissolution of classic neo-colonialism.[48]

In 1836, Brazil was just working its way out of the Regency, 1831–40, from which her most powerful regional elites emerged with a new commitment to a centralized state legitimized by a consecrated dynast, Pedro II. Principal among these elites were the coffee planters of the province of Rio de Janeiro, slave- and land-holding patriarchs who identified their interests with the peace, security, and resources of the monarchy enthroned in the port city of Rio de Janeiro.[49] Pereira Passos's father was typical of this elite – a planter of Portuguese immigrant and native descent, he had the title of Baron de Mangaratiba, and was a man of importance in São João Marcos, the *fluminense* town where Pereira Passos was born.[50]

Such an agricultural setting was characteristic of nineteenth-century Brazil. The Côrte, most populous and cosmopolitan city in the realm, was a distinct reality.[51] Yet, the distance between its urbanity and the rude traditions of countryside and colonial past was often negligible.

The ubiquity of slave labor is indicative. In 1799, nearly a third of Rio's population of roughly 43,000 were slaves; in 1821, about half of the city's 112,000 were bondsmen; and at mid-century, nearly half of Rio's almost 200,000 inhabitants continued in slavery. Indeed, in 1872, twenty years after the end of trans-Atlantic trade, about 166,000 of the slaves in the province and the Côrte were African, a living legacy of the old Portuguese *negreiros.*[52]

In fact, the Rio of 1836, with a largely enslaved population, either African or of African descent, was a quiet, tropical, traditional town, which had changed only gradually after its founding in 1565. Rio's affairs had always centered on the docks. For generations, its trade had been paltry, then, in the eighteenth century it flourished with the gold and diamond trade between its hinterland in Minas Gerais and Europe. In the 1800s, after ephemeral provincial trade in sugar and a few other tropical crops, Rio triumphed as the port for *fluminense* and *mineiro* coffee. Rio's primacy had already been enhanced in 1763, when tensions with Spain in the Rio de la Plata caused Portugal to transfer the viceroy's seat from Salvador to Rio, which remained Brazil's capital thereafter. Such status brought with it new population, new buildings, and new prestige.[53]

The city, founded on a hill (Morro do Castelo), grew around the docks that stretched along the eastern shore at the hill's foot. Until the nineteenth century, *chácaras* (small farms) could be found as close as the area between Lapa and the hills of Livramento and Conceição (see Map 1). Indeed, they framed the *cidade velha* (Old City) well into the century. In areas such as Engenho Velho, Tijuca, Engenho Novo, and the Gâvea, they grew food for the table; some even exported sugar and, in the late eighteenth and early nineteenth centuries, Brazil's first commercial coffee. Until then, even Botafogo or São Cristóvão were suitable only for holiday retreats or agriculture, being too far from the docks and the daily work of commerce and Crown bureaucracy to serve for residence.[54]

Rio's growth was hindered by its lush and varied terrain. Hills, marshes, and lakes characterized the region, leaving little room for easy expansion. Between the 1560s and 1700, the *cidade velha* was confined behind an irregular semicircle of such barriers (see Map 1).[55] The crown administrations attacked these barriers over the years by creating dry land at the city's edges. A ditch draining the Lake of Santo Antônio and the additional pipe that later supplemented it (both from the 1600s) were covered by the present Rua Uruguaiana and Rua Sete de Setembro. Part of marshy Lapa was converted into the small garden lake and streams of the Passeio Público. Even the marshy areas to the west, the present Praça Tiradentes and Campo de Santana, began to be filled in. One viceroy then forbade the nighttime use of Santana as a dump. Instead, the barrels of human waste and domestic refuse carried by slaves were now thrown into the bay, and Santana's trenchworks of raw sewage were covered. By the dusk of the colonial era, the expanding city had been graced by public fountains, fish-oil illumination, and a celebrated aqueduct between the nearby range of hills and a new public square.[56]

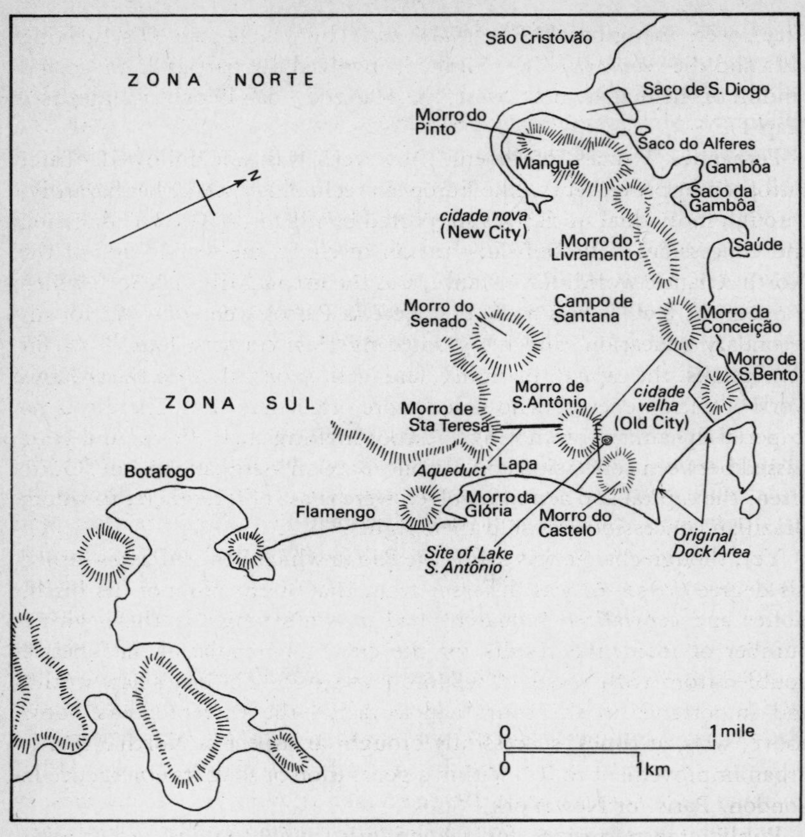

Map 1. Rio de Janeiro's geography and districts

This colonial pattern of successive minor changes endured throughout the nineteenth century, except for one dramatic moment. During the transitional era when João VI, Prince Regent, then King, of Portugal, sought refuge from Napoleon's armies and established his court in Rio (1808–21), an energetic administrator, Paulo Fernandes Viana, undertook substantial improvements to embellish and improve the city for the exiled court. While illumination and paving went on, some embarrassing aspects of colonial architecture were forbidden, such as *rótulas*, Moorish windows. Certain prominent but ugly buildings were replaced, new quays, warehouses, and public fountains constructed, the filling-in of Santana completed and a small park made there, and a few new streets and a new residential district, the *cidade nova* (New

City), were inaugurated. The *cidade nova*, by which João VI's outlying villa and the *cidade velha* were linked, involved the partial drainage and landfill of the marshy northwest; the Mangue – São Diogo complex (see Map 1).[57]

Fernandes Viana's precedent, however, was not followed. Later European improvements, like European technology, came haphazardly, through individual initiatives supported by niggardly Crown education and concessions. The only institution teaching the technology of the North Atlantic world, for instance, was the Escola Militar (1808) which trained but few. It was there that Pereira Passos went in 1852 for his secondary education, and his graduating class counted four.[58] As for concessions, the capital, planning, and realization remained the arduous work of entrepreneurs, who failed more often than not. There was no imperial dynamism promoting and coordinating such efforts, and years passed between concession and action, if action were taken at all. Quite often, the capital and action involved were those of foreigners, to whom Brazilian concessionaires sold their rights.[59]

Yet, though change was fitful, the Rio in which Pereira Passos earned his degree (1852–6) was different from that at the time of his birth. Coffee and centralized monarchy had grown strong together, with a number of incidental results for the city. Its population had nearly doubled from 1821 to 1849, to almost 200,000. The city's new wealth and importance as the court had attracted the entrepreneurs noted above, who, at times, successfully brought an aspect of North Atlantic urban improvement to Rio within a generation or so of its emergence in London, Paris, or New York.[60]

Public transportation, for the minority who could afford it, was pioneered by boats serving city shores in the late eighteenth century. By 1817, a coach line operated between the *cidade velha* and the royal villa. In 1822, there were regular sailings across the bay to Niterói, followed by a steam service after 1835. In 1837, regular, mule-drawn omnibuses were running. In 1841, there were regular *góndolas* (these were two-story, mule-drawn vehicles); in 1843, regular steamboats skirted the city; and, before 1850, regular lines of coaches were running.

Change accelerated about the century's third quarter. Regular garbage collection was started in 1847. In 1851, new portworks were begun. In 1852, the first telegraph was installed. In 1854, one of the first railroads in South America linked the court's summer capital, Petrópolis, to a station serviced by a cross-bay ferry to Rio. That same year saw the first public gas lighting. The year 1857 saw the first underground sewage system, gas lighting in private buildings, and control of the marshy Mangue area attempted with a canal. By 1858, the first major railway was baptised with its first complete section and central station, the latter being built behind the newer dock area on Rio's northern edge (see Map 5). In 1859, the first mule-drawn streetcar firm appeared; it failed in 1864. Its 1868 successor, however, brought the vehicle's definitive establishment.[61]

All public transport, especially the streetcar (*bond*), which superseded the others, made outlying areas accessible to the elite as residential districts. Indeed, the first lines of each system always extended toward these areas. They were the cooler, less fever-ridden places where the wealthy increasingly preferred to live. At first used only for regular weekly stays or genteel semi-retirement, they became practical now for daily commuting to the *cidade velha*. First, the *Zona Norte* (*cidade nova*, São Cristóvão, Tijuca, Rio Comprido), then, the *Zona Sul* (Glória, Flamengo, Laranjeiras, Cosme Velho, Botafogo) were reached, initially by the first coach, which went to the Zona Norte, then by the omnibus and the *bond*, whose first lines fed the newer, and increasingly more prestigious, *Zona Sul* (see Maps 1 and 2).[62]

In all of this, the Côrte of Pereira Passos's youth, the problematic course of change in Rio is obvious. Fundamentally, the city was of relatively little concern to imperial policy-makers. Brazil's greatest four cities represented less than a tenth of the nation's population throughout the nineteenth century. Population, capital accumulation, investment, and political power remained essentially rural, or linked to rural-based commerce. Thus, the ruling class and its imperial government were generally without driving concern for urban problems. Indeed, even when commercial or political considerations compelled their attention the paucity of capital for urban-oriented investment, the unattractively small urban market, and the prevailing ideological strictures on government action alike militated against large-scale private, public, or mixed ventures to improve urban infrastructure, amenities, or appearance.[63]

Although Brazilians envied the North Atlantic progress and civilization often associated with such urban improvements, they also thought them Europe's special achievement, and only a distant possibility for the Empire. Grander patterns of change were apparently ignored or thought inapplicable within the limits Brazil's realities imposed. Rather, Rio's steady, thin accumulation of foreign technology, customs, and capital, which reflected those neo-colonial realities, was accepted as natural. Indeed, provincials thought Rio a magnificent city, whose contact conferred urbane prestige. Only Brazil-

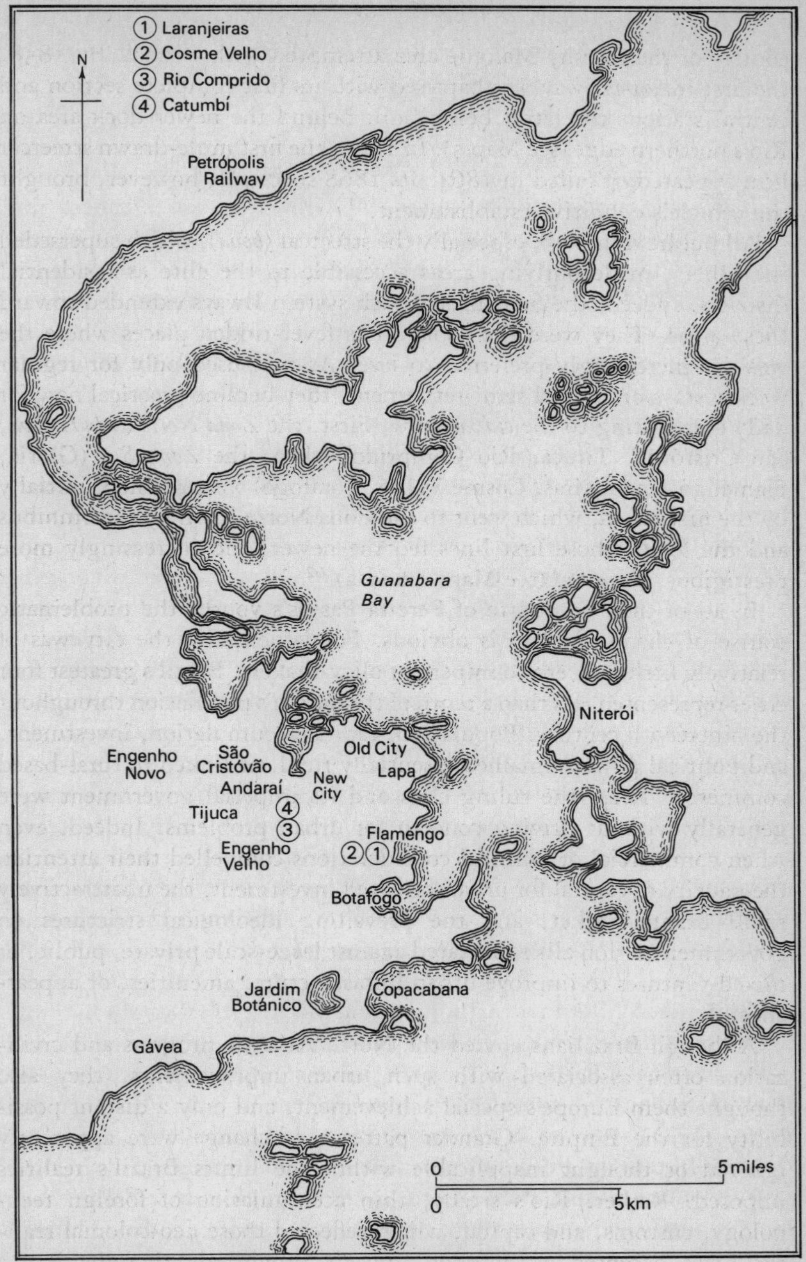

Map 2. Rio de Janeiro and its outskirts

ians who ventured abroad glimpsed the distressing distance which separated the *pátria* from Civilization.[64]

7. The Paris of the Second Empire

For nineteenth-century Brazilians, Civilization was France and England. Indeed, from colonial times, Brazilians had followed Portuguese example and looked to either country for all that was best. In modern technology, especially (although few were interested in this), both had much to offer: England, by way of example and experience, France, by way of experience and learning. The training of Pereira Passos exemplifies the importance of both, particularly France.[65]

Pereira Passos graduated from a school (Escola Militar) modeled on one of France's *grandes écoles* (probably the Ecole Militaire), where he probably studied from French texts.[66] He then parlayed his family connections to secure a sinecure as *attaché* in the Paris consulate. There, in 1857, he continued his extraordinary pursuit of a career in engineering. "Extraordinary" is used advisedly. Planters' sons were generally sent to the Faculties of Law to prepare for politics and imperial administration or magistracy, in order to link local family influence to provincial and imperial power. The elder Passos intended this for his heir, but the youth apparently demonstrated early the independence and will later typical of him. He went to Paris with one goal in mind – the Ecole des Ponts et Chaussées.[67]

The school was the traditional next step for graduates of the Polytechnique, bastion of French engineering in the era of French supremacy in the field. Foreigners with special approval were allowed to attend its courses as auditors – only students, however, spent vacations in fieldwork. Yet Pereira Passos did both, apparently winning such privileges through warm relations established with French colleagues.[68]

The milieu of his French training and warm professional relations, however, is most important here. For this was the period of the transformation of Paris – the Great Works – the first network (1853–8) of which was nearing completion when Pereira Passos arrived. No other lessons could have been as impressive for such a student.[69]

Paris, like many European cities, had become dangerously bloated with population and traffic born of industrialization. Throughout Europe, inefficient road systems and frequent epidemics called forth a chorus of utopian and then reformist responses. The latter were naturally more acceptable to the ruling classes; they posed relatively unthreatening technical and administrative solutions, rather than radical political and social ones.

Louis Napoleon, while in exile, was influenced by this reformism, especially in England. There, the government had sponsored urban public health reforms promoted by Bentham's former secretary, Edwin Chadwick. There was also the example of London. Louis Napoleon was impressed by aristocratic Hyde Park and the common relief enjoyed in the city's sprinkling of green squares. These elements and the political appeal of thriving public works employment drove Louis Napoleon to the reform of Paris immediately on becoming emperor. For success, however, he required an aggressive administrator; he found Haussmann and, thus, triumph. Together they made modern Paris in three related programs of demolition and construction between 1853 and 1870.[70]

In these programs, three main accomplishments stand out (see Map 3). First, Paris's congested and poorly articulated narrow old streets were either transformed into, or superseded by, distinct, well-orchestrated patterns of traffic. In one of these, the city was pierced by the Great Crossing of two perpendicular thoroughfares. In another, radial highways provided access between the city's suburbs and its center. In still another, the center's congestion was alleviated by providing circular boulevards around it, thus allowing traffic between suburbs without forcing it through the urban core. Articulation between these new boulevards and the older, inner ring of boulevards, as well as the new Great Crossing, were accomplished by places-carrefours, plazas where several thoroughfares met. The Place d'Etoile is the most famous of these – its function in the west was repeated by the Place de la République in the northeast, the Place de la Nation in the east, and the Observatoire in the south.[71]

Second, the Great Works destroyed or penetrated many of the crowded, unhealthy, and ancient working-class areas with many of the new thoroughfares. By so eliminating or opening up potential centers of revolt, Haussmann pursued not only a counter-revolutionary but also a reformist strategy. For the thoroughfares eased congestion, brought the city air and light, and, thus (in conjunction with a new sewage system), attacked the conditions widely blamed for recent cholera epidemics.[72]

Third, Haussmann embellished the city. He emphasized, for instance, the vistas since emblematic of Paris: long perspectives, trained on great monuments or buildings, flanked by façades meeting common requirements regarding appearance and marked by the era's Beaux-Arts style. He also refurbished or erected great public buildings, the most famous of which was the Opéra, signature of the Second Empire.

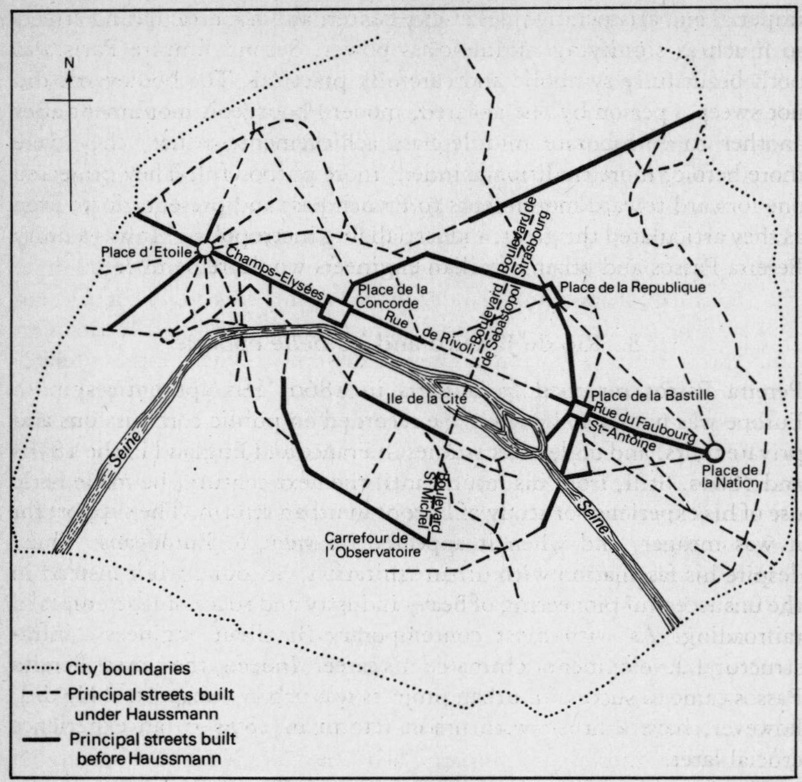

Map 3. Paris and the impact of the Haussmann reforms

Finally, he adapted the London park model Napoleon III so admired. Developed out of a tradition in English gardening, such parks were fantasies of Nature, with studied series of "unexpected" conceits. Grottoes, streams, winding paths, waterfalls – these were the English clichés out of which Haussmann created the Bois de Boulogne, the Bois de Vincennes, and the Parc des Buttes Chaumont.[73]

In all of this, the premier example of how to remake an old city practical and beautiful was put before the European world. Moreover, though perspectives and embellishments were often what fixed the imagination, the city's planners did not separate efficiency from beauty. One finds a telling contrast to this unity in the later 1860s Viennese reforms. These focussed on a "ring-street" of impressive edifices identified with the ideals of the bourgeoisie, a ring besieging the old imperial and aristocratic piles at city center, and not articulating streets so much as signifying middle-class power. Second Empire Paris was both beautifully symbolic and carefully practical. The boulevards did not sweep a person by one isolated, modern bourgeois monument after another to corroborate middle-class achievement; rather, they were more heroic, more tradition-minded, more purposeful. They projected one forward toward monuments to French past and present glory, even as they articulated the great, industrializing metropolis.[74] It was a unity Pereira Passos and other Brazilian engineers would remember.

8. Rio de Janeiro and its *belle époque*

Pereira Passos returned from Paris in 1860. His apprenticeship in Europe was not over, however; he returned on public commissions and private tours, and undertook studies in France and England in the 1870s and 1880s. Still, from his return until the next century, he made little use of his experience or study of European urban reform. The support for it was meager, and when it appeared, it went to Europeans. Thus, despite his fascination with urban sanitation, he found work instead in the unsuccessful pioneering of heavy industry and successful attempts in railroading. As with most contemporary Brazilian engineers, infrastructural development dominated his career. Indeed, the closest Pereira Passos came to successful urban projects was urban transport.[75] He did, however, have a brush with urban reform in 1874–6, an experience crucial later.

The first years following the Paraguayan War (1865–70) were an ephemeral era of imperial ambition. The Conservative ministry (1871–5) of the Viscount do Rio Branco, in imposing a program of national "modernization" (designed partially to outflank Liberal reformism), included an attack on the Côrte's perennial epidemic problems. The previous ministry's Minister of the Empire, João Alfredo Correia de Oliveira, continued in office under Rio Branco and directed the effort. He had first appointed Pereira Passos in 1870 as technical consultant when he had held the interim portfolio of Agriculture and Public Works. In 1874, he appointed Pereira Passos engineer to the Ministry of the Empire and directed him to draft the guidelines and choose his own subordinates for a commission to draw up the first comprehensive plan for Rio's improvement.

Yet, the plan was never effected. Public, professional criticism undermined it, and the Emperor opposed what he called, quite properly, "Haussmannization." More telling, perhaps, was the plan's vulnerability, since it depended upon forces that suddenly dissolved. Pereira Passos' proposals presupposed private investment and government backing. When Brazil suffered a panic in 1875, the entrepreneurial spirit and wherewithal on which the engineer counted disappeared. Worse, in the panic's aftermath, the ministry for which he had worked fell, and he lost crucial political protection.

In the end, the ministry's ambitions had accomplished little. Before the panic, for example, Pereira Passos built a few new buildings and refurbished some old ones; the new plan, however, was stillborn. Imperial reform thus remained piecemeal or decorative. Indeed, the striking urban changes of the era were parks. Auguste Marie François Glaziou, French botanist and landscape architect, englished the Campo de Santana into a proper miniature of the Bois de Boulogne between 1873 and 1880. It now had grottoes, waterfalls, and winding paths: a European "natural" garden in the midst of a tropical city rank with Nature's exuberance. A *bois*, not boulevards, was what the 1870s brought Rio.[76]

For a generation, Rio rotted within its colonial shell. Though an inadequate water system (built in 1866 after epidemics had terrified the populace, and extended by 1880) possibly helped, the port's reputation as a pesthole flourished. Travellers, at best, described Rio as exotic, with its villas, colonial architecture, black, brightly-clad multitudes of laborers and street hawkers, and lush vegetation. More often, one notes fear of yellow fever's seasonal slaughter and disdain for Rio's crowded dirty streets, tawdry public places, and stench of filth, perfumes, and sweat. Even the *Encilhamento* did little to improve matters. Again, though, there was a brush with reform. This time the reformer was another engineer, Paulo de Frontin, whose company bought up previous concessions for Rio's portworks but, in the economic collapse of the 1890s, failed to secure enough capital to carry out their modernization.[77] As for the Republic's first administrations, although reforms were studied and some minor improvements completed, they had to attend to a basic agenda – political survival and consolidation, and the reestablishment of the economy.

As discussed earlier, however, with Campos Sales' administration (1898–1902), a new era began. Political consolidation held and credit in London was won. The government had reaffirmed that European penetration was necessary and that its task was to encourage it. Moreover, it encouraged more than loans and investment; European immigration, crucial to the *paulista* elite since 1888, was increasingly described as central to European-like national development – the only sort of development contemplated. Now, in 1902, a great step forward seemed possible. The trends of the century were about to culminate at a peculiar juncture of opportunity for Rio. Although the exhausted plantations of Rio's hinterland were now superseded by newer lands in western São Paulo, the city's needs and national importance had grown. It had retained, and increased, centrality as the Republic's administrative, commercial, financial, and industrial center. After a century of gradual reform and frustrated hopes, Rio was desperate for the urban reforms that were to be the signature of its *belle époque*.[78]

In this context, it seems inevitable that the reforms should have been a *paulista*'s decision. The successor of two other *paulista* presidents, this one now set about using the fruits of their victories to refashion the Republic's capital as the showpiece of the regime and the more efficient nexus of a resurgent neo-colonial economy. This successor was [Francisco de Paula] Rodrigues Alves (1848–1919). A planter and a planter's son, a Conservative statesman during the Empire, a finance minister in the early Republic, a president of the State of São Paulo who had successfully fought disease with modern reform, and, finally, a father who still mourned a child taken by yellow fever in Rio, Rodrigues Alves was representative of the old and new forces at play and self-consciously their instrument. Arguing that the port capital's reform was central to attracting European immigration, capital, and trade (and doubtless mindful of the spectacular success of Buenos Aires' recently completed Parisian reforms), Rodrigues Alves made this program his administration's keystone. He soon appointed Pereira Passos, now nearly 70, to the federal capital's prefecture to implement the policy's urbanistic aspect. Scholars will recall Oswaldo Cruz's part, too, as the man chosen to head the effort to rid Rio of plague, yellow fever, and smallpox. Our particular interest here, though, is in the act synonymous with the *belle époque*: Rio's frenchification.[79]

9. Rio's urban reforms

It has been an unexplored commonplace that Pereira Passos' 1903–6 reforms were somehow related to his French experience or his 1870s plans. The engineer's papers and contemporary publications confirm both points and show the centrality of Haussmann. Indeed, the primacy of Haussmann among other planners is clear not only for Pereira Passos, but for the colleagues who joined in the work of 1903–6. In fact, their statements demonstrate not only that Paris' reforms were well understood, but that the subsequent reforms in Vienna, Antwerp, Lisbon,

Brussels, and Buenos Aires were common knowledge among the Brazilian engineers involved in Rio's reforms. The choice for Haussmann was both clear and informed, then, and taken by a highly professional group.[80]

The fact that there was a group involved calls for further explanation. The reforms were the joint endeavor of ministerial and municipal authorities. The Minister of Transport and Public Works, the engineer Lauro Müller, delegated the port-oriented reforms to two colleagues representing a powerful group of engineers and entrepreneurs. To Paulo de Frontin, whose earlier experience has been noted, was given the most striking of the reforms, the Avenida Central, to be thrust from the northern dock area through the *cidade velha*. To Francisco de Bicalho, Müller entrusted the portworks themselves. Pereira Passos, though collaborating with Müller's team, was granted dictatorial dispensations by Rodrigues Alves to carry out the reform of the rest of the city. The overall plan concerning the city, as opposed to its port and the latter's immediate thoroughfares, then, was that of Pereira Passos, alone. This is clear in contemporary reports and the clear linkage between the engineer's 1875–6 plan and the 1903–6 achievements. In both efforts, however, that of the Müller team and that of Pereira Passos, the influence of Haussmann is patent.[81]

Much of the *cidade velha*'s narrow, dank, and muddled working-class world was destroyed; its streets were widened, given light and air, and better connected by demolishing old buildings, changing old streets, and building new ones. For Müller's part, the northern dock area was filled in, modernized, and strung together by a great avenue (the present Avenida Rodrigues Alves). This avenue was joined to the labor and industry of the Zona Norte by another (the present Avenida Francisco Bicalho), connected to the revamped Mangue; it was joined to the *cidade velha* by the new Avenida Central (the present Avenida Rio Branco). The latter connected port traffic not only to the city center, but to a third new avenue (Pereira Passos' Avenida Beira Mar) pulling the Zona Sul into easy communication. To these three great new routes bordering and piercing the old center, Pereira Passos tied four others, two of which were new, two only widened and straightened. These four articulated specific areas of the *cidade velha* to others and the Zona Norte, without forcing traffic back through the main arteries or into the center (see Map 4).

Pereira Passos did far more, though. He paved streets, constructed sidewalks and macadamized roads, built the Leme Tunnel (the second to link the far suburb of Copacabana to the *cidade velha*'s nearer suburbs),

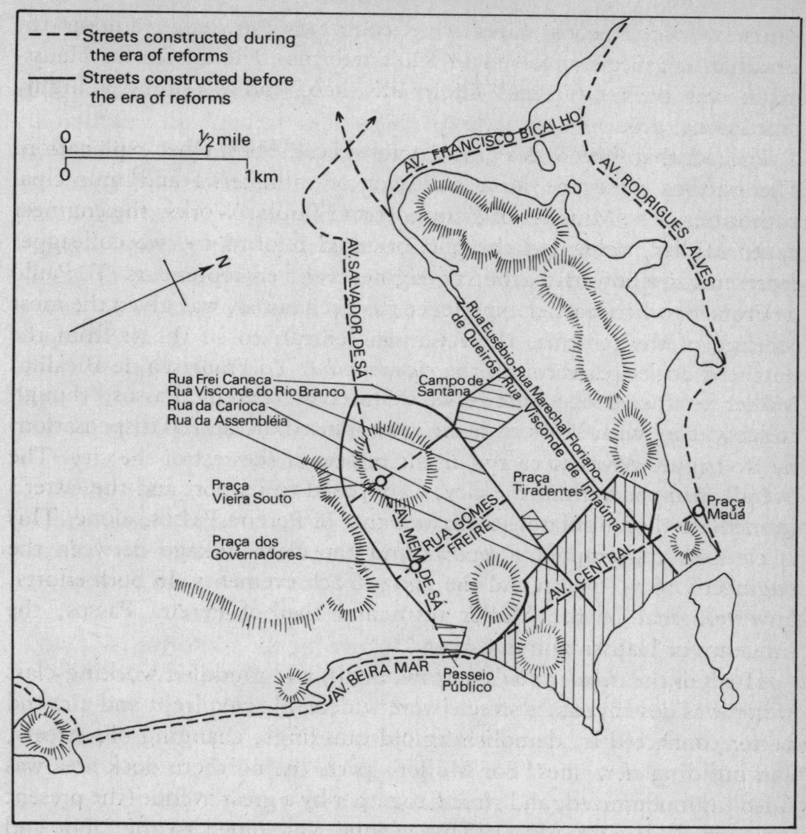

Map 4. Rio de Janeiro and the impact of the 1902–6 reforms

began Copacabana's Avenida Atlântica, built the avenue linking the Flamengo and Botafogo suburbs, improved a list of other streets, destroyed the decrepit municipal market disfiguring the Glória district and built another nearer the traffic and port facilities of the *cidade velha*, and embellished such sites as the Praças XV de Novembro, 11 de Junho, Tiradentes, Glória, the Largo do Machado, the Passeio Público, and the Campo de Santana. Pereira Passos also attacked certain Carioca traditions. He prohibited hawking food on the streets, spitting on the streetcar floors, selling milk from cows trotted door to door, raising pigs within city limits, exposing meat on butchershop entrances, allowing stray dogs to run loose, leaving building façades unpainted, continuing with the *entrudo* (wild pranks) and unregulated *cordões* (boisterous popular processions) of *Carnaval*, and a host of other "barbaric," "uncivilized" customs.[82]

Thus, principles of Paris' Great Works were adapted to Rio. The demolition in the *cidade velha* parallels Haussmann's destruction in working-class areas. The stress on light and air through broadened streets and new thoroughfares was central to both reforms. The use of thoroughfares bringing traffic from the edge of the city through the center was common to either plan, as was the use of others to direct cross-town traffic out of the center. Further, the principle of *places-carrefours* was employed at either end of the Avenida Mem de Sá: at the intersection with the Rua Frei Caneca–Rue Visconde do Rio Branco route and at the Rua Teixeira de Freitas–Avenida Beira Mar–Avenida Central combination, junctures with central and suburban routing were effected. The *place-carrefour per se* is obvious in Avenida Mem de Sá's *praças* (now Vieira Souto and dos Governadores) or in the Largo da Prainha (now Praça Mauá). Moreover, the Avenida Central's intersection with the Rua Visconde de Inhaúma – Rua Marechal Floriano route (now superseded by the intersection with Avenida Presidente Vargas) was to Rio what the Great Crossing is to Paris – two great ways across town brought together at right-angles at the city center.

In all, the impact of Paris' Great Works on Rio's reforms is obvious from Pereira Passos' 1875–6 plans to the collaborative reforms of 1903–6. The impact is also patent in more cosmetic ways. The architecture preferred, the great perspective of the Avenida Central, the planting of gardens in the city's plazas, the renewed attention to the Campo de Santana, and Pereira Passos' son's project for the Carioca version of the Paris Opéra – all these Parisian aspects were central to the meaning of the *belle époque* Rio that emerged under Rodrigues Alves.[83]

10. The Avenida Central: façades and direction in the Carioca *belle époque*

Nothing expresses this or the Carioca *belle époque* better than the Avenida Central – the great new boulevard which cut through the *cidade velha*'s colonial warren. I will discuss its larger figurative importance shortly; here I focus on the practical and symbolic aspects of the avenue itself.

The idea for the avenue was that of Lauro Müller, Rodrigues Alves' Minister of Transport, who supposedly traced out the route with a gesture and left its planning and construction to Paulo de Frontin. Though Frontin's associates considered the idea a revolutionary reorientation to traffic and commerce, the concept was at least as old as Pereira

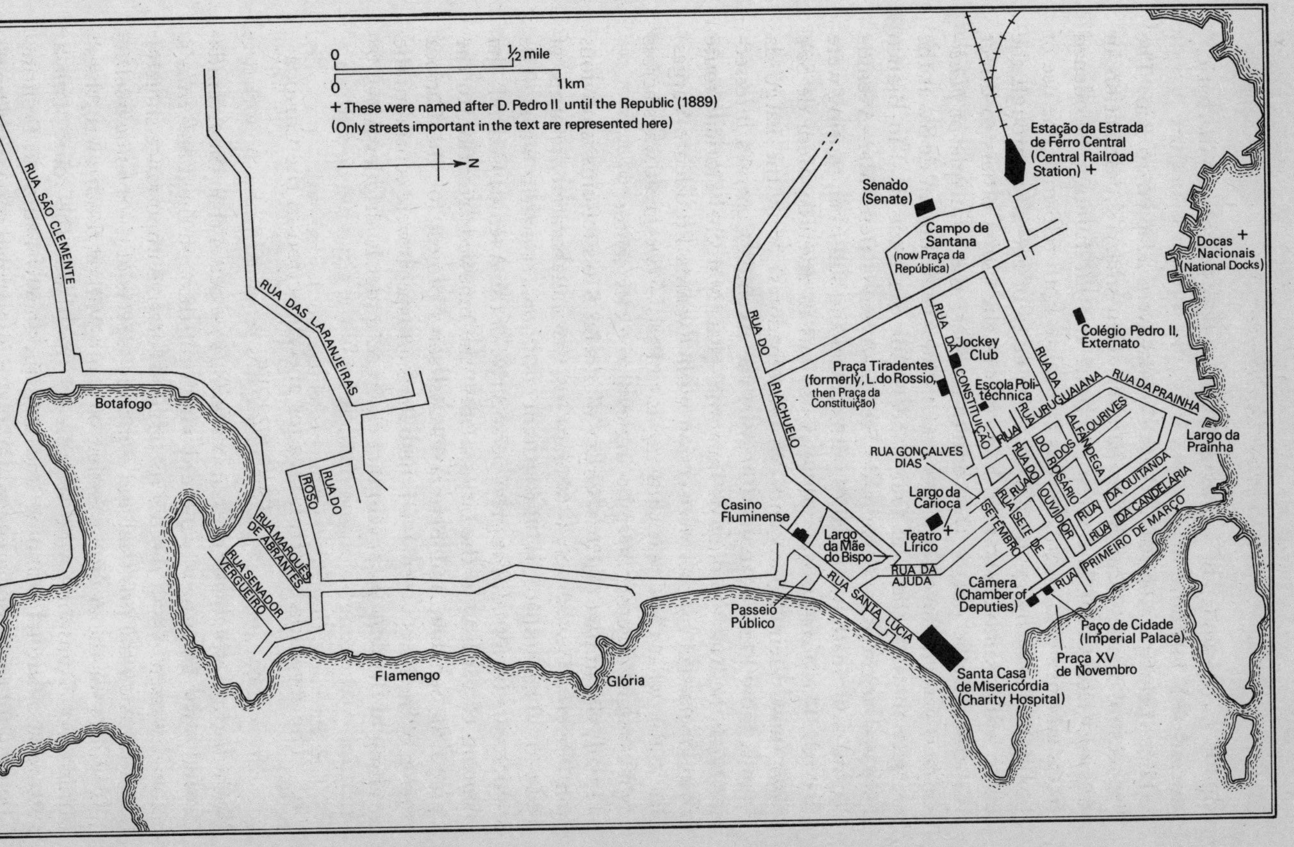

Map 5. Rio de Janeiro's Old City and elite districts *c.* 1890

Passos' 1870s plan. Then, other planners had stressed avenues articulating the city east to west, joining its public squares along the historic direction of Rio's growth. Pereira Passos agreed, but had also planned two avenues running roughly north to south. One was traced from the Rua da Prainha to the Largo da Mãe do Bispo (from the present Rua do Acre to the Praça Ferreira Viana).[84]

Pereira Passos had proposed transversing the *cidade velha* from edge to edge, using its old streets (widened and straightened where necessary): first, the Rua da Prainha to pass through the barrier of hills between the docks and the *cidade velha*, then a combination of other existing streets to cross the city and pass between the hills to the south. Müller and Frontin, however, convinced Pereira Passos to abandon his old proposal in favor of theirs. The latter was roughly congruent in route, but distinct in its radical solutions to the same problems. It was not constrained by linkage to existing streets – it cut through them with a broad, straight swath, determined only by breaks in the hills and commercial expedience. Instead of departing from the Rua da Prainha, their proposed route left from the Largo da Prainha. The Largo was to be the terminus of the new portworks avenue (Avenida dos Cais, now Avenida Rodrigues Alves) which would skirt the projected new quays. Their proposal thus superseded Pereira Passos' old solution by joining a north – south boulevard directly to the new port's possibilities. Their direct route also changed the southern terminus; instead of ending in the Largo da Mãe do Bispo, which fed into the Rua da Ajuda and thus reached the shore indirectly, their route drove straight there to meet with Pereira Passos' projected Avenida Beira Mar, which connected the *cidade velha* to the *Zona Sul*. Finally, of course, their proposed route's width and the destruction it necessitated was part of the Haussmannist solution to the congestion and inefficiency of the city's old downtown.[85]

The Avenida Central, as the projected boulevard was soon called (after the death of Rodrigues Alves' great Foreign Minister, the Baron do Rio Branco, in 1912, the Avenida was renamed in his honor), was built in eighteen months, beginning on 29th February 1904. It was inaugurated twice – in 1904, celebrating the end of demolition, on Brazil's independence day, 7th September and again in 1905, celebrating the Avenue's construction, on the anniversary of the Proclamation of the Republic, 15 November. Both inaugurations were designed as events of enormous national importance, with Rodrigues Alves presiding over crowded ceremonies recorded by solemn newspaper and photographic coverage. The achievements were considered miraculous, both for their speed and their public drama. In a year and a half, crews

1. The Avenida Central, during the genteel version of Carnaval, 1907

destroyed some 590 buildings in the *cidade velha*, and small portions of the Castelo and São Bento hills. When completed, the avenue reached 1,996 meters, with a width of 33, dimensions truly revolutionary in South America.[86]

The proposed avenue was clearly planned for far more than traffic – it was intended as an annunciation. When, by 1910, all of its buildings were constructed and the Avenida's concept thus realized, a magnificent, urbane perspective graced Rio. The Federal Capital now had a truly "civilized" boulevard – two parallel walls of buildings in the most established good taste – a monument to Brazil's Progress. The postcards demonstrate that certain private buildings, such as that of the newspaper *Jornal do Commercio*, caught the public eye, but it was the clutch of public buildings at the avenue's southern end, the Teatro Municipal (1909), the Palácio Monroe (1906), the Biblioteca Nacional (1910), the Escola Nacional de Belas Artes (1908), along with the magnificent view of façades presented by the Avenida itself, which dominated public imagination.[87] These were hardly accidental effects. Indeed, the great iconographic study of the Avenida, the 1906 album, *Avenida Central*, is a demonstration of this. In it, by a decision of Frontin and his team, the photographer Marc Ferrez matched each of the architectural elevations drawn for Avenida façades with a photograph of the finished work. Frontin and his associates were quite self-conscious in the symbolism and impetus they wished to achieve. The façades and the forces they represented and promoted were as carefully planned as the Avenida's direction.[88]

Frontin, for instance, through a careful scheme of compensation, investment criteria, and preferred purchase stipulations, ensured that the Avenida was a showcase of Civilization. Its buildings were devoted to great foreign and domestic commercial and infrastructural firms; expensive, Europhile recreation and consumption; established literature and fine arts; the Church, and the State. Frontin also, like Haussmann, stipulated the height and width of every façade. Indeed, he forced the architects involved to submit façade plans to a jury, too. This method was chosen because, like the Viennese, the Carioca façades admitted variety in their individual style. This variety may have been allowed because of the accepted architectural notion that a building's appearance should express its purpose, and Avenida buildings had varied purposes. Despite this, however, there was an underlying unity in the apparent diversity that emerged by 1906. The jury's taste and the architects' training saw to that. The façades were, above all, a Carioca celebration of French Eclecticism, the consecrated expression of the Ecole des Beaux-Arts.[89]

The Ecole emerged from France's revolutionary and Napoleonic reforms of the royal academies. Its Section d'Architecture's influence became pervasive in the European world, especially after the reform of Second Empire Paris, which featured so much of its work. I have mentioned, for example, that the Opéra was considered the signature of the period style; the Opéra was designed by the Ecole's Charles Garnier. Indeed, the Opéra has been recognized as a monument to French Eclecticism and Ecole teaching. It thus serves one well as an introduction to a discussion of Avenida façades.[90]

Late Eclecticism (c. 1860s–1920s) represented the influence of Romanticism, in the sense of both the exotic and the historical; the Classical, in the sense of a strong attachment to that style's various European manifestations; and the baroque, in the sense of a "counterpoint of visual rhythms." It was quintessentially nineteenth-century, in its pragmatic, sensitive synthesis of all of these influences to achieve an intuitive effect, and in that it frequently used the glass and cast iron newly available in the period. It was urbanistic, in that it treasured circulation within a complex of real streets and buildings, rather than simple, abstract internal articulation within a projected building.[91]

Garnier's Opéra features almost all of these Eclectic characteristics. The painting, columns, motifs, and statuary are Romantic and Classical in their display of polychromy and distinct historical phases of the Classical styles. It is superbly baroque in its use of counterpoint between the vertical of its three domed pavilions and the horizontal of its imposing crossed-rectangle main structure. Although glass does not play a striking role, cast iron graces the building's railings, gates, and lamps. It is a masterful example of eclectic synthesis, in that Garnier orchestrated his varied motifs, periods, volumes, materials, and colors into an intuitive composition of undeniable power. It is urbanistic in that Garnier stressed circulation, to the point of challenging Romantic rules regarding the correspondence of internal and external structure. For instance, rather than break up the promenade of opera-goers from street to seat, Garnier worked the exterior and interior passages, foyers, salons, and stairways to impart a smooth majesty to one's arrival, setting aside the Romantic teaching, which would have restricted the placement and size of such things as his magnificent main staircase. Indeed, Garnier's preoccupation with the opera-goer indicates another Ecole characteristic – the emphasis on actual experience in relation to the building. By the early 1800s, Ecole theorists wrote of a building as a series of tableaux perceived by a person walking into and through it. By the 1860s, Garnier wrote of architecture as tailoring for an experience of princely comfort and imperial display, something which not only had impact on those who viewed it, but shaped their perception of themselves and others while they were under its influence.[92]

Such was the architectural tradition which dominated the considerations of the jury judging the Avenida façades. Among the ten jurymen, the dominant intellectual influence was French. Müller, Frontin, Pereira Passos, Saldanha de Gama, Aarão Reis, and Jorge Lossio were all engineers trained in, or representing, the Francophile engineering institutions of Rio; the Escola Central, Escola Politécnico, and the Instituto Politécnico. Of the others, Feijó Júnior, Oswaldo Cruz, Ismael da Rocha, and Rodolfo Bernadelli, Cruz was Paris-trained (Institut Pasteur) and Bernadelli's family was long associated with the 1826 Brazilian offspring of the Ecole des Beaux-Arts – the Escola Nacional de Belas Artes. Even if French influence had been insignificant personally, however, the Beaux-Arts tradition could not fail to influence their judgment as an architectural jury. The post-Haussmann period was that of the Ecole's greatest influence (1870–1914); it was felt from Vienna to San Francisco.[93]

Beyond the Ecole's influence on the jury's judgment, one must logically expect to find it on the architects involved. Of the seventy-seven projects accepted, twenty (the greatest number from a single hand) were the work of Adolfo Morales de los Rios (1858–1928). One of his buildings won one of the jury's highest prizes; another was one of the Avenida's aesthetic hallmarks, the Escola Nacional de Belas Artes' new seat. Little wonder why one architectural historian has called him the "most prestigious architect of the epoch."[94] More to the point, this influential Spanish architect was a former student at the Ecole des Beaux-Arts, where he spent two of his six years (1877–82) in Paris studying architecture. In Rio, where he settled, Morales de los Rios was a professor at Belas Artes, where he trained, among others, Heitor de Melo, whose many buildings are also typical of the period, including the Avenida's Jockey Club, Derby Club, and Conselho Municipal. Morales de los Rios, however, if one simply counts those Avenida buildings that most impressed contemporaries, built not only the Escola de Belas Artes, but the Archiepiscopal Palace (now the old Supreme Federal Tribunal), the *O Paiz* building, the Associação dos Empregados no Comércio do Rio de Janeiro building, the Café Mourisco, the "Edifício das Aguias," and the Equitativa building. In these, the Eclectic character of Ecole architecture is marked. Whether "pure" (e.g., the classicism of the "Edifício das Aguias"), exotic (e.g., the Café Mourisco), or contemporary French (e.g., the Escola de Belas Artes, or the *O Paiz* building), the stress on composition, the exotic, the historic, the Classical, on the use of cast iron and glass, and on visual counterpoint is clear. In his *tour de force*, the Escola, where he could design a building of truly monumental scope, the Ecole stress on circulation, character, and internal tableaux were masterfully rendered – at least on paper. In the actual execution, to his chagrin, much was changed.[95]

Even in buildings where the architect was not directly linked to the Ecole, the latter's influence is patent. Take two other exemplary buildings of the Carioca *belle époque* – the Biblioteca Nacional and the Teatro Municipal. Although the putative architect of the former, Francisco Marcelino de Souza Aguiar, was only schooled in the Francophile engineering schools of Rio (he was a military engineer), this and other famous works of his (most notably, the Palácio Monroe, built in St. Louis for the 1904 Exhibition there and then brought to Rio) bear the indelible stamp of Ecole inspiration. The Biblioteca Nacional may well have been especially French in origin. As Santos' research has

2. The Teatro Municipal, from a contemporary postcard

shown,[96] the original plan, written in French, seems to have come from the hand of one M. Hector Pepin, a French architect.[97]

The French links are even stronger for the Teatro Municipal. Its plan, authored by Pereira Passos' son, Francisco de Oliveira Passos, was clearly inspired by Garnier's Opéra – façade, floor plan, lateral views, and interior demonstrate the paternity. Only changes born of the constraints of the locale (including smaller dimensions and the site's odd triangular shape) really distinguish the Carioca theater from Garnier's. Instead of Garnier's symmetrical pair of crossed rectangles, for example, Oliveira Passos used three crossed rectangles, two of which are slightly asymmetrical, to parallel the lateral and rear streets. However, the viewer is more conscious of only one great difference – the two smaller pavilions Garnier planted to either side of his central pavilion have, in the Carioca variant, been brought forward and closer together on either side of the main entrance. The visual impact and circulation of the interior demonstrate the same compromises, but also declare Garnier's influence in clear accents. No wonder – the architectural team and auxiliaries charged with construction and embellishment were made up of Frenchmen and Francophile Brazilians almost to a man.[98]

Such buildings point to the contemporary meaning of the boulevard.

The Avenida was the centerpiece of Carioca reforms and, as such, it had to demonstrate Brazil's claims to Civilization and Progress. I discuss what this entailed below, but several *unintended* symbolic aspects may be noted here. First, the Beaux-Arts role suggests the pervasive influence of the Parisian interpretation of European civilization in Brazil, a motif central to all this study. Civilization and Progress were generally rendered in French.

Second, one must note the way in which this French influence was adapted in Rio. Beyond the accommodation to local circumstances, which buildings like the Teatro Municipal display, is another which makes for an obvious cliché. Although the great public buildings of the government, the Church, literature, and the fine arts were whole, integral constructions, most of the Avenida's construction involved a Beaux-Arts façade grafted on to a plain, functional building, completely divorced aesthetically and functionally from its face; a Brazilian body with a French mask.[99] Garnier had successfully broken with Ecole dicta regarding correspondence between external and internal appearance by inspired composition that pulled the disparate elements together.[100] This Carioca divorce between the external and internal, however, was grossly different, lacking any unity in material terms. Yet, in a larger way, there was still an affinity to Ecole teachings. Beaux-Arts theorists taught that the outer appearance of the building should state the building's function. All of the Avenida's buildings did this, if in an ironic manner. Although they often lacked internal *architectural* coherence with their façades, they still fulfilled a purpose coherent with their façades' *symbolic* function. After all, no matter how Brazilian, each of these constructions was integrated into the fantasy of Civilization. Even if they lacked Beaux-Arts floor plans and spatial organization, they sold European luxuries, participated in North Atlantic trade, catered to a Europhile style of consumption, and so on. The Frenchman experiencing the Opéra viewed and moved within a fantasy of refinement and display purposely crafted by Garnier; the Carioca, in the meanest, most apparently discordant Avenida building, did the same – in Carioca terms. Though it lacked the architectural coherence of the Parisian model, such a building, through its façade, Avenida locale, and European goods or connections, successfully conveyed this neo-colonial experience of Civilization to the Carioca. The mask often shaped the features and affected the vision of its wearer.

Third, the direction of the Avenida seems allusive, too. In Haussmann's Paris, the boulevards often led the eye toward a monument of historic French grandeur; a church, a column, a triumphal arch. I contrasted this earlier to the Viennese Ringstrasse, which pulled the viewer by one newly-built bourgeois building after another, encircling an aristocratic past in decline, without being able to focus on a rooted, secure present. The Avenida Central's two termini are a third symbolic contrast: each links colony and metropolis and suggests their juncture in the *belle époque*. A monument marked each terminus, as in Paris. The northern terminus had, by 1910, a column topped with a statue of the Viscount de Mauá, pioneer of Brazilian finance and industry. The southern one had an obelisk, put up by the contractor Antônio Januzzi to celebrate the Avenida's completion. Neither marker, however, dominates the perspective it was meant to. Instead, the northern end of the Avenida points one's view toward the quays and, beyond, to the hinterland from which coffee came. The southern points to the fashionable residential districts of the elite, and, beyond, toward Pão de Açucar and the Atlantic – that is, to the site of the first colonial settlement and then to the route of the colonial and neo-colonial metropolises. The Avenida, like the *belle époque* for which it stood, pulsed between both poles, colonial realities and metropolitan dynamism, in a constant counterpoint, a tension which is basic to the explanation and experience of the world under discussion here.

11. "O Rio civiliza-se."[101]

To conclude the overture of this study, one must emphasize the contemporary perception of what was happening to Rio under Rodrigues Alves. In this perception, one picks up one of the central themes of nineteenth-century elite culture – denial and evasion. For, in the changes of the *belle époque*, the elite celebrated not only what was done, but what was undone.

To "civilize" Rio, it was clear to Rodrigues Alves' auxiliaries that the city's plan and its hygiene must be reformed. They pursued Civilization by material change along modern European (i.e., French) lines. However, while they undertook such practical measures, they shared with other members of the elite and middle sectors the passion for symbolic changes, too. I have demonstrated this in certain ways just above, but others must be stressed here. It is worth noting, for example, that the *batalhas de flores*[102] in the refurbished Campo de Santana were actively promoted by president and prefect, or recalling the ceremonies concerning the "miracle" of the Avenida Central – the city's new signs of Civilization were successfully manipulated to have enormous impact on contemporaries. The journalists, especially, trumpeted the cultural significance of the reforms. They saw Rio's frenchification not merely as a healthy, efficient new complex of thoroughfares, but as a symbol and means to Brazil's rehabilitation and "civilized" (i.e., European) future. In 1904, one writer pointed out Rio's necessary role in impressing European capitalists and immigrants: "The foreigner who disembarks here . . . brings from his brief visit to our impoverished city a sad idea of all of our country . . . To attempt to turn Rio de Janeiro into a modern, comfortable, and civilized city, then, is an undeniable and immediate necessity in our economic plight."[103]

The significance of the Avenida Central, most conspicuous of the reforms, has been explored. What it meant to contemporaries should, however, be expanded upon. One editor, for instance, argued that:

> For those who mediate . . . on the past and future of the Fatherland, the opening of this street is of an extraordinary import, not only for the greater material grandeur of this city, but for its greater moral grandeur. And as Rio de Janeiro is the center of Brazilian progress and civilization, and as it is by it that all Brazil is judged, the Avenida Central, representing comfort, hygiene, opulence, will convince those who never come here and only make assumptions as to what we are . . . that Brazil is not what they have been told.[104]

The Avenida Central, with its Parisian perspective, Beaux-Arts façades, fashionable import consumption, exuberant shoppers, stylish *flâneurs*, and monumental buildings dedicated to edifying Europhile high culture, made palpable the fantasy of Civilization common to elite Cariocas of the *belle époque*. It also suggested the magical potential they attached to that Civilization; one sanguine commentator opined that:

> The wide and extended streets, the broad gardened plazas, the tall and beautiful buildings, the varied diversions of simple pleasure or of intellectual enjoyment that necessarily accompany these transformations of the milieu in which the populace is living, ought to modify its habits, influence its character, activate its initiative, awaken in it the taste for the beautiful, the cult of the ideal, the love that translates into patriotic acts, not platonic, rhetorical love.[105]

It is only in this ideological context that the reforms can fully be understood. At this high point of the neo-colonial era, the European world generally accepted that increase in commerce, overseas investment, colonialism, and the resultant integrated overseas economies would naturally bring all peoples the same rewards – Civilization and Progress *à la européenne*. The Carioca reforms were understood to be a means to clear away the accidental obstacles to Brazil's achievement of such universal goals, and to proclaim the inevitable, happy results:

a. Rodrigues Alves

b. Pereira Passos

c. Olavo Bilac

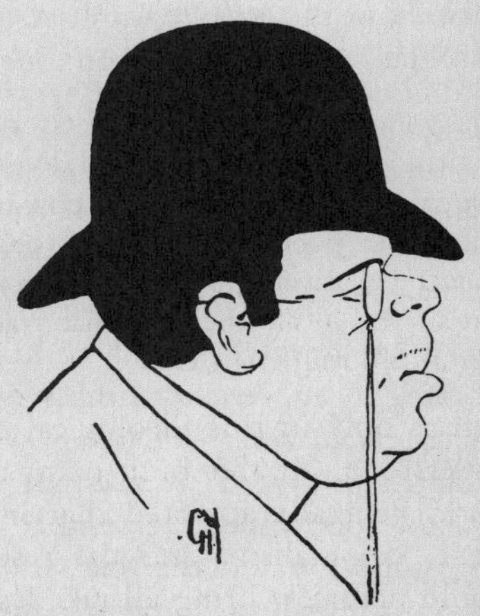

d. João do Rio
(contemporary caricature by Gil)

3. Four who made the Carioca *belle époque*

the works of sanitation and embellishment in the Republic's capital . . . are . . . going to bring innumerable and admirable advantages . . . it falls to the present government to take up the monumental labor of our resurgence as a people which wants to occupy the place to which it has unassailable rights in the concert of nations, whether by its intellectual and moral achievement, or by the vastness of its territory and the material riches that Nature has given it in a gesture of astonishing prodigality.[106]

But these beliefs and fantasies concerning Civilization, the ideological milieu of the reforms, had a negative element essential to their meaning. For, if the reforms meant that Cariocas were achieving Civilization by becoming more European, they also meant, necessarily, a negation, an ending, of much that was very Brazilian indeed. The embrace of Civilization was also the leaving-behind of what many of the Carioca elite saw as a backward, colonial past and the condemnation of the racial and cultural aspects of Carioca reality that the elite associated with that past.

The reforms were described as a tonic against "tropical lethargy," and an attack on old material circumstances conspiring to leave Brazil traditional (i.e., backward). When the Avenida's construction began, for instance, one of the city's literati, Olavo Bilac, proclaimed:

A few days ago, the picks, intoning a jubilant hymn, began the work of the Avenida Central's construction, knocking down the first condemned houses . . . we begin to stride toward our rehabilitation. In the collapse of the walls, in the crumbling of the stones, in the pulverization of the earth, there was a long groan. It was the sad and lamenting groan of the Past, of Backwardness, of Shame. The colonial city, filthy, backward, obstinate in its old traditions, was weeping with the sobs of those rotten materials falling apart. But the clear hymn of the picks smothered the impotent protest. With what happiness they sang, the regenerating picks! And how the souls of those who were there understood well what the picks were saying, in their unceasing, rhythmic clamor, celebrating the victory of hygiene, of good taste, and of art.[107]

What were these old traditions, the Backwardness, the Shame of Brazil? They were not simply unhealthy and inefficient colonial aspects of the *cidada velha* – they were symbols of a culture the Europhile Carioca wanted forgotten. It was not only filthy narrow streets that Pereira Passos condemned, remember, but unpainted façades, rural styles of consumption, and the "barbaric" aspects of *Carnaval*. Perhaps the latter is most revealing, *Carnaval*, after all, with its *entrudo* and *cordões*, partly expressed a whole Afro-Brazilian culture of which the Europhile elite were ashamed. In the same issue of the fashionable review in which he celebrated the Avenida's construction, Bilac attacked the "abominable *cordões*" as "that ancient custom of bacchic processions." "I believe," he wrote, "that, of all civilized cities, Rio de Janeiro is the only one that tolerates this shameful exhibition . . . it is revolting that these orgies spill out onto the streets, in erotic processions."[108]

João do Rio, most adventurous of contemporary journalists, pointed out that "*Carnaval* would have disappeared . . . if it were not for the enthusiasm of the groups from Gambôa, Saco [de Alferes], Saúde, S. Diogo, *cidade nova* [predominantly Afro-Brazilian, working-class districts], that burning enthusiasm . . . which captures and leads astray the entire city."[109] He also noted the *cordões*' origins:

> they come from the festival of Our Lady of the Rosary, back in colonial times. I don't know why the blacks like Our Lady of the Rosary. [However,] in that period they already liked her and went out in the street dressed like kings, animals, pagans, and policemen, playing African instruments, and they would stop in the front of the Viceroy's house to dance and sing . . . the origin of the *cordões* is the African Afoché, the day in which religion is mocked.[110]

Luís Edmundo, another contemporary journalist, recalls that it was during the reforms that such "outlandish traditions" were condemned or restrained: "Rio is becoming civilized, the papers report. And the barbarous noise is invited to disappear from a city that is beginning to worship civilization!" During *Carnaval*, he remembered, "Only the aristocrat, the *élégants*" who triumphed with the reforms did not participate.[111]

Such people wanted to put an end to that old Brazil, that "African" Brazil that threatened their claims to Civilization. And, it was a very present "Africa" for the elite. Most of the elite had probably been nursed by blacks and were surrounded by black servants, and they had known slavery, abolished only in 1888, at first hand. A substantial portion of the city's population, perhaps more than half, remained of African descent, and their traditions mingled and flourished in servants' quarters, nurseries, and the poorer *cidade velha* neighborhoods and hills. Indeed, hillside shanty-towns (*favelas*) had been founded near the newer northern dock area in the late nineteenth century, and often it was to these that refugees from the decrepit housing of the *cidade velha* fled after their homes were destroyed in the 1903–6 reforms.[112] Luís Edmundo remembers this old "African" Rio well:

> the country, until the time of the African slave trade's end, was still a land that seemed more like a corner of Africa than a nation of the New World. And, it was more or less the same until the dawn of this century. Bilac, quite accurately, called the Rio de Janeiro of his time, Old Portuguese Bantuland![113]

Skidmore[114] has demonstrated how the "scientific" racism of this era of intense European imperialism was accepted in Brazil, and how it had driven the white elite and its spokesmen to despair for their country's future. The elite, in effect, often perceived Brazil in much the same way as contemporary European colonists in other parts of the world viewed outright colonies – as an area of potential riches obstructed by an inferior race and culture. This was so especially before the time of the reforms. Luís Edmundo relates how the city was perceived as both parochial and distasteful to the white high society. Elite men rode in their imported carriages, rather than mix with "people of little or no social position," and the elite women, "agreeably disgusted," examined with *lorgnons* "the prosaic and badly dressed plebians" while thinking of the Bois de Boulogne or Hyde Park and "letting escape, from time to time, out of their polite little mouths, tender sighs which seemed to be torn from the depths of their souls . . . which might be translated thus: My God, what a horrible city, and what people!"[115]

In effect, the reforms under Rodrigues Alves, with their explicit condemnation of urban appearance and culture associated with traditions considered backward, barbaric, and colonial, were designed to stake Brazil's claim to "European" status – Civilization – partly by the explicit attack on an old, unique Brazil. And, for many among the elite, that attack was a successful one:

> the city slowly began to change. New immigration began to make its way here augmenting our population considerably and, above all, greatly diminishing the number of blacks . . . Even in our usages and customs there were transformations . . . We changed everything, until we came to change, completely, our mentality, hobbled by long years of stubborn self-absorption and routine. They were right, then, when the country's papers . . . cried out: Rio is becoming civilized! It was indeed becoming civilized! Progress, which for a long time had hovered at the door, without permission to enter, was welcomed joyously.[116]

Haussmann had included plans of a counter-revolutionary nature in his blueprints for efficiency, health, and beauty – he attacked the bastions of working-class revolt. Pereira Passos included plans of a counter-traditional nature in his blueprints for efficiency, health, and beauty *à la européenne* – he attacked bastions of an essentially Brazilian milieu and its Afro-Brazilian culture. In the Rodrigues Alves reforms, as he and his elite audience perceived them, however, the reforms' negative impact was naturally subsumed in the positive one proposed. With these changes, they held, Brazil began her rebirth and demonstrated her potential for joining a triumphant, universal Civilization.

One's own conclusion may be broader. In the new "civilized" Rio, a long-lived, colonial predisposition for the assimilation of European appearances, technology, and values triumphed, and the underlying assumptions and contradictions of the Carioca *belle époque* were made concrete.[117]

Let us now turn to a close analysis of that predisposition and explore the roots of the assumptions and contradictions of turn-of-the-century Rio.

2
Formal institutions of the elite

Our exploration of elite culture and society begins with the consideration of formal institutions charged with the intellectual and social formation of elite youth and several other institutions within which Society and high culture generally flourish. It is in these places that much of elite world-view and social domination were both expressed and promoted. The places taken up here will include schools, social clubs, and theaters. These share a public, inclusive character within the elite world which suggests separate discussion. The institutions chosen, moreover, will afford a specific notion of the historical development of the Carioca elite by providing the basis for an analysis of the changes in the origins, circumstances, and expression of elite society and culture.

1. Secondary education

Higher education in the Second Reign (1840–89) and the Old Republic (1889–1930) was generally the preserve of families of wealth and position. As time wore on, a growing number of the children of shopkeepers, lesser bureaucrats, and professionals managed to enter *colégios*, but, for the most part, those born outside elite circles were either illiterates or autodidacts. The reasons are unsurprising. Tutors and the few *colégios* that existed were expensive, were traditionally considered proper to the rich, and, of course, would take children out of the field, the shop, or wherever they were contributing to the economic survival of their families. In 1872, to pick a middling date, "for a population estimated by the census at about 10,000,000 inhabitants, the general matriculation in the primary schools was not more than 150,000 pupils."[1]

During the Monarchy and Old Republic, the sons of wealthy planters, big merchants and men of affairs, upper bureaucrats, and wealthy professionals were educated by their parents or by tutors (often

Europeans) at home for a few years. After they were old enough, they were sent to the *colégio* which was generally part of the provincial or state capital's claim to cultural preeminence. In the first half of the nineteenth century, these *colégios* were often staffed with a European or two, religious or lay; perhaps an expatriate Frenchman, like the Guinard who taught in the Rio of 1837 and complained, "I am condemned to pass some three or four years in this backward country, in the midst of this people without mettle and without shame!"[2]

Certain premises about such education, especially during the Monarchy, are apparent. It was not only an education for the few, but one with an urbanizing impact; it forced those few to come together in the more important provincial cities and the Côrte. Moreover, it was an education distinctly Eurocentric. The teachers were often from the Old World (probably French, or French influenced); the texts were often French or translations from the French; and the acknowledged presumption was that the acquisition of European culture was intended.[3] Given the origins of many of the schools, of such teachers, and of such texts, one may also assume an education much beholden to Restoration France – humanist, conservative, and Catholic.[4]

As for the girls in elite families, the situation was rather bleak for most of the century. In the earlier era, they were given very little education at all, and throughout the century, they were generally taught at home by parents or tutors. Some few attended small classes taught by foreigners, or attended the highly select nuns' schools that slowly took root, or were taken to Europe with their parents and allowed an education in French convent schools.[5]

The assumption was that a boy would get the basic intellectual formation necessary for a bureaucrat or statesman (a foundation to which he would probably add the *bachelarado* from the Faculty of Law at either Recife or São Paulo). The *colégio* also provided the humanist culture required for a European gentleman. The assumptions about a girl's education were rather different. As late as 1898, Rui Barbosa's daughter Adélia was described as "one of the ornaments of our aristocratic society. Rare are the girls who at such a tender age can show themselves to be so rich in instruction as she. She is familiar with various languages, and reveals herself a remarkable artist on the piano." That is, learning for girls comprised a list of genteel accomplishments that enhanced their reputations in the eyes of a prospective suitor and his family.[6]

It is within this context that the Colégio Pedro II and the Collège de Sion are most illustrative. Each was, in its day, the model for the secondary education of elite children. Let us consider the elder of the two first.

The Colégio Pedro II

The Colégio Pedro II was built on the eighteenth-century foundations of the Escola de São Joaquim, and was created under the imperial aegis in 1837 in response to the obvious need for a central Brazilian secondary school. It soon became the preferred alma mater of *turmas* (classes) of boys from those elite families located or relocated in the capital.[7] In fact, it only slipped from this favoured position during the Old Republic, and even when it lost many of the elite's sons, it retained its government patronage and the associated primacy with regard to establishing the national requirements in examinations and texts.[8] Certain aspects of learning at the Colégio Pedro II remained constant throughout the period of its greatness. First, a strong training in the traditional liberal arts. Second, a superb faculty under close imperial scrutiny. Third, the use of rote memorization of standard texts on consecrated subjects.

The Colégio drew its inspiration and curriculum from the classical education of the French. Ancient and modern languages and literature, religion, history, philosophy, rhetoric, and the arts long held favored positions over against mathematics and the natural sciences. Indeed, the later inclusion of such emphases, even in limited form, represented a radical change in the Brazilian tradition.[9] The prestige of scientific training grew slowly in the Colégio, parallel to that of Brazil's technological progress: both gained ground only in the later Second Reign and the Old Republic, triumphing in the radical educational reforms under the new regime. Even before those reforms, the gradual inroads made were resented by many of the traditionally-formed elite. Ferreira Viana, Colégio alumnus and outstanding lawyer and statesman wrote on the Republic's eve that,

> We ought to respect the rights of science in . . . education, but it is particularly necessary to promote culture. There is no more beautiful source of moral education, [or] better choice of virile preparation for life in society, than that of the study of the humanities, the contact with antiquity, with that antiquity full of great examples, who all, in the phrase of the great Roman orator, would be buried in the dark, if they did not fire the light of letters.[10]

It was towards the light of letters, then, that the youngsters wended, trudging through the narrow, noisy streets of the *cidade velha* to the imposing, two-storied *externato*, rebuilt in Eclectic style by Bittencourt da Silva in the 1870s, or marching through the halls of one or another of the *internatos* maintained by the colégio among the farms and villas of the outlying districts of Engenho Velho and then São Cristóvão. Within the small *turmas* (all of which, in 1865, for example, added up to 327 boys), for as many as six or seven years, young gentlemen and a sprinkling of scholarship boys,[11] studied the classics under the eye of the greatest professors of the Second Reign. One loyalist recalled that "it was said that there were only two enviable positions in Brazil: that of Senator of the Empire and that of Professor of the Colégio Pedro II." And another tells us, "The competitions for the professorial chairs consisted of very rigorous examinations. Carried out under the personal supervision and control of the Emperor, true merit always triumphed, and the impression left by these contests of knowledge remained indelible in the memory of those who witnessed them." Certainly, the list of professors is impressive, including many of the greatest names in nineteenth-century Brazilian letters, history, and science: the Baron de Tautphoeus, Sílvio Romero, Capistrano de Abreu, Carlos de Läet, Paulo de Frontin, João Ribeiro, Joaquim Caetano, the Baron de Homem de Mello, Joaquim Manuel de Macedo, Gonçalves Dias, the Baron do Rio Branco, and Coelho Neto.[12] It was under these men that the boys studied, standing to recite what had been laboriously learned by heart. One son of an alumnus recalled the "great mental strength, . . . the inductive faculties, and . . . the exhaustive gymnastics of memory" required "for the acquisition of great and varied knowledge." More prosaically, our informant tells us of the response given him when he had the chance to ask his father's old professor the reason for forcing pupils to memorize lessons:

> "Boy, the student who does not memorize only avoids saying something stupid when he understands the point, and this does not always happen. Because of this, I took the route of always demanding that the students learn the material by heart for me, because in this way, they would not say something foolish, even though they didn't understand the issue.[13]

Whether understood or not, then, the lessons were repeated, and often in the presence of Pedro II, who was inclined to pay visits to witness the progress of his protégés. One alumnus remembered that,

> The bell, . . . gave the signal for the Emperor's visit . . . I had the old monarch presiding solemnly at my final examination in French, flanked, at the enormous table, by the rectors, the vice-rectors, and the professors of the subject in both houses, the *externato* and the *internato*.[14]

As for the learning under such scrutiny, it was culled from the likes of religious such as Fr. Francisco de São Luís, P. Caldas, and P. Antônio Pereira, who all wrote on Portuguese and Latin grammar, as well as from French texts, such as Delamarche's *Atlas*, Sévene's *Grammática Francesa*, Filon's *Nouvelle narrations françaises*, de Rosoir and Dumont's *História romana*, Charles André's *Cours de littérature française*, Barbe's *Cours élémentaire de philosophie*, and the *Manuel d'études pour la préparation du baccalauréat en lettres: Histoire de temps modernes*. The English were represented by Murray's *English Spelling Book*, Goldsmith's *History of Rome*, Clifton's *Guia de conversação*, and Hillard's *First-Class Reader*. There were even some texts by Brazilians. After all, hardly anyone else wrote about Brazil then, and the professors sometimes wrote the first texts themselves. Among the earliest used were the classic by Abreu Amoroso Lima, *Historia do Brasil*, as well as P. Pompéo's *Compendio de geographia*, and A. M. da Silva Pontes' *Nova rhetorica brasileira*. But, all in all, the Ancients would seem to have enjoyed much greater attention. They marched in with Caesar in the van, followed by Phaedrus, Cornelius Nepos, Ovid, Sallust, Virgil, Cicero, Livy, and Horace, with the noble Tacitus bringing up the rear. All of the authors cited, for example, were typical of the 1862 *programa*.

In that particular epoch at the *colégio*, these were among the authors pored over in five years of Latin, four years of geography, three years of French, English, Greek, and mathematics, two years of philosophy and medieval history, and one year each of Portuguese, reading and analysis, ancient European history, sacred history, Roman history, experimental physics and chemistry, modern history, philosophical and rhetorical grammar, the history and geography of Brazil, natural history, poetry and literature, and experimental natural history. And it was under this sort of intellectual regime that the men who would come to dominate the Carioca *belle époque*, men such as Rodrigues Alves and Joaquim Nabuco, passed through the Colégio.[15]

The students' socialization conformed to the prejudices of that era in European education: submission to authority was axiomatic, and authority was ubiquitous. The boys wore a distinctive uniform; at first, a quasi-religious habit, later, a gentleman's formal attire. They were subject to a discipline that recalled the religious origins from which the *colégio* was but barely removed. One student recalled, for instance, "The bell, that marked for us the exact hour for entrance to, and departure from, the *colégio*, the beginning and end of each class, the quarter hour of recreation, [that] marked, systematized, habituated, punctuated our duties, accustoming us to discipline, to exactitude, to punctuality."[16]

Their schedule, their comportment, and their comings and goings, as well as their work itself, were all regulated, and omissions and commissions noted.[17] The 1838 *Regulamento do Colégio* is to the point:

The students will be divided into classes of 30 to 35 each and, as far as possible, into classes of the same age and of the same course; the direction and supervision of each class will be confided to an *inspetor de alunos* . . . The *inspetores* will eat at the table with them; their quarters will communicate with the dormitories, in order that they might easily inspect them. The *inspetor de alunos* is charged with: 1: dividing his class into as many subdivisions as will be judged necessary, turning over the direction of each one of them to the student who merits confidence, who will be responsible for the behavior of the subdivision; 2: writing a daily report of what has happened in his class, in which will be given a summary account of the behavior and application of the students; 3: on Saturdays organizing a chart on the progress and work of each of the students; 4: turning over his reports every night and that chart on Saturday night to the *vice-reitor*; 5: being aware of the work to be assigned to the students by the professors, and taking care that the lessons be done with exactitude; 6: taking to the students the lessons that they ought to learn by heart; and examining the written work that they have done; putting on a separate page their judgment concerning the work before turning it over to the respective professors; 7: accompanying the students every time that they leave to go out; 8: occasionally examining the books of the students, to see if all have been authorized by the *reitor*.[18]

The Colégio was thus another, perhaps more dismal, world, one which inspired a lasting bitterness in some.[19] But whatever the harshness of such discipline, hierarchy, and close supervision, the status of the school and its instructors was unquestioned. In imperial Brazil, one could do no better:

That *casa de educação* was the apple of the eye of H.M. the Emperor D. Pedro II. He attended all of the professorial competitions, the solemn graduation of the *bacheréis*, the boys' exams, where he asked them questions. This assiduity of the Sovereign gave him contact with the boys and these, when men, were those chosen by him for the positions in the upper administration of the Country.[20]

The roll of those who attended the *colégio* shows that the boys of the same and inter-related families came and went there for generations, and that among them were many of the *conselheiros*, ministers, senators, *titulares*,[21] and important bankers, lawyers, and doctors who presided over the fortunes of imperial and republican Brazil.[22] It is the pride of the school that men such as Joaquim Nabuco, the Viscount de Taunay, Rodrigues Alves, Washington Luís, Ferreira Viana, and Antônio Prado passed through its portals. There the sons of the great provincial planters, merchant princes, and imperial politicians and statesmen met, learned, and lived together in their small *turmas*, and often made the acquaintances among and with whom and whose families they would make their ways in the years to come.[23]

The next step generally taken, the Faculty of Law in either Recife or São Paulo, only enhanced such elite congregation and socialization. Often, indeed, schoolmates from the Colégio Pedro II continued rooming together, in the *repúblicas* that were rowdier adolescent equivalents of the strict childhood *dormitórios* of the *internato*.[24] The Colégio Pedro II was, in effect, the best first step in the *cursus honorum* of the Empire in which the men of the Carioca *belle époque* grew up. Moreover, it is safe to say that if the boys of the Carioca elite did not pass through the Colégio itself, they experienced the same sort of formation at the provincial level or in the Rio monastery schools of the Jesuits or other regular orders that began to gain favor toward the end of the century. Indeed, it is important to emphasize that these Carioca religious *colégios* gained favor precisely because they continued to provide the exclusive, disciplined, and humanist education that the men of the ruling class had had at the Colégio Pedro II or its provincial imitators and wanted for their heirs in turn.[25]

The Collège de Sion

For heiresses, it was different. As noted earlier, the daughters of the elite often did not even share in the limited secondary education available in the Second Reign: they were generally taught what was considered appropriate at home. The exceptions were those whose fathers, posted to Europe as diplomats, or living there in the enjoyment of their rural or commercial wealth or urban rents,[26] decided to fit out their daughters with a prestigious, Catholic schooling in the hands of one or another order of nuns. Such convent schools were, after all, good, safe places to stow the girls away while one went about one's business or pleasure, and it was entirely the aristocratic thing to do in Europe at the time. Paris' Sacré Coeur was the preferred school in the preferred city.[27]

Now, this was all very well for a good many years, but it was expensive and not very convenient to indulge in either alternative. European schooling, especially, was difficult to manage for those who, like it or not, spent most of their time in Brazil. In the last decade of the Monarchy, one of the more important *titulares* in Rio, the Countess Monteiro de Barros, and a number of her well-born friends decided that they wanted to arrange a proper education for their daughters in Brazil itself. They did not, of course, mean by this a Brazilian education, in the way a modern nationalist might. They meant an education: for them, that meant a Catholic, French education by French nuns.[28] Whereas one might argue that the Colégio Pedro II (with its Brazilian origins, instructors, and occasionally Brazilian texts) had its Europeanizing influence and direction at second hand and was partially rooted in a Carioca tradition (the Escola de São Joaquim), the *collège* the Countess had in mind was to be a direct transplant.

As the nuns of the Sacré Coeur were not to be had, despite the best efforts of the Countess and a friend high in the Papal court, the lady accepted a subsequent offer from the Congrégation de Notre Dame de Sion.[29] This congregation was a recent one, founded originally by converted Jews to proselytize among their own people. But, in the milieu of social reform and evangelical education in this period of Church history, the Congrégation constituted a teaching order ready to brave the steamy jungles and fever-ridden port capital of Brazil to instruct the daughters of the ruling families in Christian culture. They began their mission in 1888.[30]

The teaching that Sion provided over the years surely must have pleased the noble patroness of the *collège*. On the one hand, the cultural formation, many of nuns themselves, the language spoken, most of the texts, and the paradigm of pedagogy provided were all French. Moreover, the atmosphere and the aims of the *collège* were profoundly Catholic and evangelical, often leaving a distinctive trace in the religious devotion of the young women who graduated to take their places in the ruling class.

The curriculum makes much of this obvious. There were, of course, the necessary books on Portuguese grammar, and Brazilian books such as Serrano's *Epitome de historia universal*. But most of the authors who shouldered in were French, or the classics mediated by the French. There were Pichon's *Histoire de la littérature latine*, and "Jules César" and his *Commentaires sur la guerre des gaules*. There were Racine, Chateaubriand, de Vigny, Sainte-Beuve, Corneille, Molière, La Rochefoucauld, Pascal, and La Bruyère. There were "Tasse" and his *La Jérusalem délivrée*, "Xénophon," "Virgile," "Tacite," "Thucydide," "Platon," and the edifying "Plutarque," with his noble examples.[31]

However, though the humanities *à la francaise* were strongly emphasized, by the 1900s other subjects were not lacking. An *aluna* of Sion recalled that,

> With Portuguese we studied grammar, the history of the language, the regional dialect, the history of the literature and literary analysis . . . In French,

we studied . . . besides the language, the history and literature of France. English and Latin were done in the same way. There was the history of Brazil, general history (prehistory, ancient history, and modern), the history of art, music, science and philosophy and the history of the Church, all [taught] as separate subjects. Calligraphy was obligatory, music and painting optional. The natural sciences were divided into biology, natural history, zoology, and mineralogy. Geography [was taught] in imaginary voyages. Plans and spatial geometry, and even mathematics, algebra, trigonometry, physics and chemistry [were taught]. The subjects were developed over a five-year curriculum . . . Studies were based almost 80% on memorization.[32]

Yet, perhaps the best characterization of much of what seems to have stayed with Sion alumnae is in this account:

Great importance was given to the religious and moral upbringing of the *alunas* . . . On arriving, those students who wished could go to chapel for silent prayers and Communion. At the signal [for beginning class], the *mestra de classe* (the religious responsible for that group), called the roll and each student evaluated herself and gave herself the grade that she deserved for the previous day. An "Honors" when all had gone well; a "Two" when she had shown a lack of application (lessons unstudied), good behavior (talking in the class, the lines, or in the refectory), or politeness (lack of delicacy with teachers, staff, or colleagues). The behavior [expected] at home reinforced the upbringing in the school. Each student used the insignia, cross, and belt that corresponded to her *turma* . . .

The classes were regulated by chimes at the beginning and at the end, as were the hours for meals. The great bell was rung on important occasions and on Sunday for mass. The families, though of a high social level, agreed that the education received at Sion would not consist of social superficialities, [which] gave too much importance to external appearances.[33]

The status and social milieu associated with the *collège* were markedly elitist. The *collège*'s patrons were all titulares and the school enjoyed the favor of the Imperial Family. At first Sion was housed in the mansions of titulares in Rio, only to move to the old Imperial Palace in Petrópolis afterward. Sion immediately enjoyed the reputation of being the most exclusive, the best school for girls of "good family" in Brazil (whence the demand for branches in São Paulo and Minas Gerais).[34] Parents wanted their daughters brought up like those of the French nobility, and they were doubtless satisfied by what has been described. They must have rejoiced to know that their children were taught to obey the rule of silence in the *collège*, that they wore a uniform dictated by the European *congrégation* itself, that they made the required *petite plongée* before addressing a superior. Those who passed through this intellectual and social experience were different, and designedly so. "*Les enfants de Sion*" were noted for their perfect French, their refined manners, their classical literary background, and their proper submission to proper authority. One *aluna* put it succinctly:

There was . . . an element that entered into our *sionense* formation, and which I would suggest was of great importance; I refer to *harmony*, that refines, and to *aesthetics*, which perfects. In Sion simplicity, discipline, even austerity, did not exclude distinction and good taste. Life was made as rhythmic as a piece of music, to the sonorous ringing of the great bell! What harmony, in the cohesion of that society in miniature! In the observance of the hierarchy, in a respectful obedience, which did not diminish one, because she who exercised it was thereby cultivated, and that linked the girl to the *mestra de classe*, the Sisters to the Superior, and all in the same spirit![35]

It was all very wonderful and fine, but it was profoundly distinct from the larger reality outside of the Collège and the *palacetes* of Petrópolis, Laranjeiras, and Botafogo. That reality was the misery of the darker poor (who were to be given charity by those blessed by *le Bon Dieu* with the wealth and position); that was Brazil (which, they were told, "n'a pas d'histoire"); that was the Portuguese-speaking world (whose contemporary authors were not taught by the *soeurs* at Sion).[36] Sion and its later rivals made possible an education which successfully brought aristocratic France to Brazil, not only in the sense intended by the Countess Monteiro de Barros and other titulares, but in the same way that France and Europe often functioned in the Carioca *belle époque* – as the reproach and the counterpoise of the Brazilian realities over which the elite presided.

In these two schools, then, the nature and the direction of formal education for the elite are made clear. In both, small groups of children from similar social backgrounds were placed together, beginning the social interaction with peers which would continue with the same people and their families for their lifetimes, as it often had in the lives of their parents before them. In both, too, elements basic to the neocolonial class society were reinforced – disciplined obedience and belief in a hierarchical society, and the cultural skills and prejudices that corresponded to the acceptance of a world dominated by the North Atlantic powers.

To elaborate, consider the fact that the extremes of Brazilian stratification were accentuated here by schooling in which wealthy and well-to-do children were further isolated and distinguished from the urban middle sectors and the great masses of the rural and urban poor. This was so not only because these children had a formal education in a school (though this would have been enough in terms of a differentiating socio-intellectual experience), nor simply because of their being segregated and socialized along hierarchical lines. These initial aspects were compounded by the results of the inherently Eurocentric learning and experience undergone. They were not simply educated, they were Europeanized to a greater or lesser extent.

There is something inevitably alienating in an education which uses norms and models foreign to the local environment. When one also recalls the prejudices of the European world-view central to this education, the impact seems even more problematic. The assumption among Europeans (and, perhaps, especially among Frenchmen) during the nineteenth century was that their civilization was preeminent, and that most of the cultures of what we now call the Third World were, in corollary fashion, worthy only of disdain or of contempt. In 1855, for example, a Brazilian *titular* abroad found that a well-educated Parisian was quite capable of the most astonishing ignorance about South America, to the extent of not knowing where Rio de Janeiro was. In 1896, a Parisian journalist in Rio would write of the "Brazilian national character," with its "universal apathy", which he compared "in its effects, . . . to the fatalism of the Moslem, to the nihilism of the Buddhist." In 1909, the mistress of Anatole France, the hostess of a noted salon, commented, when her lover departed for a South American lecture tour, that he was "in the antipodes surrounded by monkeys and parrots and savages."[37] Thus, when elite children were implicitly and explicitly taught to measure Brazil with the contemporary European yardstick, they were effectively trained to despise her and the cultural milieu of the Brazilian masses.

If one considers the early stage at which children absorbed these lessons, and the obvious adherence of their parents and teachers to this view of things, the predicament becomes more obvious still. The result is expressed with clarity by one member of the elite, who displayed his own prejudices and, with them, those of many of his peers,[38] when he identified Europe and Civilization as synonymous, and quite distinct from Brazil:

> We, Brazilians (the same may be said of the other South American peoples), are divided between America, the new still forming sediment in our spirit, and Europe, our spirit's stratified layers. The predominance of the latter over the former begins at the point where we acquire the least culture. Our imagination cannot help but be European, that is, but be *human* . . .
>
> I do not mean to say that there may be two humanities, the high and the low, and that we are of the last; perhaps humanity will renew itself one day through

its American branches; but, in the century in which we live, the *human spirit*, that is only one and terribly centralist, belongs to the other side of the Atlantic; the New World, in everything pertaining to the aesthetic or historical imagination, is a true solitude, in which that spirit feels as far from its reminiscences, from its associations of ideas, as if all the past of the human race had been struck from memory and it had, like a child, to stammer and spell out again all that was learned under the Attic sky.[39]

Perhaps the more complete alienation of the Collège de Sion and the somewhat more "Brazilian" nature of the Colégio Pedro II make symbolic points. As though in institutional representation of the larger socio-cultural ambitions of the elite, one finds the women (charged with the inner, domestic life of the elite) more completely separated from Brazil, the better to civilize the elite's inner world, while the men (charged with the outer, public business of the elite in the neo-colonial society as it was) more partially separated, left in a mediating position. It is as though this "middling" alienation of the men's preparation represents their "middling" role of domination, between the two worlds that coexisted in the Rio of the era – a Rio divided between Europeanized, or Europeanizing whites and the Afro-Brazilian masses. The elite men were, in this respect, rather like colonialists within their own country.

But these symbolic distinctions are often more applicable, in many ways, to the formal, public world. One finds, for instance, ambiguities, attenuations, and adaptations in these polarities as they were played out in the elite home, in a far richer complex. But we must leave that aside here; it will appear in another chapter.

2. Social clubs

The historian who spends time leafing through Carioca periodicals notes the names of theaters and clubs long since dust and memory, all betraying the stillborn hopes of gentlemen and artists to find a place for two of the most common pleasures of urbane European life. In the Monarchy and the Old Republic such institutions were characteristically ephemeral, and impoverished if they did manage to survive.[40] The names of successes and failures alike, with their references to antecedents in France and in England, or to faded dreams of a Carioca tradition vigorously maintained, proclaim the pride and the peril of such institutions.

All too often Cariocas with the means simply denied their patronage to such enterprises. One finds the journalists of the *belle époque* lamenting the limited night-life of Rio, or complaining alternately about the lack of a theater-going public and the lack of a decent (i.e., comparable to a European) theater, and even proclaiming the sad lack of theaters at all. One critic sniped in 1904 that, "Our city cannot brag about possessing theaters in abundance, since of the few that exist, there are many that are constantly closed. A study on this point of our social life would only serve to humble us and to give a poor proof of our progress. We are a people which has almost no theaters."[41] And another, writing that same year of the poorly attended performance of a classical duo (made up of Bauer and Casals, no less), sneered, "Our public is one that does not think of such things, and so remains at home or goes to *kill some time* seeing worthless things."[42] And a third, in 1908, described the results with something like desperation:

> Shall we seek distraction at the theaters? But our theaters are so uncomfortable and always empty. [And] to see what? Portuguese reviews, in which every jibe is incomprehensible to us, [full of] parochial life and preoccupations? To hear more or less lively translations of wonderful French wit? Oh! no!
>
> Those who go to the theater leave anxious to be once again in the cozy warmth of home, where comfort and the traditional consolation of tea and hot bread await them.[43]

The basic problem was a general lack of sustained, varied interest on the part of the monied public, as our critics charge; people of means apparently went out, but not often enough to maintain more than a few institutions. A good deal of the apathy may have had to do with a flourishing tradition of domestic diversion. Families in the upper reaches of society enjoyed regular gatherings of kith and kin where music and recitals, and even dancing, were common within the confines and comforts of their homes.[44] This domestic aspect of Society surely helped to obviate many public institutions.

These public institutions to be discussed here, then, are those exceptions to the rule whose longevity itself points to these institutions' preeminent place in Carioca elite society. Their history will have much to tell us about the character and the transitions central to that elite as it developed toward the end of the nineteenth and the beginning of the twentieth centuries.

The Casino Fluminense

The most long-lived of Rio's social clubs was the celebrated Casino Fluminense. The Club Beethoven (founded 1882) was also important, of course. But the Club Beethoven lacked the age, the possibilities, and the social importance of the Casino. It was only a center for literati, artists, and other "appreciadores da vida educada" to meet, during presentations of chamber music and edifying cultural addresses (*conferências*). It must be admitted that its membership was impressive, including people such as Machado de Assis, Rui Barbosa, Ferreira Viana, and the Viscount de Amoroso Lima, that is, established literati, statesmen, and commercial magnates.[45] But that was apparently not enough, as its brief Second Reign existence suggests.

The Casino, was different. It was founded in 1845 by a group of the most powerful men in Rio. Further, it was established in a beautiful neo-classical edifice; it was honored with the repeated presence of the Imperial Family; and it enjoyed the official patronage of the Count d'Eu, consort of the heir apparent. Better still, it was intended as a seat for Society. It was an expensive, exclusive organization (in which the admitted members bought shares and paid dues) that gave the Second Reign's great formal balls at regular intervals and both balls and banquets on important occasions of State or Society. And, as if all this were not enough, it must also be noted that other elite clubs and organizations, in tribute to the Casino's prestige and facilities, made use of the club's building. There, they would hold their own concerts, banquets, and lectures, passing by the trees and springs of the Passeio Público to walk up the grand, carved staircase and enjoy the magnificent furnishings and expanse that delighted all who entered. Even a generally critical Englishman who did so in the early 1880s recalled the occasion with almost unmixed good feeling:

> In the evening we went to a ball, given at what is called the Casino, a magnificent room about as large as the Kensington Town Hall, with a gallery on a fine row of pillars running all round it inside, and well lighted. The floor was bad, the music fair. All the Imperialities [were] there.[46]

The Casino Fluminense's membership was a stable group from the "best society" in Rio. For that reason, the Casino gives one an important opportunity to go beyond lifeless generalizations by briefly examining some of these men, so representative of the Carioca elite. I shall pick among the entire membership in the Casino's first and last phases, to suggest the kind of people who made up the elite in Rio during the Second Reign and the early years of the Old Republic. This will be helpful in much of the discussion and analysis I hope to make in this chapter and in others to follow.[47]

One can begin, for instance, with someone of obvious importance –

the Viscount de Nogueira da Gama (1802–97), Nicolau Antônio Nogueira Valle da Gama. Nogueira, son of a *mineiro* planter, nephew of the very powerful Marquis de Baependí, son-in-law of the Countess de Itapagipe, was a planter, a personal friend of the Emperor, a preeminent member of the court, and, logically enough, the holder of any number of decorations and honorific titles. Another man figuring in the Casino's first lists was also of obvious importance – Roberto Jorge Haddock Lobo (1817–69). Though Haddock Lobo lacked the titles of the Viscount, he was also important in the city. Born in Portugal, he had emigrated to the Côrte, where he had established himself as a noted doctor and a well-known man of affairs. He had won a number of municipal appointments and imperial distinctions, which certainly suggest that he was a man to be reckoned with.

João Baptista Vianna Drummond, later Baron de Drummond, was one of the early men of affairs involved in the urban infrastructure. He was Director of the Companhia Ferro-Carril de Vila Isabel, one of the first mule-drawn streetcar companies. He was also the creator of the Jardim Zoológico on the Serra do Engenho Novo, which he left to the city.

Another Casino member was particularly favored at court; Leopoldo Augusto da Câmara Amoroso Lima, made Baron de São Nicolau (1805?–81), was the *gáucho* son of a minor provincial bureaucrat, yet he rose to be the equerry of the Empress, with a nice sinecure as *Guarda-Mór* of the Rio customs house and what was doubtless a useful marriage to the daughter of the Baron de Sorocaba.

It is important to note that several of the other Casino figures in this generation share a common pattern. Immigrant men of affairs, they rose to wealth and aristocratic titles, a dual success which served as the foundation of their families' subsequent position in the Empire. Take the Viscount da Estrela, for example. Born Joaquim Manuel Monteiro (1800–75) in Portugal, he ended up an important investor and wealthy property owner in Rio, marrying the daughter of a Counselor of State and senator. Monteiro had his title not from the Emperor, but from the Emperor's nephew, the King of Portugal, and that monarch granted the same title to Monteiro's son and namesake. Two of Monteiro's other sons became Brazilian *titulares*: the Baron de Estrela and the Baron de Maia Monteiro.

There is also the story of the Baron de Nova Friburgo, Antônio Clemente Pinto (1795–1869). Portuguese, too, he also died wealthy and successful in Rio. Indeed, he was among the richest merchants in Brazil and a Grandee of the Empire. He fathered sons who became the

Count de São Clemente and the Count de Nova Friburgo. The two apparently specialized in either province of the business empire they inherited. São Clemente became a wealthy man of affairs and property-holder, moving into finance as Director of the Caixa Econômica e Monte de Socorro of Rio (a government savings and mortgage institution). The second Nova Friburgo concentrated on coffee plantations. Both sons married daughters of *titulares* and both died loaded with imperial honorifics.

The Baron de Itamaratí (1806–83), another Portuguese, and son of the first Baron de Itamaratí (d. 1853) exemplifies the pattern, too. The first Itamaratí was a merchant who died the dean of the Carioca commercial world. The second Itamaratí, known as a property-holder and important financier and agricultural promoter, died with an impressive string of court titles, suggesting the complete success of a long career knit to the expanding possibilities of the monarchy with which it coincided.

One might also include among these Portuguese the Viscount do Rio Bonito, João Pereira Larrigue de Faro (1803–56). Not because he was Portuguese-born (he was apparently Carioca), but because his father, the Baron do Rio Bonito, was, and the two exemplify the same pattern as the others. The father, an important man of affairs, financier, and holder of various imperial honors, took care to groom his son for the handsome place he was to have. The second Rio Bonito became an enterprising planter, a noted promoter of provincial railroads, a wealthy property-holder, a member of various important commissions, a figure of note at court, a deputy and vice-president for the Province of Rio de Janeiro, a vice-president of the Banco do Brasil, and the uncle of the third baron of the title.

Finally, among the Casino's members are some of those Bahians so powerful during both Reigns. There was, for example, Joaquim Francisco Alves Branco Moniz Barreto (1800–85), a son of a member of the colonial judiciary who graduated from Coimbra and became a magistrate himself, before abandoning his robes for *fluminense* politics and political journalism. He became eminent among Brazilian journalists, founding and editing the influential *Correio Mercantil* (1848–68), from which he helped to shape the thought, literature and partisan struggles of the generations coming of age in the Second Reign.

There was also that master of imperial politics, the Marquis de Monte Alegre, José da Costa Carvalho (1796–1860), another Coimbra graduate. He began his career in the First Reign as a prominent figure among the liberal opposition. A Bahian deputy to the Assembléia Constituinte of 1823, he had seen his cause lost after the coup by which Pedro I closed the Assembly. He apparently sought to build a new base afterwards in São Paulo, where he married into an important provincial clan and soon rose in the dominant liberal party as a prominent journalist and editor. Afterwards, first as liberal deputy and then as senator for the province, he finally crowned his ascent in opposition ranks as one of the first Regents who ruled after Pedro I's abdication.

Monte Alegre, as one of many who changed their politics in the turmoil of the Regency, however, soon emerged in the new ranks of the Conservatives. It was there, as a preeminent supporter of the monarchy, that he reached new national prominence, becoming a trusted troubleshooter for the young Emperor and the centralizing forces behind him. In rapid succession, he had his rewards; his first titles, member of the Imperial Council of State, Grandee of the Empire, and, finally, the rare title of marquis.

Our last example, the Marquis de Abrantes, unlike Monte Alegre, was never a stranger to imperial favor. Born Miguel Calmon du Pin e Almeida (1796–1865) into one of the important Bahian planter families, he, too, had taken a Coimbra degree, and served as a deputy in the 1823 Assembly. His subsequent career, however, did not evidence the dramatic shifts of his colleague. It was simply a stately parade of honors. He represented Bahia in any number of the subsequent legislatures, was then a noted senator, councilor in both the Imperial Council of State and the more honorific Council of His Majesty, minister in several cabinets, special diplomat in Europe, a Grandee of Empire, the holder of a multitude of honors, a renowned philanthropist, patron of the arts, salon host, and promoter of industry and agriculture. Abrantes died one of the most powerful figures of the Second Reign, a man enjoying enormous respect crowned by a reputation as a superb orator, one of the nation's best.

These were the men who helped to make the Casino what it was in the Monarchy's palmy days; their successors secured the club's elite status in less propitious times. Among them, for example, one finds Antônio Francisco de Azeredo (1862–1936), whom we shall meet often in these pages. Linchpin in the Old Republic's hidden political struggles, Azeredo was a fixture of the Senate, of which he became vice-president, and of polite society, as the head of a noted salon. One also finds Carlos Buarque de Macedo, one of the more important urban-based entrepreneurs in the burgeoning federal capital. There is Fernando Mendes de Almeida, too; son of a senator, Cândido Mendes de Almeida, and brother of the latter's namesake, a papal count. A Carioca (b. 1857) well known as a Catholic devoted to the interests of the Church, Fernando was also noted as a journalist and an editor of literary and scientific reviews, as well as being respected as a prominent lawyer with a São Paulo degree.

Another lawyer in the Casino is typical of many elite members; his career resembles those of the earlier Casino members except that it was apparently cut off by the Republican coup of 1889. The Baron de Homem de Melo (b. 1837), was born Francisco Ignácio Marcondes Homem de Melo in the Province of São Paulo, son of the Baron de Pindamonhangaba, a high officer in the provincial Guarda Nacional. Homem de Melo had a São Paulo degree, but had apparently devoted himself to education, politics, and financial and business administration rather than the law. He was a professor at the Escola Militar and, as the reader may recall, the Colégio Pedro II. He also taught at the Escola Nacional de Belas Artes. He had been appointed president of various provinces, Inspector of Public Instruction in Rio, Director of the Banco do Brasil, and president of the board of directors that completed the crucial railroad linking Rio to São Paulo. His talents and service had been recognized in appointments to a ministry and to His Majesty's Council, as well as by a vast number of titles and memberships in a long list of literary and scientific organizations. Under the Republic, much of this was quietly abandoned; Homem de Melo resigned himself to the profession of law and the pursuit of his literary and scientific interests.

Others in the later sample, however, were successful in both Monarchy and Republic. The Baron de Quartim, Antônio Tomás Quartim (b. 1854), is typical. His father and namesake established himself as a Carioca merchant, coffee factor, coffee planter, and banker, firmly connected to the Rodrigues Torres family, one of the most important *fluminense* clans, powerful in coffee and politics alike, and headed by one of the most important Conservative statesman of the Second Reign, the Viscount de Itaboraí. The younger Quartim followed his father as the partner of a Rodrigues Torres, too, at the beginning of a career in which he also became a noted investor and financier in Rio. His positions included that of Solicitor of the Municipal Council in Rio, Director and, later, President of the Caixa Econômica e Monte Socorro, a Member of the Board of the Caixa de Amortização, co-founder and Director of the Centro de Lavoura e Comércio, and Director of the Banco de Brasil. We will meet him again, in discussing the important salons of the *belle époque*.

These, then, are the sort of men one found in Carioca high society in the generations at the beginning of the Second Reign and the beginning of the Old Republic. These are the sort of men who brought their wives and their children to meet and mingle with their peers at the Casino. Let us turn once again to the institution itself, to see what else it can tell us.

Despite the prestige of the Casino, it was dogged with financial trouble from the 1860s on, when the earlier construction and decoration of its magnificent premises failed to garner the financial rewards of increased patronage. Debt and dissolution became the constant preoccupations of its directories; by the 1880s, they began to cast about more and more frantically for a way out.[48] This decade's troubles may have been exacerbated by the economic decline of many old *fluminense* families brought on by the crisis in the coffee *fazendas*.[49] And, certainly, reading between the lines, the threats to the old elite that erupted in the 1890s did little to ease the matters. Many of the Casino directors left for Europe in the aftermath of the Republic's proclamation, doubtless unsettled by the radical challenge to the status quo, the anti-Portuguese sentiments, the coups and counter-coups of the first several years, and the economic collapse which struck the Carioca *praça*. Indeed, between 1891 and 1896, there was but one session of the Casino directory, which met only to elect replacements for those who had fled Rio.[50] A number of such elite members and their families never returned to Brazil; they simply prolonged indefinitely the periodic stays in Paris so traditional among their sort. While they lived, they helped to make up the aristocratic colony waiting out the initial events of the new-born Republic.[51]

A change of name in 1891 to the Novo Casino Fluminense and numerous makeshift measures reshuffling the cost of shares and renting out the premises did nothing but prolong the administrative and financial uncertainties of the society. In 1898, with the new era of reasserted elite control under Campos Sales and the beginning of the Carioca *belle époque*, the Casino attempted recovery. It opened daily as more of a men's club, there were games, and the use of the library. In 1900, an informal merger with the Club dos Diáros began. The latter rented the second floor of the Casino in exchange for a tidy sum and the right of Casino members to frequent the Club and use the rented floor for its own Casino functions. By 1905, near dissolution and financial bankruptcy forced complicated discussions (1906–7) of two offers of merger, from the Jockey Club and from the Diários, which finally resulted in the 1908 liquidation and merger with the latter.[52]

It should be noted that the Carioca elite represented in the Casino began a gradual change over the years in socio-economic terms. As we have seen, some Casino members of the last years were linked to the same sort of backgrounds as those associated with the early Casino.[53] However, what they did for a living, and their interests and way of life reflect changes in the socio-economic development of Rio, and, thus, the basis for elite membership over the more than half-century separating the birth and death of the club.

It would be too simple to claim that the institution's godfathers were all ennobled planters, statesmen and merchant princes and its pallbearers all bourgeois businessmen, politicians, professionals, and financiers. Yet, obviously, something in these extremes rings true enough to suggest the direction in elite society. Those who presided over the Casino's first years were men with secure positions at court and in the imperial administration, Coimbra-trained statesmen, a few professionals, titled planters and merchants and men of affairs (and merchants and men of affairs, the reader should note, of Portuguese extraction, who usually branched out from commerce into finance, real estate, and plantations). That is to say, they were the logical congeries one would expect in the capital of a monarchy that also served as the entrepôt of a colonial economy, producing an agricultural crop in exchange for imported manufactures.

Those who directed the Casino in its last years were often descendants of traditional families who had adapted to the new era and become newly successful urban-based men. There were still merchants and *titulares* among them, as we have seen. But the political men were now lawyers from the São Paulo or Recife faculties, not Coimbra-trained imperial magistrates. More important, the directors of the Casino were now more obviously men of the city: businessmen, financiers, politicians, bureaucrats, and professionals – a negligible number (in our small sample, none) were planters.

It is not that one could not find men in similar occupations in the earlier Casino documents. It is that one now finds a greater tilt toward urban occupation, urban-directed finance and business, urban professions, and, even, Carioca birth. Correspondingly, there are fewer of the elite members typical of the Second Reign, who often combined planting with commerce, were involved in three or four different ocupations, fewer who might still have one foot in the province and another in the capital in terms of investments, politics, and entrepreneurial activity.

Rio had become a "modernizing" bureaucratic secondary industry center, with a swelling immigrant population and flourishing urban commerce, infrastructure and financial institutions to match. The court and the coffee plantations had failed their aristocrats, but the commercial, industrial, and bureaucratic *urbs* had offered them and their descendants and the new men lucrative alternatives.[54]

The Club dos Diários

Indeed, the Club dos Diários (founded 1895) itself speaks to these changes in circumstances and Carioca elite occupations. Names are instructive in this regard. "Casino" and "Fluminense" suggest the older way of life. The first word hearkens to the idea of aristocratic diversion, the second, which in the Second Reign signified something of either the province or the city of Rio de Janeiro, bespeaks the traditional identity of interests between the two, the pulse of wealth and power that beat between the plantations and the port capital.

"Club" and "Diários," suggest more modish ideas. "Club" comes directly from the clubs that sprang up in seventeenth-century London and flourished in nineteenth-century London and Paris as urbane gentlemen's gathering places. More important, "Diários" pointed to a new reality of Carioca elite urban occupations. It derives from the daily (*diário*) travel of those whose wealth and position enabled them to summer in the cool mountain resort of chic Petrópolis but, at the same time, required them to journey to and from Carioca offices every morning and evening, a tedious ritual to appease the gods of fashion and wealth alike.[55]

Gone was the era when men of affairs and merchants or planters and men of the court could simply stay in Petrópolis for weeks or spend Rio's hot fever-ridden season on their plantations. During the *belle époque* the new pace and place for the getting of wealth demanded a nearly six-hour daily commute of an increasingly large number of elite men.[56]

Yet, despite these changes in the elite's way of life, it is just as important to stress the continuities. Petrópolis, for instance, had always been an elite resort since Pedro II had made summering there fashionable.[57] Furthermore, the clubmen of the Diários maintained a definite aristocratic tone, however bourgeois their occupations. Many of the founders were *titulares*, and the club itself was devoted to many of the elegant diversions and marked by the same exclusive atmosphere that had formerly been the preserve of the Casino. Not only did one enjoy matinées, but grander sorts of things. An invitation for the year 1900 reads: "The Directory of the Club dos Diários . . . advises Your Excellency that the first great Ball will take place in the Casino Fluminense, at 10 o'clock the night of the 25th of this month."[58]

There was also an important continuity in the sort of people with whom one might mix at the club. There was, for instance, the Count de Figueiredo, the notable banker, financier, and economist, a Grandee of the Empire, whom we shall meet often in these pages. There was his son-in-law, Luís Felipe de Sousa Leão, whose father we could have met in the Casino. There was also José Carlos de Figueiredo, son of the count, a man important in finance and business, too, who cut quite a figure in Society, helped by Heloísa de Figueiredo, his wife and one of the great beauties of the era. There was Carlos Buarque de Macedo, the entrepreneur whom we noted as a director of the Casino, and the Baron de Santa Margarida, one of the first several presidents of the Diários, who was a Casino director, too.

One might also glimpse Rui Barbosa, a member of His Majesty's Council and, as we have noted (and will explore later) a pivot of Old Republic politics. There might also be Luís Rocha Miranda, the son of the Baron de Bananal, and doubtless a relative of one of the two Rocha Mirandas whom one finds in the list of members of the Casino in 1856. There was João do Rego Barros, of an old Pernambuco family, a doctor and an entrepreneur in urban utilities, a patron of an important musical salon very chic in the Rio of 1898. One might also meet Henrique Chaves, the noted journalist and editor, one of the founders of the great *Gazeta de Noticias*. And he might be talking to Antônio de Azeredo, whom we have met in the Casino. For Azeredo, very much as part of the same political career which saw him to the Senate and made him a close friend of Rui Barbosa, was a political journalist and editor, too.

We would probably see Antônio Januzzi, the powerful contractor and architect, who figured heavily in the Avenida Central. And, certainly, one could expect to see Deodato C. Villela dos Santos, one of Rio's foremost lawyers, a formidable clubman, member and historian of the Casino and the Jockey Club. Perhaps he might be chatting with Harold Hime (son of Elkim Hime, a man big in importing and an old member of the Casino). Januzzi would more likely be talking to Francisco Pereira Passos, engineer, railroad builder, and urban entrepreneur, whom we have met as Rio's Haussmann and whom we will meet again in pages to come. If Pereira Passos were not there, perhaps his son, Francisco de Oliveira Passos, an engineer and designer of the Teatro Municipal, might be. And, talking with either Villela dos Santos or Januzzi, one might also find Francisco Teixeira Leite Guimarães, a lawyer out of São Paulo become urban entrepreneur and coffee factor, son-in-law of Januzzi's friend, the Baron do Rio Negro, and member himself of a very old and extensive planter-merchant family.[59]

As these members and the other aspects of the Diários noted make clear, there was a good deal of continuity between the old Society that frequented the Casino and the *belle-époque* set of the new club. Between the last directories of the Casino and the new administrations of the Diários there was practically no difference at all. The changes the Diários represented were in the way of economic transitions which could be contained within generations of the same sort of family. And this, along with the retention of Second Reign diversions and style and the continued presence of Second Reign figures, all help to explain the ease with which the Casino finally merged into the new club. Both symbolically and materially, it was a shift from an older, moribund basis of elite wealth and power (*fluminense* coffee) to a more vigorous elite basis (the *diários*' urban occupations). And, both symbolically and materially, much about the elite and the new social club remained the same. That, after all, was what was intended; the continuation of the Casino tradition, despite the passage of time and the changes in circumstances. As Vilella dos Santos put it, in a nice mix of nostalgia and proprietary sentiment:

> . . . it may be seen that the life of the Casino Fluminense, in spite of repeated difficulties, was brilliant and no other *sociedade recreativa* has more beautiful traditions. In the long period of 63 years, the most distinguished gatherings took place there . . .
>
> Happily, the disappearance of the society does not bring with it that of the beautiful building, whose restoration work is going to be executed by the Club dos Diários in a manner that will enable it to continue to fulfill the ends for which it was constructed.
>
> And this is no small thing.[60]

The Jockey Club

Many, perhaps most, of the same men who enjoyed the distinguished gatherings of the Casino and the Diários were also members of the Jockey Club.[61] The model for the club came from either the English or the French Jockey Club, each of which signified the importance of the turf to Society on either side of the Channel. Since the eighteenth-century, clubs devoted to horseracing had served as a special place for England's aristocratic gatherings and diversion. The Jockey Club in Paris had been founded in 1838 by the most fashionable of Restoration France's anglomanic aristocracy, and reigned as one of the city's most exclusive clubs thereafter.[62]

The Brazilian Jockey's foundation and ostensible purpose were of a similar nature. In 1868, a small group of enthusiasts created the club, taking the idea of the name and considerable impetus from one Major João Guilherme de Suckow. The major had first unsuccessfully courted the imperial government's support for a Jockey Club Fluminense (founded 1848) with two spectacular 1851 races. His efforts then had met with no luck. The 1868 venture, based principally on members' and spectators' purses, had much good fortune indeed. The stated purpose was simply "to race horses." By 1871, one of the horses was the Jockey's first English thoroughbred. By 1873, the land used for turf on the northeastern outskirts of the city was bought. By 1874, the first grand prize was instituted. By the early 1880s, an English traveller could report

> I do not suppose that any other racecourse in the world enjoys such a view, with the glorious mountains all round, and glimpses of the Bay . . .
>
> The grand stand is a very fine building, and could hold five thousand people. I daresay there were two thousand on it to-day; so we all had room to move about comfortably. The Imperial party drove on to the course in state carriages . . .
>
> . . . I suppose because racing is entirely an exotic from England, the horses ran round to-day as they do at Epsom, from right to left.[63]

By 1892, competitive horseshows, as an incentive to the importation and breeding of horses, completed the "horsey" picture of the club's efforts.[64]

However, the Jockey was hardly just an institution for racing horses. Nor was it a place one went to to make a fortune at the track. In fact, financially speaking, the Jockey was a rather precarious affair; during the 1890s' financial and political crises, the Jockey, like the Casino, barely avoided dissolution.[65] Why, then, did the Jockey endure, enjoying perennial elite favor? Even the failed 1851 attempts of de Suckow, after all, had brought out the imperial court and the rest of Society. The reason is simple. They and the long roll of Jockey members afterward were probably there not for the love of the turf and a fine-looking animal, but because the Jockey was an expensive, aristocratic, prestigious kind of institution with which to be associated. Just reporting horseracing imparted chic, a wonderful connection to the Ascot races, the select membership of the Parisian Jockey, and the fashionable turnouts at Longchamps. In 1910, for instance, "The Directing Council of the Sports Writers' Center, resolved to officiate collectively in the presentation to the Minister of England of their sympathies for the death of the great sportman [*sic*] Edward VII."[66]

The 1851 report of the presence of the imperial court metamorphoses easily into the *belle-époque* photographs of the Republic's presidents and their ministers, who are glimpsed leaving the track in top hats, with a cane in the crook of one arm and the white-gloved hand of a lady in the other.[67] Monarchies might fall, Republics might rise, Society and the Jockey remained.

I have already mentioned the Jockey's bid to merge with the Casino in 1906. I should also note that in the *belle époque* the club held afternoon teas with dancing in the magnificent seat it had on the Avenida Central.[68] On one occasion, too, the sports writer for the *Rua do Ouvidor* informed his readers of

> *A Chic Note* – Tomorrow Sr. Alvaro Martins, the concessionaire for the bars of the Jockey-Club, will begin serving tea, in small kiosks in the Japanese style, in the garden of the enclosure for that society's exhibitions. It is a novelty for our turfmen [*] and a chic note for the parties of the old Fluminense Field.[69]

Most prestigious of the horseracing clubs, absorbing even its closest rival, the Derby Club,[70] the Jockey had, with these Society diversions, merely broadened its enormous appeal to fashionable Rio. The membership list was flush with the old and the new names important in Carioca elite society, a society which admired itself in the splendours of the club's Eclectic-style palace, far indeed from the sound or smell of horses neighing at the *hipódromo*.

It is interesting to speculate about the reasons for the Jockey's continued good health. Unlike the Casino, the Jockey has long survived both the financial troubles and socio-economic shifts of the turn of the century. Perhaps the Jockey retains its elite patronage and monied vigor because it has proven eminently elastic in the face of the successive changes in elite composition and tastes.

The Jockey's structure was fairly simple and of perennial attraction: horseracing (and thus the imprimatur of European aristocracy), expense (erecting the welcome barrier of class exclusion), and snob appeal (the most venerable and most exclusive club of its kind, it was consecrated with a tradition of elitism, especially appealing given the instability and relative novelty of so much about the Carioca elite).

Now, while much of the same could be said about the Casino and its heir, something else set the Jockey apart from them. The Jockey was an institution inviting only passive participation in its essential diversion – one watched; the horses performed. In the Casino and the Diários, one was expected to perform oneself. And the sort of performance was not perennial in nature; it was integrally a part of the old Society of the Second Reign. One danced complicated dances in great balls and practiced other social graces which were part of a mannered, courtly society most of whose members were dying off by the 1920s.

The Jockey had its phase of dances, as we have seen, but they were tea dances, not stately formal balls, and endured only so long as the taste of the elite still demanded it. When the composition and the culture of the elite began to change, and courtly functions became too rare, the Casino's legitimate heir, the Diários, would be forced to close its doors (1924). The Jockey simply changed some of its menu; its entrée remains the same, and the Jockey survives and flourishes.[71] The Jockey is a tradition in which newly arrived families without tradition (and traditional families who have lost the practice of, or taste for, some aspects of their past) can participate.

3. The Opera Theater

The last institution to be discussed here is the only exception to the dismal fate reserved for nineteenth-century Carioca theaters: the Teatro Lírico.[72] This theater, founded in 1871 on the Largo da Carioca near the center of the *cidade velha*, existed until 1934, and enjoyed an exceptional social importance in both the Second Reign and the Old Republic. It owed its stature not to any luxury in its appointments, nor to any excellence in its acoustic construction. It was *the* theater because it was there that opera was performed, and opera, central to Society in Europe, was crucial to the Carioca elite, too. Opera was the centerpiece of the Season, the temporal stage on which the Carioca elite played.[73]

One American cynic noted spitefully what price Cariocas were willing to pay for opera, and what he thought of it:

> Those who have more money than they know what to do with, or who wish to while away the happy hour before the exchange goes down to 16 and the summer dream of the patriotic optimist is rudely dispelled, will find a very fine opportunity to spend a small fortune by subscribing for the impending season of Italian opera . . . The unhappy individual whose modest income will permit but one night's dissipation, will of course pay more proportionately.[74]

Whatever the value of the entertainment, the theater itself was once described by the celebrated Parisian actress, Réjane, as "une cirque," and, doubtless, the plain edifice and its threadbare outfittings hardly demanded respect or kindness from someone used to Paris.[75] Still, for two or three generations of the elite, it was the Teatro Lírico where one bought expensive subscription seats to listen to what was considered the highest form of music, and to do so in the company of the most fashionable of one's fellow citizens. If the American was left cool by the sum spent, and if the Frenchwoman disdained the setting, the Carioca theater critic waxed enthusiastic:

Last Tuesday night the lyric company of the well known and untiring empressario, cavaliere Giovanni Sansone, made its debut in the Teatro Lírico, the theater being almost full.

All that is most fine in beauty, talent, and elegance, decorated the boxes, seats, and balconies.

Like great and splendid fleshy flowers, the seductive forms of the gentle ladies and damsels appeared, framed in the boxes, giving the theater the appearance of an enormous animated flowerbed.[76]

The other theaters, and there were many that came and went, presented Brazilian and Portuguese comedy reviews, French light comedy and vaudeville and drama, and so on. Only the Lírico traditionally claimed the works of the great operatic composers. The 1898 advertisement for the returning Italian touring company offered the faithful these delicacies: *Africana, Aïda, La Gioconda, Otelo, Les Huguenotes, Fauste, Rigoletto, Roberto il Diavolo, La Bohème, Méphistophélès, I Lombardi, La Juive, Carmen, Cavalleria Rusticana*, and, of course, *Il Guarany*. That year, there would also be new offerings: "*André Chenier*, by maestro Giordano, *Samson et Dalila*, by Saint-Saëns, *La Navarraise*, by maestro Massenet."[77]

The Lírico's patrons had their opera served up to them, at least once in a while, by the most renowned European artists (e.g., Tito Rufo, Caruso, and others), just as they had other dramatic and melodic offerings there, by the European touring companies that regularly thrilled or tormented the upper crust of Rio every year. One might add that, at times, it must have been hard to tell the difference between the thrill and the torment – the passion for a singer or an actress was an esteemed rite of elite youth. Our American cynic observed,

An actress here had the following effect upon a critic: "she does not produce ecstacy, she impresses; she does not attract, she dominates and crushes; she does not always move one, but she always subjugates." We do not know if the critic, subjected to such wear and tear still exists, or whether he has succumbed.[78]

The importance of the opera in terms of Society can be gauged by the treatment accorded it in the press. Periodicals, of course, regularly reported the artists' performances. However, much more important was the detail it gave of what prominent women were wearing (men, need one add, always wore formal evening dress). These descriptions were given, in French, by the theater critic, who specified the box or seat thus decorated. Indeed, Carioca readers of, say, the report on *La Bohème* learned more about the audience than they did about poor Mimi. While that impoverished *bohémienne* was suffering lyrically on stage, the critic informed his readers that

Among the beautiful and very rich *toilettes* the following were exceptional: First-class box to the right, no. 21, *Mme. et Mlle. Rodolpho Miranda, Mme. en satin bleu brodé, de jais noir, Mlle., en satin jaune d'oeuf.*

Idem, no. 23, *Mme. F. Casemiro Alberto et Mlle. Diedriche. Mme., en soie rose recouverte de tulle . . . en soie gami de perles et broderie nuancée pailletée d'or. Mlle., en soie crème.*

Idem., no. 23, *Mme. et Mlles. Eduardo Guinle. Mme. en soie blanche recouverte de tulle noir brodé et jais. Mlles, en crêpe de chine blanche.*[79]

One went to the theater knowing precisely which great lady would be in which subscribed seat, and that she would be wearing an imported gown, to be worn only on that occasion.[80] One young lady remembers:

. . . above all, one was careful about toilettes. They said that certain ladies of the *haute gomme* competed in showing off dresses and very rich jewelry, that, unhappily, were never allowed to be repeated. Those of more humble origin, who had had access [to Society] through money, were real walking shop-windows. Known rivals inspired factions during the evening, and picturesque episodes took place.[81]

What was being measured was the wealth and taste of elite members within a context and a language consecrated by a most important European paradigm.[82] Beyond this aspect, however, lies another. For the Lírico, in a way common to the social clubs discussed, served as a place where the elite went to meet and to talk "informally" about their affairs. One foreigner remarked on the unusual length of the intermissions, which allowed for such exchanges, and memoirs recall the importance a night at the opera might have for one's career.[83] In a phrase, the Lírico was most important not for the representation of elite fantasy on stage, but for the manifestation of elite reality in the boxes.

One might argue, in concluding, that perhaps for the same reason as the Jockey, the Lírico survived because its essential attraction was similar. The Lírico involved the elements common to the Casino, the Diários, and the Jockey (an activity designated fashionable by European model, a discriminating expense, and a snob appeal born of elite tradition), but shared only with the Jockey the element of a passive, thus perennial, central activity. The Lírico, too, offered an attraction in which new generations or new men could take part without a traditional preparation. Like horse-racing, opera demanded only passive participation. While some familiarity with the art would have made it more palatable to those squirming in white tie or Parisian corset, everyone accepted that the opera itself was secondary to the conspicuous consumption and elite congregation at the heart of what was really going on. Some of the audience, or so one is told, had little idea of what they were hearing[84], but they doubtless did have a precise idea of what they were doing.

A number of common points are apparent in the analysis of these last two sections. The sorts of activities to which these institutions were ostensibly devoted; the barriers erected to membership by the price of entry; and the social exclusion actively practiced in at least some of them (the Casino, for example, or the Jockey), all make it clear that these were effectively elite institutions, as intended. Our survey of a number of important members, too, has certainly corroborated that fact. Most important, from our point of view, however, is something only slightly less obvious. Whatever putative ends they served (ballroom dancing, conviviality, elegant diversions, horseracing, and opera performances), it is also clear that these institutions also had strictly socio-political effects. They served as the informal setting for the display of one's financial worth, for the announcement of one's socio-economic position, and for the proclamation of one's personal cultivation. In Rio's high society, the model for which derived from a European aristocratic paradigm, such social institutions allowed one to demonstrate one's place (or one's right to such a place) among the Carioca elite by assimilation to the style and behaviour of a European aristocrat.

Besides those aspects, however, these institutions facilitated other things just as integral a part of Society. For, as was pointed out regarding the Teatro Lírico, such places allowed for the larger, public congregation of members (and would-be-members) of the elite and the sort of activities that naturally might follow: discreet discussion of business and politics during pauses and intermissions, for instance, or alliance-making and cabals over lunch. It was convenient, after all, in a small elite in a small city where so much was done face to face, to have such places at hand, integral parts of one's routine, to make the important contacts that stitched wealth to power to influence.

Such things are not so distinct from our own world, even with its greater size and means for communication, as to need further explanation, but the following example may prove interesting. In it, one gets a rare glimpse into the informal workings of the Carioca elite. The example derives from a 1903 letter from one senator to another:

> Ruy,
>
> Rio Branco came to the Senate and was with me and Pinheiro until after 2:30 in the afternoon, . . . because he very much wanted to talk to you . . . Pinheiro, however, [then] mentioned our luncheon date together tomorrow, upon which we agreed [as the solution].

Accepting Pinheiro's idea, I agreed that we shall lunch in the Club dos Diários, just the three of us, at 11:30 tomorrow, it being my task to advise you that R. Alves asked me, with much insistence, that I promote your meeting with Rio Branco.

Have patience, and let us put up with the man tomorrow, and, so that we can talk before lunch about something, such as R. Alves, I will remain at your disposal from 9 on . . .

I kiss D. Cota's hand and await your orders.

Your devoted friend.

[sig.] Antonio de Azeredo[85]

The nature of informal meetings in such institutions as the Diários and their importance are captured here. Especially when one reflects on the people involved in this instance. Here, the Ruy is, of course, Rui Barbosa; the Pinheiro is José Gomes Pinheiro Machado; the Rio Branco is, of course, the baron of that title; and R. Alves is Francisco de Paula Rodrigues Alves. That is, the letter gives us three of the most important men in the political machine run in the Senate sitting down to lunch with the architect of Brazilian foreign policy, at the insistence of the president of the country. It seems safe to suggest that the next ball at the Diários probably did not figure much in the ensuing conversation.

Broadly, then, these institutions helped make possible the social conviviality among the powerful and their families that made for the ongoing friendships, the courtships, and the personal introductions and contacts that made class solidarity and the business of ruling the personal, perhaps warm, and certainly effective things they often were among the elite in the Carioca *belle époque*. The Casino, the Diários, the Jockey, and the Lírico were traditional parts of but one of the important, shaping frameworks within which moved the realities of power.

3

The salon and the emergence of high society

Our glimpse of the Club dos Diários was our first of the Carioca *alto mundo* around 1900. In order to give our exploration more texture and depth, we will now go much further into biographical detail, focussing on a carefully selected cross-section of that world in the era 1898–1914. In this way, the complexity and highly personalized nature of elite origins, elite relations, and elite careers will be made clear. It will also help one to get a better sense of the "lived" reality of the social phenomenon under discussion. It is only after trying to recapture something of this rather elusive milieu through personal introductions that analytical generalizations can properly be made.

1. High society and its salons in the Carioca *belle époque*

A study of the *belle époque* periodicals and later accounts of Society yield a sizable list of social lions and noted Society women. As one searches to learn more about these people, interrelated members of the various groups that made up the *alto mundo*, certain pivotal figures become apparent. Some of these are familiar to the reader from previous pages, others only now make their introductions.[1] For this analysis I have used the salon as the criterion of selection. This institution, because it was crucial to elite society (as will be seen further on in this chapter), is a useful way to pick out those who typify the era's dominant elements.

One begins with someone noted in the Diários, the famous engineer and rebuilder of Rio, Francisco Pereira Passos (1838–1913).[2] It is no surprise to find him there for Pereira Passos was a member of Carioca high society for many years and, besides his membership in the Diários and the Jockey, was known as a friend of polite society and a man of recognized charm (whatever the gruff, aggressive tone of his official persona).[3] With his wife, whose gifts as a hostess were fondly remembered later on, Pereira Passos presided over a salon in his comfortable home on the fashionable Rua das Laranjeiras,[4] and his two sons, Paulo and Francisco ("Chico"), known for their charm and accomplishments, enjoyed reputations as men-about-town.[5]

Pereira Passos had come to this envied social position through both "good" birth and a good deal of work, much of it both innovative and crucial to the infrastructural development that marked Brazil in his lifetime. Chapter 1 noted the trajectory of his career: the unusual engineering vocation, the French training and European experience, the railroads and urban planning, and the crowning glory of the great reform of Rio under the Rodrigues Alves administration.

In all of this activity (as well as in his private business as the owner of a sizeable sawmill) Pereira Passos made a formidable professional reputation and a considerable fortune that provided social esteem, his handsome Laranjeiras home, the European education for his sons, extensive trips abroad, and various collections of *objets d'art* which paid tribute to his taste and to his wallet. As a *belle-époque homme du monde*, he was noted for his English taste in fine clothing and gentlemanly reserve, the French refinement of his domestic decor, his weakness for pretty women (he made no bones about promenading with a French mistress in Rio),[6] and the pleasure he took in entertaining the *alto mundo.* His many photographs show us a man of erect, dominating posture, fierce eyes, thick white hair, mustaches, and sharply pointed beard. (See photograph in illustration 3.) His biographer notes that,

> . . . he frequented the elegant public functions and enjoyed receiving friends. The politicians of greatest influence sought him out at home . . . . He was interested in social cliques, delighted in elegant get-togethers, and was considered perfectly at ease in a feminine milieu. He was a refined charmer, a witty *causeur*, and he knew how to make himself admired among young people.[7]

An old friend recalled fondly that,

> Passos died when he was more than 70, but he always had a youthful spirit. It was a pleasure to have a conversation with him. When we both left the Prefecture, we met and visited each other more than once in Paris, and I took great pleasure in listening to him. His age did not prevent him from engaging in amorous escapades.[8]

Another familiar member of the Diários was also a fixture of Society, the illustrious senator from Bahia, Rui Barbosa (1849–1923).[9] Rui shared with Pereira Passos a strong link to the rural-based elite. Although his father, João José Barbosa de Oliveira, was a Bahian doctor and sometime deputy and bureaucrat, marriage had united the Barbosa de Oliveira family in other branches to planter families in Bahia, Minas Gerais, Rio de Janeiro, and São Paulo boasting numerous *titulares*.[10] Like Pereira Passos, however, Rui had made his way in urban-based professions: law, journalism, and politics.

A *bacharel* out of São Paulo, Rui had risen from inherited debts and a provincial law practice to deputyships in the Côrte and a fiery reputation as an Abolitionist and oppositionist journalist that helped to win him the portfolio of Minister of Finance in the Provisional Government of 1889.[11] Rui's crucial role in the early years of the Republic as a minister, senator, and celebrated jurist proved a mixed blessing. It was Rui who was largely held responsible for the *Encilhamento*, the ephemeral boom of inflated currency, easy credit, bogus corporations, wild stock speculation, and occasional enrichment, that was followed by a general economic collapse. Nor did Rui escape rumors of collusion with one of the most notorious profiteers. Then, in his fall from ministerial power and opposition to the administration of Floriano Peixoto, Rui became a target for elimination. The early nineties soon found him in a bitter London exile.

With Floriano's mid-nineties eclipse, however, one finds Rui back in Rio and in a position of increasing professional, political, and social esteem. Elected senator again for Bahia, he would enjoy a seeming lifetime chair in the Senate thereafter, and with this public position as a base, made any number of celebrated stands against the first two civilian governments (Prudente de Morais, 1894–8; Campos Sales, 1898–1902), refurbishing a somewhat tarnished reputation with the championship of the constitution and the public welfare. To this initial stock of a reputation for a superb mind, peerless oratory, and maverick courage, Rui would add, under the Rodrigues Alves administration of 1902–6, an opportune reintegration with the newly established Republican order and its emergent political machine, the *bloco*.[12]

To prestige and power were soon added national popularity, with Rui's triumphant representation of Brazil at the Hague's International Peace Conference in 1907. Then, things began to fall apart. Rui lost a key internal struggle over his presidential hopes. He broke with the machine and, using the issues of civilian rule and electoral morality as sticks with which to beat Hermes da Fonseca, the military candidate of the *bloco*, ran for the presidency. This, the famous *civilista* campaign of 1910, won Rui enormous admiration. Although the *bloco* made sure, through heavy-handed fraud, that it won him no victory, long after this defeat Rui would bask in public esteem, remembered as the

"Eagle of the Hague," and the dauntless opponent of political corruption.[13]

Rui's public laurels were gilded with private success. While in exile, he had tried to make a living representing British clients with interests in Brazil. On his return, Rui was again retained by foreign clients, as well as wealthy Brazilian ones, with much greater rewards. His greatest success was being made the chief lawyer for The Light and Power Company of Rio de Janeiro. This Canadian company, having capital available for expansion, had moved triumphantly against its competitors, bought up many of Rio's public utilities, and constituted a marked example of the type of monopoly against which Rui had railed as an oppositionist journalist in the 1880s and 1890s. Nonetheless, in 1905, in the phase of his political reintegration, Rui's brother-in-law acted on Rui's behalf to ask Pinheiro Machado (the acknowledged chief of the *bloco* and senator for Rio Grande do Sul) to arrange for Light to make Rui the offer. It was all nicely arranged, complete with monthly retainer, fat fees for the inevitable special problems in court at which Rui was so good, and an agreeable bit of nepotism for the trusty brother-in-law. But Light only secured and enlarged the credit and tidy fortune Rui possessed as early as 1895. By then, Rui was already able to purchase the *palacete* of the Baron da Lagoa on the Rua São Clemente in Botafogo. As the years passed, he furnished it with the eclectic taste of the nineteenth-century bourgeois, complete with his matchless library and surrounding gardens, heavy with the scent of the roses he loved to cultivate.[14]

It is hard to recognize in this well-to-do lawyer and respected statesman the demon-ridden figure a French journalist observed in 1890, when Rui was in the midst of his controversial ministry:

> Small, nervous, irritable, and authoritarian, M. Ruy Barbosa is a son of Bahia: born under the vertical sun of the Equator, his passions are of an extraordinary vivacity, his style of a monstrous abundance [*ampleur tarasconnaise*]. On seeing that enormous head on that stick-like body, those burning eyes, those excited gestures, it seems that that man must be constantly ill with ideas, and his brain ready to explode.[15]

A decade of changing fortunes had wrought wonders. By 1900, when an Argentine diplomat and littérateur paid a visit to Rui, it was to a "superior" sort of man, a wonderful conversationalist of beautiful manners, who did the Argentine the honors of his enormous library.[16] Indeed, though Rui had an office in the heart of the *cidade velha*, it was in his Botafogo home that he spent most of his time. There he prepared his articles and briefs; there he studied; there he received his business and political acquaintances. (See photograph in illustration 4.)

These included old friends, like Antônio de Azeredo, or, more rarely, Azeredo's crony and Rui's new ally, Pinheiro Machado.[17] Pinheiro Machado would leave his own mansion, at Morro da Graça, to chat with Rui over lunch or in his dressing room, where he might finger Rui's collection of ties, perhaps, as Rui dressed for his drive to the Senate or the Supreme Tribunal, and a late afternoon walk through the Rua do Ouvidor bookstores or a pleasant session at the cinema.[18]

It was also at Rui's mansion, graced with the presence of his beautiful wife and fashionable daughters, weighted with the presence of his powerful friends, and charming with the *regimento* (as Pinheiro Machado called them) of beautiful socialites, that Rui had his own *salões*. His women folk recalled his style:

> [His] habits were very simple. He dressed with sobriety . . . He wore dark blue or grey suits made by Raunier or Brandão, a felt hat, a starched shirt-front and white tie. . . . He never went to parties, but enjoyed parties at home. He liked to see young, happy people around him. The receptions at the Rua São Clemente house were attended by notable artists, such as Magdalena Tagliaferro, Antonieta Rudge, [and] Claudia Muzzio.[19]

These affairs were the same sort of gestures of power and social prominence obvious in the salons noted at Pereira Passos's home. For both men, the salon had a useful symbolic and instrumental function – both for acquiring and demonstrating the prestige associated with European culture and for providing the setting for important, discreet contacts and conversations.[20]

If Pereira Passos and Rui Barbosa are examples of the *belle-époque* elite who began their careers under the Second Reign, so are the three to follow now: Figueiredo, Frontin, and Quartim. The difference is that these three had their origins in the Carioca world of urban-based business, rather than in traditional rural or provincial circles. We have already noted the Count de Figueiredo (1843–1917)[21] among the Diários. He also figured in the older Society of the Second Reign, as a member of the Casino Fluminense, for instance, and as a frequent guest at the *salões* of that imperial statesman, the Baron de Cotegipe. These social triumphs were closely knit to conquests in commerce and finance. Son of one of the wealthiest Carioca Portuguese merchants, José Antônio de Figueiredo, Francisco had left school early, beginning in his father's firm at thirteen. By eighteen, he was its manager. Soon thereafter, Figueiredo began an apprenticeship with another firm in

Bahia, where he began to move in Society. It was the overture to his career.

In the next movement, Figueiredo moved from commerce into urban-based industry, infrastructure, and high finance, riding the expanding potential of Brazilian cities. By forty, Figueiredo was in insurance, urban transport, coastal shipping, and, most important, banking. After his 1879 election to head the Banco do Brasil, a contemporary reports, "there was no company that did not desire to have him on its board of directors."[22] Among others, these companies came to include ones concerned with flour milling and urban utilities. An 1880 commentator wrote of Figueiredo that, "Possessor of an impressive fortune and enjoying great credit in the Rio de Janeiro market, he has before him the horizon of a splendid future."[23]

By the *belle époque*, that future had long been realized. Figueiredo had not only enjoyed great credit, he had come to dispense it as the founder of the Banco Internacional do Brasil and the impressively endowed Banco Nacional. An innovative economist and industrial promoter, he was one of the epoch's two great financiers, along with Francisco de Paula Mayrink, and a pivotal figure in the reorganization of imperial finances undertaken by the Viscount de Ouro Preto immediately before the 1889 coup. Despite the reversal to his hegemony the coup represented, Figueiredo was hardly undone, though he was put on the defensive. Figueiredo quickly found himself cut out of the initial reorganization of banking central to the *Encilhamento*, a reorganization largely allotted by Rui Barbosa to Mayrink, whom Rui took as his financial mentor (and, shortly thereafter, as a business partner). Still, the Count retained enough power to force himself back into the picture, albeit as something of a junior partner, and strengthened his foothold by taking a dip into the new regime's politics, arranging for his election as the deputy for Rio de Janeiro, the newly-created Federal Capital.[24] In effect, the *belle époque* found Figueiredo still a figure of considerable prestige, with various addresses in the commercial and financial streets of the *cidade velha* bearing witness to his manifold interests.

Figueiredo won his place in Society in this business ascent by the careful acquisition of various prizes. His first title, Viscount de Figueiredo, was the reward for charity pleasing to the Emperor (Figueiredo was involved in aiding drought victims in Ceará, in 1879); his second was a reward from his ally, Ouro Preto. Figueiredo, however, added good connections to patents of nobility; he did not depend on honorifics alone. His daughters married well,[25] and he sought social and cultural legitimization as a member of the aristocratic, well-respected

Instituto Histórico e Geográfico Brasileiro. He also arranged for religious prestige as a member of the Venerável Ordem Terceira dos Mínimos de São Francisco de Paula, one of the most prestigious lay orders in Rio, and as president of the Irmandade de Santa Casa de Misericórdia, another fashionable lay order with charitable ends. As noted, he also belonged to the most exclusive social clubs.

It is thus unsurprising that Figueiredo's Rua da Constituição residence should have a salon.[26] It was the obvious culmination of Figueiredo's conquest of Carioca business and high society. Indeed, it is with an air of quiet satisfaction that Figueiredo contemplates the viewer from his portrait.[27] Somewhat stout, he is quite firm in his gaze, comfortable in his frockcoat, resplendent in his thick "muttonchops," straddling an ornate chair back-to-front, arms folded calmly on the back with an air of relaxed arrogance. It is unsurprising too, to find the Count's heir, José Carlos de Figueiredo, married to the most beautiful woman of the epoch, Heloisa de Godoy, and figuring nicely in both stock market and clubs. He had, after all, inherited the great financier's wealth and connections, the trophies of a half-century, the inseparable portions of the Count's legacy of power and prestige.[28]

The place of André Gustavo Paulo de Frontin (1860–1932) in the *alto mundo* was also won as part and parcel of a long, successful career, part of which has already been noted.[29] His father (a French engineer turned businessman in Rio) died young with diminished fortune, and left Frontin with nothing like the opportunities Figueiredo had had. The elder Frontin had, nonetheless, bequeathed his son the connections that made his education at the Colégio Pedro II possible, and that was all the start Frontin needed. He was to win his way as professor, engineer, and entrepreneur in a dynamic unfolding of precocious talent and success.

By 1882, Frontin had taken bachelor's and doctor's degrees in civil and mining engineering, respectively, had won one chair in the Colégio Pedro II and two in the Escola Politécnica. Even before his 1880 doctorate, however, the youth had already begun professional work in landfill project organization under the direction of two prestigious engineers of the epoch, Vieira Souto and Paula Freitas. By 1880, in fact, he was working on Rio's water reservoir system, leaving it later for private work dealing with water supply in Bahia. In all of this difficult work, his skills were tested and honed.

Frontin thus unknowingly prepared for a series of unexpected challenges and opportunities that would make his career. The first challenge made his name for him. In 1889, Rio was stricken with drought, and the possibility of popular unrest in that turbulent period charged the atmosphere. Frontin promised the authorities and the populace to bring water to the city in six days, in a daring bid to keep a lid on the situation.[30] It was a nervy thing to do, but Frontin succeeded, and was never forgotten for it.[31] The other challenges came in quick succession. At the Republic's birth, in spite of the turmoil of the economic situation, Frontin founded the Empresa Industrial de Melhoramentos in 1890, and undertook preliminary work on the quays of Rio and, most important, various railroads. In 1896, he worked on Rio's sanitation commission, later going on to direct the government's Estrada de Ferro Central, a powerful position he would be given again in 1910. As we have seen, Frontin was also one of the celebrated professionals who undertook Rio's urban reformation under Rodrigues Alves (1902–6). It was Frontin, in fact, who oversaw the reform's showpiece: the Avenida Central.[32]

Through all of these accomplishments, Frontin's power in municipal affairs became enormous, a position enhanced by his prestige in Carioca business circles. Later, he would convert much of this capital into political coin, and be elected senator. From the Second Reign, when he had won academic chairs under the eyes of the Emperor and began his professional career, through the early years of the Republic and into the *belle époque*, when he had constructed an unassailable position as entrepreneur and municipal power broker, Frontin had moved with vigor and skill from the edges to the center of the Carioca structure of power.

Frontin had begun the conquest of social esteem, something indivisible from such professional and political success, in the decade his career began. Already in the Jockey in the 1880s, Frontin founded the Derby Club in 1885 with other unsatisfied members of the older club, and became its president (a position he held until his death).[33] He was also a moving spirit and perennial president of the Club de Engenharia, an association of the most powerful entrepreneurs and engineers in the country,[34] and the Sociedade Geográfica, a scientific club largely populated with elite savants (such as the Marquis de Paranaguá, the Baron de Loreto, and the Baron Homem de Melo).[35] Frontin eventually capped all these clubs with membership of the papal aristocracy, being made a count, despite the Huguenot tradition of his family.[36]

It was thus as a man prominently established as a professor, engineer, entrepreneur, politician, and clubman that Paulo de Frontin presided over yet another *belle-époque* salon.[37] This one, whether at the prestigious Flamengo district address he first had on the Rua Marquês de Abrantes, or at the equally fashionable Rua Senador Vergueiro address he later boasted, became well known over his career. As a man whom "everyone" knew, and one with the useful knack of recalling one's name at sight, Frontin's professorial air did not deprive his salons of a worldly elegance. Aided by his wife and daughters, his home was familiar to Society, and one might find there intellectuals mixing with ministers and diplomats. Again, as in the other cases noted, the conclusion seems obvious. Frontin's salon, an extension of his place in the *alto mundo*, was both a celebration and a component of a successful career.[38]

The life of Antônio Tomás Quartim (1857–1911?)[39] bears resemblances to those of both Frontin and Figueiredo. As has been noted elsewhere,[40] Quartim's father was an important Portuguese merchant in Rio de Janeiro and its hinterland, where he was involved in coffee export and credit to planters, and was linked to the Rodrigues Torres family, the important clan of planters, bankers, and political chieftains.[41] Quartim came to Brazil a youth and worked in his father's business, now with the next generation of the Rodrigues Torres family.

Quartim, however, like Figueiredo, was not content to follow his father's path. He turned away from *fluminense* coffee (increasingly precarious by the 1880s in any case),[42] into the expanding urban-based economy, utilizing his connections in the world of Portuguese entrepreneurs and Carioca finance. He moved into banking and investment, starting as a director of the Banco do Comércio, a director and, later, fiscal, of the Banco do Brasil, a stockholder in a railway company and a mining enterprise in the 1880s, and a director and president (in 1888 and 1898, respectively) of the Caixa Econômica e Monte Socorro (a government savings and mortgage institution). He also married the daughter of one of his coffee business partners, and joined with another relative in importing the materials necessary for his urban industrial interests in ironworks and shipbuilding.

Quartim maintained crucial links to the Portuguese commercial community through the Gabinete Português de Leitura and the Retiro Literário Português, prominent literary societies patronized by such wealthy immigrants. His place and prestige in this world are suggested by his lengthy return to Portugal during the turbulent Lusophobe 1890s and by his membership in scientific, literary, and commercial organizations in Lisbon. By 1907, Quartim's prominent position among Rio's Portuguese was an established fact. It was he who gave the keynote speech in the Gabinete that year (before a select audience including the Portuguese diplomatic representative)[43] and acted as a voting member of the directory of Propaganda de Portugal in the old country.

Quartim's Portuguese links only partly explain his success; he also enjoyed a secure position in Carioca high society. This, of course, is not surprising. There was complete acceptance, among the Brazilian elite, of the elite of the Portuguese colony. Such Portuguese, as was seen in chapter 2, frequently married into Brazilian elite families and founded some of the most important dynasties (recall the origins of the Rio Bonito, Itamaratí, Nova Friburgo, and Estrela families). This apparent harmony between Brazilian and Portuguese at the level of the elite, implicit throughout much of this study, had a firm basis in the common economic interests of both groups, broadly defined, during the nineteenth century.[44] Quartim was only one of many Portuguese immigrant commercial success stories. He had won his title from Pedro II, he wrote for various Carioca newspapers, his daughters married into wealthy Carioca families,[45] he had been a councilman in the Câmara Municipal of Rio as early as 1881, and the Baroness figured in the same prestigious religious order to which the Count de Figueiredo belonged. Like the others', then, Quartim's salon, at his traditional Rua do Riachuelo residence (which boasted the Baron's celebrated collection of paintings) was almost to be expected; it crowned yet another career of recognized success and power in the Carioca *belle époque*.[46]

If some of these *salões* were aspects of lives begun in traditional circumstances (e.g., families tied to planting, commerce, and the old combination of liberal profession cum politics) and of careers carried forward under the Empire, other high society salons of the *belle époque* were different. They represent, in a more full-blown fashion, the achievement Frontin's prominence suggests; the importance of the urban professional under the Old Republic, emerging out of the strengthening trend in that direction obvious in the Second Reign.

Though some connection to traditional sources of power probably existed in their families, what differentiates these people from the pattern Rui or Figueiredo exemplifies is their origin in circumstances doubly removed from such traditions. These are people who are not only urban professionals, but the children of urban-based professionals. The new opportunities and the break with traditional restraints brought by the urban expansion of the late nineteenth century and the broad changes signaled by the Republican coup provided these people their strength and potential.

The senator for Mato Grosso, noted earlier as a clubman and a friend of Rui Barbosa was certainly one of them. Antônio Francisco de Azeredo (1861–1936)[47] not only rose to prominence in the Republic – one could say that he was made by it. Son of a *doutor* in Cuiabá, Mato Grosso,

Azeredo left to try the opportunities in the turbulent Rio of the 1880s. His academic career was erratic, but his public one showed a clear sense of direction. Azeredo wandered from the Escola Politécnica to the newly-founded Faculdade Livre de Direito of Rio,[48] where he eventually took a *bacharelado* in 1895. In all three years of academic vacillation and delay, his real passion was politics, which Azeredo embraced early as a Republican journalist in José do Patrocínio's Abolitionist paper, *Gazeta da Tarde.* During the Monarchy's death agony, Azeredo acquired the *Diário de Notícias* (1889) for political purposes. He promptly handed over its direction to Rui Barbosa, thus beginning a long and profitable personal and political friendship.[49]

With the Republic proclaimed, all the pieces were in place for Azeredo. Having established his Republican credentials through journalism and secured his partisan base by alliance with the more dominant of the two great warring political clans of Mato Grosso,[50] Azeredo began his climb through the last narrow passes of political power. First a deputy in the Constituent Congress, he went on to represent his state in the first several legislatures of the regime (1890–6). He then replaced Joaquim Murtinho (his personal protector and a chieftain of the Mato Grosso clan to which Azeredo was allied) as Mato Grosso's senator, when Murtinho was selected by Campos Sales as Minister of Finance. Azeredo held his senatorial chair for more than a generation. Only the Revolution of 1930, which tore through the fabric he had helped to weave, put an end to his tenure.

That, however, was a world away at the beginning of the *belle époque*. Then, when Republicans triumphed nationally and the regional elites were reorganized with the *política dos governadores*,[51] then it was that Azeredo came into his own. In that epoch he worked not only with Murtinho and Rui, but, most important, with that *chefão* of the Senate, Pinheiro Machado. It was with the *gaúcho* that he helped to put together the national political machinery that was known as the *bloco*. Here is a glimpse of the working partnership between the two, in the *gaúcho*'s famous mansion, the Morro da Graça:

> One entered through a hall . . . There was leather everywhere. The setting was made up of *gaúcho* decorations and motifs . . . Next to this, the billiard room, where, in the morning, Pinheiro received, in casual clothes of heavy linen and leather-heeled slippers . . . until the moment to go upstairs to dress and go out, generally at eleven. At times, he came down already dressed in frockcoat and striped pants. He had visits to make before lunch. Then Azeredo arrived early, his hair white, his voice clear, his mouth full of fine talk, addressing Pinheiro with intimacy and displaying every Brazilian charm. One of the few senators

who did not wear a frockcoat, he adorned his pale cashmere jacket with a yellow carnation or a red rosebud. Pinheiro almost always rose to talk with him in a corner at a whisper.[52]

By the late 1890s, then, Azeredo had begun a palmy period which some have charged was tainted with corruption. One contemporary put it rather literarily. He referred to Azeredo and Pinheiro Machado as being comparable to Fouché and Talleyrand "in an immortal page" of Chateaubriand, where the two Frenchmen are described as, "the vision incarnate of Crime fraternising with Vice."[53] Corrupt Azeredo may well have been, successful he surely was. In 1915, when Pinheiro Machado was knifed as he arrived to talk with another politician in a posh Flamengo hotel, it was Azeredo who took his friend's place as Vice-President of the Senate.

It comes as no surprise, then, to find that Azeredo and his gifted wife formed an important couple in the *alto mundo*; the senator had taken care to underwrite his political prominence with the social kind. The couple's Botafogo salon became a tradition. Azeredo, short, stout, but with a leonine shock of white hair, an eye for smart clothing, and a way with women, was considered an engaging, affable host, famous as a good friend and a passionate poker player.[54] His daughters and his wife, like Rui's, were frequently noted in the Teatro Lírico, and visited with Rui's womenfolk, the feminine, family counterpart to Rui and Azeredo's constant lunching at the São Clemente mansion or the Club dos Diários.[55] The various strands bound tightly. In the highly personalized wheeling and dealing of Old Republic politics, the salon, the clubs, and the Lírico were just as much a part of Azeredo's *impedimenta* as his newspapers. In the small world of Rio's powerful, they all spelled contacts and influence for the man known as "the great operator."

The salon over which Herculano Marcos Inglês de Sousa (1853–1918)[56] presided had a different tone, more the pleasant recreation of a highly successful lawyer of literary and musical tastes. Like Azeredo's, Inglês de Sousa's father was a provincial *doutor*, in this case a chief magistrate, for a time in Pará, the Amazon-region province from which his family hailed, and later in the powerful and dynamic province of São Paulo. Inglês de Sousa's was a "good" traditional *paraense* family. Doubtless it was this provincial standing that explains why the boy was sent away; they wanted him to acquire a traditional elite education. Inglês de Sousa went to one *colégio* in Maranhão and another in Rio, and then was safely placed on the next usual rung – the Faculty of Law. He began in 1872 at Recife and, in 1876, completed his degree at the faculty in São Paulo.

It was in law school and as a new *bacharel* in São Paulo that Inglês de Sousa began to write fiction seriously. At the same time, he began journalistic and political activity, working in the *paulista* judiciary and associating himself with Antônio Carlos.[57] In 1878, Inglês de Sousa made an excellent marriage to one of Antônio Carlos' relatives, Carlota Emília Peixoto, and began to climb, entering the Liberal circles in Santos, founding partisan newspapers, securing election as a provincial deputy, and being named provincial president of Sergipe in 1880 and of Espírito Santo afterward. In both provinces, he was remembered for political fair play, institutional reform, integrity and efficiency. Nonetheless, his political career suddenly foundered. He lost his next bid, election to the national legislature. Disappointed, Inglês de Sousa retired to practice law in Santos and support a growing family. In the calm of this prosaic provincial life, he wrote his masterpiece, *O missionário* (1888).[58]

Inglês de Sousa was thus hardly distinguishable among the *bacharéis* of that epoch – a nicely-connected provincial lawyer and literary dilettante. The events of 1889 changed all that; the years of national turmoil took apart and re-arranged what seemed to be a finished life. Inglês de Sousa knew important Republicans in São Paulo and in Rio. On hand by chance in November 1889, he knew immediately before the 15th of what was afoot. On the strength of his Republican connections, he managed an introduction to Deodoro and secured an offer of governorships in one or another state within that first, heady week following the coup. The offers, however, soon dissolved before his eyes, dropped in the strong acid of political convenience.[59] Inglês de Sousa seems, though, to have found the drift of events and possibilities. He returned to Santos, picked up everything, and moved to São Paulo. In 1890, apparently with the help of the great financier, Mayrink,[60] he got rich in the *Encilhamento* by organizing the Banco de Melhoramentos and the Companhia Agrícola, Industrial e Colonizadora of São Paulo.

Again, however, Inglês de Sousa suffered a reversal. In 1891, his health gave way. The doctors diagnosed asthma and recommended moving, so, at thirty-eight, politics forgotten, his Santos law practice abandoned, family increasing, and businesses liquidated, Inglês de Sousa made his stand anew, this time in Rio. Without a sinecure, without a protector, without a circle of clients, he took up law again. Yet, in three years of constant work he created the basis of one of the most respected professional reputations in Carioca legal circles. Aristocratic in style, bearded, quiet, polite, Inglês de Sousa moved softly but firmly through many of the great legal questions of the day, was retained by companies and the wealthy, worked on the reform of the Civil Code, retained a prominent place in Rio's prestigious Instituto da Ordem dos Advogados Brasileiros, and lectured from the chair of commercial law at the Faculdade Livre. His literary preoccupations, vital in his early manhood, took color now only in memory, in his treasured library, and in his part in founding the Academia Brasileira de Letras, of which he was treasurer for more than a decade.[61] (See group portrait in illustration 6.)

One realizes, in reading the reminsicences of Inglês de Sousa's son (interviewed fittingly in a comfortable chair at the Jockey Club), that culture was the pleasure and the regret alike of the well-to-do bourgeois Inglês de Sousa had become. After success and failure in three occupations common to men of his background, Inglês de Sousa seems to have felt frustrated that he had not continued to pursue literature. His son recalled him commenting, toward the end of his life, "Who would have imagined that I would have to write a Code?!"[62] His success as a lawyer brought him wealth, recognition, and an assured place in the Carioca *alto mundo*. It had provided the life thought proper to his sort of family. After 1892, however, it had not brought him the time to write.

Inglês de Sousa worked not only at his *cidade velha* office, but all morning in the library of his residence, where his novels silently reproached him from the shelves. True, he could be found browsing and chatting at Laemmert's or Garnier's bookstore during the late afternoon on the Rua do Ouvidor, when men of affairs, politicians, professionals, and bureaucrats traditionally met and talked.[63] True, the literary and musical salons at his "seigneurial home" on the Rua São Clemente were well known.[64] But one senses that this role in fashionable *belle époque* culture was, for Inglês de Sousa, an older man's compensatory gesture toward a cultural prestige he had hoped for as a youth, and now could only mourn.

The alternatives to Inglês de Sousa's choice among men of a similar background make his decision understandable. Literary endeavor (as we shall see in chapter 6) was impractical for someone desiring a "respectable" standard of living without independent income. It forced one into dependency and, often, a sinecure in which one never made much money and thus lacked the style of life and independence commonly desired by men of middle-sector or better background. Still, some went ahead, if only part-time, drawn by their skills or dreams or temperament – or lack of alternative paths to prestige – and, at times, they made an important contribution to the elite culture and society of the period. An exemplar of this sort of successful dilettante, a sort of link between the more literary and the more social aspects of the Carioca *belle époque*, is Escragnolle Dória.

Luís Gastão d'Escragnolle Dória (b. 1869)[65] was the son of Luís Manuel das Chagas Dória, officer and professor at the Escola Superior de Guerra, and of Adelaide d'Escragnolle Taunay, daughter of the Baron de Taunay. Escragnolle Dória's paternal relatives were soldiers and engineers involved with technical education and the development of urban transport; his maternal relatives were interrelated descendants of the French aristocratic *émigrés* of the First Reign who served the Empire as soldiers, court functionaries, and upper bureaucrats, and went into the liberal professions, engineering, literature, the arts, and urban capitalist investment.[66] In effect, Escragnolle Dória was born into a family devoted to Rio's material and cultural Europeanization; he simply continued in this tradition.

Carioca by birth, Escragnolle Dória was educated at home by his mother and then went on to two private *colégios* and the São Paulo Faculty of Law. A *bacharel* by 1890, by the turn of the century he seemed just another lawyer of scholarly tastes. He wrote a financial history of Brazil, contributed to *A Gazeta Comercial Financeira*, and taught at the Colégio Pedro II and the Faculdade Livre. However, the thirst for a literary name, doubtless made burning by the example of his uncle, the Viscount de Taunay,[67] drove Escragnolle Dória to *belles lettres*. He began early to contribute translations and literary pieces of his own to the most popular Carioca literary and Society periodicals. These included *Brazileira*, *A Semana*, *Gazeta de Noticias*, *Noticias*, *O Pais*, *Kósmos*, and *Rua do Ouvidor*. It was naturally French literature that benefited most from his attention. His profile in the *Rua do Ouvidor* established his credentials in a fashion characteristic of Carioca literary prejudice, by noting the praise Escragnolle Dória's prose had won among the consecrated *littérateurs* of Paris. Thus, one was able "to read in the celebrated *Journal des Goncourts* an honorable reference to our compatriot, and to see that he, besides this, has earned the literary esteem of Jules Verne, of Pierre Loti, of Edmund Rostand, Maurice Rollinat, and of other illustrious men of letters of France. . . ."[68] The profile clinches matters with the provocative mention of his translation of Prévost's work, *Les demivierges*.

More interesting than this translation for the discussion here were the weekly pieces Escragnolle Dória turned out. In these, he translated *feuilletons* of the fashionable French authors and wrote brief biographical and critical columns to help orient the reader.[69] In this work, Escragnolle Dória not only polished the overwhelming prestige of French literary culture, he also provided the *alto mundo* with the information and the opinions so useful in polite social conversation at the Lírico or a salon or reception. In other words, he did for Carioca salon culture what some of his relatives helped to do for Carioca transportation; he provided an infrastructure.[70]

If one thinks of Escragnolle Dória as an important "auxiliary" to the Carioca salon one might think of a certain kind of woman in the same way. Typical aspects of the era's salon included poetry recitation or singing from the French or Italian operatic repertoire. In general, the *declamadora* (the woman who recited) and the singer were the single young women from among the host's family or the guests. This was part of being a well-bred young woman.[71]

No one displayed salon skills with more aplomb than the lovely Bebê Lima e Castro (b. *c.* 1880).[72] Her family background suggests again the importance of the liberal professions in elite culture and society discussed here. Bebê's father, João da Costa Lima e Castro (b. 1855), was a prominent surgeon and professor of medicine, born in Rio and the son of a chief magistrate of the same name who, too, was Carioca-born. Lima e Castro took his degree from Rio's Faculty of Medicine, where he later held a chair in surgery. His social and professional prestige is indicated by his fashionable Flamengo district residence, his marriage connections to important, landed families, his position in the charity hospital of the Santa Casa da Misericórdia, his ranking membership in the Academy of Medicine, his early association with another socially prominent physician, Dr. Hilário de Gouveia,[73] and his family's ties with Rui Barbosa, a distant relative, with whom they regularly traded calling cards and birthday telegrams.[74]

Bebê, born Violeta Lima e Castro, was a frequent trooper in Rui's "*regimento*" of fashionable beauties, but his was not the only chic gathering place in which Bebê appeared. One finds references to her presence at the Lírico as early as 1898, in João do Rego Barros' musical salons of that same year, as well as in the 1908 National Exposition.[75] She appears in memoirs and a study of the literary life of the period, and there are people alive today in Rio who will still call her "a star of the first magnitude" or remember the rumor of her cachet.[76] One is still told stories of her charms: they were held to be such that a thief, on entering her boudoir and hiding on hearing her return unexpectedly, was so awed by the beauty revealed to his unsuspected eyes that, after Bebê had dressed and gone, he left his spoils behind, with a note of apology and explanation.[77]

If one balks at this tale of thievish gallantry, one can still accept firmer proofs of Bebê's sway. She was publicly acclaimed by vote in a beauty contest organized by the *Rua do Ouvidor* at the turn of the century, for instance, and she was well-known as the inspiration of at least one requisitely tubercular poet.[78] Appearing with such famous *galants* as Humberto Gottuzo (fashionable doctor and society chronicler) and Ataúlfo Paiva (whom we shall meet shortly), Bebê was important not only for the wit, beauty, and manner she exemplified and attracted in her set, but, as suggested earlier, for a celebrated voice.[79] In both the more literary and the more social salons of the *belle époque*, she was the exemplar of that union of "good" family, personal attraction, and artistic cultivation central to the values of the contemporary *alto mundo*.

Another woman famous in the salons of the era, however, speaks more to the exception than the rule. Laurinda Santos Lobo was one of the few *belle-époque* women who were important in the *alto mundo* in their own right. In her case, her husband accepted her obvious preeminence, and resigned himself to being something of a cipher.[80] D. Laurinda was anything but – she stood out. She did so, first, because of a celebrated fortune inherited from her uncle and protector, Joaquim Murtinho (Azeredo's old patron, and a one-time business partner of Rui and Mayrink),[81] and, second, because she used this fortune to host one of the most noted salons of the era and to protect many of the artists and literati who appeared there.

Denied personal refinement or great beauty, D. Laurinda possessed an instinct for people and for talent and a sparkling gift for conversation. One of the men who frequented her salon recalled with warmth its pleasant routine and D. Laurinda's *grande simpatia*. There was a reception on the fourth of every month, and a tea every Sunday. One brought an artist friend to introduce him, one chatted until tea was served, and, afterward, one enjoyed the singing or the music provided by one or another of the day's guests for that day.[82] Another contemporary wrote of an older D. Laurinda of the 1920s in a manner that suggests a crystallized version of the woman's style:

> At forty years old, which she seemed eternally to be, it was difficult to say if she had been pretty as a girl, but the humor of her glance, and the incessant movement of joy in her smile, dispensed with any perfection of features that one might demand of her. She attracted one, too – very much indeed – by her voice, low and sonorous, vibrating with warmth, as everything about her did, and with throaty notes that were the neighbors of laughter and beckoned to it. She was the first to be diverted with the wit that she herself displayed. She was also prodigal with jokes, at times caustic ones; ready with repartee, and exuberant, almost even to the point of vulgarity. The aura that surrounded her obliged her to attempt elegance in her dress, but a certain lack of taste or of discretion, and

a figure tending to the heavy side, did not help her in the eyes of the most demanding critics. Her gowns, from Paris or no, were always uncommon. They might be commensurate with her position in social functions; however, at times, they were more appropriate to the stage than to salons.[83]

The delicate censure of these lines, written by a daughter of a distinguished family, suggests D. Laurinda's maverick quality. Propelled upward and forward by circumstances particular to the era, independently wealthy and a woman, D. Laurinda and her salon were creatures of the *belle époque*. They could not have happened in the Second Reign, and seemed odd in the Old Republic, where so many prejudices of the old society held true. Yet, monied by the financial turmoil of the early 1890s, and profiting from the increasing breadth of women's roles in elite society (something to which we turn in the next chapter) D. Laurinda hosted salons in the Santa Teresa district that became a tradition, as did her presence in Society, complete with her inseparable lapdog, Poupée.

Others besides D. Laurinda demonstrated special social mobility in their era. These "new men" were without traditional families, wealth, connections, or urban professional or political positions; they "arrived," however, for very traditional reasons – new wealth, won at the end of the Empire and the beginnings of the Republic.[84] Perhaps the most famous among these new rich were the Guinles,[85] famous for personal charms and a style of life cultivated at the expense of a fabulous fortune, born of the era's particular circumstances.

The founder of the family fortune, Eduardo Pallassin Guinle (d. 1912), had simply been another French entrepreneur in Rio. Guinle took up the import of electric machinery, along with a capable partner, Cândido Gaffrée (d. 1919). In the last years of the Empire, however, Guinle and Gaffrée managed a coup of incredible proportions. They won a ninety-year concession to build and operate the docks at Santos, the entrepôt for São Paulo, just as that province was assuming the primacy in coffee production that helped make Brazil the foremost coffee exporter in the world. Gaffrée, godfather of at least one of Guinle's sons, died childless himself, and thus this concession, along with the other interests of the firm, became the milch cow of the Guinles' fortune, placing them, ever since, in an enviable economic and social position. By 1914, an Englishman noted:

> . . . you cannot stay long in Rio without learning the name "Guinle," which looms with equal prominence in industrial, financial, trading and social circles. Immensely wealthy and enterprising is the general verdict. . . . A word about

[the firm's] operations cannot but be informing – for they are nothing if not ambitious and resourceful, and as a private house the firm is, I suppose, the biggest property-owner in Rio and Brazil.[86]

Long before the elder Guinle or his partner died, then, there was plenty of money for all, and the two founders and Guinle's sons (all born in the 1880s) had begun to enjoy a marked social prominence. Da Costa recalls Eduardo (*filho*) and his brother Carlos as popular men about town, and Carlos, Otávio, and Guilherme were all involved in the Club dos Diários.[87] Carlos (b. 1883) took a medical degree in Rio's Faculty of Medicine, married an Oliveira Rocha, and continued in the family businesses (later branching out into banking). He was a renowned club man, active not only in the Diários, or the Club de Engenharia and the Jockey (to both of which his father and Gaffrée had belonged), but also in the Derby, the Fluminense Futbol Club, and, in France, the Cercle du Bois de Boulogne and the Polo de Paris. The magnificent house his brother, Guilherme, and old Gaffrée had built on Botafogo Beach became his, and thereafter a rendezvous for Society in the 1930s.[88]

The same profile could be sketched for his brothers – *bacharéis* from Rio schools, they, too, worked in the family firms, pursued their own businesses, enjoyed life in Society and its clubs. To the residence on Rua São Clemente and the *cidade velha* office on Rua da Quitanda, the social and economic poles between which their father had spun out his initial success in the 1880s, were added the imposing Eclectic-style building on the new Avenida Central and the various Guinle residences in smart locations such as Flamengo Beach, Botafogo, and the Rua Marquês de São Vicente. The portrait is clear enough, and gilt-edged.

Another figure in *belle-époque* high society might be suggested as a final example of its nature: Ataúlfo de Paiva.[89] Ataúlfo [Napoles] de Paiva was born in 1865 in the same *fluminense* coffee town as Francisco Pereira Passos: São João Marcos. He was the son of a merchant fallen on hard times, who brought him, in 1871, from that town to another, similar one, Barra Mansa, where the elder Paiva used what wealth he still had to put the boy through primary schooling. From then on, it was Ataúlfo's own intelligence, ambition, and ability to win patrons that made his way for him.

While still at the primary school, he put together a weekly paper which impressed the town's merchants enough to pay the boy's way in *colégio*. Then, however, the well-connected educator and majority leader in the *fluminense* provincial assembly, Alberto Brandão, heard of the boy. He persuaded the merchants to allow him to educate Ataúlfo free of any charge, as a *pensionista* of his celebrated Colégio Brandão, in Vassouras, center of the prosperous Paraíba Valley.

Ataúlfo graduated early and remained to teach in Brandão's school until he was old enough for the São Paulo faculty. In his days there, he worked his way through by preparing students for entrance to the Colégio Pedro II. He completed his degree in 1887 and returned to Barra Mansa to practice.

Patronage rescued Ataúlfo from the provinces, again, this time in the new era of the Republic. Prudente de Morais, then governor of the State of São Paulo, nominated him municipal judge of Pindamonhagaba. After a year, he was named a *pretor* (lesser municipal judge) in Rio. Less than three years later, Prudente, since become President of the Republic, named him judge of the Civil and Criminal Tribunal. After nine years in all the districts of the Tribunal's jurisdiction, he was nominated chief magistrate of the Court of Appeals, and re-nominated six years later.

In all this time, Ataúlfo participated in commissions dealing with the "Social Question": labor, orphans, and the like. He represented Brazil in Paris at an international conference on charity in 1900. While there, he took part in the International Congress of Comparative Law, of which he was elected vice-president, all of which won him the praise of the Instituto da Ordem dos Advogados on his return. His position put him prestigiously in the center of the reformist responses to urban social ills that were in the air at the time.

Reformism and international conferences, commissions and judgeships were not Ataúlfo's only media for a prestigious public image. A member of the Academia Brasileira de Letras by 1916, he was its secretary general by 1918. If literature served his purpose, so did foreign decorations – he seems to have been awarded all of them, from the French Legion of Honor to the Chinese Order of the Precious Stones. Before he died he also had been made president of the Academia and minister of the Supreme Federal Tribunal. He once admitted that the only thing he was denied in life was the hand of the woman whom he wished to marry, a daughter of the Baron do Rio Negro. Considering the rival who won the lady, Ataúlfo doubtless took the defeat graciously; the heiress refused the magistrate in order to take the veil.[90]

Ataúlfo's successes speak directly to a crucial aspect of elite society throughout the period in question. He was president of the Academia "without ever having written a book" and held the highest position in the judiciary without any reputation as a jurist. Whatever substantive talent he had, and his early successes demonstrate a great deal, it was subordinated to what one man remembers as a "career made by good manners," by "pleasing the strong."[91] Paiva was as famous for his *politesse* as for his handsome appearance, his vanity, and his very stylish dressing.[92] Known as a leader from his *colégio* days on, he used his skills at domination and at pleasing in an adroit combination which impressed and attracted patrons willing to promote him to positions where he made the most of his opportunities and obtained positions still more impressive. Inseparable companion of the fashionable, he shared D. Laurinda's box at the Lírico and bestrode the Rua do Ouvidor's fashionable curbs like the colossus of Society he was. He displays the interpenetration of the *alto mundo* and the structure of power, by showing how triumph in the former might lead to important positions in the latter. A key to Society could be the key to place and power.

The alto mundo: people and places

In this review of the careers of these members of the *belle-époque alto mundo*, the basis and the nature of much of that world has emerged. Each of these people helped to make up Society, an existence of luxury and glamor heavily beholden to foreign cultural models. They did this, however, as part of careers that were inseparable from domestic realities. One glimpses here Cariocas and provincials who came together over years spent in Rio's expanding urban economy, in the elaboration of the nation's infrastructure and in Rio's urban reforms, in the movements which helped to destroy slavery and monarchy, in participation in the *Encilhamento*, in the matted undergrowth of Republican politics, in the growing legal apparatus associated with the burgeoning port capital, and in the flourishing world of Carioca journalism and fashionable European cultural styles. The *alto mundo*, in a phrase, was foreign cultural influence interwoven with the emergent Carioca fabric of power.

An important aspect of that fabric is that these people were not only representative of leadership in all these areas, but representative of a leadership knotted together personally. Though hardly unique, this is essential for understanding culture and society in the Rio of 1900. This knotting up of socio-economic power, distinct cultural usages and vision, and close interpersonal relationships is basic to this analysis.

One glimpses precisely what is meant here in recalling the ways in which these particular members of the elite crossed one another's paths. Thus, one notes that Figueiredo was a fellow clubman with Pereira Passos, Azeredo, Rui, Inglês de Sousa, Frontin, and the Guinles. One remembers that Ataúlfo was a friend of both Bebê Lima e Castro and D. Laurinda. One recalls that D. Laurinda's uncle, Joaquim Murtinho, was a patron of Azeredo, which explains how Azeredo knew D. Laurinda. Azeredo, in turn, was a close political ally of Rui, who, in turn was related to Bebê, his frequent guest at salons where Azeredo and Pinheiro Machado also appeared. Rui was not only a salon host, but a member of the Academia Brasileira de Letras, where he doubtless met with Ataúlfo and Inglês de Sousa. Quartim, though not a member of the Academia, certainly belonged to the Casino, along with Azeredo, Rui, and Figueiredo, whom he would have known, in any case, as another of the handful of prominent financiers in the capital.

Escragnolle Dória, as a journalist, would have known Azeredo and Rui, and, as a São Paulo-trained lawyer, financial writer, and scion of important aristocratic families who summered in the intimate resort of Petrópolis with the rest of the elite, may well have known Inglês de Sousa, Ataúlfo, Rui, Quartim, the Guinles and Figueiredo. Even without their high profile in Society, the Guinles would probably have known Pereira Passos and Frontin, entrepreneurial colleagues of their father in the Club de Engenharia, and just about everyone else, because they themselves were clubmen in the Jockey and the Diários.

When one adds to these personal connections the probability of meeting simply as a function of workplace, leisure, residence, and the size of the elite, the *alto mundo* squeezes smaller still. The *cidade velha*, where every one of these men had an office and a club, and where the women shopped, took tea, and promenaded, was a tightly jammed space about a mile square, within whose narrow gambit the city's heart beat – perhaps a dozen streets, accounting for all that was most important for the elite.[93] Primeiro de Março, Quitanda, Rosário, Candelária, Alfândega: these were the streets that encompassed import and export, finance and law. Ouvidor, Gonçalves Dias, and, after 1904, the Avenida Central (later Avenida Rio Branco), were the streets for luxury retail, journalism and bookstores, chic cafés, restaurants, and teahouses, and the exclusive clubs. The old mansions now housing the public bureaucracy, along with the theaters and a few clubs, were scattered, most of them lining the various squares and small parks – the Praça 15 de Novembro, the Praça da República, the Praça Tiradentes (once Largo do Rócio), the Largo da Carioca, and the Passeio Público. As for the residential areas, one may recall how many homes noted above had Flamengo or Botafogo district addresses – it was a neighborly elite indeed (see Map 5). If one considers that what is being discussed is a group of probably less than five hundred families,[94] and then recalls the relationships discussed in this and in chapter 2, many of which spanned generations, the personalized nature of the elite's world is patent.

In effect, Carioca high society in the *belle époque* had roots deeply embedded and densely interwoven in the creation and ongoing vitality of the urban and the national political and economic structure. The seeming superficial frivolity of much in the elite culture should not obscure the processes in which it played a part. It was a small world, and one within whose compass the dynamic of a changing Brazil was caught up. As one moves from the discussion of the kind of individuals making up high society to the analysis of the salon, *per se*, this relationship between elite culture and elite power will become clearer still.

2. The Carioca salon under the Monarchy and Old Republic

The salon is a kind of transitional institution between such formal institutions as clubs or schools and such domestic institutions as the extended family. Something of the role the salon played has already been seen in the various lives just traced. Other insights can be gathered now as one picks up the strand of the salon in its own right. For this strand is a long one, pulling at historical contexts which will point again to the elite of the *belle époque* in yet another light, not only that of the powerful of the Republic, but as the successors to the Monarchy's powerful, a continuity and metamorphosis suggested in the previous chapters. In the salon's pleasant milieu, one sees again both shifts in elite membership and certain perennial qualities of the Carioca elite and its world.

The Second Reign was remembered by many *fin-de-siècle* Cariocas as a far better epoch for the elite and its salons. One fashionable writer noted in 1911:

> Thirty or forty years ago in Rio de Janeiro, society was supremely distinguished and delicate, with habits of refined sociability and a notably gracious stamp . . . Gallantry was so much the mark of the time that, to put political events in their proper contexts, the historian has to narrate at each step the soirées, recitals and balls that took place. This was, undoubtedly, the golden age of Carioca society.[95]

It has been seen, in institutions such as the Casino Fluminense, that the elite of Rio in the Second Reign (1840–89) was characterized by ennobled men of affairs, planters, upper bureaucrats, and statesmen.[96] It was such figures and their wives, daughters, and sons who dominated the most important salons of the period, too.

These gatherings were generally of a common pattern. The host and his wife made a private dinner for a select group of friends and relations. Afterwards, the larger circle of guests arrived, and a number of genteel pastimes were enjoyed: chamber music, operatic selections or poetry recitation (generally performed by a musical protégé, by women of the host's family, or by a guest), or, perhaps, the performance of a bit of light theater (perhaps written by a favored man of letters and acted by guest and family members). Dancing, cards, and highly polished conversation were common. The women wore imported gowns, the men frockcoats or formal evening dress. What distinguished such an occasion from a simple party was regular repetition, generally on a certain day of the week every week, ever other week, or every month.

Such get-togethers, coincident with the increasing wealth of the Côrte during the Second Reign, and the consequent spread of luxury goods from Europe and European contacts, allowed the most powerful men of the plantations, the counting-houses, the boards of directors, the political cliques, and the imperial cabinets and ministries to bring together family, friends, and acquaintances during the cooler months of the year in a festive milieu of imported refinement. In such gatherings, they could make contacts, smooth over divisions, and vindicate their preeminence by an obvious personal statement of wealth and refinement.[97]

A brief acquaintance with imperial Society is enough to demonstrate this. The most important salons of the period were those of the Marquis de Abrantes, of the Councillor Nabuco de Araújo, of the Baron de Cotegipe, of the Viscount de Meriti, and of the Haritoffs, the Estrelas, the São Clementes, and the Nova Friburgos.[98] From our discussion of club membership in the last chapter, one may remember that the Estrela, São Clemente, and Nova Friburgo families were associated with Portuguese merchant founders and dynasties involved with commerce, finance, plantations, and railroads. As for the new names mentioned here, the Haritoffs had their wealth from coffee planting and Meriti was a banker of Portuguese birth. Cotegipe, one of the great party chieftains of the Second Reign, was a member of the Wanderley clan of Pernambuco planters, just as Nabuco de Araújo, another major statesman of the epoch, was also married into important planter families of Pernambuco. Abrantes we have met before – a statesman representative of Bahia's great merchant and planter families.

Of these salons, the most important were those of the political figures because of the clear overlap between the period's high society and elite statesmen in Rio. The Côrte, as the seat of Empire and the most Europeanized of Brazil's cities, attracted the best of the powerful provincial families as deputies, senators, and ministers. Further, the cooler winter months (from May or June through September or October) saw Society's annual round of pleasures, the Season, take place at the same time as the annual round of political activity in the Chamber and the Senate. The salon of Abrantes in the first decades of the Second Reign, and that of Cotegipe, in the last, with Nabuco de Araújo's bridging the two epochs – thus formed the most important centers of elite society and culture (outside of, say, the Casino and the Lírico) and were unrivaled by the mere luxury of the balls and regular receptions of their more monied merchant acquaintances.[99]

The style of these later salons was modeled directly on that of the Parisian society that varnished France's Second Empire (1852–70).[100] The splendor of Napoleon III's court served to reinforce the French influence on Brazilian elite society which has already been discussed and will be analysed even more thoroughly in the chapters to come. Here, however, it should be noted that, with the vigorous policy of embellishment and of stylish refinement pursued by the imperial court in Paris, Carioca elite frenchification increased dramatically. This was possible because of the growing wealth born of coffee which made contacts and commerce with France more pervasive with logical consequences for everything about the elite and its institutions. In the salons, the décor, the dances, the music, the gowns, and the conversational catch-phrases all reflected the tastes of the aristocratic Paris which so charmed the increasing numbers from the Brazilian elite who now began to make frequent visits there. As early as the 1850s, a contemporary journalist wrote of Catete, a part of one of the fashionable residential districts, as "the district of coquettishness, of foppishness, of *bom-tom* [*sic*], of elegance, of wit, of aristocracy – the Faubourg Saint Germain of Rio de Janeiro."[101]

Metamorphosis

The most striking difference between these Second Reign salons and those of the *belle époque* has to do with the fragmentation of salon life in the later epoch. Where the Second Reign did have its more literary salons, these were clearly the exception – most salons were of the broader, Society variety. Though these latter included artists and literati, surely, they focussed on the elegant and the worldly among the powerful – arts and letters served the function of cachet and light diversion.[102]

Belle-époque salons were more varied and only one or two were hosted by important political figures (e.g., those of Azeredo, say, or of Rui). One finds a strong literary and musical flavor in the salon of Inglês de Sousa, a decidedly artistic strain in that of D. Laurinda, and broader salons hosted by urban professionals and men of affairs.[103]

The cases of Pereira Passos and Paulo de Frontin have already been discussed (engineer entrepreneurs), and of Figueiredo and Quartim (urban-based financier capitalists) – we might add to them salon hosts such as Paulo Leuzinger (publisher), Heitor Cordeiro (lawyer), Oscar Varadí (lawyer, banker, and businessman), Luís Rafael Vieira Souto (Pereira Passos' old critic, another engineer entrepreneur), and João do Rego Barros (physician, banker, administrator in urban utilities).[104]

In this shift from salons hosted by an elite of planter statesmen and great merchants to salons hosted by urban professionals and businessmen, one glimpses the same phenomenon discussed earlier with regard to the Casino and Club dos Diários.[105] Here, again, is the shift from Côrte, coffee and rural/urban commerce to an expanding urban center for professional, business, and bureaucratic careers.

Instead of the great provincial chiefs representing the great plantation and commercial fortunes of the Northeast or the *fluminense fazendas*, men who resided in Rio for years at a time to gain leverage within the centralized Monarchy, the political men most important and most present in the Capital Federal during the Old Republic were power-brokers attempting to defend their state oligarchies' interests within the decentralized structure of the Republic. In the Republic, truly great political chieftains often only came and went to and from Rio as presidents and ministers. The capital was not politically vital in the same way it had been as the Côrte. Then, the party that the Emperor favored ruled the Empire from Rio, by dispensing favors, appointments, and small delegations of power. Now, Rio was more the brokerage house where Federal rewards and punishments, ultimately founded on the strength or weakness of the various state oligarchies, were sorted out and haggled over. The nation's wealth continued to center on plantation export crops and power continued in the hands of planters; only now, those in control of the most powerful states had constructed a regime with a decentralized political structure. Such men no longer needed to reside for years in Rio themselves to watch over the security and imposition of their desires; that could be left to professional politicos. They themselves needed to secure their positions by tightly organized political power at the state level, so as to manage their affairs profitably and to gain leverage at the federal level for the favors necessary to their local interests.[106]

The hosts of *belle-époque* salons indicate the change in the origins of Carioca power and wealth in the new era. Now, men of traditional families and new men alike were attracted to Rio as businessmen, engineers, lawyers, doctors, politicians, journalists and writers, diplomats, and other members of the State bureaucracy. Abrantes and Cotegipe and their salons were replaced by hosts who were politicos like Azeredo and Rui, and entrepreneurs like Pereira Passos and Frontin. Rui's case, again, is instructive. A man who seems closest to the "type" of the older statesmen, he represented little real weight as Bahia's senator, and divided his time between a doomed pursuit of national power in the face of the new political realities and a very successful pursuit of fortune in the midst of the new urban variety.

Continuity

As I argued in discussing clubs, the shifts born of Rio's changing role in the nation were hardly as disruptive or abrupt as one might think. Members of the older Carioca-based elite families could often see and adapt to the gradual economic and social developments to which political conflict and change corresponded in more sudden fashion. The growing weakness of *fluminense* coffee or Bahian cotton and sugar, and the growing importance of other regions and of urban-based professions – these were apparent years before the Monarchy's fall, and the success of many at anticipating the possibilities emerging helps to explain why so many of the *belle-époque* elite were not all new men, but, rather, scions of old families who had adapted to circumstances.

This is illustrated by the case of the Paranaguá family.[107] The family's place among the Carioca elite was established by João Lustosa da Cunha Paranaguá (1821–1912), son of a modest provincial *coronel* of Piauí. The colonel's son began his ascent when he took a *bacharelado* from Olinda[108] and a wife from a Bahian elite family; he climbed swiftly from deputy in the provincial assembly to deputy and then senator for Piauí in the Côrte. There, he secured various provincial presidencies, in Piauí, Maranhão, and Pernambuco, as well as a number of judicial appointments in Rio itself, a string of ministerial portfolios, and the imperial nod to organize the cabinet of 1882, which followed his being ennobled with the title of viscount. At Empire's dusk, his long service to the crown was recognized with the title of marquis (1888).

Paranaguá, a personal friend of the Emperor (his daughter was very close to the imperial heiress and, later, when Baroness de Loreto, accompanied the imperial family into exile), retired to practice law after the coup of 1889, passing his time with many historical and scientific interests. His traditional *solar* in the old Glória district (legacy of his father-in-law, the Viscount de Montserate) was the modest home where he continued to entertain friends – old colleagues from the aristocratic ranks of the Second Reign's Conservative Party who gathered around him on Sundays with his family.

Although Paranaguá retreated, his sons advanced in the new age. One, Júlio, had early engaged the era on its own terms and had gone into engineering. He became an associate and good friend of Paulo de Frontin, with whom he worked on the celebrated feat of delivering water to Rio in six days. The other son, José, shifted later, and successfully, in this age of transition. He began with the same kind of career his father had had – one presupposing the Monarchy's centralized power and imperial patronage. He went to the Colégio Pedro II, the Faculties of Law at Recife and São Paulo, and then on to Amazonas, as provincial president at twenty-eight. However, this career, so typical of the imperial *cursus honorum*, was apparently snapped off in 1889; the Marquis' son turned to commerce. Until 1913, José spent his time in Europe and Rio, as a representative of the rubber interests with which he had come in contact in the Amazon region as governor. He married into a Carioca commercial family of French extraction. He used the capital he acquired on both counts to invest in Carioca real estate, both in the Avenida Central (the pet project of his brother's friend, Paulo de Frontin), and in Copacabana Beach, when it was still largely sand and poor fishermen's huts.

Like many others, José had thus successfully crossed over from the careers of the older to those of the newer era. Groomed to be an imperial statesman, he had become, instead, an entrepreneur and *rentier* in the expanding Carioca economy. The cultural influence, wealth, and the Catholic devotion of his wife, yoked to a persevering social ambition, reinforced their position in elite culture and society. José became a papal count, read *L'Illustration*, *La Revue des Deux Mondes*, and travelled regularly to Paris.

By 1916, the couple were fixtures of the *alto mundo* chronicled in the social columns.[109] In a beautiful new French-style house, the imperial statesman's son, made wealthy by a new regional agricultural export, by an urban commercial fortune, and by urban investment in the expanding Federal Capital, presided over a twice-monthly salon for family, friends, artists, and foreign diplomats.

3. The salon and elite culture and society

Two elements, then, were constant features in the salons of the Second Reign and the *belle époque*, and will serve to close our discussion. In each era, the salon was, first, an important informal aspect of power in the

Carioca socio-economic structure, and, second, it was defined and expressed in the same cultural terms.

Their historian has noted that Second Reign salons served an instrumental purpose in imperial politics – something I have argued, too. In politics, finance, and business this warrants little debate. The reason the salon was useful derives from the highly personalized nature of the elite, something strengthened in turn by the small number of people involved. As I note elsewhere, the Côrte's entire population in 1872 was 275,000. One can imagine, then, the correspondingly small size of the elite, which I have estimated at a maximum of *c.* 1,000 households.[110]

Think, too, of the fact that men of the elite were often former classmates in the Colégio Pedro II, the Faculties of Law, or, possibly, the Faculty of Medicine or the Escola Politécnica. Consider, as well, that such men married each other's womenfolk, went to the same clubs, theaters, and balls, often had similar or complementary economic interests and professional associations, and journeyed to the same summer resort in Petrópolis. The conclusions for the Second Reign salon and its importance follow easily. It was a superb setting for the personal contacts and patronage natural in such a milieu. Nabuco de Araújo's youngest son, recalling people typically at his father's salon, listed the most powerful Liberals of the Northeast and family names of those powerful in coffee, the court, and commerce:

> The center of this agreeable society . . . was formed by the so-called Lions of the North, Monte Alegre, Pedro Chaves (Quarahim), Dantas, Pinto Lima, Sinimbú, and other intimate friends of Nabuco [de Araújo], like Madureira, Pedro Muniz, José Caetano de Andrade e Pinto, [and] the Baron do Catete, with whom the Marquise de Abrantes would afterwards marry. . . . [The] young *fluminense* beauties [also] made their debut [there:] the daughter of Quarahim, the future Baroness de S. Clemente; the daughter of Nogueira da Gama, future Countess de Penamacôr; . . . [and] the daughter of Lins Gomes Ferreira. Mme. de Saint-Georges, wife of the French minister; D. Belizara de Paiva; D. Maria de Nazareth Costa Pinto; [and] *senhora* de Souza Franco, "The Star of the North," also provoked admiration.[111]

One of Abrantes' relatives notes just as telling a list of names among the Marquis' frequent guests: Olinda, Itanhaem, Sapucahí, Abaeté, Caxias, Tamandaré, Silva Paranhos, Zacharias, Cotegipe, Ferraz, Junqueira, Saraiva, Maciel Monteiro, Boa Vista, Joaquim Manuel de Macedo, José de Alencar, Menezes e Souza, Torres Homem, Justiniano da Rocha, and Mauá. That is to say, the chieftains of the Monarchy's two great parties, as well as men noted in letters and the dean of Brazilian entrepreneurs.[112] Such salons were, then, simply more select and relaxed media for the contacts and exchange of views that one finds in more formal institutions such as the Casino, the Jockey, and the Lírico.

Clearly, this instrumental aspect held true for the *belle-époque* salon as well. Indeed, considering the growth of the city's population and the increased pace of change, the importance of the salon's role would logically be enhanced. It must have helped to maintain relationships as conveniently personalized as they were. As Nabuco de Araújo's granddaughter remembered "It was a familiar society whose doors no one tried to force."[113] The size of the elite itself was still conducive to this result, remaining, quite possibly, below five hundred families.[114] This size and the institutions discussed here would allow for that comfortably select atmosphere so useful for conducting the affairs of the ruling class. That it was the ruling class in which the *belle-époque* salons (and the clubs, schools, and Lírico) found their place has also been made rather clear. Men such as Figueiredo, Frontin, Pereira Passos, Azeredo, Rui Barbosa, Inglês de Sousa, the Guinles were not just salon hosts, clubmen, or men of fashion; they were such as part of their being men of power in the Federal Capital.

The question of how these socio-cultural institutions fit into the construction of a position of power raises our second concluding point – the centrality of the cultural values figuring in the salon's make-up. In both Monarchy and Old Republic, the elite self-consciously identified with the same European paradigm in the salon that figured in the schools, clubs, and opera theater – an aristocratic paradigm of Franco-English derivation. Let us examine this, in its salon variation, a bit closer.

In the salon, this paradigm is most striking in the qualities that made certain salon figures admirable to their contemporaries. In the Second Reign, perhaps the most admired man in Society was Antônio Peregrino Maciel Monteiro, second Baron de Itamaracá (1804–68),[115] a *pernambucano* educated in Olinda and Paris, a physician, a deputy, a president of the Chamber of Deputies, a minister for foreign affairs, and Brazil's *ministro plenipotenciário* to Portugal. A contemporary claimed that Maciel Monteiro could have been one of Brazil's greatest poets, had he chosen.[116] He had not. He preferred Society: the salon, the soirée, numerous affairs, all of which he graced with a singular gift for the improvisation of Romantic poetry.

He was celebrated for his literary cultivation and poetic gift, the "fluent, unhesitating cadence" of his oratory, his pleasant round of theaters and balls, as well as his invitations to join in the "societies of the most elegant circles."[117] He was most distinguished, however, by his personal style

> . . . of the most demanding and whimsical elegance, in that he always dressed rigorously in fashion, and in that he always spoke using gentilities of a delicacy and a refined courtesy that, without any pretensions or excess, softly and enchantingly radiated his subtle spirit and his poet's imagination.[118]

The Franco-English aristocratic paradigm is obvious here. The literary cultivation, the way of life, the personal style, these are patently modeled on the behavior of men of contemporary French and English aristocratic society. While one expects that his oratory and dress[119] owed something to the great models of England's Parliament, his greatest debts were to France. The beauties of his conversation, for instance, and the emphasis on poetic inspiration and *amours*, clearly reflect aristocratic French influence. A modish writer of 1911 wrote, quite rightly, of Maciel Monteiro, that,

> The worldly splendors of Paris, where he lived some years, the sensual atmosphere of the salons, of the clubs, and of the restaurants, of the aristocratic boulevards, the Romanticism of her heroes and of her poets, revealed a new world to Maciel Monteiro, and made of him an original creature in our milieu.[120]

Original he may have been, but only in the sense of his consummate accomplishment of a cultural assimilation commonly desired by his peers. French salon society, long established and famously refined, had taught Maciel Monteiro the arts of conversation and other aspects of style, as well as, one would expect, graceful pointers regarding the skillfully executed love affair. Nor had French Romanticism been without impact, as the *pernambucano*'s flair for timely improvisation of Romantic poetry attests. It is indicative that one of the few of Maciel Monteiro's poems still extant was printed by contemporaries in a collection entitled *Lamartinianas*, and that he himself had taken the trouble to translate Lamartine for the edification of his less polished countrymen.[121] Maciel Monteiro had learned his lessons well; Carioca high society was only too charmed to witness his performances.

In the next elite generation Wanderley Pinho notes that the qualities for which Maciel Monteiro was admired recurred in another, and with the same Society approbation. This lion of the 1870s salons was Joaquim Nabuco (1849–1910),[122] son of the Nabuco de Araújo who hosted one of the great salons of the Second Reign. Nabuco, too, like Maciel Monteiro, was *pernambucano*, a *bacharel* (São Paulo, then Recife), and a

a. Joaquim Nabuco in 1888, *homme du monde* and triumphant abolitionist

b. Rui Barbosa in 1913, elder statesman

4. Two exemplary figures of the Carioca *belle époque*

noted diplomat, *littérateur*, deputy, and orator. Among the dissimilarities, one must note Nabuco's central role in the Abolition movement and his justly respected legacy as an historian. These, however, are beside our point. What is striking is the parallel Nabuco traced with Maciel Monteiro as an *homme du monde*. (See photograph in illustration 4.)

Like his predecessor, Nabuco was noted for his facility of expression, his taste for fashionable dress, his conversational aplomb, the amorous escapades of his youth, and his mastery of French literary culture. Unlike Maciel Monteiro, though, Nabuco was heavily influenced by the English aristocratic model in certain matters of polite society – table manners and personal courtesies, for instance, were of English origin in Nabuco's home.[123] Still, in Nabuco, French influence was marked. Steeped in French literature and thought, and with a profound admiration for Renan, Nabuco's intellectual ease with French went to the extent of writing and publishing in the language, not only prose and poetry, but a long diplomatic treatise. Even his wit apparently took its wings, or its edge, in that tongue.[124]

Again, as with the Maciel Monteiro, the essential point in this foreign influence on Nabuco's style is the aristocratic image they helped to project. The result was a triumphant one, if not one that all Nabuco's contemporaries found easy to live with. One of these sniped that "Nabuco was an aristocrat. . . . [After] being in contact with the people, he went to soap his hands and perfume himself, before dressing in his Poole coat."[125] Another contemporary, however, was doubtless closer to the *alto mundo* consensus when he wrote, in a chic review in 1905:

> when to distinction in manners is allied a good education, when to gallantry is joined a perfect science of, and sensitivity to, life, when one possesses tact and a great knowledge of men and of things, when one has the cultivation of a Morny and the wit of a Talleyrand – when, in sum, one is a Nabuco. . . . – one realizes the type of the true diplomat, according to the old school.[126]

Though Nabuco suffices to express the salon values of both the late Monarchy and the *belle époque* (being a contemporary of both the young gallants on the first and of the established hosts of the second);[127] one may also consider the style of the other *belle-époque* men and salons described to see the continuities.[128] For the matter of care in fashionable dress, one might recall Pereira Passos, Rui Barbosa, Azeredo, and Ataúlfo de Paiva. Refinement and skill in conversation were noted in Rui, Pereira Passos, Paiva, and Inglês de Sousa. As for amours, more difficult to detect in the documentation available, one still reads of the reputation of both Pereira Passos and Azeredo.

If the point of personal style is obvious, so is that of the French aristocratic influence on the literature, music, and poetry likely to be featured in salon life. A fashionable young poet later recalled that, for example: "The prestige of the French book . . . continued immoderate and unconditional. With what eagerness we read it! . . . we remained French in spirit. . . ."[129] The same poet, in describing fashionable receptions, betrays our paradigm again in the terms he uses for those performing, chatting, and simply attending such salons: "*diseur*," "*causeur*," and "*gentleman*."[130] Afrânio Peixoto's contemporary Society novel, *A esfinje* (1911), mentions such typical salon fare as the recitation of "Le chien," "Matelot," "Les bottines," and "C'est le vent,"[131] and Broca, in observations on the salons of 1900, writes, "What was the preferred topic of conversation in such milieux? Most of all, Parisian novelties, then, the latest novel by Anatole France, the failure of *Chantecler* by Rostand, the most recent play by Bataille, etc."[132]

It was the same *mélange* of cultivated, frenchified small talk and entertainment boasted by the Second Reign salons. If the dancing, the card-games, and some other bits and pieces of the Second Reign salon now no longer appeared, neither did they in contemporary French salons. Rio had merely remained *au courant*.[133]

The activities of the salon and the "type" admired there in both the Monarchy and the Old Republic demonstrate, then, the continued vitality of the Franco-English aristocratic paradigm. Whether in the poetry declaimed, the songs sung, the music played, the sort of personal style respected, or the French dropped, whether in the champagne drunk, or the other wines served, whether in the pastries nibbled, or the *dîners* eaten, European, and predominantly French, fashions changed, but the fashion for such things did not.[134]

Just as with the role of the salon in elite society, as yet another useful intersection of the interlocking circles of a very small world, the aristocratic European values that informed the salon's pastimes and its members' behavior were enduring. Maintained for contacts, conversation, and prestigious forms of consumption, the salons of the *belle époque* also demonstrate the importance of such values, once again, in the projection of the elite's self-image to itself. As with their education and formal institutions, the elite salon's association with European civilization was central to the elite's sense of what it was supposed to be. In the changing world in which members, and would-be members, of the elite sought to retain, or gain position, these values were among the few things that suggested continuity and the legitimization that comes with tradition and identification with power.

4

Domestic institutions of the elite

The reader may have noted that one's attention has slowly been drawn from the grander, more obvious features of the *alto mundo* to the individuals and social reality behind them. Now, we explore the nature and development of still more fundamental institutions which have only partially emerged heretofore. Here, I discuss the elite family and its world, the domestic institutions essential to comprehending elite culture and society.

1. The family

As both travellers and scholars have observed, the family in colonial and much of post-colonial Brazil is best understood as an instrument for survival and triumph in a hostile environment relatively untouched by State intervention. Indeed, colonial and monarchical Brazil was largely the creation of great clans who held the wealth and power and sought to secure them over the years to survive. Brazil's economy has always been precarious, ebbing and flowing with the North Atlantic demand for certain crops or precious natural resources. The State, traditionally impoverished, delegated its authority to those on the coasts and in their hinterlands who wielded power informally, possessing the family resources in land and men which counted for everything.[1]

With political and economic realities cast in these terms the social results are unsurprising. One's possibilities in life were circumscribed by one's position in a family, by that family's position in the region's politico-economic hierarchy, and by the region's position *vis-à-vis* the Brazilian and Atlantic economies. By the nineteenth century, some fluidity, at least in urban careers, allowed for greater opportunities for the individual, as we have seen. Immigrants' children might find new choices open to them in the expanding potential of the ports, as might the children of the provincial and urban middle sectors – one has only to think of Paulo de Frontin, Antônio de Azeredo, or Ataúlfo de Paiva.

In these examples, however, certain variables must be remembered. None of these men could have won his chance without an education bought him, at least initially, with family money, and all of these men, with the possible exception of Frontin, made their way through the patronage of the powerful. Such patronage, as we shall see, was traditionally integral to the elite family. The dominant aspect of elite social mobility, then, remained the limitations and possibilities inherent in the institution of the family.[2]

An image that might be useful for the institution is that of a net – a net woven of flesh and blood, bone and brain, stretched as wide as possible to catch and hold whatever possibilities treacherous economic and political currents washed through, yet flexible, easily pulled in and shifted about when the catch was poor and another spot beckoned. All students of Brazil know of the successive triumph and collapse of each regional economy – seventeenth-century sugar in the Northeast, eighteenth-century gold and diamonds in Minas Gerais, the early nineteenth-century ephemeral possibilities in sugar and cotton in various provinces, the turn-of-the-century boom and bust of rubber in the North, and the ongoing, shifting triumph of coffee since the 1830s, a crop that has favored various valleys and plateaus within the South-central region at various times.

Indeed, the story of coffee families is typical of the perennial predicament noted here. The reader will recall, for instance, how coffee and its corollary commercial activities were the basis of *fluminense* fortunes until the 1880s. The crop had known its first triumph in Rio de Janeiro Province by mid-century, while spreading to Minas Gerais and São Paulo. By the 1880s, however, it was leaving *fluminense* plantations behind, the exhausted fields of memory rather than great wealth.

It was against this backdrop of roving regional decline, or sudden failure that might blight the world of one's youth (or haunt it in the poorly hidden preoccupations of one's parents) that elite children grew up.[3] It was that human net of the extended family upon which one relied to reinforce one's position or save oneself in the face of these traditional threats.

2. Matrimony

Climbing elite family trees helps to see behind these preliminary observations. One gets at the pivotal institution of marriage: one way in

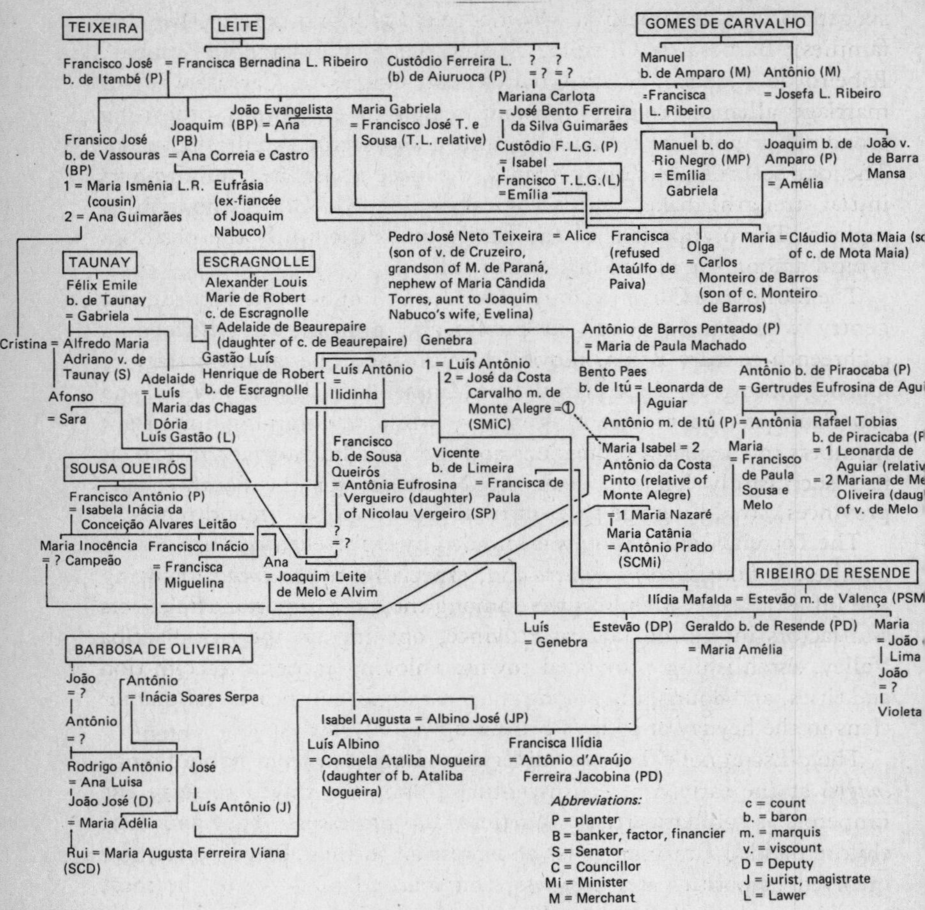

Figure 1. Elite families and matrimonial strategy

which elite families sought to second-guess economic ruin. Let us discuss two examples to demonstrate the importance of families and matrimonial alliances among the elite.

The more complex family tree (Figure 1), like the simpler (Figure 2), is incomplete, showing only members important for linkage and certain successes. One may recognize members of the elite from the earlier chapters. If that is not enough to make the point that marriage served to unite fortune and power and to maintain and increase them, two other observations will be.

First, one should note that the complex tree, including from four to six generations, is actually six distinct trees (with branches to other elite families): Barbosa de Oliveira, Teixeira Leite, d'Escragnolle Taunay, Ribeiro de Resende, Sousa Queirós, and Gomes de Carvalho. Their marriage alliances trace a constant search to enter into promising economic or political terrain to improve and secure familial position. The local seats of each family (that is, the place where the family won its initial strength) make a chronological catalogue of Brazil's flourishing regions. The occupations of the family heads exemplify the positions typical among the nineteenth-century elite.

The Barbosa de Oliveira family, founded by impoverished Portuguese gentry who "made good" in public and professional positions in eighteenth-century Bahia, moved through the imperial magistracy to marriage into great landed families of Minas Gerais, Rio de Janeiro, and São Paulo in the nineteenth century, while maintaining important members in the urban professions and the State bureaucracy in Rio. It had successfully left the declining Northeast for the South-central provinces, straddling the poles of rural and urban wealth and power.[4]

The Teixeira Leite family was founded by eighteenth-century *mineiro* families. It flourished in *mineiro* and, especially, in *fluminense* financing and infrastructure. Members were among the most important financiers and factors in Rio de Janeiro Province, opening up the rich Paraíba Valley, establishing provincial towns, enjoying imperial recognition and titles, and flourishing among the most important provincial planter clans in the heyday of coffee's beginning.[5]

The d'Escragnolle Taunay family was descended from noble French *émigrés* at the early nineteenth-century Côrte who stayed to serve the Emperors as soldiers, artists, courtiers, and professors. They and their children added Brazilian titles and prestige to their French ones, got involved in politics and business, and married into two of the most prestigious planter families of Brazil – the *fluminense* Teixeira Leite and the *paulista* Sousa Queirós.[6]

The Ribeiro de Resende family, of noble eighteenth-century Portuguese origins, enriched itself through extensive urban and rural landholdings in the provinces of Minas Gerais and Rio de Janeiro and considerable prestige at Côrte. The family's patriarch, the Marquis de Valença, won imperial favor as a loyal magistrate and statesman and was granted successive titles of nobility, all of which added weight to his own and his descendants' matrimonial pretensions, facilitating their enviable alliances with important *paulista* families.[7]

Among these, again, were the Sousa Queirós. This family, like two of the others, claimed a Portuguese blazon and eighteenth-century beginnings in Brazil. Like the Teixeira Leite, they were among the earliest big planters in their province, holding numerous plantations, boasting titles and marital relations with the few clans and political favorites who were their peers then in the province of São Paulo.[8]

The Gomes de Carvalho family, finally, illustrates the shifts in provincial and urban economies so often discussed earlier. Like so many of the families noted in the Casino Fluminense membership[9] during the period 1850–1900, this one derived from nineteenth-century Portuguese merchants who married into *fluminense* planter families. Likewise, the Gomes de Carvalhos completed this pattern in the end, as *rentiers* and urban professionals with investments in coffee, commerce, and urban real estate.[10]

The second observation is that the marriages here involve not only movement outward (to families of comparable planter status, attractive professional and Côrte positions and prestige, or financial and entrepreneurial connections), but a striking movement inward (toward those families within the same clan which seemed to promise security). Basic to this second movement was the desire to consolidate and maintain holdings. For the law declared that the children following the first-born must inherit, and families strove to keep such legacies within the closest circle of kin possible, rather than see property dissipated through a division in extra-familial marriages. Though uncles marrying nieces were uncommon, cousins marrying cousins were very common indeed.

One might suspect that this endogamy was due to a rather circumscribed rural social life, in which the only prospect one was likely to have was but another one of yet another uncle's ten children. However, as most marriages, even into this century's last third, were arranged by parents, this question of choice seems moot. Even were the parents uninvolved, though, one must take into account that elite planter families commonly passed part of the year in the townhouses in the capital or provincial towns, and that the young men often spent several years in the São Paulo or Recife law faculty. The chance to be paired with another well-born prospect was not, then, limited to those with one's own family names. Rather, what was at play was the desire to reaffirm the economic and emotional bonds within circles of extended kin who shared interests, past links, and the confidence born of conviviality.[11]

The simpler family tree (Figure 2) illustrates a third point – Rio's role as a marriage market for provincial families advancing their interests. Joaquim Nabuco's family (Nabuco de Araújo) was illustrious, but circumscribed by the economic decadence of its region, the Northeast. Joaquim's father, *Conselheiro* José Tomás Nabuco de Araújo, had already

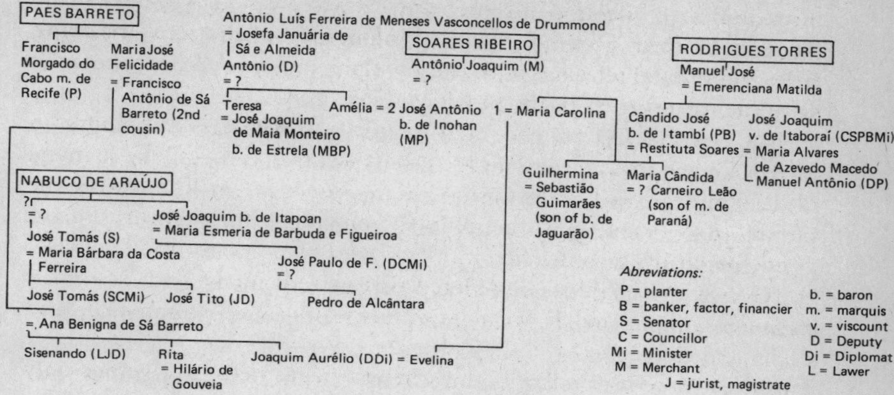

Figure. 2 Rio de Janeiro's role in elite matrimony

made the best marriage possible in such surroundings. The connections his bride brought were impressive; her family names, Sá Barreto, denote a clutch of families descended from a sixteenth-century noble who helped to plant Pernambuco, and whose line (Paes Barreto), was distinguished for nine generations by an hereditary title: Morgado do Cabo.[12]

Still, past glory gave but some stature in Brazil; only wealth or political power gave weight. Joaquim nearly won the wealth in his courtship of Eufrásia Teixeira Leite. This first attempt, however, failed. His luck with politics proved better. He made a brilliant reputation early in the Chamber of Deputies and in the campaign for Abolition. That accomplished, Nabuco returned to the marital lists, this time successfully winning another wealthy heiress, Evelina Torres Soares Ribeiro.[13] In both courtships, the Côrte was indispensable. What other setting served so well for a young man of "good family" to meet and marry someone who could secure his prestige by an alliance to families of perhaps briefer pedigrees, but certainly longer purses? Rio, the political, economic, and social center of the empire, was irreplaceable.

It may be objected that Nabuco's case is not conclusive, but, certainly, his wife's is. A glance at her family tree (grown in the Côrte or its shadow) makes Rio's role in strategic marriages clear. It is clear, first, by the number of titles claimed by the bride's ancestors and contemporary relatives. It is clear, second, by the principal roots of the tree. Evelina Torres Soares Ribeiro's paternal family (Soares Ribeiro) had grown unusually wealthy in Carioca commerce and rural and urban entrepreneurial activity and had intermarried with similar families (such as the Estrelas, the Vasconcellos de Drumonds, et al.). Through her maternal family (Rodrigues Torres), D. Evelina was connected to *fluminense* planters, coffee factors, bankers, and statesmen who intermarried into titled military and magisterial families of provincial origins (but Côrte residence).[14] The possibilities for alliances with families of wealth, power, and connnections increased enormously through the generations, if one's family remained suitable, and located in nineteenth-century Rio.

If these arboreal exercises help us to see the most important consideration in marriage – the improvement or conservation of familial status and opportunity – they obscure the personal one. One might marry as part of one's relatives' ambitions, but the union of families was, necessarily, a union of bodies as well. In 1847, Albino José Barbosa de Oliveira, aged 38 and a Carioca magistrate, was informed that a marriage had been arranged for him by the bride's godmother and his father. He agreed to the match (his father was "very satisfied" with the acquisition – the bride, a Sousa Queirós, was goddaughter to the Marquise de Valença), though he confesses, "I began to cry, because, in spite of desiring and needing to marry very much, and in spite of this marriage seeming very acceptable, I lamented the loss of my freedom and the burden that I was going to take up."[15] He only met his fiancée (who was clearly very frightened and embarrassed) shortly before their wedding; they never had a moment alone until they faced each other in the bridal chamber. A generation later, the magistrate could recall his bride's timidity and the embarrassingly long time it took for her to murmur formal acceptance of him at the wedding ceremony. Yet, for all these matters, common among the elite at mid-century, this marriage was happy, at least for the magistrate. He asked that a verse from Virgil celebrating his "conjugal felicity" mark the tomb under which he and his "Isabelinha" were to sleep together forever.[16]

Matters were different by the 1870s. Joaquim Nabuco's courtship of Eufrásia Teixeira Leite then was carried out on a European tour, far from intervention by his father or the lady's relatives; and, when the engagement foundered, it was because of the couple themselves.[17] Again, when Nabuco courted a second time, in the 1880s, he did so on his own behalf. When he asked D. Evelina's hand at the door of a Petrópolis church, where he encountered her, by chance, alone (something improbable in the earlier generation, as will be seen), their exchange was deeply personal. Nabuco spoke of his poor health and fear of dying before they had much time together. D. Evelina, twenty-three and long impressed with the brilliant deputy, was not discouraged; when Nabuco told her he might survive but five years more, she replied, "That's enough."[18]

Yet, despite the differences in the intimate, romantic aspect of marriage suggested in these two examples, the continuities are much more important. In both cases, the pressures toward a union beneficial in familial terms is apparent. Barbosa de Oliveira's match was obviously a familial alliance, arranged by the principles of each family and involving considerable wealth. The father's part in the match has been noted; his happiness regarding the wealth may be surmised. Certainly, in writing to his father, Barbosa de Oliveira carefully itemized his bride's dowry and jewelry with a sharp, appraising eye.[19] This was expected, but it was also hedged about with calculation and regard for family appearances. Barbosa de Oliveira confided to his daughter that he carefully avoided disputing with his wife's family over her rights to certain inheritances in order to demonstrate the aristocratic tone of his family. As he explained the ploy's outcome, ". . . at first they showed themselves unhappy with my marriage, and in the end, made it clear that they adored me, as your father, far from being a starveling, was a gentleman."[20]

Such concerns also affected Nabuco's generation. Though his father did not arrange Nabuco's first betrothal, he did encourage it and then displayed disappointment when his son backed away: "So, you did not marry? I . . . attribute the blame to you and your lack of worldliness. You abandon a beautiful, rich, intelligent girl because of words and apprehensions about the future."[21] This familial interest, keen on the Nabuco de Araújo side, weighed negatively on the Teixeira Leite side during the courtship. This clan, headed by the Baron de Vassouras, was bound to oppose an alliance with an Abolitionist, anathema to the slave-owning traditions long associated with such *fluminense* planter families. Nabuco was so preoccupied with the threat that he and his father acted secretly to prepare the documents for the wedding.[22]

The familial role in courtship was present in Nabuco's second attempt, as well. Though Nabuco proposed to D. Evelina alone, for example, his way was made straight by others. Introductions, mutual family acquaintances, and the active favor of one of the lady's godmothers – all these powerful sanctions came into play. It was hardly an elopement.

Nor, or, so one might suspect, did love alone play a part. Nabuco, the youngest of several children, had spent the inheritance left him by a landed godmother, and depended on his deputy's salary. Marriage may have seemed promising in this respect – his daughter notes that D. Evelina brought a substantial dowry. It is to the credit of the couple and their love that they survived the loss of this fortune in a financial reverse in 1890. They got by in the fine house D. Evelina inherited, while Nabuco struggled successfully to make ends meet as a lawyer and journalist.[23]

We might conclude noting that marriages were celebrated with very suggestive traditions. Among the other ritual usages, the display of wedding presents and the presence of several *padrinhos* (ritual sponsors of the bride and groom)[24] might be emphasized. The display of wedding presents, common in Western tradition, is an obvious demonstration of the status of the couple's relations. In Rio, the presents also suggest the peculiar nature of the Carioca elite. Two sorts of presents were common – the immediate families of the couple gave bondsmen, and everyone gave fashionable European luxuries. Slaves to serve as personal servants in the new house, and china, silver, crystal and the rest to adorn it.[25] Such presents were both practical and symbolic. They were, on the one hand, necessary to the domestic life proper to members of the elite. On the other, they bespoke the Europhile ruling class of a society built on plantation slavery.

The second usage, involving *padrinhos*, speaks to the system of familial alliance just discussed. *Padrinho* and *madrinha*, the words used for the couple's sponsors, recall parents in their etymology because, as in the institution of godfather- and godmotherhood (in which the same words serve), the persons selected were expected to play a parental role, if only to the extent of the protection and promotion of the couple's interests.[26] To be chosen *padrinho* was thus not only an honor, it also implied, however attenuated over the century, a responsibility and a familial bond. Further, like the display of presents, *padrinhos* were also a demonstration of status: prominent *padrinhos*, at times along with the china and the silver, were generally listed in the newspaper announcements.

3. Socialization in the use of manners

The wedding was only the couple's initial projection of their particular status into Society. How they comported themselves publicly, how they received and entertained, how they figured in the intimate circles of family and relations, these were at once an issue, as they sought to maintain and improve upon a social status explicit in their wedding. Now, usages demonstrating proper socialization came into play.

These usages, once again, often had aristocratic Franco-English origins. It had not always been so. Elite domestic culture, in the sense of social manners, became greatly complicated during the century. Travelers' accounts and local memoirs suggest that extrafamilial social functions were rare for most of those years, and, when they did occur, involved some few great figures and their relations, as in the Second Reign salon, for instance.[27]

For the most part, while these few great figures might have salons and birthday balls and the like, they and everyone else in the elite kept mostly to the circles established by blood, marriage, and long friendship. Further, except on the rare occasions noted, the display of European food and drink was rather less prominent, up through the century's second third. However, the distinctive European style of dress, music, and ballroom dancing, all signifying elite status, would still obtain in family get-togethers. What happened would seem to be something belonging to the rural, planter tradition: the relaxed, regular reunion of kith and kin at the home of the most powerful kinsman, perhaps once a week, for talk, food, a bit of piano and operatic repertoire, and perhaps dancing among the cousins. Manners pivoted on gracious talk and showing respect "where it was due" and, as one informant put it, "knowing how to enter a room and how to leave it" – maintaining a sense of decorum.[28]

These narrower, family gatherings did not disappear at the end of the century, rather they were crowded by a host of domestic rituals of a much more elaborate and often extrafamiliar nature. These derive from broader changes which have been noted earlier and from European models, a two-winged backdrop for Society's new stage.

One may recall that the Côrte of the 1850s was a small port capital dependent upon provincial coffee and imperial politics, while the Rio of 1900 was a citified nexus, where professional, bureaucratic, and entrepreneurial elite careers were the rule. The world of the elite was more urban and urbane. More frequently city-born and bred, more exposed to foreign influence, gaining new wealth, or spending old coffee fortunes, the *alto mundo* was increasingly drawn to, and capable of, emulating European aristocratic forms. These shifts figured in the backdrop of Casino Fluminense members from 1850 to the turn of the century and explain the contrasts between mid-century Casino and the *belle époque*'s Club dos Diários. These shifts also informed our discussion of the careers of the *belle-époque* high society representatives and their salons.[29] Here, the point to be made is that urban setting and access, combined with increased travel to Europe, and the consequent increase in elite members with acquired European tastes, had a marked impact on elite domestic life in Rio by the era of our focus – 1898–1914. It increasingly became the signature of elite status to display a distinct, recognizable social persona of clear Franco-English derivation, and to do so in certain rituals that became part of the formerly more private, familial life traditionally the rule in the elite home.

A striking proof of this is the newspaper columns catering to anxiety about fashionable appearance and style, an anxiety apparently widespread in the middle and upper reaches of Carioca society by at least the 1890s.[30] Many established elite families were probably familiar enough with Paris and London not to need instruction in European social style.[31] However, other old elite families (less well-traveled, perhaps), as well as the new rich (and the increasingly comfortable and Europhile middle sectors) were not. The newspapers of the *belle époque* sensed and cultivated this anxiety about social propriety

The most important exemplar of this response was the celebrated column "Binoculo" ("Opera Glasses"), which appeared daily from 1907 to 1914 in the *Gazeta de Noticias*. In the style of an *homme du monde*, concerned with the continual *faux pas* of erring brethren, Figueiredo Pimentel pronounced on everything from the urban reform of Rio to the proper way to wear one's monocle: "Fashion," he once wrote, "is a work of art, and there is no work of art worthy of the name that does not display the delightful personal tic of the mind that created it."[32] Certainly, Figueiredo Pimentel's own distinctive touch helped make "Binoculo" the arbiter of all that fashion meant in the *belle époque*. A contemporary recalls:

> The "Binoculo" commanded and was rigorously obeyed. Ladies and gentlemen obeyed the *Gazeta*'s column on whatever it directed regarding dress and public and private behavior, as well . . . The tables for banquets followed the regulations dictated by the columnist, [and even] family parties were regulated according to his advice.[33]

One of the columnist's basic ideas is a concept that is both contradictory and essential to the anxiety about proper behavior in Society. This influential critic of manners assured his readers that true elegance was not to be gotten by wealth, but by breeding:

> A person can keep up with fashion, dressing as the latest fashion plates do and not be elegant. Why? Because elegance is a special gift, a particularity, a gift as difficult, praiseworthy, and precious as grace and intelligence . . .
> What is being discussed here is the "gentleman," who knows how to wear his clothes and handle himself with dignity and beauty, the refined man who does

not stand out and dresses himself without fuss within the fashion and elegance of his epoch.[34]

Another time, he noted, "the essential thing is not wealth, which brings luxury and pleasure. The most difficult thing is, precisely, knowing how to use the advantages of wealth . . ."[35]

The contradiction is wicked – if elegance was characteristic of a person, like grace or intelligence, and defined him as a "gentleman," then Figueiredo Pimentel's elite readers were surely ill-bred boors. Otherwise, Figueiredo Pimentel would not have had to prescribe dress and manners in all the complicated detail he regularly served up. Indeed, this contradictory situation underscores the meaning of the period's new anxiety. The Carioca *alto mundo* read "Binoculo" because it made the equation between the identification "gentleman" (member of the elite) and elegance (the successful display of elite Franco-English Society manners and style) and wished to employ the second to signify their rightful claim to the first. They doubtless understood Figueiredo Pimentel's point not as the threat it logically suggests (if one needs to learn elegance in a column, one is not really elegant nor, therefore, a gentleman), but as the guarantee of social success the journalist's instructions implied (the secrets of elegance, the signs of the gentleman, are made available to the discerning reader in this column).

Another such column was concerned with manner and style at home. This exemplar was published in *Rua do Ouvidor* (1898–1913), a weekly devoted to the sort of readers anxious to take part in the new urbanity of the *belle époque*.[36] These readers were probably women of the new middle and upper reaches of urban society, ladies paying regularly for vicarious participation in the world enjoyed by the Carioca elite.[37] Besides the profiles of celebrities and the reviews of the opera boxes, salons, and racing clubs, there was also the column of our interest: "Indicações Úteis" ("Useful Suggestions"), apparently changed shortly after appearing to "Normas de Polidez" ("Rules for Good Manners"). Both titles make the point; it was to be a primer (seemingly written by a woman who was an established member of the elite[38]) on how to socialize oneself and one's household into the desired facsimile of the style and manners of one's "betters" in Rio and Europe.

As such, "Normas de Polidez" gives us a detailed look inside the running of an elite home (at least, in ideal form), as opposed to the glimpse afforded us elsewhere. Elite informants can tell us of learning their manners from example, family preference for British or French table manners or protocol, the ridicule earned by one's gaffes, the importance of calling cards, and paying afternoon visits in proper form.

Memoirs note the restrictions on language, the formality of public address and expression, the gestures of respect due women, formal teas and fixed days for one's receptions (the English "at home"), the importance of proper attire for receiving visitors of a certain "category," or for coming to the dinner table.[39] Correspondence is full of elegantly inscribed calling cards,[40] and novels, articles, and short stories betray the obsession with European aristocratic ways.[41]

It is, however, in columns like "Normas de Polidez" that the minutiae of elite domestic institutions are most painfully clear. In one example, various formal visits are defined and categorized, and the "at home" described, along with the proper attire and behavior for all the actors on the domestic stage.[42] A subsequent example helps with advice to the guests for managing everything from hat and cane to one's neighbor's hand (with proper regard for rank and degree of acquaintance).[43] Another example concerns organizing a proper menu and discusses the visits and invitations and dress and manners attendant upon the proper execution of that most feared and prized maneuver, the *jantar de etiqueta* (formal dinner party).[44] Yet another defines the behavior of "*o verdadeiro* gentleman."[45] Yet another makes numerous criticisms, observations, and recommendations on the art of conversation.[46]

It would be foolish to conclude, however, that such columns demonstrate an extraordinary Brazilian preoccupation. They demonstrate, rather, Brazilian emulation of the extraordinary European preoccupation with such matters. Acute contemporary observers of such things, such as Proust, as well as recent scholarly studies of the subject, show how deeply concerned the French and the English were with such things as introductions, clothes, and small pieces of hard paper imprinted with one's name. The regular, stylized promenades, the worries about visits and the "right" introductions, the place to set one's hat upon sitting down, the number and sort of cards one "left on" someone and the correct manner of response, the protocol, placing, and precision of a dinner-party, all were common to the elites of all three countries.[47]

One study argues that the rigidity and complexity of English manners in Society were an attempt to confront and manage the challenge posed to the ruling class by the increasing number of new aspirants to place and power in Victorian England.[48] Another shows the role society and manners played in the maintenance of a network of kith and kin crucial to the security and advancement of one's immediate family.[49] In thinking of the expansion of wealth and social mobility in

Rio and the erratic quality of the economy or the patronage in the State bureaucracy, one logically assumes these factors obtained in Brazil, too.[50]

However, in raising this issue in comparative terms, it is crucial to point out that while aristocratic style was integral to domestic institutions in all these ruling classes, distinctions must be made. English and French elite members learned an amalgam of usages derived from their cultures,[51] usages that identified them as aristocratic within their societies and the European world. Brazilians, in order to accomplish the same ends, adopted the same usages.[52] In Brazil, however, their meanings were different. For such usages not only distinguished members of the elite from other Brazilians in terms of class-based culture, but in terms of national culture. They adopted practices in their homes that identified them not just with aristocratic status, but, *ipso facto*, with Europe. As with their education, as with their clubs and opera, as with their salons, so with aspects of their domestic culture – the *alto mundo* was characterized by metropolitan identification within a neo-colonial context.

4. Socialization in the use of power

The house was not only the setting for elite socialization through cultural practices, but for socialization in the use of power, as well. Here, the focus is on patronage within the household (or that extension of domestic "space," private correspondence).

Such patronage was traditionally part of extended families' relationships in Brazil, something central to such families' usefulness.[53] Patronage in our period came in many guises. Take the sort portrayed in Machado de Assis' work, *A mão e a luva*, in which an aged baroness raises her goddaughter to take the place of her own dead child. Here, patronage corrects an accident of nature. It also restores proper order to hierarchical relationships; the girl, as the baroness states, is beautiful and talented, and, thus, "naturally" ought to be a member of an elite family.[54]

In another case, the problem of skewed birth and status is also resolved by patronage. Here the descendant of a noted surgeon and his black servant cannot, of course, be legitimized, but she can be provided an education and affection within her master's family. Her husband, dedicated partisan of a political chieftain, also enjoys patronage, receiving positions in the hand of his patron. The son of the two will, as it were, share the profits of such capital by a secure childhood and the exceptional luxury of secondary education. All of this was to help clients to a status commensurate with their familial relations and in just reward for exceptional talents and partisan loyalty.[55]

In a third case, a petty bureaucrat and man of letters tries to impose on his literary and social relations with a pivotal politician. He does this through visits and family invitations. He hopes to advance his career and, thus, make the salary necessary to maintain the level of consumption expected after a "good" marriage.[56]

In each case here, patronage is set in the milieu of domestic and familial relations. In each, patronage is invoked to maintain a certain hierarchical order by raising dependants of the elite to a socio-economic status to which they claim some right within the order in question.

Patronage, however, is also commonly observed between putative equals (in the exchange of favors) or as a regular relationship between superiors and inferiors, in both of which no change in relative status is expected. An example of the first would be a case noted earlier. There, a power-broker politician is asked, by a powerful lawyer's intermediary (who, himself, looks on the lawyer, a relative, as *his* patron) to arrange an important corporate client for the lawyer. The broker does so, thus strengthening the bonds between the two on the valid expectation that the bonds are convertible into political currency.[57]

Examples of the second often involve use of a patron as intermediary by an inferior (a place-seeker, say) who will come to a second powerful person, patron's letter of recommendation in hand, to ask for his favor. The elite's correspondence is flush with such letters.[58] Nor was such use of a patron limited to men without family names of importance. Men whose fortunes had dissolved in the economy's vagaries and the sons of fathers prematurely dead asked family friends to use their influence, their "palavrinha" ("little word") to maintain them in comfortable situations. It was, after all, partially to guarantee this sort of thing that kith and kin had been knit together in the first place.[59]

This socialization in the use of protection among interwoven families and friends should not be seen as contradicting the Europhile cultural socialization analyzed earlier. It was not a case of an urbane, modern way of dealing with one another grating against atavistic relations proper only to rural patriarchy. Rather, these two types of intercourse should be seen as complementary. One student of European *belle-époque* Society suggests the point I wish to make for Brazil:

> The circle of acquaintance had to be wide, as the time-honoured expression was, and this was not so much an expression of snobbery as an insurance against "reversals of fortune," a tribal interaid system. "Decent people" knew that

somebody's uncle, a councillor of state, someone else's nephew, the heir to an important legal practice, could one day help a husband or marry a daughter, and they paid visits and gave dinners to consolidate links with these connections and create a milieu.[60]

In both Europe and Brazil, it was not a question of style versus substance, but of style being integrally a part of substance. Relations within the *alto mundo*, in which patronage was a central element, were ordered and reinforced by etiquette crafted abroad for that purpose. Thus, socialization in cultural usages not only won the status conferred by the acquisition of European aristocratic attributes, but enhanced the use of power to maintain and promote traditional social relations within enduring socio-economic realities.

5. Women

The role of women in elite society has been glimpsed repeatedly in our analysis. This attests to its ubiquity in the *alto mundo*, but it also suggests women's subordination, for they only appear there in a supporting role. The point is sharpened by their introduction here, because here the focus is on the domestic world, almost always the defining frontier of elite women's existence.[61]

Yet, as previous mention of women will have indicated, their subordination to fathers and husbands did not mean unimportance. Within a traditionally patriarchal world the position of women was both dependent and pivotal.

This is obvious in discussing the household. The family alliances analyzed earlier, as well as the children who sealed the bonds and maintained elite lineage, these were both "women's work," however subject to men's ambition and desire. Also, as memoirs attest, widows in the hinterland often managed *fazendas* in their husbands' stead. Further, as travellers or relatives recall, nineteenth-century elite women were charged with the household's running; no petty affair, with the large houses, the number of slaves or servants, the organization of purchasing, preparing, and serving food, and the attention to menfolk, children, and guests.[62]

Beyond domestic administration, women were principals in the play of Society. For it was the woman's display of clothing and jewelry, her comportment in salon and at a tea, and the grace brought to her weekly receptions that helped signal her family's position. Every Society function necessarily involved a woman, and, thus, her preparation for her part in elite culture and society is central to our discussion.

Elite women's education and their scope of activity enlarged in direct relationship to the evolution of Society in the nineteenth century, which, again, points to their essential subordination. For, clearly, Society, however often feminine in expression, was masculine in purpose. It served to maintain and promote elite families' interests, as defined by the fathers and husbands who oversaw them.[63]

As observed earlier, Society, fairly primitive in the earlier part of the century, gained its greater complexity and splendor as a function of the increase in wealth, European contacts, and urbanization that marked the Carioca elite as the years wore on. This functional link is made painfully clear if one makes regional comparisons within Brazil. In Bahia, for example, a province enjoying ephemeral profits from sugar and other crops during the nineteenth century, there was a notable elite social life the capital of poorer São Paulo province could not possibly match. By the end of the century, however, coffee had transformed São Paulo from a wretched provincial backwater to the increasingly sophisticated regional seat of wealthy planters.[64]

In Rio, of course, political hegemony had ensured preeminence to Carioca Society long before *fluminense* coffee reinforced it with new wealth. Despite this inherent superiority, however, Rio's early nineteenth-century Society, with rare exceptions like the salons of the Marquis de Abrantes[65], was unimpressive, as noted in discussing manners. Gatherings outside the family were few, the sexes generally separated, and refinement confined to frockcoats and French gowns, imported china, European *objets d'art*, bits and snatches of French, and the inevitable piano playing and ballroom dancing. As late as 1882, an Englishman could describe an exalted Society function, a *partida* at the imperial heiress' residence, in this way:

> During the music, ladies only were admitted into the room with the piano, and the men hung about the hall and looked at the *fruit défendu* sitting round the walls of the carpetless room, and showing a great variety of shoes, feet, and ankles.
>
> Ices and light refreshments were handed round when the concert was over, and then a nigger [*sic*] band in a corridor behind struck up a quadrille, the social barrier was broken down, and the black coats invaded the sanctuary. Quadrilles were danced on an Aubusson carpet in the opposite room, as well as on the excellent floor of the concert room, and the band, though without a conductor, did not play badly . . .
>
> . . . There was a small *buffet* with sandwiches and iced orangeade, *à la* Berkeley Street, in the corridor, and I had a glass of very good port wine at 12 o'clock, when the emperor and empress left, and all the guests followed in a body.[66]

Indeed, it is noteworthy that Abrantes' salon was distinguished for "making a bridge" between the ways of aristocratic Europe and the rougher customs of Brazil (Abrantes usually invited European diplomats and artists)[67] – well beyond mid-century, elite society in Brazil was noted for its parochial, family quality. Wealth, travel, and luxury trade had not yet had enough strength and time to wear through the stifling traditions shrouding the extended familial conviviality that passed as Society for so long.[68]

Elite women's lives through into the second half of the century were correspondingly narrow. They were generally traded to their suitors (usually established men in their thirties or older) as girls in their mid-teens. They had already been taught what the Society just described required of them. They could manage a bit of French, read Portuguese, play piano, dance, and sing operatic arias or other agreeable airs.[69]

Women learned most of these things at home from foreign tutors. On the few occasions when girls did leave the house, male relatives escorted them lest their reputations suffer. Church and domestic get-togethers were the only places where the discreet signals and glances of anything like a flirtation might take place. These would be perhaps heated, but surely muffled exchanges, and of little actual moment in the fate of either party. Even after the girls were safely married, this strictly secluded life continued, immured within the family circle, administering households in loose cotton gowns fit for the tropical heat, sitting on floormats or swinging in hammocks, surrounded by favored slave women and the variously-hued children of the household. Their husbands, to ensure their lineage's continuity, took their girl brides to bed to make them pregnant, expecting the usual annual childbearing, a duty done for ten years or more. Aside from this familial effort, the *mulata* domestic slaves could be used to satisfy the husband's desire. At the end of ten years or so and as many children, the little girl bride was nearly thirty, fat, heavily jeweled, terribly jealous of her women slaves, and seeing to her daughters' preparation for the same sort of "conjugal felicity." That is, if she had survived her childbirths. Many husbands had to make another young cousin a second wife if their first had died in her teens, or succumbed, exhausted in her twenties, providing their husbands with yet another child.[70]

Given such a life, the travelers' generally poor impression of elite women in Society seems understandable. One Englishman complained in 1882:

the Brazilians are a very dull people, the women more so than the men . . . And . . . they have no manners, nor does the language lend itself to pretty, scarcely to polite speeches in social life. Indeed, when men and women meet in what you may call society, they never seem to speak at all. But all the women play the pianoforte. It seems to be the only thing they can do; and they play airs from the *Trovatore* and *Traviata*, the march from *Norma* and the *Carnaval de Venise* with variations; some correctly, some incorrectly, but few with expression. They all seem to dance well, but they waltz very fast, which in so hot a country is doubly a mistake.[71]

That this dullness derived from the closed environment described seems obvious. Women found themselves so constrained within the walls of home and convention that a semaphore using various flowers was developed, by which girls could communicate with those admirers who dared appear on the street or in church to eye them soulfully.[72] Indeed, the term Society seems premature for a social life limited to the extended family, church, and the rare court functions and balls.[73] It is indicative that the first ball which was "public" (i.e., subscription, rather than private) took place only in 1844.[74]

There was, then simply no reason to give women education and experience beyond the little required for the family and primitive society functions just described. Although one must question the motives of such travelers' "exposés" and the range of their experience, their remarks on women's ignorance, lack of conversational skill, and timidity cannot be simply dismissed – they make too much sense. Except in the case of the few most wealthy and well-traveled contemporary women, one can hardly expect more in the face of the brutally narrowed existence this relatively impoverished, isolated society and its conventions allotted women. What this meant in terms of personal fulfillment may well be imagined. It may be apposite to note that the three pleasures thought characteristic among them were gluttony, gazing out of the window and gossiping about passers-by, and indulging in *cafuné* (a traditional recreation consisting of placing one's head in the lap of a favored slavegirl for a scalp massage and, as some suggest, for delousing).[75]

Travelers' accounts and memoirs suggest that such matters changed slowly. The changes, when they came, were dramatically symbolized by the advent of the *bond* (streetcar). This vehicle was established in 1868, and, for the first time, made it convenient for elite women to venture from the home and the distant residential districts to visit the *cidade velha* shopping area for imported luxury goods.[76]

The *bond* and the new world it opened to women point to the means and results of the new age of the latter nineteenth century. With increased wealth born of expanding exports and urban services and with the impact of new European technology, novel experiences, refinements, and complexities were to be had which forced a metamorphosis on women and what was expected of them. In conformity with their alloted role as the ornament and projection of their families' social position, women began to acquire a greater refinement and greater experience in the outside world hitherto impractical and unnecessary. Not only the *bond* to the downtown shopping area, with its increasingly affordable imported luxuries, but the steamship to Europe itself now brushed aside the domestic veil and made up the face of Society with new arts and sophistication.

Certain expectations endured – French, dancing, dress, piano, singing, and recitation remained characteristic of the well-bred girl. Now, however, other languages, a greater familiarity with the arts (particularly French novels, the opera, and the theater), and a greater confidence in the company of men, even foreign men, began to be noticed. Women learned these things because they were expected and because they were exposed, in Europe and the Côrte, to an increasing amount of European culture (to the point where, in those increasingly longer stays in Paris, some elite women were comfortably married into French aristocratic families). The ideal result was described by one fashionable writer this way:

> The Carioca is prepared for all the demands of contemporary life. She plays tennis and bridge, discusses politics and art, drives a car and rides a horse with the same ease with which she does the honors of a salon. If she knows that the dresses of Paquin are light and vaporous and that Redfern is more hieratic than Doucet, she also appreciates aesthetic motifs, worldly *causeries*, and literary periodicals . . . In sum, she possesses the fascinating gift of knowing how to dress, to walk, to smile, to glance, and to talk.[77]

By 1910, it was possible for women to walk alone while shopping downtown (so long as they neither looked at, nor talked to, men, acquaintances or no) and for João do Rio and Afrânio Peixoto to write fiction in which elite women having affairs is something delightfully and fashionably scandalous.[78]

It is best, however, not to mistake the greater worldliness of the *belle-époque* woman for liberation. A more active role and broader experience do not constitute freedom – women were more experienced, refined, and educated as the fitting response to, and medium of, their menfolk's changed needs and ambitions in the new era.

The attitudes of Júlia Lopes de Almeida (b. 1862) are indicative of the changes and the continuities at issue. Daughter of a *titular* and someone of literary renown (a successful novelist in her own right, she was the wife of a noted poet, too), she represents the era's possibilities for the elite woman perhaps more faithfully than Laurinda Santos Lobo and Bebê Lima e Castro do.[79] D. Júlia wrote a book of advice to young wives (the oft-edited *Livro das noivas* – "Book of Brides")[80] which made explicit her concept of women's modern position.

The necessity of subordination to the husband's desires and weaknesses is repeated throughout *Livro das noivas*: "man," opined D. Júlia, "is selfish and authoritarian and . . . to make him happy, as falls to your lot, you have to renounce the sweet leisure in which your thought wavers and have it always vigilant and active."[81] D. Júlia also states, repeatedly, the centrality of motherhood and being the well-ordered household administrator:

> With your hands dirty with charcoal, in the kitchen, lighting the fire to make the lunch for your husband, sewing clothes, nursing children [*], sweeping the house or interpreting Chopin, painting a watercolor or arranging a *bouquet*, the woman always has the same poetry: that of working to be pleasant, useful, and good, to satisfy a moral or intellectual necessity of her husband or of her family, revealing herself loving and worthy of the sweet and heavy charge for which society destined her.[82]

As for education, D. Júlia urges a profession as useful insurance should father or husband die, and complains that women's education is too superficial. She feels strongly, however, that books of the naughty sort (by which she probably intended the lighter, popular French novels) should be shunned and sees the improvement of women's education primarily as a benefit for the better instruction of their children.[83] D. Júlia also condemns taking Society's approbation more seriously than the husband's, and taking jewels, fashion, and flirtation (the era's new possibilities, after all) more seriously than domestic simplicity and accomplishments.[84] Clearly, there is much here representing an early reaction *against* many of the new opportunities of the *belle époque*.

Elite women, raised in the family, silent and discreet in public, mindful of the formalities implying respect and subordination, and groomed for Society and marriage at seventeen or earlier (and cut out of Society should that marriage fail), enjoyed a fuller life in the era, but not a free one.[85] The *belle époque* had not cut away the old prejudices so much as modified them in a necessarily more Europeanized Carioca world.

Indeed, one might recall how faithful elite women were to the models evolved in France and England. Arranged and early marriages, a private but superficial education, a jealously guarded childhood and adolescence, and a strict regimen of prejudice surrounding virginity, Society, and marriage, all directed toward preserving family status and lineage, were as much a part of the elite French and English girls' lot as the Brazilians' up through the *belle époque* and the Edwardian age.[86] Indeed, the anecdotes suggest that the rigidity of prejudice regarding comportment was, if anything, greater for the European. One Brazilian diplomat's daughter remembers attending class in London and being told that her manners were neither good nor bad; rather, she really did not possess any of which to speak.[87]

One concludes that Brazil's elite women, by the *belle époque*, were not suffering the effects of "underdevelopment," so much as those of a very successful development indeed, for the transplantation of European forms, in this area at least, would seem to have taken place without much of a hitch. Carioca women had emerged from their particular colonial tradition into a comparatively richer set of restrictions, defined by more universal rituals and prejudices.

6. Children

Elite children hardly play about the edges of our exploration so far, nor do they figure much in other period studies.[88] Still, there is information in the primary sources, and one can hazard initial observations and analysis.

Let us begin at the beginning. Those adolescent girls forced into labor so often were pitted against a high infant mortality rate. It seems clear that death visited plantation big-house and Carioca *palacete* constantly. Death is a fixture in every memory of childhood, and, despite others' arguments,[89] my sources suggest that this repeated loss was neither easily accepted nor borne by parents, no matter how many other children survived. One magistrate in Rio recalled that, during the first ravages of yellow fever in the city (1850), he prayed God,

> in the event a sacrifice were demanded, to prefer taking from me my children, because they were innocent, and I could have others. Ah! I did not know what I was saying. My son died on the sixth of April . . . My Mariquinhas died on the ninth . . . And for many years I did not recall this misfortune without tears.[90]

Names, at times, repeat in the brood of the living and the dead, perhaps as an attempted compensation for losses deeply felt, and sickbed, nursing, and tears were the common portion of young mothers.[91]

This warmth of attachment was balanced by certain distancing aspects of elite child-rearing. Most important was the interposition of black women and their children between elite children and their parents, black people who served as the most proximate, affective element of the young white child's world.

Well into the *belle époque*, a black wetnurse (*ama de leite*) was the rule for elite children. Often the same servant played surrogate mother for years, becoming an honored matriarch to the next generation. Her so-called *cria* (litter), or those of other favored domestics, were often captive playthings for the young whites – *negrinhos* (little Negroes) and *negrinhas* (little Negresses) for the *sinhazinha* (little mistress) or *nhô moço* (young master), who thus began to learn what it was to be rich and white in a country where most were terribly poor and of obvious African descent. These were lessons taught in the innocence of childhood games and in the warmth of their first, most intimate relationships. To these lessons were added, one must assume, those taught by black mother, black playmates, and the black companion who accompanied one to *colégio*, the lessons about the hidden order of the world, the stories and beliefs of an Afro-Brazilian culture only one or two generations distant from African roots.[92]

On this upbringing in affection, power, and folk-belief was superimposed the education taught by one's mother, a religious, or a foreign (generally French) governess. These introduced the child to European high culture and socialization. It was not unusual to give the child marvelous imported French and English toys, nor to teach the child to read in French, at times without instructing him to read in Portuguese. Children's literature included the *Bibliothèque Rose*, or the series written by the Countess de Ségur. This first formal education was rigorous and deeply personal, with a daily regimen and a governess who often stayed on for years, a second surrogate mother after the *ama de leite*. It was a phase of education strengthened later by the *colégio* education described earlier and by foreign texts read even before adolescence began.[93]

This second phase of education, like the first, comprised not only an intellectual vision of the world, but a social one. Just as one had learned about the relationships between master and servant, white and black, now one began to learn about "civilized" behavior, the comportment and appearance becoming to ruling-class children. Here is the place of that increased European complexity of social ritual discussed above. From the sailor suits and imported frocks of childhood, little Cariocas soon graduated to the three-piece woolen suits and longer dresses as adolescence, often in a regime of corporal punishment and authoritarian discipline, unfolded. The boys learned circumspection and public sophistication, the girls, silence, French courtesies, the usual parlor refinements, and the like.[94]

Respect between children and older relations was learned with language and gesture. It was remarkable if fathers did *not* require the formal address of *senhor* (sir), rather than *você*, and children bowed to make the old obeisance of the *beija-mão* (hand-kiss), with its customary plea for *a benção* (the parental blessing), upon coming home or chance meeting. Indeed, a number of honorific variations distinguished the degree of respect one wanted to demonstrate, and the child, like all subordinates, had to learn which to use for whom, from *senhor* or *doutor* to *vossa senhoria, vossa excelência*, and *vosmecê* (sir or doctor – in the sense of someone with a secondary school degree – to your lordship, your excellency, and your mercy).[95]

Memory of father often tended to an image of stern, demanding demeanor, removed by ritualized distancing. One's father did not discuss, he talked or taught. He never appeared outside of his room or his study without coat and tie. His business, his world, were kept outside the home; he did not share his preoccupations there, except, perhaps, with his wife. His time with the family tended to be ritualized, too: certain hours to take daughters shopping in the *cidade velha*, to give lessons to sons, to ride over the plantation, to relax at dinner, to read the newspaper aloud, or to listen to the girls perform at piano, recite, and the like. Moreover, this implied a relationship really established for the first time in early adolescence. One's mother tended to be the lesser god; after all, she commonly took part in one's early education, and she organized the domestic world to which children belonged. Even one's mother, however, might be restrained in her shows of affection, and expect proper respect. One looked to one's black mother for easy warmth, it would seem.[96]

Yet, one must also note that even more distant, dominant *papai* was deeply attached to his children. In stark contrast to the cold dearth of contact that often characterized relations between elite parents and children in England and France,[97] one discovers a surge of affection between Brazilian generations. Foreigners, especially Englishmen, were shocked that Brazilian parents persisted in keeping their children close and would even have servants take them along to society functions. In 1887, a Briton noted that,

> The Brazilian father and mother live with their children always about them, and spoil them to the utmost. A Brazilian child is worse than a mosquito on the

warpath. Brazilian houses have no nurseries, and, as it is considered cruel to put the poor little dear to bed during the day, one has the pleasure of their company without any intermission.[98]

In 1914, from the height of his column, Figueiredo Pimentel inveighed against the enduring custom, uncorrected in even the smarter circles:

Among the various, the multiple habits of little elegance existing among us, perhaps one of the most irritating and easy to correct might be the custom of bringing children to the theaters and "*jeunes filles*" to the important balls. . . . In Europe, the young ladies are only introduced to society after a certain age, after having finished their studies. . . . Here, no. We are accustomed to see . . . girls and boys . . . everywhere, in every corner: in the cinemas, in the cafés, in the theaters, in the salons making "*blagues*" and – above all, the boys – speaking badly about others.[99]

Affection crops up in letters, too. One imperial magistrate customarily closed his correspondence to his daughters with "your loving father," "your father and true friend," and other endearments.[100] One finds fathers taking keen interest in their children's progress, happiness, and birthdays; one finds them welcoming their children into their studies and taking pains with their preoccupations and desires. Here, for instance, is the son of a *fluminense* political chieftain, sending father on a shopping errand:

Papa,

You forgot, sir, to take with you the little note that I wrote about how I want my clothes, and so I am sending it written in this letter.

1 coat of white flannel cloth, long enough for a 13-year-old; three little collars in the Santos Dumont style and a white tie, to be bought in Casa Colombo, and, if it isn't there, from the Torre Eiffel.

From your son and friend
Paulino Jr.

N.B. If the cloth can't be found in flannel, bring the same cut in drill.[101]

In another case, one finds a boy raised by a black nurse and a white godmother in the provinces, sent to his father's Carioca mansion at eight, and then to boarding school. Yet one still finds that son, as a man some twenty years after his father's death, writing of the very strong personal relationship he and his father had had, something corroborated in their letters, marked by a profound filial respect on his part and close paternal concern and pride on that of his father.[102]

Perhaps anxieties born of the ubiquity of infant mortality and the perennial economic uncertainty of the country combined to offset the impact of surrogates, distance, and traditional respect. One was too much aware of what one could lose to take children and the family for granted. More certainly, domestic relationships were rigidly defined in role but apparently quite fluid in affective bonds. The ritualized distancing of parents from their children, just as with the Europeanization of the whites, in a household labored in by Afro-Brazilians, distinguished members of the elite home, but did not separate them.

Indeed, the child grew up within a household including, perhaps, three generations, visiting kith and kin, established dependants, and the half-score or score of family servants.[103] His domestic world was thus a crowded, close one, hierarchically organized, with particular categories of people who followed particular patterns of behavior and were clearly differentiated by combinations of color, culture, and power. In this way, the home prepared the child for the place he was to have in the larger world.

Moreover, this domestic world was a whole, interdependent, affective place. Roles were realized within an emotionally charged web in which affection and informal relationships constantly smoothed sharp edges and broadened narrow roles: the family was an organism, after all, not a diagram. In many Carioca families, the slaves one ordered about were also, so to speak, only darker members of one's, and one's parents' family. The dependant one patronized gave one influence and a sense of superiority, but also represented an obligation. A child was not only an object of discipline, but one's hope; and one's father was not just the respected, perhaps feared, patriarch, but one's loving guarantor. One was taught French and refined manners that signified separate, superior status, yet one knew of an Afro-Brazilian lore that was part of a larger, matted reality. One voyaged to Europe, but one lived with one's intimates and inferiors in a common, comfortable Brazil.

7. Domestic architecture and décor

The domestic matters with which this chapter is concerned had their setting, of course, in the home. For most of the nineteenth century, elite members made this home in three places – a plantation house, a city residence, and a summer place in Petrópolis. Let us turn to the latter two, the proper concerns of our urban preoccupations.

For the longest time, nineteenth-century domestic architecture was hardly inviting. Traditional townhouses (*sobrados de moradia*) in the *cidade velha*, although big, were an uncomfortable legacy from colonial architecture. Façades flush with the street, they rose two stories: the first, for carriage or litters, the great reception and dining rooms, storage space, slaves' quarters, and (probably separated, in a small structure) a kitchen; the second, divided between larger rooms and a corridor leading off to a series of dank, stifling *alcovas* on either side, into which one stuffed oneself at night. The whole house probably framed three or four sides of a patio, if it were large. If not, it might be L-shaped, with the longer wing flanking an open space that served the patio's function and led off to a larger ground behind.

In mid-Second Reign, one Carioca physician gave his diagnosis:

> On examining the houses, one would imagine they were buildings for the Eskimo . . .; small, narrow windows, low, narrow doors, no facilities for ventilation, hot, close rooms, damp, dark, suffocating bedrooms, hallways through which one could barely pass, and always that open drain in the kitchen, that filth close to where the daily meals are prepared, beside a pestilential, evil-smelling place where the piled-up refuse produced all sorts of miasmas.[104]

The consensus about these thick-walled piles is that they were poorly constructed, unhygienic, and lamentably enduring: their red-tiled roofs and dirty white walls marked the cityscape in three centuries of paintings. The most pleasant feature was the garden, laid out behind or in the patio with fountain and songbirds, and colored with beautiful and useful flowers and plants plucked from the far-flung shores of the old Portuguese empire.[105]

Sobrados, long after they were abandoned for bigger mansions (*solares, palacetes*) just outside the *cidade velha*, remained, first floor given over to commerce, their second to offices for the burgeoning liberal professions.[106] Grander things awaited the newer *solares* when they, in turn, were left by the elite. Built in French style (two stories, classical pilasters, two orders of windows, plaster statues, fruit, or floral decorations of classical inspiration at the corners and vertical structural divisions, and a row of small curved posts rimming the façade's top), they survived into the Republic on the newer streets and *praças* gradually incorporated into the city, serving the nation's growing bureaucracy. Some few, like Palácio Itamaratí, stand today.[107]

Indeed, from the 1820s, Rio's wealthy increasingly built their *solares* away from the old center. Many went beyond the urban edge to begin the *bairros residenciais* (residential districts). There, on the hills and beaches, they enjoyed what was newly considered a genteel way of life, in nature's more pleasant surroundings. Their houses were built in the Neo-Classical style described, at least initially. Such *solares* had salons for entertaining and receiving (drawing rooms, libraries, dining rooms, billiard rooms, etc.) on the first floor, living space on the second, a detached kitchen, and slave quarters behind the *solar* or in the basement.

These *solares* also differed from traditional *cidade velha* dwellings in having larger grounds. There they laid out fine gardens, in the "Andalusian" style (small hills, ceramic jars, groves and fountains, occasional classical statutary, tiled paths, and ornamental bushes) or in the French or English fashions (in a style stressing geometric symmetry or a style suggesting the "natural" irregularities and surprises of English rural seats). Combined with their irrepressible luxury of tropical plants and fruit trees, the effect was both aristocratic and exotic. An American recalled their success:

> The town-residences in the old city always seemed to me gloomy beyond description. But the same cannot be said of the new houses, and of the lovely suburban villas, with their surroundings of embowering foliage, profusion of bowers, and overhanging fruits. Some portions of the Santa Theresa [Hill], Laranjeiras, Botafogo, Catumby, Engenho Velho, Praia Grande, and San Domingo, cannot be surpassed for beautiful and picturesque houses.[108]

After the 1860s, this neo-classical phase slowly ripened into the Eclectic, which, like its predecessor, derived principally from Paris's Ecole des Beaux-Arts. It employed a varying composite of traditions, through typically joining variations of the classical's many reincarnations in French and Italian architectural history to the new technical potential of iron and glass. Eventually, mansard roofs, domes, wrought iron, and a broad chromatic interior palette in lavish embellishment were characteristic. Its greatest public examples, as discussed earlier, would be imposing piles on the Avenida Central, completed by 1910.

The Eclectic-style homes were generally big; at times, even grandiose. They were called *palácios* or *palacetes*, with their two stories set back from the street in French or English gardens, with a wrought iron fence at the edge of the lot, punctuated by classically cut stone or masonry posts, the entrance framed by two huge monoliths inevitably crested with baskets of fruit. The walls were white or somber grey; not the *solares*' lively pinks or yellows or blues but the proper, moribund colors of architecture *grande bourgeoise*.[109]

The generations with whom we are concerned, then, lived in houses beholden to European, especially French, taste. Even those who lived during the First Reign and inhabited traditional *sobrados* displayed in their interiors traces of the French influence that eventually dominated the century. The tendency was gradual at first. The catalogues of furnishings suggest that First Reign taste was catholic. Wealthy people had furniture, wall decorations, *objets d'art*, bedding, and tableware reflecting the colonial heritage. Faint echoes of the gorgeous Orient, ancient prize of the Portuguese, were captured in Chinese porcelain and Macao ivory. The frequent painting of furniture in white and red may have demonstrated African or Asian influence. The ubiquitous hammock betrayed Amerindian tradition, as the floormats for sitting suggested the Moorish, and tiles and furniture patterns recalled Portugal and India. Colonial traditions could best be savored at table, where English silver jostled Portuguese, and African food was eaten with Amerindian, served up, at times, with Amerindian gourds.[110]

Even early on, however, when the opening of the ports encouraged so much English and North American trade in furniture, and when the worked beauty of native adaptations of Portuguese and Oriental designs held their own, the superb line of French furnishings began to appear. Among Oriental wall-hangings could be found Gallic ones, and walls themselves might be painted with French designs or papered with a French import. Among the Macao knick-knacks might be French *bibelots*. Among the Oriental and Portuguese ceramics and porcelains, one began to find Sèvres. Among English and Portuguese silver might shine French pieces, in the much imitated *rocaille* style. However, the clearest evidence was in furniture. The Portuguese style still popular around 1800, for example, *estilo* João V, bore the decisive accent of the French Regency. Soon, French taste not only lent grace to Portuguese style, it was sought out in its own right. Among the most favored styles of 1800–50 were Louis XV, Empire, Restoration, and Louis Philippe. The demand for these styles was such that Carioca artisans turned out copies of the Gallic imports.[111]

By the 1860s, the heyday of the province's coffee and the great *fluminense* fortunes, the consolidation of French taste in domestic furnishings matched its conquest of architecture. The descriptions and illustrations make the same impression contemporary French interiors do.[112]

Domestic décor though the Carioca *belle époque*, like that in France since the Second Empire, was crowded with furniture arranged for conversation. The classical pattern dictated a sofa, flanked at right angles by two brief rows of chairs. The pieces were generally Louis XV or Louis XVI, rarely Empire. The piano was an important, even inevitable, monument to elite taste and respectability. The walls hung with French patterned silk or velvet, or, more commonly, a French wallpaper, with a pattern of small bunches of flowers or something else discreet. Crystal chandeliers supplemented gas lamps to pick out

5. Contemporary interior style from the Palácio Itamaratí

porcelains from Sèvres and Saxony, the midget armies of *bibelots* swarming over every horizontal surface, and to reflect in the magnificent wall mirrors. Ornately framed paintings hung ponderously, portraits of the family *titulares* and statesmen or European pictures of various schools. Finally, the basic finished aspects of the interior, from wrought iron to woodwork to marble and glass, were imported from France, the varnished, fitted framework to a tasteful work of wealth. The material splendor of the home was a monument to the Carioca passion for a domestic style of life exquisitely French.[113]

8. The French tradition in Brazilian taste

The reasons for this passion are complex. Two best help one to an explanation: first, the French reputation for quality; second, a Luso-Brazilian tradition of official patronage.

French quality in architecture and decoration is rooted in a history of royal patronage (bringing not only Crown protection, direction, and purchase, but those of a wealthy court and provincial aristocracy and bourgeoisie) dating from the seventeenth-century establishment of the academies under the hand of Louis XIV's minister, Colbert. The protection imposed on the arts, joined to the prestige of Louis XIV's court, established French art, artisanship and academic institutions as models for the European world. They were only enhanced by the refinements successively introduced to add to the charms of the later French reigns.[114]

I have mentioned how the Portuguese (in *estilo* João V) adopted Gallic motifs. That was in the mid-eighteenth century, and was a response typical of this European admiration for French craftsmanship and for the premier courtly establishment on the Continent. In the nineteenth century, French prestige continued undisputed. The English made beautiful furniture in the eighteenth century, but they saw their tradition of craftsmanship wither with industrial mass production. The French maintained their craftsmen and their tradition with courtly and bourgeois patronage. Even after 1789, the tradition of luxury artisanship, now established in French taste, remained unrivaled. The English admitted as much in the 1851 Great Exhibition.[115]

Portugal, like the other Francophile European monarchies, had thus only acquired a taste synonymous with courtly elegance. Brazil's elites, as a function of their colonial relationship, merely followed suit. The tradition of French influence in metropole and colony were secure by the eighteenth century[116] – it became quite official by the nineteenth.

This happened quite ironically. The Prince Regent, João VI, forced to leave Portugal for Brazil by French arms (1807), would later seek to embellish his tropical kingdom by French arts in the aftermath of Waterloo. When cordial relations between the Portuguese empire and France were restored, João VI decided to enlist French artists and artisans in his efforts to strengthen the monarchy in Brazil by the promotion of the arts and sciences within royal institutions. French academies had already proved useful means in eighteenth-century Portugal for similar ends;[117] now, after his earlier establishment of a printing press, a national library, an engineering military school, a botanical garden, and a medical school, and the dissolution of many restrictions on trade and manufacture, João VI wanted a French-style Royal School of Sciences, Arts, and Trades. Thus, seventeen men (nearly all directly associated with France's official academic institutions) were recruited, in the Missão Artística Francesa (1816).[118]

This official patronage was reinforced by the tastes of João's new Carioca court, which insured a Portuguese aristocratic market for luxury French goods.[119] These two elements, with the established colonial Francophile tradition, formed the foundations for the splendid edifice of

French material culture in nineteenth-century Brazil, an edifice constantly renovated by French immigrant tradespeople and artisans and the elite's long Parisian holidays.

It is illustrative that in the 1840s, the Marquis de Abrantes refurbished his Botafogo *palacete* in French Renaissance style.[120] Curiously enough, the canons of the Missão Artística's Escola de Belas Artes (founded 1826) called for the consecrated neo-classical, which, indeed, was prevalent in *solares* up to the 1850s.[121] Abrantes was apparently more sensitive to the vagaries of Parisian architectural fashions. His recent voyages seem to have educated his tastes to accept the style which was *au courant* under Louis Philippe.[122]

Abrantes' fashionable taste introduces an apposite problem in the relation between culture and society in nineteenth-century France and Brazil. This Renaissance fashion under Louis Philippe was ephemeral, part of a more enduring Romantic reaction against "pure" Classicism and the emerging industrial, rational culture of the times. This reaction championed architectural models recalling the various glories of old France, the actual archeological reconstruction of the classical age, or architectural styles allusive of non-Western traditions. Looking backward or abroad (or both), it was an evasion of the European present.[123]

Where the political and cultural pretensions of the *ancien régime* had made classical architecture its expression by a long process of academic refinement and aristocratic patronage, bourgeois France was clearly different. It had arisen suffused with aristocratic cultural traditions but without any of its own; indeed, this very lack of an "organic" culture was to be integral to its cultural expression.

Obsessed with claiming the stable legitimacy denied by the recent realities of its ascent, bourgeois culture was marked by an attachment to symbols of traditional establishment, symbols easily purchased in the new mock-ups furnished by industrial mass production. Symbolic legitimacy was accomplished through conspicuous consumption of mass-produced copies. The relative respectability of one's taste helped legitimize one's position in a society where nothing was so common as parvenus – and the contempt for parvenus. Perhaps the taste for Oriental and Levantine bric-à-brac and décor could be ascribed to the same response (the desire for symbolic legitimacy conveyed by identification with traditional cultures) combined with a kind of passion for trophies. Scholarship suggests that the nineteenth-century bourgeois home resembles a cluttered museum of all the cultures dispossessed or conquered by a triumphant new class.[124]

This wedding of traditional and exotic canons driven to consummation by the revolutionary needs and techniques of the bourgeois of industrializing countries begot Eclecticism. Its theoretical basis is associated with the ideology (also called Eclecticism) of the 1830s French bourgeoisie. This ideology, joining the liberal ambitions for progress and bourgeois advancement to the conservative fear of socio-political upheaval and longing for traditional institutional safeguards, expressed itself in the compromises integral to the July Monarchy (1830–48). The Eclectic style was this eclectic ideology's aesthetic complement. It united modern techniques to traditional motifs, much as the liberal bourgeoisie married constitutionalism and dynastic authority. Eclecticism, fittingly enough, flourished in the Ecole des Beaux-Arts during the Second Empire and the Third Republic, the palmy days of the grande bourgeoisie.[125]

Where the new French ruling class sought legitimacy in the symbols of traditional, aristocratic cultures, the same Eclecticism served the Brazilian elite's needs in a similar but distinct fashion. The juncture between modern technology and traditional styles, essential in French Eclecticism, for instance, was also essential in Brazil.[126] Moreover, as Goulart Reis argues (following Cruz Costa), Eclecticism, in the ideological sense, was also important in Brazil. There, the elite's consensus on Second Reign politics ensured that radical opposition was evaded for fear of social upheaval; instead, constitutional monarchism and compromise between elite fractions obtained.[127]

The difference between French and Brazilian Eclecticism is in the symbolic accomplishment of cultural Eclecticism for each elite, and it derives from Brazil's predicament as a country on the European world's periphery. If the French bourgeoisie sought legitimacy in identification with traditional aristocratic culture, Goulart Reis supports the argument basic to this study, that the Brazilian elite sought legitimacy in identification with Europe.

One might put it this way – the French bourgeois fantasy was of the past and exotica, symbolic of the order they craved for their well-being. The Brazilian fantasy was of the contemporary French and English aristocracies and their styles, *per se*, symbolic of the perceived superior culture of Europe – the metropolis in the neo-colonial epoch in which the Brazilian elite had their place. Goulart Reis' point about the distinction between the way the Romantic element in Eclecticism "worked" for the European in one way, and for the Brazilian in another, is suggestive of the point. The European reproduced a classical, medieval, or rural milieu as a *reaction* to modern European industrializing culture. The Brazilian reproduced the same milieu in Rio to create something *associated with* modern European culture. The European's is a negative response, the Brazilian's positive, but both use the same aesthetic motifs from other milieux (periods, places, or combinations thereof) without regard for their original "organic" purpose, and thus both examples are variants of Eclecticism.[128]

The parallel between this passion for association with Europe and conclusions in earlier pages regarding such cultural manifestations as Rio's "civilizing" itself, the salon, the Jockey Club, secondary education, and the rest, is patent.

9. The domestic realization of the European fantasy

Two manifestations of this European fantasy in Carioca domestic institutions are especially interesting here: Petrópolis and the internal organization of the elite home. Petrópolis is apposite because it was the most complete realization of the European fantasy possible. Visitors always commented on the pleasant (that is, European) difference between the resort and Rio. It was not only the summer capital's temperate climate that pleased them and the elite, it was the distinctly European ambience. For some, it crystallized prejudices common in this high tide of European racism and imperialism. In 1882, an Englishman, seeing the Germans previously settled as colonists by the government in 1845 reflected that

> Petrópolis itself is a German colony, which, together with the difference in the climate, makes it a far more civilized place than Rio . . . I wonder how much is race and how much climate? But I feel sure that if the English had colonized Rio de Janeiro, it would have been one of the most prosperous cities in the world. Even the yellow fever is not indigenous, but has been created quite within the last few years by accumulation of Portuguese filth.[129]

Another Briton, in 1887, contented himself with noting that "Petrópolis is a fashionable watering place, with smart houses and well-kept roads; the population is remarkably free from duskiness, and generally prides itself upon its European aspect."[130]

Founded by Pedro II in 1844, Petrópolis became established as a refuge from the heat and (after 1850) yellow fever of the Carioca summer.[131] Considering the coincidence with the Second Reign's consolidation and the florescence of *fluminense* plantations and exports, the wealth and palatial quality of the town's architecture is hardly surprising. The best example is obvious: the imperial palace, a superb neo-classical rendering by a disciple of the Missão Artística.[132] Moreover, with the increase in wealth and population brought by the advent of the *diários* in the 1890s,[133] one is not surprised to find the Eclectic evident in the well-known mansions of men of affairs and the foreign diplomatic community.[134]

By 1900, Petrópolis was thought of as a bit of aristocratic Europe, at more than one kind of remove from Rio's tropical realities. It was the *alto-mundo* fantasy cultivated and made real, set apart from the neo-colonial port. Elísio de Carvalho captures (and constructs) the fantasy in a piece on diplomats in Petrópolis for the fashionable *belle-époque* review, *Kósmos*:

In *fluminense* society, the foreign diplomatic corps always constituted . . . an element of worldly preponderance . . . now animating the world of good taste with suggestive visions. . . . [the men] in their gold-braided uniforms, [the women] showing off Redfern [*] dresses, . . . *bien nées*, and living sumptuously, they bring with them that admirable science of sociability, made of sybaritism and worldliness, that is one of the most brilliant characteristics of modern cosmopolitanism.
With the exception of the *soirées* of the Club dos Diários, always organized with much *entrain* by the Baron de Santa Margarida, and of the *bal de têtes* of the Pensão Central, of the *fâte masquée* that a ladies' commission promoted in the Palacio de Crystal to benefit some establishments of charity and of the *garden party* at the Villa Laurinda [**] in honor of the minister of Chile, it is to the initiative of the diplomats that are owed the principal parties of the summer of 1909 in Petrópolis, from the sumptuous ball with which the Minister of Uruguay inaugurated the *season* to the enchanting *redoutes* of the Baroness Riedel von Riedenau, the beautiful wife of the minister of Austria, an American beauty formed of smiles, glances, and the manners of Gainsboroug's [*sic*] ladies.[135]

The internal organization of the home is also to the point here because it paralleled the relationship between Petrópolis and Rio: the rooms were distinguished from one another by the symbolic value of European appearance. Some rooms, notably the drawing room, and any other designated for Society functions (the billiard room, the library, the entrance hall, and the formal dining room) were those most carefully Europeanized in their finish and furnishing. They clearly acted as the public statement of family status and had to demonstrate the requisite wealth and taste in conformity with the Europhile values under discussion.[136]

However, those rooms designated for the use of family and servants suggested the traditional Brazilian culture glimpsed in the child's domestic world. The servants, often descendants of the family's plantation slaves, generally lived in basement, attic, or backyard quarters (a kind of urban *senzala*). The family passed their time in the bedrooms and the family dining room, where no one but very intimate relations were admitted, the finish was less splendid, and furnishings were traditional, even including hammocks and floor mats up through the Second Reign.[137]

There, relations were intimate and familiar. Even meals changed; there, food was served all at once, instead of French style, in sequential courses (something for special occasions, except in families accustomed to living in Europe.)[138] An incident indicative of the symbolic values of rooms at issue appears in the memoirs of Nabuco's daughter:

> I laughed a good deal once, when a dear friend . . . came to see Mama . . . The maid . . . asked her to wait in the drawing room while she informed mama. Dona Tita protested: – I am not a drawing room visit. I am a dining room visit.[139]

In the organization of domestic space, then, the instrumental and symbolic value given European culture is made obvious once again. As one stepped from one room to another, one might also move from one cultural expression, and associated statement of role, to another. One's formal Society persona was more European, one's family one, more Brazilian. They coexisted, elements to be emphasized in turn as circumstances dictated.

10. The direction of fashionable residence

Our final word concerns the urban geography of fashionable residence. Carioca residence in the early eighteenth century was confined to the *cidade velha*; i.e. between Rua da Prainha and Rua da Ajuda, north to south, and the Bay and Rua da Vala, east to west (now, the Ruas of Acre, Chile, and Uruguaiana, respectively). By the late eighteenth century, some few great merchants and crown officials had country places, especially in São Cristóvão, Botafogo, and even Gávea – for the most part, however, few lived so far away. The regular orders and some magnates might have chapels or churches, small farms or villas as close as the Carioca Aqueduct, the areas between Morro Santo Antônio and present-day Rua Sete de Setembro and Praça Tiradentes, around present-day Ruas do Lavradio and do Senado, and the area now traversed by Avenida Presidente Vargas between the Campo de Santana and Rua Uruguaiana. That is, those elite residents who lived outside the *cidade velha* generally lived very close indeed.[140] (see Maps 1, 2 and 5.)

However, with the Arrival of the Court (1808), this changed dramatically. The Côrte and the Opening of the Ports (1808), brought a surge of foreign commerce. Many of the Britons came to stay, and established villas in areas sparsely populated by men of means. Initially attracted to São Cristóvão, they soon settled mostly in the Southern Zone – Glória, Catete, Flamengo, Laranjeiras, Cosme Velho, and Botafogo. The court nobles and bureaucrats, as well as elite members, either remained at the city's edge or bought villas in the north – São Cristóvão region, near the royal Quinta da Boa Vista, and Andaraí, Catumbí, Rio Comprido, and Mata Porcos (now the more euphonious Estácio de Sá). The French sought out the further areas of Tijuca and Engenho Velho.[141]

By 1850, although some men of affairs hung on at the fringes of the *cidade velha*, the elite had already began moving out of the Northern Zone and into the South. Indeed, *titulares* such as Baependí, Montserate, Abrantes, and Paraná built their *solares* from Lapa to Botafogo by the 1840s. By the 1860s, the *palacetes* of Nova Friburgo (now Palácio do Catete) and Itambí stood in Botafogo, and the *solar* of Nabuco de Araújo and the Palácio Isabel (now Palácio Guanabara) graced Flamengo, with a host of other fine mansions. The elite predilection for the southern *bairros residenciais*, principally Botafogo and Laranjeiras, lasted well into the *belle époque*. In 1898, a Carioca journalist trumpeted:

> Botafogo is the aristocratic district *par excellence*. There it is that fashion, luxury's ostentation, reveals itself in all its glory . . . there it is that the nights pass lightly, spent in intimate but splendid and inviting gatherings; there it is that one enjoys the peerless panorama of the beautiful bay . . .; there it is that nature reveals . . . harmonious, imposing, incomparable grandeur . . . Oh! Botafogo is the paradise of Rio de Janeiro.[142]

It seems rather obvious why the first successful *bond* line (The Botanical Garden Railroad, 1868) was routed from the *cidade velha* to Flamengo, Botafogo, and the Jardim Botânico – the entrepreneurs were well aware of the direction of wealthy residential growth.[143]

This history of residential change suggests again the direction of elite cultural impulse in domestic institutions. First, because Brazilians followed European cues in locale. Until the English and other foreigners had shown the way, Brazilians and Portuguese had generally preferred homes in the *cidade velha* near the beaches. It was the English who first moved north and south in numbers and, with other foreigners, built villas in hilly valleys to enjoy the cool breezes and wonderful views there.[144]

Second, because, just as Petrópolis was, these *bairros residenciais* were, architecturally, aristocratic European settlements. In them, the Ecole des Beaux-Arts influence was clear in the neo-classical and, then, the Eclectic.[145]

Both points signal a break with Rio's past. Before, rich and poor lived and worked all together in the teeming, fetid streets of the colonial port. In the nineteenth century, the elite left tasks in sweltering urban ministries, counting houses, or professional offices to return to European-style *solares* and *palacetes* which proclaimed their status and removed them from the places and labor that made that status possible. Not only had European forms been reproduced; so had, if only symbolically, the separation of "civilized" metropolis and "uncouth" colony.

Conclusion: adaptation on the periphery

In this long exploration of elite domestic institutions certain patterns play themselves out and repeat. The focus on one institution after another demonstrates how each responded to general shifts in the world of the elite. The word Freyre employed for much discussed here is "re-Europeanization," implying the reemergence of Brazil into the circle of "European" influence after the isolation of the colonial period initiated by European discovery and settlement.[146]

The idea of re-Europeanization, however, implicitly denies a key, underlying, continual process, involving essential tensions. It is more useful to see what we have discussed here – the increasingly important role of Franco-English culture within nineteenth-century Carioca domestic institutions – as but part of the latest phase in an ongoing colonial relationship. This, never broken, simply grew in impact and became more complex in its cultural influence as a function of larger processes dependent upon Brazil's relationship to a world market revolving around the North Atlantic.

European cultural influence on Brazil never stopped after 1500. Even as a restricted Portuguese holding, much in the larger European world was felt in Brazil, however circuitously or faintly.[147] What is different about the nineteenth century is the degree of impact, a function of the old colonial order's end and the gradual, sure emergence of the neo-colonial order.

Integral to the new order's beginnings were the increasing play of British commercial, financial, and technological interests in Brazil, alongside those of others (always keeping in mind the extraordinary

French cultural impact).[148] The neo-colonial order only came into its own, however, in the century's last third, rising on bases made firm in the second. These included the discovery of a highly profitable crop (coffee), with markets among the European and American working classes; political consolidation and domestic stability; the development of the European technology useful in exploiting coffee (e.g., railroads); and the available investment capital (mostly British). It is the combination of these developments that brought Brazil what has been called the "maturity of the neo-colonial order" – within which the changes in elite domestic institutions must be understood.[149]

I have noted here and in the other chapters the growing complexity and luxury of European, and especially French, cultural forms in the lives of the Carioca elite. Moreover, I have done so while discussing the local changes of which they were a part – the splendor of the Côrte as the center for *fluminense* coffee wealth and the Second Reign's statesmen, and then the more urbane refinement of the capital become a nexus of new urban professions and continued commercial and financial affairs. Both the cultural and the urban socio-economic changes cannot be understood without the larger neo-colonial relations in which they figured. As has been pointed out in discussing the growing complexity of Society usage, the increasingly cosmopolitan nature of Society itself, the more active role of women in Society, and the pervasive luxury and Europeanization of domestic architecture and décor, cultural Europeanization is to be understood as something possible to the extent that increased wealth, travel, and foreign influence in a growing port made it so.

It is not, then, a "re-Europeanization" one finds in the nineteenth century, so much as a level of Europeanization newly possible, due to changes within an enduring colonial relationship. European influences, like the larger colonial relationship of which they were a part, had always obtained – what one sees in this century is not their introduction, but their triumph.

In this new phase, Franco-English aristocratic cultural forms served to reinforce and legitimate the distinction and superiority of the Carioca elite. They did this by conspicuously adorning the elite with symbols of European aristocratic derivation (thus associating it with that aristocracy's traditional legitimacy, as well as with the power and prestige of the neo-colonial metropolis), symbols adapted in many of the most important rituals, relationships, and milieux of elite domestic life. The use of Franco-English forms, in effect, newly legitimized the traditional relations between masters and slaves, whites and blacks, patrons and clients, Europeans and non-Europeans, elite and everybody else.

In this chapter moreover – more than in any other hitherto – one glimpses the subtlety and limits of the adaptation. This use of new cultural forms to express and maintain old relations, despite these forms' inherently alien quality, did not dissolve the bonding elements essential to the old ways. Outside the home, there was remove and alienating fantasy, as argued in the last section, but there were, within the home, especially, strong continuities. The French governess came after the Afro-Brazilian *ama de leite*; the family dining room coexisted with the formal drawing room; the chic lady, active in Society, still functioned in instrumental terms established by patriarchal families. It is symbolic of the adaptation that an elite family might decide to bring one of its old plantation house-slaves with it to Paris – not suffering, even in the metropolis, the complete loss of old and intimate relations.[150] In elite domestic institutions, in an especially important way, both the "Carioca" and the "*belle époque*" of our subject are seen to come together.

5

The rise of consumer fetishism

In domestic institutions, striking adaptations of European paradigms to Carioca realities are evident. However, more jarring adaptations also became apparent in nineteenth-century Rio; their awkwardness has much to tell one. As the neo-colonial relationships between Brazil and the North Atlantic strengthened, particularly after 1850, the absorption of European cultural phenomena increased, as has been discussed. This chapter explores three – luxury shopping, fashion in clothing, and fashionable prostitution – which, linking deeply individual desires to a social display in stark contrast to Brazilian conditions, are very suggestive of just how compelling European culture was among the Carioca elite. We begin with the analysis of the emergence of the European cultural phenomena in question. In this way, I hope to make clear their European meaning, the better to distinguish their substance and significance in Rio.

1 The emergence of commodity fetishism in bourgeois Europe

The meaning of commodity fetishism in nineteenth-century Europe derives from marketing and technological shifts linked to tensions springing from social status insecurity and anxiety. Although this can be seen in many aspects of material culture, it is clearest, perhaps, in clothing. There, certain lesser tensions were national – between France and England – and soon subsided. The most important tensions were class-based – between the aristocracy and the emergent bourgeoisie – and long endured. The national tension is important to Brazil only because it explains the origins of the fashions later adopted there. After the 1820s, for instance, aristocratic fashion was established by the elite circles of the nobilities resident in Paris and London; Paris dominated feminine fashion, London dominated masculine. Before, up through the eighteenth century, both masculine and feminine had been ruled by the

French; the Revolution and the subsequent wars, by destroying the old French court and establishing English hegemony, had ended all that. English masculine fashion, which had already succeeded in influencing French models and, through them, those adopted throughout the European world, now exercised its sway directly. The French regained feminine fashion through their unique traditional skills and strong government support. What remained in both London and Paris from *ancien-régime* fashion was the primacy of aristocratic values: these were essential, however seemingly contradictory in an era identified with the triumph of the bourgeoisie.[1]

I write "seemingly contradictory" because it was the very rise of the bourgeoisie in societies suffused with aristocratic values that created the motor of modern fashion, through class-based anxieties, industrialization, and the formation of the urban bourgeois market. In the *ancien régime*, one's social status was signaled by certain prescribed marks, like the *talon rouge* which only nobles might wear. After the Revolution, legal distinctions between estates' proper attire vanished, although class prejudice and social anxiety remained, exacerbated, perhaps, by the uncertainties of less rigid class structure. Now, one might only suggest one's social status by one's taste. One distinguished oneself in the anonymity of the urban setting by the "right" choice, associated with a certain way of life subtly different from one of mere wealth. After all, anyone with money, any bourgeois, could pay for costly clothing; the aristocrats, or the bourgeois hoping to pass for them, could only separate themselves by choices demonstrating distinctive taste.[2]

The way that this aristocratic urge to distinction functioned to create modern fashion might be compared to Poggioli's theory of the way a "cliché" functioned in nineteenth-century aesthetic trends.[3] That is, a revolutionary breakthrough would occur, seize the imagination of the avant-garde, and then be successively modified, popularized, and mass-produced as it was assimilated by the bourgeoisie and became common taste. The same pattern plays itself out in modern fashion. In the nineteenth century, someone within the elite circle of the aristocracy adopted a distinct article or style of clothing; then, it seized the imagination of that circle as something setting it apart from the common taste. The wider circle of the aristocracy quickly adopted the innovation to remain in fashion, and thus established the innovation as the very best good taste. The upper reaches of the bourgeoisie followed nearly simultaneously to maintain itself on par with a class whose established legitimacy it continued to envy but could only imitate. The bourgeoisie as a whole followed, making allowances for cost in material and practicality of cut, in order to remain "respectable" – that is, to conform to the tastes now consecrated by their "betters" in societies still dominated socially by the aristocracy. The last step was made ever more quickly and cheaply by the emergence of mass production of clothing in the early stages of industrialization. By mid-nineteenth century, ready-made clothing for men, for example, had begun to answer the need of the bourgeois and their inferiors for respectable attire in increasingly large, wealthy, and sophisticated urban markets. What this meant, of course, was that an innovation in attire was more and more quickly made "common," and, thus, vulgar – which drove the innovators within elite circles to yet another change in order to continue to distinguish themselves, which, in turn, galvanized the entire process yet again.[4]

Aristocratic values, anxiety about social status, new manufacturing capacity, and an expanding urban market, then, combined to explain the centrality of fashion in bourgeois culture; they also introduce the key concept of commodity fetishism. Commodity fetishism – the investment of objects manufactured for sale with ideological values[5] – may be analyzed here in three new phenomena exemplifying the patterns just sketched: the evolution of the department store, the actual beginnings of modern fashion in attire, and the creation of the *demi-monde*.

The origins of the department store spring directly from the interlinking forces of the growing urban market, the capacity of the textile industry, and the social tensions and changes noted above. The French *maisons de nouveautés* and the English bazaars were both prototypes that grew out of drapers' shops into establishments selling not only cloth, but various manufactured articles of clothing and dress accessories in the period between the 1780s and the 1830s. Along the way, they cultivated elements of both a commercial and ideological nature that led to the first department stores in mid-century Paris: plate-glass display windows, bulk-buying and selling cheap for rapid turnover, fixed prices, speciality divisions, and the concept of shopping as a leisurely adventure for the wealthy, in which courtesy, novelty, artful display, and a beguiling promenade made the purchase of commodities an absorption into socio-cultural fantasy that reached theatric proportions.[6] Early on, commodity fetishism's grip on the bourgeois was tight. One no longer sent one's servants shopping or expected a tradesman's visit – one went oneself for the pleasure of fantasy consumption, buying objects whose value lay not in what they were in themselves, but in what they represented socially. One went shopping to purchase one's bid at aristocracy. As early as 1830, Balzac, in *La Mode* (itself typical of the new era's periodical), proclaimed that "The elegant life is the perfection of the material and exterior life. . . . Nobility is translated into things." He added that "The exterior life is a sort of organized system that represents a man exactly as the colors of the snail are reproduced on his shell."[7] By 1888, one *homme du monde* noted a department store where "for a modest sum, you can buy a small kit for a man-about-town."[8] The elegant life, identified with the aristocracy, had "trickled down" to the commodities for sale behind the *vitrine*. Let us see how.

Beau Brummell and the Empress Eugénie[9] demonstrate how Poggioli's process of the cliché was crucial to this trickling down and to the beginnings of modern fashion. Brummell is apposite because, precisely in the milieu in which the forces discussed first formed, he provided the basic clichés for masculine attire and style *par excellence*: the origin of the modern business suit and the exemplar of the dandy. Although no noble himself, Brummell's aristocratic tone and appearance captured the admiration of the elite circles of London during the Regency; this enabled him to set fashions in personal style and attire in those circles which, in turn, automatically commanded the attention of the English and French *émigré* aristocracies and, thence, the obedience of the bourgeoisie and the European world. His unique emphasis on fit, cut, cloth, and color combination, as well as his affectations in society, became aristocratic styles, and the clothing acquired an appropriate fetish value as a sign of aristocratic status.[10] Brummell's social ascent also represented the wish-fulfillment of individual bourgeois anxious over social position in a more mobile world. Thus, he stands not for a triumphant bourgeoisie,[11] but for uncommon success at the common bourgeois socio-cultural "treason" of the period: identification with aristocratic values. After all, the sources for bourgeois fashion, the Anglo-French dandy and the *homme du monde*, were aristocratic in the traits subsumed in their style and thus increasingly appropriated by the bourgeoisie: wealth, leisure, studied physical grace, restrained taste, hauteur, and exclusive social relations.[12]

Eugénie's importance for the beginnings of modern fashion owes much to her collaboration with Charles Frederick Worth, the first *haut couturier*. What she brought to the match were her beauty, considered near perfect by contemporary aristocratic standards, and a personal *cachet* derived from her social position as foreign aristocrat raised to the throne of imperial France.[13]

What Worth brought were his gifts for handling cloth, for entrepreneurial innovation, and for divining the fetish quality in the fashionable commodity.[14] Essentially, Worth played on fetishism by matching his dresses to women, above all to Eugénie, whose personal manner and public position showed that they were likely to establish fashions by the chic[15] with which they wore them. Moreover, he capitalized on Eugénie's special quality as a sort of lightning rod for social fantasy by inventing the idea of reproducing and selling the dress model she established, as a commodity to whomever had the price. Before, women had imitated styles that they observed or they copied from fashion plates; now they were able to buy exact duplicates of styles associated with the glamor of Napoleon III's Paris. Worth and his successors thus harnessed the old value of aristocratic distinction to the new potential for mass production, selling to the wealthy in France and abroad the fantasy identification with the imperial court. After 1870, *haut couturiers* perfected the same process with women models who often merely embodied aristocratic values in their appearance or way of life, just as Brummell had. Now, however, the fantasy was often projected by women whose profession was fantasy – the celebrated actresses or prostitutes of the *belle époque*.[16]

The fantasies raveled round either of these two professions were often closely related by the nineteenth century; indeed, many of the stage professionals, from the ballet dancers to the great *tragédiennes*, sold their public and private charms to the best range of clients that they could command. Other times, the stage was used simply to secure such patronage by would-be mistresses. The mid-century and *fin-de-siècle* prototypes were celebrated in literature and the theater – *La dame aux camélias*, *Nana*, and *A la recherche du temps perdu* alike have given us their images, and Dumas fils' piece their place – the *demi-monde*. They are important here because of the patent conflation of the basis of their appeal with urban commodity fetishism. From the poorest categories of such women, who were associated with the sale of luxury commodities either as shop girls or by the area in which they chose to work, to the most expensive and exclusive, who were associated with a very costly public way of life, such women were purposely reduced to living commodities whose display and distinction by price and use were part of the same "phantasmagoria" Benjamin analyzes in Parisian consumption.[17]

The identification between fantasies and commodities was enriched by the use of celebrated actresses and cocottes as advertisements by *haut couturiers* and conspicuous consumption by lovers. Both fused "their" women to expensive commodities in a mutually reflective process – the designers to demonstrate the chic of their commodities through association with an expensive, stylish sexual object; the lovers to demonstrate their own wealth and chic by showing the expense and taste of the women whose favors they were known to have purchased. Indeed, the most exclusive cocottes, the *horizontales*, were often at least as well dressed, kept, and cultivated as the wives and daughters of their clients, so that certain understandings were employed to distinguish them publicly and avoid embarrassment – be it in words like *cocodette* (for fashionable society women who flirted "like" cocottes, but did not trade in coitus) or in restricted seating at Longchamps.[18]

The value of the *horizontale*-commodity was thus collapsed into the fetish objects carefully associated with her display. Such women were publicly admired for their style and their purchasers, as luxury commodities are generally.[19] They, in themselves, capture for us the extent to which, in the bourgeois culture emerging under European industrial capitalism, fantasy and personal status were identified with objects of aristocratic derivation made for sale.

2. The emergence of commodity fetishism in Rio de Janeiro

Commodity fetishism in nineteenth-century Rio de Janeiro resembled the Franco-English phenomenon just explored. The tendency's development only differed in realization and chronology because of the limits imposed by Carioca material circumstances.

The French Revolution, watershed for the European socio-cultural developments just discussed, had its Carioca counterpart in the Arrival of the Court in 1808. The Revolution, in destroying the *ancien régime*, loosed the dynamics explored above; 1808, however, in bringing the Portuguese *ancien régime* to Brazil, gave greater strength to those dynamics in Rio. Let us first examine this in the Carioca emergence of the same three phenomena analyzed above: luxury shopping, fashion in dress, and fashionable prostitution.

The mid-century European department store only emerged in Rio by the 1870s.[20] A flourishing trade in luxuries began after 1808, however, and it found its permanent home on the Rua do Ouvidor by the 1820s. There the French merchant community took root, ousting English trade in grosser products and coexisting with the Portuguese. The shops tended toward luxuries – jewelry, clothing, wigs, haircutting and shaving, accessories, artificial flowers, beverages, foods, periodicals, and books. The Ouvidor was celebrated for precisely those aspects of the proto-department store common in contemporary Paris – window displays, variety, luxury goods, chic, and leisure within a small physical area. One went there for *flânerie* and the "interiorization" (leisured personal identification with the displayed commodities) Benjamin emphasizes as essential in the fantasy experience central to commodity fetishism.[21]

The *maison-de-nouveautés* type of establishment probably remained the limit of Brazilian consumerism until late because the element crucial to contemporary European commerce was missing: Rio lacked an urban market comparable to that which luxury commerce enjoyed in Paris and London. This also obviously made impossible an industry manufacturing luxury goods (Brazilian industry did date from around mid-century, but naturally produced mass-oriented goods, such as soap and cheap cloth).

When, around 1870, Carioca department stores did emerge, finally made possible by the slow growth of the urban middle-sector market, there was still no important luxury manufacture. Customers probably would have been unwilling to buy something without a well-established European *cachet*. Instead, the increased market allowed only for the commercial florescence of stores like Notre Dame de Paris, which sold nothing but expensive imports.[22]

Whatever the limitations, however, the nature of the commodities sold demonstrates Carioca sensitivity to European fashions, not least in dress. The milliners' shops on the Ouvidor, as well as the Cariocas in Europe who sent home trunks of the latest modes, ensured Carioca stylishness from early on. Indeed, certain tailors' names survive from mid-nineteenth century on as the fashionable elite's outfitters: Raunier, for instance, or Almeida Rabello. The period portraits make clear how mindful the Carioca was of the proper image. This aspect of commodity fetishism, then, developed according to the Parisian timetable, if only for a bare fraction of the population. By the *belle époque*, the passion to be "up-to-date" in European fashion became nearly as feral in Rio as in Europe. That wonderfully smart chronicler of the mode, Figueiredo Pimentel, began to spy out fashion and the lack of it with his "Binoculo," regularly censuring the recalcitrant or slovenly within the small world of the elite.[23]

Finally, again, only a small portion of Cariocas enjoyed a replication of the third phenomenon, prostitution – at least, of the "better" Parisian sort. Further, in Rio the development of this commodity was staggered, while the Parisian could purchase all grades of this "object" from early on. For example, the Carioca exploitation of French shopgirls was possible only after the 1820s frenchification of the Ouvidor. The pursuit of actresses and singers was possible only after mid-century, with the advent of dance halls, *cafés cantantes*, and, especially, the Alcazar Lyrique Française.[24] As for the *courtisane* sort, though hidden, kept Frenchwomen probably existed from early on (exalted Ouvidor *modistes*, perhaps), the *horizontale*, an expensive, publicly acknowledged mistress, did not appear until the last third of the century.[25]

The phasing of development *à la parisienne* corresponds rather neatly to the city's socio-economic metamorphosis. The shopgirls come with the Opening of the Ports in 1808, the limited luxury market, and the frenchification of the Rua do Ouvidor. The actresses and singers come with the economic expansion and urbanity born of *fluminense* coffee and imperial consolidation *c.* 1850. The *horizontale* came with the increasingly urbane Rio of the later Second Reign and the *belle époque*, when wealth, European travel and experience, large-scale luxury imports, and an urban style of life were established aspects of elite Carioca society and culture.

Like other aspects of Carioca commodity fetishism and the European phenomena which they replicated, such prostitution must be understood within the context of socio-economic limitations and tendencies. Its particular meaning, however, and that of Carioca commodity fetishism as a whole, cannot be understood simply in terms of the possibility of its reproduction in Rio. Rather, it has to be analyzed with regard to the reasons for its reproduction. One must turn to the consumer and his fantasies.

3. The distinct fetishism – the fantasy of the Carioca consumer

In the commodity fetishism analyzed in France and England, the essential fantasy through which the consumer related to luxury manufactures had to do with class. The commodity was both medium to, and a realization of, one's aristocratic aspirations. As Cobban put it: "The French élite in the nineteenth century was an élite of bourgeois, but their aim was to be, as in the eighteenth century, *bourgeois vivant noblement*."[26]

Carioca fetishism was different. The consumer of luxuries, for example, was already in the elite. Unlike the bourgeois' case in Europe, these Carioca consumers' fantasies did not coil around aspirations to rise in society – at least not until the rise of the middle sectors from about the 1870s. Further, even then, the fantasy projected into the commodities drew its basic power from the same source of anxiety and desire that obtained during the 1820s. What Carioca consumers projected into imported luxury commodities was the same aristocratic fantasy the

European bourgeois nurtured. Only that, for the Cariocas, this fantasy had distinct meaning. In Rio, it was not simply a case of class identification, but, rather, cultural identification as well. The fetish Cariocas worshiped in luxury imports had to do with being a European aristocrat. Let us unravel this Carioca meaning in our three phenomena.

The Rua do Ouvidor

In symbolic terms, the Rua do Ouvidor (like Petrópolis and, in many ways, parts of elite homes) was Europe. This street, a half-mile in length, was like no other in this small city. From the 1820s, the heart of elite culture and society beat there; only the very metamorphosis of the city would change this, with the construction of the Avenida Central, in 1906.[27] Within a block on either side, the grosser trade and most traditional aspects of Brazil might rule – within the Ouvidor, only the finest European luxuries and newest "improvements" reigned. There, everything novel and "civilized" made its first appearance: shopwindows, ice cream, streetcars, literature, gaslighting, and *la mode*.

The Ouvidor was more, however, than just a Carioca version of the Palais Royal, a shrine to fashionable purchase. It was also Rio's Boulevard des Italiens, meeting place of the elite, the fashionable promenade, at the expense of the colonial gardens of the Passeio Público, or the Campo de Santana, newly landscaped by Glaziou in the 1870s. Each day, especially after streetcars[28] made access to the Ouvidor easy from the fashionable residential districts, the street was mobbed with the elite making their regular, *de rigueur* appearance.

The Ouvidor was the public place for the expression of elite fantasy identification, not simply by participation, as in the Lírico, the Casino Fluminense, and the Jockey Club, but by self-identification and acting-out. The other institutions gathered all of the elite together indiscriminately, in a common space associated with European culture. That, in functional terms, was one of their main advantages and purposes. The Ouvidor, did the same; it also, however, facilitated gratifying distinctions corresponding to European categories:

> It was the rare place in Brazil where all was concentrated. On the days in which there were no sessions in the Chamber of Deputies or in the Senate, the parade of parliamentarians began at one in the afternoon; when, however, the two houses of Parliament functioned, the murmur of the deputies and senators, to which was joined that of the bankers, brokers, the upper bureaucrats, the officers of the army and the navy, . . . journalists, men of letters, actors,

etc., [began] after four o'clock. Groups formed here and there, at the doors of the various establishments of important commerce.[29]

Thus, the politicians of each set met in one *confeitaria* or another; the literati met in bookstores or newspaper offices or *confeitarias* according to each literary clique; the engineers and entrepreneurs gathered in one shop (the origin of their Club de Engenharia); the men about town congregated at certain shops or corners, often according to generations; the fashionable women, after a ritual promenade down the street, met their various cliques at a certain hour, at certain tea houses or *confeitarias*; and the cocottes would drift in to certain cafés at certain hours when "honest" women had left. The press was so great in the late afternoon, after Parliament and the ministries closed, that pedestrians found the going difficult and carriages were forbidden altogether.[30]

Now, the explicit models for the Ouvidor were the streets for fashionable concourse in Paris or London. There, however, elements from each culture were exchanged and modified (e.g., the English use of French, French wines, French feminine fashions; the French passion for English suits, clubs, and horseracing).[31] In Rio, matters were different. There, there was no exchange and little modification. What could be, was brought over intact and implanted proudly, in edged contrast to the rest of the old port city and its largely Afro-Brazilian population. Luís Edmundo, remembering the Ouvidor, noted:

In the midst of that parade of elegance, . . . it was not rare to see a pitch-black Negro burst in, drunk, to stagger, shoving and driving away the passers-by, [or,] on the sidewalk, a *cabrocha*, exposing a shiny, jelly-like breast outside of a ragged blouse, or a *capoeira* from Saúde or Saco de Alferes with his odd gait, a soft hat drooping down the back of his head, a cigarette behind his ear, and a club in his hand, smelling of cheap rum, shouting like a madman.[32]

Questions of incongruity with the Carioca milieu, however, were of little importance; the emphasis was on the studied modeling of the Franco–English aristocratic urban culture. Indeed, that is the point. What distinguishes the Ouvidor (with regard to Paris or London – the pattern is common enough in the colonial and neo-colonial world) is precisely the passion for replicating European aristocratic life publicly, identifying oneself (through association with the consumption of consecrated commodities) as a worthy member of the elite by virtue of being Europeanized. One Carioca *homme du monde* suggests this passion in recalling the 1870s:

In my youth, the Alcazar Lyrique Française was the favorite theater for all of the citizens of the best *fluminense* society. In the orchestra chairs of that elegant theater, one saw almost daily the same persons, all of the elite. . . .

> Until nearly five o'clock in the afternoon, the elegant world was at the Rua do Ouvidor; afterwards, it was in good taste to take a turn through Botafogo Beach, where the dandys [sic], the actresses, and the *demi-mondaines*, showed themselves off in open carriages.
>
> At the dinner hour, from 6.30 to 7.30 in the evening, the fashionable restaurants filled up: Aux Frères Provençaux, . . . Hôtel d'Europe, . . . Hôtel Ravot, . . . Hôtel du Brésil, . . . Hôtel des Princes, . . . Hôtel de Paris, . . .
>
> At night, after the shows, the *viveurs* of good or wealthy families and the *horizontaes* [sic] of the stage drove off in innumerable carriages to dine in Botafogo . . . at the Hôtel de Londres and others, when they did not go to dine in the famous restaurants just cited, in the center of the city.[33]

There, in the tropical port capital, along its sandy beaches and jungled hills, the Cariocas remade Paris, with its theaters, boulevards, *bois*, women and restaurants – an incongruous vision, with all the details coffee could buy.

Proper Dress

Carioca concern with European fashion in dress, no matter how impractical, is a dramatic example of the particular fetishism under discussion. I do not mean to imply here that European fashions were practical in Europe, and followed as such by a hard-headed, rational populace. The nature of fashion, as has been seen, is a function of expressing and attempting to realize social aspirations through the consumption and display of a fetishized commodity. In this, there is no difference between Parisians and Cariocas. Rather, it is the consumer's relationship to the fantasy the fetishism involves that is different.

The Carioca stepped into a foreign culture when, to demonstrate a superior status, he followed fashions; the Parisian stayed in, or attempted to step up to, a social class in doing the same. For him, the cultural fantasy Brazilian adoption of such clothing signified was absent – the difference is qualitative. Indeed, it should be emphasized how much the aristocracies of France and England shared, adapting each other's modes and usages and creating something of a common culture in which influences were mutual. The Parisian aristocrats, on taking up the English suit, for example, were adopting something to which Frenchmen, too, had contributed over time. More important, neither the French nor the English looked on the other as the source of civilization; they assimilated the others' culture to strong traditions they maintained as superior. The Brazilians, however, had no sense of such a superior cultural tradition; they tended to see themselves as backward. Thus, one *paulista* planter, though staunchly proud of Brazil, looked to Parisian high society as a school of manners, where one might acquire, "... the good customs and those that we ought to introduce into our country."[34]

The qualitative extent of the absurdity of the clothing should also be noted. Again, I do not argue that European clothing was comfortable in Europe. In Rio, however, what was merely uncomfortable and impractical in Paris or London became a vivid act of self-martyrdom, indicating commitment worthy of analysis. Examples come easily to mind.

Men's apparel during the nineteenth century consisted of numerous garments of wool, over cotton or linen. The latter were white; the outer garments varied, at least during the first half of the century. One generally wore blue or black cutaway coats and skin-tight knee-breeches, pantaloons, or, increasingly, trousers. Vests were the rule and, along with what one wore on one's legs, tended to lighter colors and weights than the coat. Less formal, sporty occasions, might allow for wearing a heavy woolen plaid, tweed, or other woolen of lighter colors. From about 1860, proper daytime wear settled into a somber, heavy, woolen black, with only the occasional concession of woolen grey, check or stripe trousers, and vests of varied possibilities. Even such concessions, however, were dominated by black frockcoat or cutaway. Indeed such woolen coats, in lighter weight, were worn in summer, possibly relieved by white or buff vests and trousers, with lighter materials, like drill, for the latter.

Under these two layers of wool were long cotton or linen drawers and shirts, with attached tight, white, wing collars, starched and firmly bound up with one of the ancestors of the tie or bow tie. One's feet were wedged into high button shoes, and one's hands sheathed into neat, delicate gloves. Crowning it all would be the top hat, unrivaled until the century's latter years, when derbies came into vogue.

In the evenings, for the whole century long, one might wear only the "penguin suit." Cutaways were used and a generally white (rather than black) vest, both tailored to achieve the proper svelte look. These were trimmed with white gloves, bow tie, and hard shirtfront and collar, with a top hat to complete.[35]

All of this was costuming with little concession to ease of movement, blood circulation, temperature, or economy. Still, one might recall the European setting, where men of wealth confined their movements to leisure or office activities, the winter was cold and heating poor, and other seasons relatively mild, and one's servants saw to the cleanliness of one's clothing. One might also recall that woolens, England's traditional manufacture, would also be practical for England's climate. Yet, these factors are really beside the point. Fashion is essentially blind to convenience or creature comfort.

This last argument is even more painfully made regarding the plight of well-dressed women. Illustrated books of fashion make a few descriptive generalizations possible. Women began the century in clothing that displayed their bodies nearly *au naturel*; they completed it in clothing that exaggerated its nature, accentuating hips, buttocks, and breasts. During the interval, women's clothing blended exaggeration of one's attributes with their complete elimination beneath a vast yardage of precious cloths buoyed up by cunning artifices and punctuated with costly conceits.[36]

A few analytic generalizations may be noted, too. First, the expense of dressing well was certainly high. One paid small fortunes to exhibit a Worth, and any formal occasion demanded a different, if not new, dress. One must also mention the considerable expense of jewelry, which as early as the *Directoire* was indispensable in lavish display and varied to combine with one's costume. Second, constriction was essential in every period – even the women *à la grecque* who wafted about the Napoleonic era were, on occasion, held together by a flexible undergarment. They were unfettered, however, compared to their daughters. These were forced into corseting, as their eighteenth-century grandmothers had been, and very serious corseting, indeed. Kroeber makes the fashionable measure out to be one that would leave a woman of 5' 2" with a waist of from about four to five inches in diameter over the period from 1844 to 1907.[37]

Third, for most of the century, warmth and awkwardness were integrally part of one's skirts. These were exaggerated for purely aesthetic reasons with no relationship to how a body is constructed. Thus, from about the 1820s, women wore increasingly large numbers of petticoats and whatnot to keep matters mysteriously flared out to increasingly larger circumferences. Indeed, the crinoline was apparently conceived as a liberation from this burgeoning infrastructure; it allowed enormous circumferences to be taken up under a flexible basket of steel.[38] When the crinoline withered slowly away (it was unavoidable from 1856 to about 1868), it did so in the form of an atrophy, the bustle, which rose and fell through the 1870s and 1880s in various festooned exaggerations of the buttocks. These finally drooped entirely away (the bustle's variations, that is) into luxurious trains by the 1890s and 1900s.

In all this skirting, one was forced to adopt extraordinary grace in one's movements. In the crinoline period, especially, one transported an enormous, rustling, silken exemplar of the Eclectic style so typical of contemporary taste. As Eugénie's *dame d'honneur* primly recalls,

> . . . it required the greatest skill to manage in the crowded salons. It was a commingling of all styles. Draperies *à la grecque* were disposed upon *paniers* of Louis XVI's time, and the *basquines* of the Amazons of *La Fronde* were supplemented by the flowing sleeves of the Renaissance. . . . it required all the grace which proceeds from perfection of form and habit of observation to cope with the difficulties which impeded an easy carriage, a gliding gait and freedom of movement . . . Distinction of manner and bearing, that elegant quality of breeding that we so seldom remark nowadays, established an absolute line of caste among the different social clasess.[39]

The men, it will be admitted, clearly had the easier situation, despite carnivorous collars and tight strata of wool.

Still, however uncomfortable such clothing was for Europeans, it was more obviously torture for Cariocas, and, hence, a much more powerful statement. One morning in the Rio of 1908, say, when Figueiredo Pimentel was making recommendations for daytime use of gloves, the next day's temperature forecast was for 17.3° to 22°C. (i.e., 62° to 71°F.).[40] Moreover, this was mid-winter. Picture, then, the daily agony of dressing as has been described in Rio.

The *cidade velha*, where elite men spent the day's hottest hours, and where elite women came to join them for several hours in the afternoon, was a teeming, narrow-streeted, odiferous port town, thick with the humidity of the tropics, a city where the offices were cramped, thick, colonial *sobrados* divided up into workspace. And the summer! Though the women and children escaped to Petrópolis, think of the *diários* forced to battle in the old city each day, before the evening retreat to the mountains. They worked through the tropical, vaporous, fever-ridden summer in stolid black English wool. A Parisian journalist observed the carnage in 1890 and filed this report:

> Under a killing climate, in a town where the thermometer attains 40°C [104°F] in the shade at times, where the rays of the sun are, in summer, so broiling that one dies in a flash, the Brazilian stubbornly continues to live and to dress himself in the European manner. He works during the hottest hours of the day; he goes to his office from nine to four o'clock, like the London businessman; he walks about in a black frockcoat, capped with a tophat. imposing martyrdom on himself with the most perfect lack of concern.[41]

Perhaps the perfect lack of concern was *para francês ver.* When Pereira Passos was still young and fit, he reported one summer's tribulations this way: "It has been 94°F. in my office; the endless sweating rids one of all desire to write. For three days so far I have limited myself to visiting the workshops, despite having important affairs to see to in the Côrte: I don't leave because I cannot work up the enthusiasm to get into my top coat."[42]

Nor was such martyrdom cheap. Even today, in an old city shop renting evening wear one can find the era's detritus: there, cutaways, striped pants, and top hats lie, a mournful monument to doughty dandies long dead. Even if famed local tailors put them together, the hats and cloth came from England, just as the Ouvidor *modistes* put their confections together with materials from France. Imported ready-mades, or imported cloth to be cut and sewn by prestigious fingers, were extravagances, more costly than if bought in Europe.[43]

Yet, they were worn; after all, they were Civilization. "Dress," Figueiredo Pimentel opined, "is the index by which we may reconstruct the usages and customs of peoples; we can recompose civilizations and understand and explain them in their glorious periods and in their depressing decadencies. . . . Fashion is a consequence of the moral state of an individual or of a people."[44] This theme, that one's dress was a reflection of one's level of civilization, is one of the principal motifs of "Binoculo."[45] That such opinions were common was obvious wherever the elite gathered:

All wear English cashmeres, thick, stiff, and very hot for a climate like ours, vests in which one drowns, very high collars and, not unusually, woolen . . . or satin ties, making an appearance in the "great artery" [the Rua do Ouvidor] from four until six, top hats, derbies, or boaters being tipped to the ladies, walking along in shoes from . . . Cadete or . . . the Incroyable, displaying shirts tailored for them in the Casa Coulon or bought ready-made in the Casa Dol.

The ladies coming from Largo da Carioca take Rua Gonçalves Dias, between . . . gentlemen who crowd the corners . . . their mustaches with fine points, waxed with pomade *hongroise* or Kaiser-style in vertical spouts . . . They smoke *bout doré* cigarettes and use perfumes on their handkerchiefs and hair, carrying *papier poudre* in their pockets to lessen the sweat on their faces, drenched in the heat.

The women dress in long, full skirts, thick with underskirts, displaying tiny wasp waists . . . thrown into relief by corsets. All have long hair, piled high on the head and on which balances a hat . . . They wear taffeta, [and] merino . . . boots buttoned or tied high, and always carry a silk or gauze fan in a well-gloved hand. They wear no makeup . . . Carioca women are figures of ivory or wax . . . When they pass in groups, they remind one of a procession of cadavers.[46]

It was considered a scandal when a group of physicians tried to change matters, and put on white suits of light material, more appropriate for the climate.[47] The point of dark, heavy clothing was too clearly understood. Distinctly European, it signified aristocracy, civilization, and, *ipso facto*, one's superior rank in Carioca society, and thus enjoyed a sacrosanct prestige, proof against all pain. A contemporary later confided:

I ask myself: How did they bear the heat? . . . Years after, I saw Quintino Bocaiuva in Rio . . . at the corner of the Rua do Ouvidor, wearing a topcoat of heavy material and gloves. . . . In Pernambuco, we . . . Faculty students dressed with frockcoats. . . . At . . . the *Diário de Pernambuco* Aníbal Freire never arrived except with frockcoat and top hat. How did we manage this? In my time in Pernambuco, except for common people, I never saw, anyone with light clothing . . . A well-to-do family was distinguished by the thickness of the cloth that it wore.[48]

Another contemporary declares that anyone "who courageously attempted, even in the vigor of the most raging summer, to cross our streets dressed in white clothing, even if of good cloth and cut, would be booed or taken for a madman."[49] The fantasy investment in this commodity, its fetishization, was too great to admit compromise. So the elite, in black wool topcoats and vests, in narrow corsets and thick skirts, endured the swelter, satisfyingly European, satisfyingly distinct from the darker, cooler poor who went about half-naked, openly proclaiming uncouth inferiority.

Expensive French prostitutes

The fetishism involved in Carioca prostitution is just as clear a case of fantasy projection. This is as patent in the national ranking of available prostitutes as it is in the sexual dynamics implicit in one's choice, dynamics fired by the hypocrisy characterizing sexual relations within the elite.

Like their counterparts in Europe, Carioca elite youths successfully made domestics and poor women in general the sexual targets for bribes or threats. Indeed, the supposed sexual availability of women of color, vulnerable as slaves or dependants, was a prejudice so deeply worked into the fabric of society that it persists today.[50] Once a man grew up or came to town, however, he had other choices, and fantasies, in his sexual repertoire. In a culture where extramarital relations for men were assumed, he did not hesitate to play.

During the century's first half, women immigrants from the Azores, working as domestics and shopgirls, were often forced into common prostitution by poverty.[51] In the 1820s, as noted earlier, French women became available, and, with them, the choices allowing an analysis of cultural taste. The French *modistes* and shopgirls to whom I refer took clients from the elite who frequented the Rua do Ouvidor and who could pay well for such carnal commerce. That the elite were interested, however, is the point.[52] One must note that this was not a racial preference for whites rather than blacks, for the elite had the Azoran women available, too. Was it, then, the exoticism of non-Portuguese-speaking women that proved attractive? The next generation of prostitutes argues against exoticism, and suggests that it was the Frenchwoman, *per se*, that was attractive in these prostitutes.

Two distinct elements emerged betwen 1840 and 1870. The first, mentioned earlier, was the establishment of dance halls, *cafés cantantes*, and the Alcazar theater, places offering French sirens for sexual hire, tropical variations on the famous themes of Rachel and Blanche d'Antigny.[53] The second element was less glamorous. In 1867, the first *polacas* arrived; such women, often Jews, came from Eastern Europe and made up the majority sold into the infamous white slave trade to South America.[54]

Now, both the French women and the *polacas* were exotic, yet their ranking was obvious to the Carioca – sex with a white woman was not the issue, nor sex with someone exotic in the Portuguese world – sex with women who had French *cachet* was. *Polacas* were the commodity for the middle sectors' poorer extremes and for sailors; Frenchwomen were merchandise for the elite. Distinct milieux suggest the fetishism in question. *Polacas*, like prostitutes of color, suffered in the bordellos of the "red-light" districts of the *cidade velha*: around Praça Tiradentes and the Campo de Santana, and the streets Sete de Setembro, Treze de Maio, Senador Dantas, Mangue, etc. Such women walked the streets or, more likely, displayed their bodies from windows; perhaps, as Pires de Almeida has it, with a parrot perched there to make a lewd sales pitch.[55] They were "run" by entrepreneurs, often Jews as well, who promised husbands and new lives in the Americas to the impoverished women of the Russian Pale, then raped them and sent them on to the brothels of Rio and Buenos Aires.[56]

Though Frenchwomen (generally recognized as the most lucrative commodity)[57] sometimes came by way of white slave organizations, many apparently operated on their own or through local madames or theatrical procurers. As an actress, café entertainer, or a more obvious cocotte, they chose those locales and styles that capitalized on the established fantasies that made them so attractive in the first place. In effect, like other imported commodities (and the prostitutes of Paris' Palais Royal area), they were established luxuries of the European center of town. Such women joined their admirers not only at theater or café, but in the prestigious restaurants and hotels of the Ouvidor. Indeed, the Ouvidor hotels, boasting French names and the pleasures of the table, were considered little more than chic bordellos. By the late nineteenth century, fancier brothels staffed with such women were celebrated (often as "*pensions d'artistes*"), and their patronage conferred prestige, so much so that their madames became celebrities and their parlors clubs to which the Republic's Senators were quite pleased to belong.[58]

The cocottes' attractions derived not only from studied association with Parisian paradigms, but from the contrast they made with the perception of elite Carioca women. As has been mentioned, elite Frenchwomen sometimes approximated the *demi-monde* in behavior. During the Second Empire, some did so in their flirtatious style; throughout the century, many did so in dress and the promiscuity of their private lives.[59] However, as discussed earlier, anything like this was distinctly foreign to expected Carioca elite comportment. Sexual promiscuity in the elite home was notorious, but excluded white women. Elite youths dealt circumspectly with white girls: they kept their distance, wooing discreetly with signals and glances at family dances or weekly mass. Kissing between fiancés was scandalous, and a promenade without a chaperone from the woman's household was unheard of. Women, save for ritualized afternoons on the Ouvidor and *visitas* to other "respectable" women, kept to home save for formal functions; only the men went out at night.[60]

Certainly, when women did go out, there should be nothing of the *cocodette* about them. The cocottes' style was well known, and one took pains to avoid it and to maintain the silence, respect, and company tradition demanded. The *alto mundo* was a small world in which one was under observation; if one drew attention to oneself, reprimand was sure to follow. As one advice columnist suggested, even ostentatious and modishness could taint: "I can never repeat often enough that in the street simplicity is the enchanting distinction of good taste and high society; costly dresses in loud colors and pretentious jewels are for the dubious women who live from scandal and need to call public attention to themselves."[61]

If, then, one did break away from the sexual propriety expected (and some surely did) one undertook the most elaborate subterfuges to safeguard one's reputation. One tradition for the wayward involved go-betweens, rented rooms in the *cidade velha*'s notorious streets, and furtive midnight use. The continued tension about elite women's adultery in the *belle époque* is clear in the fiction and memoirs – it happened, but was clearly regarded as scandalous or decadent.[62]

In contemporary Europe, sexual tension and activity were more diffuse in the elite expectations of women. This is clear, for example, in fashionable painting. Take Giovanni Boldini, one of the era's pre-eminent society painters;[63] he displays both blatant conventions of male fantasy to convey feminine sexuality and subtle painterly conventions to convey a continuum of sexual potential between *demi-monde* and Society ladies.

The sexuality and blatant conventions are obvious in Boldini's examples of seemingly genteel pornography. The cocottes in these are naked – to use Hollander's distinction[64] – they have clothing or bedsheets falling away from their legs, and with their horizontal positions, pubic hair, spread thighs, and out-thrust breasts and buttocks, suggest the uses to which they were put.[65]

Boldini's continuum and subtle conventions in portraits are, in some ways, more interesting. Society ladies are barely distinguished by their poses and facial signals from actresses, singers, and other subjects conventionally available sexually. The ladies face one calmly, with a light smile at best and a direct glance either to the viewer or to the distance, their hands busy with tasteful accoutrements, and the tactile possibilities of their décollatages muted by the use of light, which often erases cleavages and emphasizes, rather, expensive toilettes.[66] Sexual attraction is indirect; one is drawn by discreet, possibly unattainable beauty, breeding, and wealth, where cautious wooing and one's station must be brought to bear.

The "available" women are proclaimed by the invitation of their smiles or laughter, sidelong, or very direct, looks, deeply shadowed cleavages, and arms raised away from the body to show the path to a caress. Here, then, were women whose social position had to be made plain by artifices showing them as indiscreet, interested women, with whom a bit of charm, words, and money might suffice.[67]

The reason I write "had to be made plain" is central. Parisian Society was apparently such that these conventional artifices were necessary to distinguish the "type" of woman, since both *demi-mondaines* and ladies mixed in Society, dressed in the same style, and, in some cases, were available. Indeed, with some of Boldini's aristocrats, only the title clarifies the "type". The distinctions have dissolved, perhaps tribute to the portraitist's candor.

Contrast the relative subtlety and diffusion of sexual roles such paintings suggest with the harsh oppositions demanded in Rio. There, the same perceptions of women influenced tastes through the European images that suffused Carioca books and newspapers, and the Parisian holidays and illustrated magazines subscribed to that helped to make up the elite style of life.[68] Yet, of the "good" and the "bad" women in Rio, surely it was the latter in whom either of Boldini's extremes melded, the woman who best fulfilled the elite man's sexual fantasies.

Their own women (bound by familial constraints and de-sexualized by traditions ascribing carnal passion solely to coitus with subordinated women of color) must have seemed tidy shrines of domestic virtue, where one worshipped and, almost uneventfully, begat heirs, but did not linger. The *demi-mondaines*, though, embodied not only the fetish of an expensive Parisian commodity, but one suffused with that elegant sexuality which neither elegant wives nor Rio's brutalized *polacas* could match. Something of this is captured in this memoir of the most notorious of the Alcazar actresses:

> . . . the famous Mlle. Aimée very graciously ruined many admirers . . .
>
> As the fortunes of her admirers, who in that time were called *paios*, were not, in general, extraordinarily great, because great fortunes in Brazil were still rare . . . Aimée soon liquidated them and, having ruined these men, continued to give them a place at her table as a consolation prize, preserving them in this way at her side as witnesses to and aids in her task of plucking new birds, who succeeded one another in rapid succession.
>
> I knew two of these plucked fellows, whose greatest concern in the afternoon was the elegance of their dress and arriving on time for dinner at the . . . Rua dos Ciganos . . . *chez la belle*; they would not trade this for the best party, for the most replete banquet, since there they would not be under the dominion of the eye, the voice, the enchantment of that fantastic being.[69]

Beyond the strong sexual–cultural contrast such a woman presented was another: the cultural, *per se.* For elite wives were only more or less successful facsimiles of Frenchwomen. The Alcazar actress and her colleagues *were* Frenchwomen; they could teach the refinements of civilization which one craved.[70] The passion for such women, then, demonstrates the particular fetishism of the Carioca in any number of ways that, when joined, were powerful indeed.

4. Conclusion: fantasy knit to reality – reality knit to fantasy

The fetishism apparent in Carioca consumerism sharply discloses the fantasy central to so much of the elite culture and society analyzed in earlier pages. Here, in private choices made in public places about intimate aspects of one's existence – personal consumption, clothing, and sexual preferences – one sees again the identification with aristocratic Franco–English paradigms as an essential element in elite culture and society, the red thread traced in every previous chapter.

What generally varies is the socio-economic capacity for successful replication of the paradigms. The felt need to express and promote one's position in Carioca society by means of such replication is constant. As has been noted, this tendency is obvious, if weakly realized, in colonial society; it simply increases in strength of expression over the course of history to the florescence of the neo-colonial context, with its greater wealth and communication. By the Carioca *belle époque*, the fantasy of European identification was knit to the elite's Carioca reality of domination. It was the parallel of a larger paradox – the reality of Brazil's neo-colonial relations with the North Atlantic being knit to the fantasy of a universal Franco–English culture, the fantasy of Civilization.

These three particular examples of public demonstration of that Civilization are especially jarring, however, because they are inserted so deftly into one's intimate world. In moving back and forth easily between private experience and public expression, they emphasize the ubiquity and importance of Europhile culture in elite life. One's expression of one's taste and position in the Rua do Ouvidor was informed by European paradigms, as was one's choice of public and self-image in clothing and the projection of one's sexual desires.

This is, often, a more telling pattern of choice than that obvious in the elite home. There, one may recall, one finds a private/public dichotomy in the organization of domestic space. In décor and the use of various rooms, one finds a more European style for more public, formal use and a more traditional style for more private. Thus, the presence of European culture in the home might be ascribed to the idea of "show": it served as a public, instrumental demonstration of superior status, and might seem simply functional.

One cannot say this as easily regarding the phenomena in this chapter. Though they were shown and served a purpose in the showing, they make up too personal a selection not to suggest how profoundly permeated Cariocas were with a fetishization of Franco–English aristocratic values. This was a Europhile fantasy so closely woven into the elite fabric that it cannot be picked apart without unraveling the whole.

To mob daily into one thin, short street full of expensive bric-à-brac, over-priced cloth, and hot, expensive cafés and restaurants; to wear those clothes with such sweaty, steady devotion; to discriminate so obviously in one's lovemaking is to make manifest the internalization of this fantasy and to point the way to the reality of its meaning. A fantasy so deeply internalized is the stuff in which a vision of the world is obvious. Carioca consumer fetishism discloses the wholeness of the world whose separate levels all these pages have torn apart for analysis. It makes clear the place Civilization had in the Carioca *belle époque*, as the central ideology of domination and identity. Now we turn to its explicit expression.

6

The literary *belle époque* in Rio
The end of the Brazilian nineteenth century

The strengthening fantasy of Civilization central here is most dramatic in the elite's high culture, to which we now turn. Though the points to be made could be found in the fine arts, we will explore literature. This is not for lack of interest in the arts, but for the clarity and texture offered our analysis in the case of letters.

An analysis of music, for example, would necessarily touch on a social complexity taking us far afield from the Carioca elite, our central preoccupation here. Nineteenth-century Brazilian music, after all, was replete in popular motifs, techniques, and evolving renditions. For, unlike literature in Brazil's largely illiterate society, music was accessible to all Brazilians, and the mass's influence was pervasive and rich, whether in the various incarnations of, say, the *modinha*, rooted in the colonial past, or in the new music of nineteenth-century elite salons, such as the Brazilian tango. Even were one to consider the refinements of such Europeanized *belle époque* Brazilian composers as Alberto Nepumuceno (1864–1920) or Ernesto Nazaré (1863–1934), who looked to the concert piano repertoire for inspiration, their milieu and (European) Romantic preoccupation with native themes necessarily touched their works with the "exotica" of Afro-Brazilian popular culture. As for the work of Heitor Villa-Lobos (1887–1959), its characteristically successful adaptation of Brazilian musical tradition is announced in the *choros* of his earliest published work, *Suite popular brasileira* (1908–12). Yet, to repeat, if one wished, the strengthening fantasy of Civilization could be traced on the other side of this coin. Although popular influence made it richer and more complex, an abiding quality of the music that the *elite* cultivated was the steady increase in European influence. From the mid-century salon music of polkas and *schottisches* (so influential in the development of the popular *choro*) to the Franco-Cuban *havaneiras* and French musical review songs of later decades (crucial to the tango and popular *maxixe*), many of them introduced in the Alcazar Lyrique

Français, the musical prestige and encroachment of Europe was pervasive. Obviously, in the "higher" forms, the opera and chamber music, enjoyed in the Teatro Lírico or, say, the Club Beethoven, Europe's domination was even clearer. Here, of course, was the elite ambience within which men like Nepumuceno and Nazaré wrote. A more extreme, but indicative, case was that of [Antônio] Carlos Gomes, the era's great musical figure, whose consecration, for example, was possible only in Verdi's Italy, where his *Il Guarany* (with its Italian libretto) triumphed at La Scala (1870). Thus, although popular influence might meld with it, the stages and progressively stronger quality of European musical influence would be familiar to the reader from earlier pages.[1]

This pattern is even more marked in painting. Indeed, while music quickened with the creative sensibilities of the Carioca masses, painting, to an extent qualitatively distinct even from literature, reflected solely the increasing influence of France. Our reason for pursuing literature, instead, has to do with the latter's telling contradictions. As we shall see, Brazilian writers went beyond derivative origins to failure and success at making a *Brazilian* literature; this is what makes literary history more interesting to explore here. Art historians rarely grant such independent tendencies to Brazilian painting of the period. This is so not simply because of the hegemonic Eurocentric schooling institutionalized by the French Artistic Mission of 1816 in the Escola de Belas Artes (1826). It was also because of the dependence of the very small group of Côrte artists on the patronage of a traditional, academically minded elite, as well as the artists' training and long years of experience in the Parisian *ateliers* of only the most accepted academic masters. The great works of the century, whether of French *émigrés* like Nicolas-Antoine Taunay (1755–1830) or Adrien-Aimé Taunay (1803–28), or of frenchified Brazilians like Vitor Meireles [de Lima] (1832–1903), Pedro Américo [de Figueiredo e Melo] (1843–1905), Rodolfo Amoeda (1857–1914), Henrique Bernadelli [1858–1936], and Eliseu [d'Angelo] Visconti (1866–1944), flourished in the academic genres of portraits, classical allegories, heroic or edifying historical or biblical scenes, or allegorical nudes. Their achievements were and are measured according to the European standards they and their patrons assumed. The tension between Brazilian milieu and French technique in this era of painting, save, perhaps, for the isolated successes of [José Ferraz de] Almeida Júnior (1850–99), is not rich enough for the kind of analysis one can make for literature. There, this tension, the expression of explicit values and perspectives, and the impact of the elite audience allow us a useful concluding discussion for these pages. Indeed, only the architecture of the Avenida Central, perhaps, is so evocative of the Carioca elite's *belle époque* as the period's literature, whose important links with the style of life and cultural assumptions analyzed in earlier chapters is manifest.[2]

As with painting and elite musical tastes, Brazilian literature was associated primarily with Rio either in origin or in diffusion. As I will show, the Côrte and, then, the Federal Capital performed the role most national capitals did in nineteenth-century literary history. The greater poverty of provincial cities in Brazil only strengthened the appeal of the political, social, and economic center of the nation. To be accepted as a man of letters meant to live, or, at the very least, to publish in Rio.[3] The work published, naturally, always formed an important element in the capital's elite milieu. As has been seen, the education a member of the elite received was classical, with great literary emphasis. To know literature, especially French literature, was the mark of someone properly brought up. Hence familiarity with letters, adolescent verse, and an enduring respect for literati were common to those in, or aspiring to, the Carioca elite.[4] What the years with governesses and *colégios* promoted was often seconded by the Church. The traditional pleasure in a good sermon was reflected in the perennial strengths of Brazilian letters – poetry, declamation, theater, and oratory.[5] This narrow, fertile milieu will be the subject here. Not so much in literary analysis *per se*, as in the analysis of the values and the social history in which literature and men of letters played a part. First, however, I must put the *belle époque* in literary and historical context, to show how the period was, as in so much else, the culmination of social and cultural trends.

THE COURSE OF NINETEENTH-CENTURY LITERATURE

1. The role of France

The reader who has come this far may have assumed France's dynamic influence over Brazilian letters. The roots for this, once again, thrust into the eighteenth century. Just as Portugal found delight and instruction in the French Enlightenment, so did the colony. Higher education under the enlightened despotism of José I's minister, the Marquis de Pombal, crowned earlier trends. From the creation of French-style academies, Portugal went on to reform the University of Coimbra and set up enlightened *colégios*. Royal patronage, Pombal's support, diplomatic and student voyages, and the wealth born of Brazilian gold and precious stones fostered a Francophile era in literature which only gained strength with the nineteenth century. Brazil, too, enjoyed academies, and, although these flourished and faded quickly, some of the colony's elite and middle sectors picked up an enduring taste for French literature fostered at the Viceroy's court at Rio, the reformed school at Olinda, or at Coimbra, Paris, and Lisbon, where the wealthy often sent their sons for education and proper connections.[6]

This tradition explains the natural quality of early nineteenth-century interest in French literature. This was strengthened, however, by the same circumstances reinforcing French cultural influences in schooling, architecture, fashion, furniture, and the rest: the Arrival of the Court in 1808. João VI's Rio, as has been shown, became a haven for many French *émigrés* and the goal of the French Artistic Mission of 1816. Together, they provided a singularly well-connected French colony which helped make early French Romanticism fashionable in Rio.[7] Thus, cultural tradition and French residents alike predisposed the first generation of Brazilian literati to look to France. Indeed, the initially rather reflexive nature of their story seems almost too tidy. For a century and more, a similar, if increasingly complex, relationship would prevail of influence, inspiration, and adaptation. As with so much in these pages, fashions changed, but the elite affair with France continued passionate.

2. Romanticism: literary mission

The formulae of French Romanticism fired the imaginations and ambitions of Brazilian writers for obvious reasons. Calling for a national literature derived from folk traditions, relishing untamed nature, and dwelling on the particularities of each people's past, Romanticism was especially appealing to the Brazilian generations that witnessed the new Empire's consolidation. Matters were actually initiated by a kind of Franco-Brazilian proto-Romanticism in which French voyagers or *émigrés* wrote essays or novels in response to the Brazil they found. The most important of these precursors was Ferdinand Denis (1788–1846), who, after youthful travels in the Portuguese empire, attempted to distinguish a Brazilian literary tradition from the Portuguese, and noted the Brazilian elements propitious for the Romantic endeavor. He wrote of the singular glories of the country's past and national character, and of the exotic grandeur of its setting. Thus, a Frenchman introduced the Amerindian and the tropical forest to the Brazilian Romantics.[8]

The first Romantics declared themselves and their mission in Paris, where, under the influence of both French and Portuguese Romantics, a few banded together and published a short-lived review, *Niterói*

(1836).[9] Afterward, some followed Denis and began cataloguing colonial literature to order the tradition from which the national literature could grow. Others defined the ideology of literary mission, explaining literature's central role in the nation's Progress and Civilization. This idea stressed the necessity of each nation having a literature, since the national literature was the nation's soul, memory, and conscience. Still others wrote the first Romantic poetry and novels of Brazil. It was all of these men, writing generally in newspapers or short-lived literary reviews, who quite self-consciously constructed the first essentially Brazilian literature.[10]

The second Romantic generation was led by men whose names remain resonant: the novelists José [Martiniano] de Alencar (1829–72) and Joaquim Manuel de Macedo (1820–82), for example, or the poets [Antônio] Gonçalves Dias (1823–64) and [Antônio] Castro Alves (1847–71) crowned Romanticism with its finest works. Alencar did so with popular novels, in which Denis' Indianist theme played a powerful role. In *O Guaraní* (1857) and *Iracema* (1865), Alencar realized the promise of early Romanticism and helped found the Brazilian prose tradition: he died acknowledged chief of Brazilian letters. Others, Macedo and Manuel Antônio de Almeida (1831–61), for example, had won success with novels of bourgeois Carioca life, and, indeed, Alencar wrote such works as well. However, the Romantic nationalism that pulsed strong in the reading public found the Tupís and tropical jungle of the Empire more seductive than what could be worked up about mundane, Europeanized realities in the Côrte.[11]

3. Determinism: science and progress

Romanticism owed much to the German response to French classicism and the traumas of 1789–1815. Its historicism, mingled and submerged within English empiricism and the influence of the Industrial Revolution's manifest triumphs, permeated the milieu in which the great thinkers of the second and third quarters of the century worked. These men, Auguste Comte (1798–1857), Ernest Renan (1823–92), and Hippolyte Taine (1828–93), along with Charles Darwin (1809–82), Herbert Spencer (1820–1903), and Ernst Haeckel (1834–1919), dominated the intellectual horizons of Europe and Latin America, establishing the materialism, positivism, scientism, and evolutionism that provided the literary infrastructure of "modern" notions from which new authors derived much of their power. The Realism of Balzac (1799–1850) and Flaubert (1821–80) emerged in the century's second third, and, then, in the last, Naturalism and Zola (1840–1902) triumphed in the monumental "Rougon-Macquart" series (1869–93) and its international following. Religion and idealism were disdained now as metaphysical remnants of a benighted past, Romantic writing and criticism as overdone, vague, idealistic, and out of touch with scientific progress. Literature and criticism should be objective and scientific, to engage in the dissection of the harshest realities of society. From such would come the liberating destruction of retarding institutions and the possibility of progressive reform.[12]

It was in this way, too, that Brazilian literati understood the age. Again, as with Romanticism, this diffuse ideological revolution had particular ramifications for the Empire. Naturalism dominated novelists from the Amazon to Rio to São Paulo, men like [Herculano Marcos] Inglês de Sousa (1853–1918) and Aluísio [Tancredo Gonçalves de] Azevedo (1857–1913), men admiring not only Zola, but his Portuguese disciple, Eça de Queirós (1845–1900). There was also the rise of spectacular Parnassian poets, such as Olavo [Braz Martins dos Guimarães] Bilac (1865–1918), whom we met celebrating the Avenida Central, and Alberto de Oliveira (d. 1937), both patient shapers of perfect phrasing.[13]

Just as important was the dramatic shift in critical thought. A generation, many of whom later presided over the culture of the Carioca *belle époque*, looked to European scientism (generally in its French or German version) to break with the Church and French Eclecticism, dominant in the Empire, and to criticise the Second Reign's institutions, principally slavery and the monarchy, as retrograde. This generation, *a geracão de setenta* (the Generation of 1870), was often associated with the iconoclast Tobias Barreto [de Menezes] (1839–89), whose influence at the Faculty of Law at Recife around 1870 gave to his particular followers the name *a escola de Recife* (the School of Recife). This generation's influence, triumphant in the Côrte, was felt throughout urban Brazil in the movements for Abolition and for the Republic that wracked the Empire in the 1880s.[14]

4. *Fin de siècle:* consumption and antagonism

The socio-political importance of Naturalism and the nationalist significance of Romanticism have continued to attract the sympathetic attention of scholars from across the great divide of the Modernist movement of 1922. The period between, however, which is the most important to this discussion, has generally suffered from disdainful neglect. Heirs of the Modernists, recent readers and critics usually accept the Modernist condemnation of the Brazilian *fin de siècle* as affected and superficial, though critics note its occasionally anticipatory importance.[15] The era's greatest student, Brito Broca (1903–61), observed a characteristic which is apposite: the style of literary life and production then was often more important than the literature itself.[16] *Mundanismo*, the fashionable, Europhile way of life emphasized in these pages, saturated the literary world and subordinated literature. As will be seen, the figure an author cut in Society, as well as the way of life he portrayed, often determined his success with the narrow Carioca readership of the period. As one author bitterly confided, "it was the *moças brancas botafoganas daqui*" (the white Botafogan girls here) who sealed literary acceptance; the Carioca reader "asked only one thing of the author: position. . . ."[17]

That the readership of fashionable districts like Botafogo was interested in worldly literature and literati will not surprise the reader, who has seen earlier the increasing importance of such taste in every other aspect of elite life as well. As with so much else, the readers wooed by Brazilian authors had acquired tastes from travel and schooling that centered on Paris. In this case, the models dictating fashion were French authors who, like their Brazilian counterparts, are generally *passé* today. Some readers will recall Anatole France from among them, a writer and a wit whose reputation, for a generation, was unassailable; other names may be even less familiar now, though all were once very much in vogue – Pierre Loti, Edmond Rostand, Paul Bourget, Jean Lorraine, and Joris Karl Huysmans. In any case, it was the qualities characteristic of these writers' works – amorous intrigue, irony, decadence, and exoticism – that became the themes to conjure with in Carioca literature. By swimming in the French tide, many Brazilian literati produced works that served as just another aspect of the way of life cultivated by the elite: the light, exciting, fashionable *divertissements* that helped keep one *au courant* at tea, reception, or salon.[18] As Gilberto Amado remembers,

> Mundanismo and Aestheticism ruled, under the sign of Frivolity, not only society but literature as well. And even politics. To be *mundano* constituted a title, a reason for prestige. . . . Aestheticism and Mundanismo were the two wheels of the Byzantine chariot in which the flaccid athletes of frivolity exhibited themselves.[19]

Literature, then, was an integral aspect of the consumer fetishism and ideology of Civilization I have discussed. Yet, as will be explored, in literature and criticism, disjunctions and antagonism are always possible; they were certainly present in the Carioca *fin de siècle*. A more precise sense of how this *belle-époque* literary fetishism and disjunction emerged in relation to Carioca society will take up most of the analysis here. I turn first to the relations between the literati and the elite.

THE REPUBLIC OF LETTERS

5. Genteel marginality: the Romantics

The literati of the Romantic generations (c. 1820s–70s) formed only an allusive Republic of Letters. What institutionalization there was, was quite tenuous. These founders of a self-conscious Brazilian literary culture generally indulged in literary pursuits as a kind of part-time passion. Born to relative wealth and closely associated with the urban elite and middle sectors as liberal professionals and state bureaucrats, they had the education, contacts, and leisure to write and publish. Typically, they were the sons of educated planters or urban-based families and enjoyed a classical schooling, European education or travel, a professional degree, and a career in the bureaucracy, the Colégio Pedro II, the parliament, political journalism, and diplomacy. Their early years might involve some hardship, but only because they *chose* to eschew law or medicine to pursue the Muse. That they had the choice was a measure of their favored status. Many soon had the Emperor's favor, in sinecures and honors; a few finally received a title, like Maciel Monteiro, second baron de Itamaracá, or Gonçalves de Magalhães, viscount de Araguáia, Torres Homem, viscount de Inhomerim, and Araújo Porto-Alegre, baron de Santo Ângelo.[20]

One should note, however, that literature was not only the pastime of such dilettantes. For a few Romantics, it was also the path to advancement, for they were born poor, or illegitimate, or were men of color, or bore the stigma of some combination of these. Their education, won through sacrifice, disclosed the world of letters, their talent there, the way up and out of the ignominy to which their birth would have otherwise condemned them. Rather than obscure, despised existences, Romanticism offered the glory of being the nation's voices and the patronage that came with recognized literary talent. Thus, for those at the edge of privilege, literature appeared not only a pleasure, but a passageway.[21]

There were two great centers for the Romantics, one temporary, the other enduring. São Paulo, with its Faculty of Law, was often the testing ground of students who, after their *colégio* verse, went on to their *bachelarado* and *belles-lettres* in that provincial setting, forming a close-knit, idealistic corporation far more absorbed in literature than in law. Rio, the Empire's literary and political center, was where the acclaimed next went, as literary and political hopefuls.

The life that called to all these men was, alas, only what one could expect of mid-century Rio.[22] Antônio Cândido aptly calls the city *acanhado* (backward, narrow, timid) and the literary milieu matched it – a highly personalized, spatially restricted backwater. From its beginnings through to the *belle époque*, it had found its place around a short, narrow street – the Rua do Ouvidor – Rio's "outdoor salon."[23] I have shown how central Ouvidor was for fashionable life and luxury import consumption; its centrality for literature derived from the same impulses. Around Ouvidor were the ephemeral reviews and all the great newspapers, many founded or managed by immigrant Frenchmen – the *Jornal do Commercio* (1827), the *Correio Mercantil* (1848–68), and the *Diário do Rio de Janeiro* (1821–78) – all packed in narrow offices in old *sobrados de moradia.* Since most literati, facing a very restricted market, necessarily published their work in periodicals, they spent much of their time in the jostling, frock-coated world of gossip, printer's ink, and clubby *bonhomie* of this street's presses, cafés, and restaurants. It was also around Ouvidor that the few booksellers were established. As in the presses, here, too, Frenchmen dominated from early on, symbolic of the Parisian aspirations pervasive in this world.[24]

For the few great literati, bookshops were the altars of their consecration, for only the elect actually commanded the audience necessary to sell their works in book form. For most literati, such shops were simply the understood afternoon spots to gather, talk, read aloud, and make important contacts. Newspapers, however, served all, for all purposes; they beckoned to would-be politicians and would-be literati alike. The portal between favor and political and literary journalism was a narrow, but oft-traveled one; a man good with words would see the door of patronage open. Brought through by a patron, he found regular journalistic work for one party or the other, and, then, greater opportunities to write and publish or to secure election, appointment, or a ministerial sinecure. With talent and time, came a name, sinecures or opportunities improved and politicians might look to the Senate, while literati might look to the Colégio Pedro II or other honorable positions. The centrality of Ouvidor for literati, then, was wed to its centrality for the elite: it was a medium for those who were either using power or needed to serve power to advance.[25]

The case of [Joaquim Marial] Machado de Assis (1839–1908)

suggests much of this. Poor, mulatto, possessing little schooling, he learned to read at home and picked up French from a pastry cook, learning what he could in the girls' *colégio* where he sold sweets. For him, the only road to respectability was Ouvidor. He began as an adolescent, making contact with [Francisco de] Paula Brito (1809–61), another mulatto who had also begun poor at the edges of the literary world, and whose bookstore cum press two blocks from Ouvidor on the Rócio (now Praça Tiradentes) was a gathering point for young literati, journalists, and politicians. Perhaps from contacts there, Machado found work in the National Press; it was also in Paulo Brito's review, *A Marmota* (1849–61), that he began serious publishing, in 1855. At the National Press, he was the protégé of Manuel Antônio de Almeida, author of *O sargento de milícias* (1854–55), and recently appointed head of the press through patronage, in recognition of his literary laurels. Almeida promoted Machado at the press; Paula Brito hired Machado at *A Marmota.* The literary contacts made around Ouvidor then brought Machado work in a paper with powerful Liberal Party ties, and led, in time, to Machado's first bureaucratic rung and other official positions and honors. Ouvidor also brought Machado more opportunities to publish poetry, short stories, critical essays, and regular columns of personal observation (*crônicas*). By his mid-thirties, Machado was nearing the upper bureaucracy and was recognized as a great literary figure in the Côrte. He had also left terrible penury for the comforts of financial security and marriage to a Portuguese, D. Carolina de Novais, sister of a fellow poet. Machado had won this all on Ouvidor, up which he walked every working day, from the ministry where he worked, by the newspapers, bookstores, and cafés along its length, to the streetcar stop near its end, where he boarded to reach his home in a fashionable southern district. Similar, if less spectacular, lives of humble beginnings redeemed by literary success are glimpsed in the biographies of Teixeira e Sousa (1812–64), Joaquim Manuel de Macedo, and Manuel Antônio de Almeida.[26]

Although Ouvidor could achieve this in such extreme cases, it generally did not have to. Gentility of birth, excellent connections, assured careers, and imperial patronage were far more common, and they suggest that, if peripheral to the concerns of most elite careers, literature was essential to those of some elite members and an activity respected by all. The Emperor's benevolence, the links between Côrte politics, journalism, and literature, and the elite's literary formation ensured that, although literary life was marginal to elite society, among the Romantics it was not foreign or hostile to it. A youthful phase for many elite boys, a common recreation for elite women, and an adult passion for some elite men, it was a genteel and accepted endeavor.

6. Embattled marginality: the bohemians

Though the intellectual impact of scientism and the *geração de setenta* in Brazil was tremendous, their political influence on those supporting reform and a break with colonial traditions was formidable. Novels, poetry, and essays questioned slavery, the monarchy, provincialism, illiteracy, the plight of the poor, and the like. The Romantics had felt that by writing they helped to form the nation. Journalism aside, their literary efforts were usually apolitical, with the important exception of late Romantic abolitionism, exemplified by Castro Alves, who fired the movement posthumously with verse. The youthful literati who came of age in the 1870s and 1880s, however, were often entirely caught up in such movements. Moreover, unlike Romanticism, born in Paris and fostered in Rio and São Paulo, the new movements were not exclusively French in origin and found their first Brazilian strength in various provincial capitals. Again, however, the best provincials were invariably drawn to Rio, just as ideas born in England and Prussia were generally brought to Brazil after Parisian acceptance and in French translations.[27]

Carioca or provincial, these new men were characteristically both critical and combative. They were hungry to make a new world; in 1884, one confided to another

> I agree . . . with what you think about the deplorable mental and moral state of our country. . . . it is enough to glance at our journalism and literature, where an icy lack of animation paralyzes in us all ardent impetus and generous aspiration . . . the influences of the milieu are omnipotent; I believe, it is true, in the power of great men, whose genius and whose sovereign *will* can extend to galvanize the cadaver of indifference and, modifying the milieu and injecting new blood into men, [can bring about] . . . a new direction in matters. But when will we have our V[ictor] Hugo? Rio de Janeiro is an essentially mercantile city. Sciences, letters, arts, industry, government, politics, morality, religions, all ideas, all sentiments are subordinated to the *so much per cent* and to the daily exchange [rate].[28]

Such men would challenge this stagnant pragmatism with aspirations born of scientism. One writer recalled the ferment among Carioca students as new ideas began to spread from Recife and abroad:

> Comte and Spencer exercised great influence in the intellectual milieu . . . A breeze of liberty of thought ran through Brazil – doctrines were debated,

concepts established, schools [of thought] organized. A beautiful epoch! Thinkers hastened to battle – energetic, violent at times, but never rude.[29]

By 1875, the Côrte these youths knew had grown considerably from the Regency's seat or the newly flourishing port capital of mid-century, and so had its literary opportunities. The population had grown by a fourth (to 235,000 by 1870) and the number of readers had increased even more. By the 1880s, the first truly popular papers had begun – *Gazeta de Noticias*, 1875; *Gazeta da Tarde*, 1880; *Diário de Notícias*, 1885; *Cidade do Rio*, 1888; *O Paiz*, 1884 – tied to the urban politicization part of the Republican and Abolitionist movements. The literary world changed dramatically. Though periodicals had always been the chief medium of men of letters, they had never provided dependable employment for more than a few. Now it became possible to eke out a desperate living, and, thus, the means had emerged for a true bohemia: a life independent of established society and devoted completely to letters.[30]

During Romanticism, *a boêmia* flickered during a brief phase of one's literary apprenticeship. At São Paulo's law faculty, for example, many had only lived for literature, study, drinking and whoring. For most, however, this was a pleasant interlude just before securing the degree necessary for a "respectable" career. As such, this *paulista* bohemia continued after Romanticism, as a regular, accepted tradition.[31]

What emerged now in Rio was different. Though the Faculty of Medicine and the Politécnica provided some recruits, the literary life continued to focus on Ouvidor, whose newspapers, employing many of the literati, made possible a small corps of writers living exclusively for literature and reform politics. These bohemians, self-consciously living out the fantasies of their well-thumbed *Scènes de la vie de bohème*,[32] roomed together, staffed the mass-circulation papers, and charged café and *confeitaria* life with a new energy. They lived out a fantasy of the Paris of which they all dreamed, within the thin, pulsing artery of Ouvidor. They saw themselves as an embattled minority of selfless rebels, struggling for national regeneration by attacking the monarchy's moribund institutions and writing great, scandalous Naturalist novels and pure, chiseled Parnassian poetry. The age's great national movements and the aspirations of a literary generation joined; small wonder that, afterwards, none of these men forgot the decade or its hopes.[33]

With few exceptions, most of this generation came from the same favored backgrounds as most of their Romantic predecessors. Few poor autodidacts were recruited to this special poverty. The men searching for literary glory in *cidade velha* attics and chosen spots like the Café Londres, Cailteau's restaurant, and the Confeitaria Colombo, had *chosen* to abandon the expected comforts promised by law or medicine. They had classical schooling and a year or more of *faculdade* behind them. They were *boêmios* because they could be full-time literati in that way alone and because it was compelling as a form of literary self-identification.[34]

Men like José [Carlos] do Patrocínio (1854–1902), Olavo Bilac, [Henrique Maximiano] Coelho Neto (1864–1934), Aluísio Azevedo, [Sebastião Cícero] Guimarães Passos (1867–*c.* 1909), and [Francisco de] Paula Nei (d. 1897), perhaps the most famous bohemians, had all been born to families of relative wealth and status. Even Patrocínio, mulatto and illegitimate, had paternal support for his studies and a father-in-law behind his newspaper. Most were provincial by birth and early schooling, most were Republicans, all were Abolitionists and Francophiles. All wrote for the papers, attended political mass meetings, drank and ran after Ouvidor cocottes and actresses, and spent long hours in Ouvidor cafés and restaurants, going to one after another from late afternoon to early morning. There they made their reputations and reigned, rhyming, declaiming, gossiping, and debating their ideals and dreams.[35] Coelho Neto recalled how

> They went out to the theaters, for conversation at Garnier's [bookstore] or at the Deroche [café], or remained [at home] talking about the future, making literary plans – a great work of art that would shatter the indifference of a lazy public, a strong work, made with love and talent, the form well-studied, the analysis minute; a book magisterial in style that would cross the ocean and make the foreigner talk of the Fatherland and its artists.[36]

Patrocínio was their chief, foremost orator of Abolition, editor of the *Cidade do Rio*, and a propagandist of explosive imagery. Olavo Bilac was an acclaimed poet, perhaps chief of the Parnassians, and a lifelong journalist. Coelho Neto, a prolific stylist, later became a preeminent novelist and essayist. Aluisio Azevedo, most important of Brazil's Naturalists, wrote several novels, aspiring to be his nation's Zola. Guimarães Passos, Parnassian poet and humorist, remained an unrepentant symbol of bohemia until his premature death in middle age. Paula Nei went further – bohemian *par excellence*, no book bore his name; his reputation was defined by Ouvidor. He was famous for popular, personal epigrams and poetry, which he only recited at cafés. From there, however, his words flew down the street's length, a realm he thus dominated by a verbal facility extraordinary even among this tribe of poets and orators.[37]

These, then, were the men and the milieu dominant in literature just before the *belle époque*. Unlike the Romantics, often comfortably attached to the Second Reign and the Côrte elite, the bohemians and other literati of their generation placed themselves apart. The Romantics were marginal to the elite style of life and its values only to the extent that they valued writing serious literature. Even their tubercular poets died in imperial favor. Their generation was *ambitious* for integration into the elite, eagerly seeking out ministerial or diplomatic positions, prizing aristocratic titles and orders, taking part in salons and clubs, and restricting politics, if they had any, to participation in one of the two traditional parties.[38] The bohemians made serious literature and political movements their only concern and identified with the marginal existence such foci ensured. Even older, staid members of this generation, such as Joaquim Nabuco (1849–1910), or Sílvio [Vasconcelos da Silveira Ramos] Romero (1851–1914), José Veríssimo [Dias de Matos] (1857–1916), and another old acquaintance, Rui Barbosa (1849–1923), who, like the Romantics, made a living in more "respectable" styles (as professors, deputies, and lawyers) were still embattled and marginal to the extent that they, like the bohemians, attacked the monarchy's basic institutions and worked for the *pátria*'s regeneration as a "modern" nation.[39] Veríssimo later recalled the 1880s in this way:

> Ten years ago there arose a literary movement that, perhaps having its origin in the north, was concentrated and developed here, producing a new generation like no other since our Romanticism . . . a great social concern, the emancipation of the slaves, justly motivated all spirits. Literature and poetry, to their honor, put themselves at the service of a cause of which one may speak with pleasure.[40]

That Veríssimo spoke only of Abolition, omitting the Republic, is suggestive. This generation's triumph was ambiguous. The decade between Abolition (1888) and Campos Sales' administration (1898–1902) represents its agony. Not because Abolition and the Republic did not materialize, but because of the results when they did. Abolition brought emancipation, but no great regeneration by socio-economic reform; the Republic brought the centralized monarchy's end and the emergence of new regional political power, but no new democratization or direction. Thus, among those who had been the young or middle-aged literati of the 1880s, there was typically a disappointment with political participation and a sense of failure regarding their role in changing society. Along with Machado de Assis (a member of the last

Romantic generation), it would be these disillusioned men who now presided over the culture of the Carioca *belle époque*.

7. Repectable *littérateurs*: the Academy

The conflicts and repressions of 1889–97 dissolved the classic bohemia of the 1880s through attacks on newspapers and the exile of dissidents, just as it divided and embittered the literary world, separating monarchists from Republicans and *florianistas* from the rest. Some literati enjoyed occasional or steady employment within the successive administrations. Others lost their positions forever, or held aloof, faithful to the old dynasty or disgusted with the realities of the Republic. For all, however, the period was a watershed. Most accepted marginalization from the struggle for national regeneration and sought, instead, to piece together a secure (that is, a bourgeois) way of life, while maintaining their identity as creators of the national culture.[41] Most suggestive of these trends was the founding (1897) and nature of the Academia Brasileira de Letras.

The Academy was not the first attempt at founding an organization serving Francophile savants or the interests of the literati. The historicist elements in European Romanticism bore fruit in France's Institut Historique by the 1830s, and had, among the Brazilian Romantics, spurred creation of the Instituto Histórico e Geográfico Brasileiro, in 1838. Enjoying Pedro II's patronage and a distinguished membership of *titulares*, it was sturdy, although a bit sterile – more a club for elite dilettantes and antiquarians than an intellectual or literary institution. It survived the years, though, while various literary associations that increasingly sprang up or were proposed did not. Machado de Assis participated in nearly all of them, as each surfaced and burst in the small pond of literary activity. Now, a prematurely old man in his late fifties, Machado was elected president of yet another.[42]

Machado was an obvious choice for his colleagues, and one that has symbolic significance here. It seemed obvious to literati, because Machado was at the apex of his exceptional career. By 1896, he had published three volumes of poetry, four of short prose pieces, and six novels, and had filled periodicals with fiction and columns for over four decades. Indeed, for two of them, he had been a principal, and, finally, the predominant figure in Carioca letters. In picking Machado, his colleagues dramatically formalized the homage widely paid the doyen of Brazilian writers.[43] The symbolism here derives from Machado's politics and social position, which represent the retreat from active engagement and thirst for security common, again, among the literati.

Machado, the reader will remember, had made his way in life through literature and patronage to the tenuous security of the bureaucratic *cursus honorum*. His image as a man cool to political (or any) passion, particularly Abolition, has been ably disputed. Machado first attracted Liberal patronage by his political journalism, after all, and his devoted biographers point to many occasions where the journalist was politically outspoken. They can also show how this mulatto clearly associated himself with Abolition. Still, Machado did both in the style of his generation and with the caution of a writer without dependable resources save his bureaucratic salary. A Liberal monarchist, Machado expressed opinions with an increasing reserve born of illness, disillusion, and maturity as he rose, and as the new generation's polemics destroyed the Second Reign political gentility to which he had been accustomed. Under the Republic, he was circumspect indeed. He was no rich man's son of independent means or professional options. He was a bureaucrat who served Liberal and Conservative, *florianista* and *paulista*, indifferently, with a nicety and skill rewarded by near ministerial responsibilites. He reserved convictions and passions for his literature, his wife and her family, and his friends – the means and the ends which had made a great man out of the little mulatto boy who had sold sweets to schoolgirls and learned his French in a bakery. He had survived, he had published, he had prevailed.[44] The Academy was set up very much in his image.

The Academy sprang from one of the regular literary gatherings commonly associated with Carioca periodicals. In the course of the turbulent 1890s, José Veríssimo, provincial Naturalist, esteemed essayist, and critic, began a third phase (1895–99) of the *Revista Brasileira* and recruited the best writers to contribute.[45] Some had already been meeting in an Ouvidor bookstore; now, these and the others all began to meet in the crowded offices of the review, just off Ouvidor, for afternoon talk and tea. In the decade's bitter milieu, these meetings were exceptional, in that they were apolitical. The memoirs make much of the fact that monarchists like Joaquim Nabuco, the Viscount de Taunay, and Carlos de Läet sat and chatted with Republicans like Patrocínio, Lúcio de Mendonça, and Coelho Neto. By 1896, the decision was taken to found an institution modeled on the Académie Française de Lettres and to attempt to secure government support. Government support was problematic and piecemeal through the first decade or so, but the Academy itself assembled in 1897, with all the pomp and circumstance threadbare conditions allowed. When Veríssimo's review failed, they continued to meet, moving from one office to another, depending on where members could arrange matters best. And the institution survived.[46]

Though sparsely attended, the Academy commanded enough prestige early on to draw fire from those excluded and public criticism from disgruntled members over its activities, lack of activities, and elections. Its members were illustrious in letters, many were from illustrious families. The forty "Immortals" took their number from Richelieu's institution and also adapted its ritual of chairs passed from holder to holder, by naming their chairs after "founders," thus instantly fabricating their chairs' literary pedigree. They also followed the French usage of the welcome and acceptance of new members by speeches commemorating successors and predecessors. These academic customs underscore what the inaugural speeches made explicit – that this was an organization *à la française*, created to strengthen literary tradition, maintain linguistic purity, and promote in the new-born nation respect for literary accomplishment and encouragement for a truly national literature.[47]

Machado, for example, spoke of the necessity for unity in Portuguese usage in a new era of political decentralization, and added "the baptism of your chairs now with well-known and lamented names from national fiction, poetry, criticism, and oratory is indicative that tradition is your primary desire."[48] Nabuco, speaking of political differences among literati, argued

> we part from opposite points . . . but like stars that are born, some to the west and others to the east, we have to pass through the same circle . . . thus the cycle is common to us, the social milieu that bends the most rebellious and weighs down the most refractory; there are the interstices of role, of character, of group and literary school, of each of us; there is the invincible good faith of true talent. The usefulness of this company will be . . . in proportion to its results for the approximation, or better, the meeting . . . of these contrary ideals, the suspension of reciprocal fears in the name of a common admiration.[49]

Nabuco added, hopefully, that

> We do not yet have a great national work [of literature], though I think that the Brazilian soul is defined, framed, and expressed in the works of her writers; it is just that it is not all in one work . . . Let us hope that the Academy might be a force for isolation, and that from its repose, from its calm, might emerge the work in which [is present] . . . the sign of literary sinew, of strength.[50]

The heroic overtures of Romanticism and Parnassianism were thus sounded, if in muffled tones. There were the old Romantic passion for a national literary tradition, and the great work expressing the national soul; the Parnassian penchant for a chaste, classic linguistic instrumentality is also glimpsed, in Machado's talk of Portuguese usage; and the removed, select nature of literary artistry and fellowship, the worship of genius common to Romantic and post-Romantic ideas is clear. What is lacking is the engagement with the larger society which was so integral to the *geração de setenta*'s posture. No longer did literati presume a role in *political* regeneration; they had retreated to the Romantics' redoubt. Their mission was, once again, literary in the stricter sense. Like that of the first national literary generations, their task was to define the national soul through its vigorous literary expression. Nabuco, ten years before a great Abolitionist and political reformer, now argued

> We only hope to defend the sources of genius . . . which lie almost all in the prestige, or, rather, in the dignity of the literary profession . . . Politics, that is, the feeling for danger and glory, the grandeur or the decline of the country, is a source of inspiration. . . , but for politics . . . to enter the Academy, it is necessary that it should not be its own object; that it disappear in the creation that it produced, like mercury in the amalgams of gold and silver.[51]

Indeed, for their patriotic, apolitical creation, the new academicians expected recognition, respect, . . . and funding. They accepted a certain distance from society for their proper sphere, but they no longer accepted marginality, genteel or embattled. As José Veríssimo noted, they deserved better; they questioned "whether there is in a nationality any organ more essential than literature, which is the expression, superior to the contingencies of politics and of history, of the nationality itself."[52]

Retreat from political activism, desire for official recognition as the arbiters and makers of culture, implied acceptance of the values dominating society, the values of the nation's elite. Some few, as will be seen, would not go so far, but the Academy's "respectability" under the direction of Machado and his clique was clear. It was patent, even in small matters, that bohemia's glory was past. Machado's personal circumspection and his comment that the Academy was one of *boa companhia* (polite society) made for literati of sober tastes and habits. Though apparently extravagant uniforms were later countenanced (Anatole France's secretary remembered a 1901 visit, in which "We never saw uniforms so gilded. There were more sashes than seams. And

6. An informal gathering of literati and artists, Laranjeiras, 1901

the swords, plumes, and metal buttons, big as bucklers. And the decorations . . . "[53]), hard drinking, nasty-mouthed, and unkempt bohemians were not even nominated during Machado's tenure.[54]

As Broca notes,[55] however, few really prominent bohemians of the 1880s were left by 1900. Death, disillusion, and desire to find the security once dramatically spurned had thinned the ranks. Only odd incorrigibles survived, still writing as journalists. Most literati now known as bohemians were either poor, unsuccessful literati or Symbolists righteously isolated in their private world. Now, the established literati no longer included riotous iconoclasts, but comprised an Academy of men who were prosaically aging as bureaucrats, professors, diplomats, and lawyers.[56] Often indistinguishable in their black coats, derbies, or top hats from less cultivated colleagues thronging Ouvidor of a late afternoon, they could be picked out, perhaps, for only two reasons: their faces were often well known in the highly personalized world of the elite, and they continued to meet in certain consecrated Ouvidor cafés and bookshops. As we shall see now, a third factor was less obvious, if more distinctive; they not only shared in the consumer fetishism associated with elite Europhile culture; they helped to reproduce it.

THE LITERARY *BELLE ÉPOQUE*

8. Media, the readers, and their tastes

The roles of the literati in *belle-époque* culture were played mainly in the era's expanding journalism and the chic reviews typical of the *fin de siècle*. If Rio's wealth and demographic expansion after 1870 had helped to make the popular press of the 1880s possible, the period 1898–1914 brought new sophistication and technology to bear in increased competition for an expanding elite and middle-sector market. Such established papers as the *Jornal do Commercio*, the *Gazeta de Noticias*, and *O Paiz* were joined by the *Jornal do Brasil* (1891) and the *Correio da Manhã* (1901). In 1898 came a fashionable weekly, *Rua do Ouvidor*; a simple taste of what was to follow. In 1904, with the Paris-style urban reforms of 1902–6,[57] two stylish and expensive reviews began: *Kósmos* and *Renascença*. To the established genres of verse, crônica, short story, and serial novel, nearly all these periodicals added the era's innovations: sensationalist reporting, increasingly personalized material (interviews and profiles), a preoccupation with the *alto mundo*, and (especially in *Kósmos* and *Renascença*) lavish use of illustration featuring photography and art-nouveau vignettes.[58]

All of these provided literati income and a chance to publish, but they also dictated the terms of cultural production. As had always been the case, the books Brazilians published were few, and the size of editions small. Generally, one established one's reputation through periodicals and, perhaps, republished the same material as a book. Although a favorable announcement or critique by an established critic might make a difference, the periodical readership was thus essentially the group which decided an author's success. Great dependence on periodical readership involved obvious limitations, as alluded to earlier. By 1900, this essentially narrow sector of the Carioca population (for provincial and rural readers were far less important numerically, and tended to follow Rio's tastes) was probably composed of elite women, middle-sector women of elite tastes, and a masculine contingent of students, literati, and would-be literati. These were the only people with the leisure, wealth, and interest to pursue high culture.[59] And, as one author noted, this audience was narrow in more than one sense: "The intellectual in Brazil is obliged to get along with people of the upper class, though everything separates him from it, because that [class] is the only one that knows how to read . . . and, even so! how? what? In general . . . the 'cultivated' draw on very 'spotty' reading."[60]

The readers' taste has been noted earlier. It was Francophile, modish, and fetishistic (in the sense used in chapter 5). One may recall how the elite's education was very literary and very French. Moreover, as has been seen often enough, the cumulative weight of Francophile tradition in Rio was only strengthened over the course of the century. By 1900, elite life assumed the use of French and familiarity with French culture. Most elite women read French literature; most elite men did, too. Indeed, many of the literati wrote, and some thought, in that language, and when Brazilians did read works by Englishmen or Germans, they were generally in French translations. As for the middle sector, if they did not know French culture as well, they appreciated its accomplishments and the status associated with them. How else can one explain the readers for whom many Brazilian literati regularly translated French serial novels in the papers, or the popularity of French drama in translation?[61]

To the influence of schooling, tradition, and fashion, one must add the impact of the press and the book trade. From the very beginning, as remarked before, Carioca booksellers, typesetters, and publishers were often French. Naturally, their shops promoted French works and periodicals, just as they promoted the French style of Carioca periodicals in format, illustration, and content. Such places, much more than elite travel, also explain how Brazilians kept up with French literary fashions; Garnier's and Briguiet's were the Carioca lifeline to literary Paris.[62]

The result was a *fin-de-siècle* Carioca taste formed and nourished by Gallic works in both cumulative and discriminatory fashion. The first Romantic generation throve on Chateaubriand, Musset, Lamartine, Belzac, Sue, and Hugo; the second added Cherbuliez, Feydeau, Feuillet, Dumas fils, Sandeau, and Scribe. The readers of the 1880s retained Hugo, Balzac and Flaubert, and prized Zola, the Goncourts, Taine, Renan, and Maupassant. By 1900, whether older members of the *geração de setenta*, former bohemians of the 1880s, or new men, the readers continued to prize Hugo, Balzac, Flaubert, Zola, Renan, and Taine, and had added to them the very fashionable Anatole France, Paul Bourget, Pierre Loti, J. K. Huysmans, and Marcel Prévost.[63]

Given the influence such authors had on the tastes of the Carioca reader, one must note certain of their characteristics to put contemporary Carioca works in context. Since the older authors are better known and the *fin-de-siècle* writers most fashionable in the *belle époque*, these brief comments will address only the latter. Anatole France, with his celebrated irony and sense of worldly disillusion, gave the era its preeminent literary perspective. The most fashionable author of his day,

France liked to portray himself as a man of the world who had seen enough of it to step back and chat about it with an amused interest, bereft of passion, and expressed with a classical style and an "attic" wit. Pierre Loti was quite different. He served up the pleasures of refined escapism, projecting his needs and inadequacies into the colonial world, in an egocentric travelogue of exotic settings punctuated by *amours* with submissive mistresses of various hues.

Prévost's escapism was more domestic. He worked in Parisian settings of worldly pleasure, creating a hybrid of moralism and erotic tension quite successful among his feminine bourgeois audience. Huysmans and Bourget were hardly so coy. They explored aspects of bourgeois and aristocratic life (or, rather, fantasies of such life) that were both exotic and very French, and soon defined as decadent. Huysmans depicted, in his character Des Esseintes, the modern aesthete's flight from boredom to an over-refined, cultivated life that his readers found fascinating. Bourget, in his first phase, did much the same, vicariously celebrating decadence before the change of heart that led to his trenchant condemnation of modern atheism and materialism in novels of psychological trauma and disaster.[64]

Fin-de-siècle literature, often associated with the words Impressionist and Decadent (because of its subjective approach and its preoccupation with refined self-indulgence, materialism, and moral decline), or with the school of Symbolism (because of its subjective and suggestive use of language), was turned inward toward the self – narcissistic, disengaged, escapist, sensual, aristocratically refined. In many ways, it expresses one response to a tormented period of French high culture. Bereft of religious solace or imperial glories, traumatized by the defeat of 1870, increasingly troubled by a problematic future, French writers seem to have retreated to this reserved classicism or these sensual and exotic pleasures as part of a general malaise of disillusion and doubt. In time, others would remake idealism, the irrational, and religion; now, however, the materialist determinism of the nineteenth century was twisting on its own hook – the future seemed both grim and inevitable, and only distance or pleasure brought relief.[65]

As Brazilians kept *au courant* with these trends, they naturally assimilated and adapted them; there was no simple copying. The new schools found echos among Brazilian writers seeking to make reputations by reworking fashionable trends in their own ways, and in the Carioca elite, which, for the usual reasons, attached prestige to being knowledgable about Parisian literature. For established writers, a shift to new trends might be adaptive, problematic, or even impossible.

Machado, for example, picked and chose in adapting from new schools, and did not simply adopt them; nor did Sílvio Romero, one of the era's two greatest critics, who seems to have dismissed post-1880s trends. José Veríssimo, the other great critic, did accept something of Anatole France's irony and the subjective, impressionistic approach of the critic Jules Lemaître (1853–1914) – but remained completely hostile to Symbolism. Indeed, the fate of Symbolism in Brazil is instructive. This new poetic school, enjoying rarified success in France after 1880, caught on among the younger poets in Rio.[66] The latter failed, however, to dislodge the older dominant school of Parnassianism; *le Parnasse*'s followers, for reasons peculiar to Carioca literature, continued in power throughout the *belle époque*. The circumstances explaining these various peculiarities of the Carioca *belle époque* are best explained in the context of the lives and works of the period's great writers. It is to this that we turn now, beginning with an evocation of the era through its typical authors.

9. Literary consumer fetishism and its artisans

In Rio, the champion of *le Parnasse* was Olavo Bilac, crowned Prince of Poets by his fellows in 1907.[67] (See photograph in illustration 3.) One of the *novos* remembers Bilac at the Confeitaria Colombo:

> At the entrance, behold, suddenly a prince of letters arrives – Olavo Braz Martins dos Guimarães Bilac. Tall, elegant, thin, displaying two pupils dilated by extreme myopia. He squints. Over his frank, sensual mouth, a small mustache . . . A great name. Great popularity. Everyone knows him. Everyone recites him. Everyone discusses him . . . The *novos* are dumbstruck when he shakes hands with them for the first time, and the old generation speak of him as a great master. His defects are those of his circle. Defects of the epoch. He loves *boutades*, *blagues*, and *mots d'esprit*.[68]

Bilac serves well to introduce the dominant tendencies of the Carioca *belle époque*. First, the *mundanismo* remarked earlier. Carioca, the son of a physician who expected his son to follow in his footsteps, Bilac rebelled early and devoted most of his time at medical school to literature and journalism. After trying law at São Paulo with similar results, he abandoned his father's home and good graces for those of the Ouvidor. A bohemian of the 1880s, Bilac soon exemplified the transition represented by the Academy. In the 1890s, like many bohemians, he suffered both exile and jail. By the end of the decade, with a successful volume of poetry to his name, he helped found the Academy and contributed regularly to the *Gazeta de Noticias*, taking over the column Machado de

Assis resigned in 1901. In keeping with his age, his position, and his failing liver, Bilac drank a good deal less now, though he still visited unreformed bohemians and his old cafés. By the 1900s, his respected journalist's image and the consequent useful contacts with successive presidential administrations led to a series of comfortable government positions that helped finance yearly trips to Paris. In 1904, he had a position in Pereira Passos' municipal administration and was championing the prefect's reforms, especially from his regular column in *Kósmos*. During the rage for literary public lectures (another Parisian import), Bilac's talks were considered among the smartest. It suggests the nature of *belle époque* literary success that, now, when elite women came to Ouvidor and the Avenida Central to display expensive tastes and buy modish imports, they also paid for a poet as a *pièce de résistance*, last in their pleasant stops sampling chic items to which the scent of Paris clung.[69]

In his writing, Bilac maintained a duality. His poetry was now out of fashion in France, his prose very much in step. Parnassianism, originally a reaction against Romanticism's emotional extravagance and an embrace of "scientific" remove and precision, began in Paris in the 1860s and triumphed in Brazil by the 1880s. There, as mentioned, it prevailed against Symbolism, which had buried Parnassianism in France by 1880. This paradox may be explained by the greater limitations of literary activity in Brazil, and invites examination.

Parnassianism may have better served the particular predispositions of Brazil's narrower and less refined public. Though the school lacked the vivid appeal of the Romantics (who remained popular in Rio long after Romanticism was *passé* among literati), it did stress verbal dexterity, comprehensible images, and adherence to classical images and form, happy coincidences with traditional Brazilian strengths. Its Greek images and myths were especially welcome cultural identifications for cultivated poet and lay audience alike; they linked one to both French classicism and an edifying European past. French interest in the classical Mediterranean grew strong by the 1860s, partly as an ideological weapon against Anglo-Prussian imperial rivalry, and, after 1870, partly as an ideological compensation (one notes that Greco-Roman civilization became a particularly French "property" then, with Frenchmen attempting to appropriate "Latin Civilization" and "Latinity").[70] Such classicism was pleasing to Brazilians, however, for reasons of their own. Broca has suggested how soothing such "Latinity" could be when Brazil's racial composition was a subject of consternation, fear, and denial among the elite.[71]

Perhaps, then, these were the reasons that Bilac's school retained considerable appeal; refined, French, "Latin," and accessible, Parnassianism had much to offer. Symbolism offered little. It was purposely obscure; stressing the author's subjective understanding of a word's suggestion, it made for an oblique, metaphorical poetry seemingly bereft of accessible form or content. It had neither the obvious pleasures nor gratifying cultural associations of the earlier Romanticism or the prevailing Parnassianism. Moreover, as Dimas notes, when this was added to the Parnassians' control of the established periodicals and the Symbolists' self-isolation in purist cliques, the latter's popular failure is easy to understand. A multitude of Symbolists arose throughout Brazil, marshalled ranks in their own cafés, barricaded themselves behind impenetrable verse, and published ephemeral reviews, never achieving acceptance.[72]

If his Parnassianism casts Bilac as a conservative poet, his more voluminous prose and his *mundanismo* declare him up to date. His position in high society has been suggested; now one might note how that persona melded into his prose. The title of an essay collection, *Ironia e piedade*,[73] ties this aspect of Bilac to the figure of Anatole France. The phrase is the Frenchman's, as was Bilac's pose as a Parnassian aesthete and a cosmopolitan essayist. Still, it was a Carioca who was posing. Indeed, one finds in Bilac, as the purveyor of Civilization and the critic of Carioca urban "backwardness," a perfect voice of the Carioca *belle époque*. Here is his key. His irony and pity were reserved for his countrymen, and largely masked shame and anger. His position on Pereira Passos' staff was not mere convenience, but the strongest possible coincidence of ideological interests – he desperately identified himself with a "civilized" Rio, a metamorphsis of city and citizen he could only imagine in terms of French culture. One speculates that these passions derived from the profound contrasts in his upbringing, contrasts common to his generation. Bilac, after all, was born in the *cidade velha*'s heart; he was bred within the "Africa" of nineteenth-century Rio. He knew its religion, rituals, and practices at first hand. Yet he was also the son of a physician and a student of medicine in the age of scientism and a student and a poet wholly trained within Rio's Francophile high culture. His complete devotion to poetry meant a concomitant identity with French culture and Paris, where he tried unsuccessfully to establish permanent residence. His attitudes towards Rio thus become quite comprehensible – he wanted his city to be transformed as he had, and despised it as it was. The racism and Eurocentricity of his prose is egregious, and typically *belle époque*. The reader may recall the poet's reference to Rio (in chapter 1.11) as "Old Portuguese Bantuland,"[74] or his paean to the Avenida Central, centerpiece of Rio's Parisian metamorphosis, where he trumpeted, "we begin to stride toward our rehabilitation,"[75] or, finally, his condemnation of *Carnaval*'s "shameful exhibition" of "erotic processions."[76] In such phrases, the period's and the poet's ambivalence is clear. Bilac was progressive and a patriot in the sense that he was devoted to a "civilized" culture yet to be made in Brazil. Like so much about the Carioca *belle époque*, however, this signified a profound discomfort with Brazilian civilization as it actually was.[77]

If Bilac was recognized as the outstanding poet of the era, something similar was true for his old companion, Coelho Neto. Until Machado de Assis' death (1908), Coelho Neto's position was clearly secondary; afterwards, it assumed preeminence. By 1922, his style was considered synonymous with the era's taste. This would be his bane later, when Modernism's attack on that taste triumphed.[78]

Coelho Neto's biography lays bare the turbulence of a literary generation. Son of a modest Portuguese merchant in Maranhão, Coelho Neto's vocation, like Bilac's, was opposed by his father, who feared penury for his son. The boy hid his first verses "like a thief, in the pages of the dictionary."[79] The penury and the dictionary seem a portent – Coelho Neto struggled to defeat poverty all his life, and he did so with an army of words, using a famously obscure vocabulary in an output estimated as the equivalent of four hundred volumes.[80]

Coelho Neto's family arrived at the Côrte in 1870. There, his bookkeeper uncle taught him Latin and the Portuguese classics. He had secondary schooling, including five years at the Colégio Pedro II, because of his father's sacrifices and his mother's sewing. When his father died, Coelho Neto, aged fifteen, helped to support the family and his ambitions by giving private lessons. At seventeen, he published his first poem. The next year, 1882, he entered Rio's medical school, which he abandoned in 1883 for law in São Paulo. Between 1883 and 1885 in São Paulo and Recife, Coelho Neto completed three years of law; more important, he began to meet the men becoming important in letters, journalism, and politics. The politics, of course, were those of Abolition and the Republic and Coelho Neto's radicalism led to conflict with a Recife professor. Like Bilac, again, he left law for literature, returning to Rio. There, the bohemia of the 1880s brought Coelho Neto to Bilac and the others, completing his crucial network of the young men who would count among the established literari, bureaucrats, and political chieftains of the *belle époque* as men of middle age.[81]

In 1890, Coelho Neto ended his bohemian days in clichéd fashion. He married. Maria Gabriela "D. Gaby" Brandão was the daughter of Dr. Alberto Brandão, noted educator of Vassouras (patron of Ataúlfo Paiva[82]) and well-connected representative of the *fluminense* elite. We are told that the match was spurred by love at first sight, when the bohemian came to meet Dr. Alberto with a friend. Still, it must be admitted that the bride's connections were felicitous, adding to those Coelho Neto had already, after several years' struggle on what had just become the winning side. His wife's *padrinho*[83] at the wedding was Marshal Deodoro da Fonseca, new president of the republic. Others in the fashionable Matriz da Glória that day included established men of letters, such as Machado de Assis, Bilac, and Luís Murat, and all of the republic's ministers, along with Francisco Portela, governor of the new State of Rio de Janeiro. Portela promptly made the new groom his secretary, just as he scattered appointments to other former bohemians.

After 1890, this pattern of patronage set. While writing constantly, Coelho Neto obtained political appointments, offices, or academic positions to support his proper family in proper fashion. During periods when such positions were unavailable, Coelho Neto relied entirely on literary journalism, turning out columns and *folhetim romances* at a pace difficult to believe, working ten or twelve hours at a stretch in the study he regarded as an altar to his muse.

Still, despite the hardships literary life implied in the era, the social rewards for the successful could be appreciable. Like Bilac, by 1896 Coelho Neto was already respected enough to be one of the handful who founded the Academy. The writer of very popular novels and columns, with twenty-seven volumes to his name by 1900, Coelho Neto's prestige in the Carioca *alto mundo* was unshakeable.[84] As the *belle époque* wore on, he presided over a famed salon in the Flamengo district (near the elite Fluminense Futebol Club where the author and his sons were noted members) in which, mixed in among writers, painters, and musicians, his son remembers figures more often associated with politics, diplomacy, and pure celebrity than with any muse whatever.

Something of the period's literary style is captured in memoirs of this salon. Its hostess, D. Gaby, won praise as the attentive mistress of the gracious, studied, aesthetic atmosphere; its host compelled attention, with his Prussian haircut, handlebar mustache, piercing glance behind metal-rimmed glasses, simple manner, slight build, and dramatic conversation. One visitor remembered the drawing room:

> The great jacaranda table in the center, the Manueline armoires overburdened with good books. . . ; the small branch of willow from the tomb of Musset,

picked by the master; the sketches of Antônio Parreiras; the bric-à-brac; a bronze bust of Eça [de Queirós] of surprising expression, and, hovering over all, the peerless grace of D. Gaby, enhancing everything.[85]

Another memoir recalls that

> The meetings generally occurred on Saturdays. In the corridors, in the rooms and in the garden, figures of the new and old generations met one another . . . Not just writers: pianists, violinists, singers young and old, painters, sculptors . . . also went there . . . But the best spectacle of these gatherings was Coelho Neto himself, with his imaginative and fertile conversation, describing the novels and short stories he hoped to write, recalling episodes of his youth, passing on his impressions from reading, his voice precise . . . his gestures perfect, playing a role, often, like a true actor.[86]

In effect, Coelho Neto's salon demonstrates how closely knit *belle-époque* elite culture and Society were, and, again, how closely knit one's *alto-mundo* position and one's literary position were. Coelho Neto's "artistic" salon was a useful extension of his Society identity as an established man of letters; his son's memory of the Society lions who showed up is the proud record of trophies taken in *a conquista* of a Society position.

Here one must go deeper into Coelho Neto's work itself. It not only helps to explain his Society success; it is also, in two ways, a superb expression of *belle-époque* literature. First, it was nearly all produced quickly for publication in periodicals. Second, in both style and substance, it drew on the Francophile tendencies of the period, combining echoes of Romanticism, the florescence of Naturalism, and the triumph of the *fin de siècle*. In a phrase, it was marred by hasty writing, directed toward facile, unrefined taste, and was clearly derivative in origin. Bilac once spoke to the common plight which was largely to blame. Posed comfortably against the milk-white drapes of his *fin-de-siècle* décor, he confessed, when speaking of writing for newspapers, "Oh! yes, it is a good thing. But if a young writer came . . . to seek guidance from my sadness, in my disconsolate autumn, I would only say: Love your art above all things and have the courage, that I had not, to die of hunger so as not to prostitute your talent!"[87]

Like Bilac, Coelho Neto had not died of hunger; he had turned out what pleased as quickly as possible. There were Romantic, Realist novels (*Miragem* and *Turbilhão*) like those of Balzac, exoticist pieces (*O rei phantasma*) in the style of Flaubert's *Salammbo* or Loti, there were post-Naturalist novels (*Inverno em flor* and *Tormenta*) in the psychological fashion established by Bourget, and at least one piece (*Esfinje*) playing with the occult. Besides this varied fare, he had also served up volume after volume of short stories, collected from his vast periodical production, as well as a volume or two of the fashionable public lectures with which he, like Bilac and others, entertained society women.[88]

Coelho Neto was painfully conscious of the failure of his creative hopes and the nature of his success. He once chose an early piece as his favorite in this way: "I prefer *Pelo amor!* because of its time. In that period, I was still judged capable of something in Brazil [by the critics]."[89] Then he confessed

> The truth is that while I write, I feel a great pleasure, and afterwards, I am surprised by the defects. I work constantly. Only my *novelas* were finished and retouched before being turned over to the editors. The rest of my work has been written day by day for the newspapers . . . No one knows that, my style being subordinate to my concept, my pen works almost mechanically . . . [The public and the critics] refuse to understand the plight of a writer who resolves to live only by his pen.[90]

As post-Modernist critics note, it is the style characteristic of his vast production that was so disdained after 1922.[91] As one would expect from Coelho Neto's position in *belle-époque* culture, this touches on a question of period taste; in this case, the era's passion for ornate, sensual, fantastic, over-refined superficiality. Bosi has referred to this as a Parnassian quality, because of that school's emphasis on verbal technique, as well as its association with form, refinement, and classical images and myths.[92] Even Coelho Neto's handwriting, with its studied Greek lettering, betrays his "Hellenism." However, one may also connect this quality to the *fin de siècle* and to the consumer fetishism central to the *belle époque*.

In this connection, one might recall the sensual, decadent quality of such writers as Huysmans and the predilection of *fin-de-siècle* authors for exotic, materialist escape and aristocratic, refined consumption. These emphasized, as a compositional correlate, adjectives, unusual words, and exaggerated phrasing. Coelho Neto, like such authors, had an almost tactile obsession with complex descriptions of sensual reality. Like the protagonist of his novel, *Tormenta*, Coelho Neto recalled

> . . . things in minute detail – the piano, with its acanthus-form candelabra, over which naked cupids strummed lyres; the sideboard with its precious Japanese porcelain service. . . ; the grotesque *cuspidor* in his study, [made of] Portuguese faience: a great frog, with eyes bugging out, sprawled on the ground with its immense open mouth; his mahogany bed and writing desk.[93]

The sensual nature of descriptions of rooms, decor, people, and clothes suggests the commodity fetishism integral to the era. In effect, by making descriptions as palpable as possible, the author invited the reader to enjoy vicariously the expensive, aristocratic, exciting settings and pleasures. Indeed, José Veríssimo once noted this quality in Coelho Neto's style with frustration:

> the imagination of Sr. Coelho Neto, limited, if I am not mistaken, on the creative side, truly overflows [in a most] unfortunately undisciplined [manner] on the other, what I will call, decorative side. And then it is shored up with all that exotic bric-à-brac. . . , biblical orientalism, Hellenic or Scandinavian mythology, German or Saxon legends, medieval superstitions.[94]

Like a chic department store window, such pages were another enticement to enter into the fantasies linked to material consumption. There, between the advertisements in the papers, his fiction pulled the reader into the thrills or horrors of oriental palaces or bourgeois decadence, complete with plush sets. Coelho Neto's one-man literary production line simply turned out such wordy commodities quickly. He knew better than to suggest they were turned out well. The point was that they sold.[95]

Another exemplar of the Carioca *belle époque* displays many of these distinguishing traits with even greater extravagance. If journalistic production, a taste for French models, an attachment to the decadent, the occult, the refined, conspicuous consumption, and disillusioned irony were characteristic of the era, no one was more native to it than Paulo Barreto, its most eminent journalist. If Bilac and Coelho Neto were among the era's established cultural celebrities, its *mestres* [João] Paulo [Alberto Coelho] Barreto (1881–1921)[96] was its plump, gluttonous *maître de plaisir*. The journalist, like Bilac, was born Carioca, in the milieu of the liberal professions. His father was a professor, his mother's father chief of the Santa Casa de Misericórdia clinic. He was educated at home, and began writing for the newspapers as an adolescent. Despite this apparently comfortable situation, however, factors peculiar to his family and his tastes set him apart; they may also have spurred his accomplishments.

Paulo's father, Dr. [Alfredo] Coelho Barreto, a mathematician, was a Positivist and Republican who proselytized for both causes for years at the Colégio Pedro II.[97] His mother, possessive, egocentric, and mercurial, bequeathed the lad not only traces of her affective greed and affected emotionalism, but a color suggesting African descent, something incompatible with the elite's racism.[98] Educated by a father committed to a critical view of the surrounding milieu and with the grating personal characteristics and disdained racial features of the mother who pampered him, it seems possible that Paulo may have had a sense of being unacceptably different from early on. If so, it was a sense doubtless strengthened by Paulo's own particular social stigma, his obvious homosexuality, which surely did nothing to help matters.[99]

However, if these might be reasons enough why one would not expect Paulo Barreto to triumph in the *belle époque* and its *alto mundo*, there were better reasons explaining why, in fact, he did. Paulo, as noted, began to write for the papers as an adolescent. Unlike others, however, he chose to continue at it: not for lack of another means to make a living writing, but because it was his *métier*. He worked for many papers and mastered, while still quite young, a sensationalist style exactly fitted to *belle-époque* tastes. He never pursued law or medicine; instead, without thought for formal degrees, he carried on varied studies in the vast library he collected at home and in the streets and cafés of the Rio which he came to know and about which he wrote as no one else had before him.

In doing so, Paulo Barreto revolutionized Carioca journalism. He broke with the traditional armchair reflections of Rio's press to hunt stories moving in the *cidade velha*'s steaming, twisted streets and in the wretched *favelas* of the *cidade nova* and the hills, with their traditions, their *mélange* of beliefs, their types, and their rich variety of cultural experience. He interviewed Rio's warlocks (*pais de santo*) and its literary celebrities; he flourished the flamboyant, bric-à-brac style of the era; explored with an ironic, critical eye, every aspect of modern Carioca life in fashionable afternoon public lectures. The applause became deafening. The early, French-influenced phase of urban reporting brought him, under the famous pseudonym of João do Rio, a delicious notoriety, an unfailing audience, a nice bit of money, and a certain respectability. By 1910, it also brought him consecration as the youngest member of the Academy, at the unprecedented age of twenty-nine.[100] As a result of these triumphs, Paulo Barreto's journalism inevitably brought him access to a Society charmed and excited by his work.

Paulo Barreto's pleasure in his rapid success was apparent. A contemporary portrait has him staring at us through heavy lids from a soft face, got up smartly in a well-tailored suit, stylishly cocked hat, sharp tie, and crisp winged collar. He was considered one of Rio's great dandies, sporting a monocle and indulging in afternoon baths at the best hotels, before changing into a second suit. (See photograph in illustration 3.) A good friend, Gilberto Amado, captures him at his height in this memoir:

I found him at night ... in a restaurant, the Sul-America, on Rua Sete de Setembro. He was eating with ... Cândido Campos. They both puffed vigorously at cigars that seemed ... enormous. Paulo Barreto, voluminous, thick-lipped, very dark, and loose-skinned, spoke, and the much younger Cândido Campos, still almost an adolescent, very white, with a wide forehead, laughed freely, his eyes held by those of the writer. They both wore silk shirts ... I had the impression ... that life stood still for them in an oasis of happiness, such was the joy they displayed. Paulo found himself at the apogee of journalistic and literary triumph.[101]

Amado has shown that Society's embrace of Paulo ushered in a second phase in his writing, in which exploration and criticism of the bizarre, the novel, and the miserable aspects of modern Carioca society lost ground to a celebration of the *alto mundo.*[102] He no longer excited the *alto mundo* with vicarious experiences of modernity; instead, he fed its narcissism with gossip, charming reflections, fashionable commentary, and naughty *divertissements.* It was the phase of his chic social column and light fiction for fashionable women, set in modish spas, Petrópolis, and expensive restaurants – far indeed from the social critiques and the dives and *favelas* which had drawn the journalist as a youth.

Increasingly, then, Paulo Barreto fostered the milieu from which much elite culture drew substance and form.[103] He dealt in French literary models and fashions, he groomed affectations for display, he loosed whole flocks of ideas and prejudices poached from the Continent's "high life." Most important, though, he wrote about the Carioca elite's own world, not as it was, but as the elite *wanted* it. In the fantasies thus created of the Carioca *belle époque* he helped make the Carioca elite self-conscious, and delightedly so. Moreover, by making elite culture and society the center of his flattering attention, he helped to legitimize it. In the end, though perhaps in unanticipated fashion, he thus realized the goals announced in his 1910 Academy reception speech:

the increased crush of superfluity, the formidable flower of parasitism and of vice, love, the life of the senses multiplied a hundredfold, oblige the artist to see and to feel in another way, to love in another fashion, to recreate in another manner ... The aspiration of the new artists should be that of capturing through their own personalities the great moment of their country's social transformation in the miracle of contemporary life.[104]

It is worth noting how typical this approach to writing was. Others also plunged self-consciously into the glittering modern fantasies of the period to titillate or lecture Carioca readers about it afterward. Such didactic narcissism is evident, for instance, in the columns of Figueiredo Pimentel, explored elsewhere here,[105] which stoop so far to social column and fashion material that they fail to qualify as literature at all. The columnist's appearance in a chic Musso photograph is in the best *belle-époque* tradition. His thin face is framed by close-cropped hair and a goatee, and sports turned-up mustaches. His suit is well-cut, his tie daring, and his collar turned down, in the latest fashion.[106] Figueiredo Pimentel began as a mercenary servant of popular taste who wrote advice to the lovelorn in *Manual de namorados* ("Sweethearts' Handbook"), children's books, and introductions to Brazilian literature for the *Mercure de France.* Matters apparently picked up for him as the *Gazeta de Noticias*' arbiter of consumerist chic. It seems fitting that, once established, this erstwhile hack turned Society columnist alluded to the role of literature in the era as a status commodity for conspicuous consumption:

> The elegance of any party or get-together resides in the way one socializes, in the refinement of one's manners, gestures, and attitudes, in the grace, wit, and elevation of conversations. It is never elegant to speak of others, and much less of oneself. The matters for casual conversations in a salon, in a "chic" restaurant, or in a theater, ought to be general topics. One ought to speak, in a "soirée," about music, poetry, literature, choosing the subject best suited to the conversationalist.[107]

Figueiredo here merely states the place of literature in the *alto mundo.* Perhaps Paulo Barreto and others like him did worse, in writing literature only suitable for such a place.

Falling between Paulo Barreto and Figueiredo Pimentel in this sense was the "aesthete," Elísio de Carvalho.[108] Along with the other two, he exemplifies the gilded bohemia (*boêmia dourada*, doubtless from the French original, *bohème dorée*) of 1900, whose concubinage of *mundanismo* and letters was characteristic of the era. A period caricature of this well-known figure shows him smartly turned out in derby, striped pants, black cutaway, full mustache, cane, monocle, and lapel carnation. He had married an heiress and had, at twenty, a Riachuelo mansion and one of the city's best libraries of imported books, a collection rivaling that of Pereira Passos. Like João do Rio and Figueiredo Pimentel, his place in Society and his writing were symbiotic. Elísio affected, however, a more serious profile. He published studies of contemporary literature and of the Carioca elite, for example, and proclaimed himself an Anarchist. Still, far more typical were the fashionable sorts of things he published in *Kósmos*: pieces on Petrópolis diplomats and the "high life." It was also this self-proclaimed Anarchist who, several years after founding the Universidade Popular for workingmen, dedicated his decadent *Five o'clock* to Paulo Barreto, noting it was a

book where I gathered the most personal, emotional, most lived pages I have composed, into which I poured many illusions, bitternesses, many melancholies and a few hatreds, where I spilled the essence of my vibrant, sickly, exacerbated, and purified nerves, a book written with the blood of my spirit and with the soul of my flesh.[109]

This piece is a favorite of period historians because its prose captures the hothouse style of the *belle époque* so well. Elísio wrote it as a sort of diary of decadence; its attractions *vis-à-vis* vicarious Europhile consumption are patent:

Monday the 15th. [Sra.] Souza Barros and I enjoyed . . . the tepid perfumed ambience of a luxurious apartment, a model of discrete and artistic comfort, revealing the mark of the most subtle feminine good taste, a nest of delicate and refined things, with precious bibelots and, spread over the rich furniture, adorable objects of love, photographs, beautiful illustrated works and small volumes, some pastels of Guilhaume on the walls representing scenes of life at Monte Carlo and a sweet landscape of the Luxembourg Gardens signed by Chabas, Sèvres vases [filled with] many rare, disturbing and voluptuous flowers, whose perfume went together well with that feminine spirit which reigned, mistress of French beauty and grace, in that small domain. Souza Barros, stretched out lazily on a divan, launched the light smoke of her *Bird's Eye* cigarette into the air, her eyes fixed on [the] animated [Mme.] de Fernay who completed that very Parisian décor with her sinuous profile, [and] spoke to me of her last voyage to Europe . . . and . . . her latest love affairs.[110]

Afrânio Peixoto, a well-connected physician, was even more successful at exploiting such material. A one-time Symbolist in Bahia, Afrânio had done well in Rio, winning important government positions through powerful connections and moving with ease in the *alto mundo*. I mention him not simply as another exemplar of gilded bohemia, but as the author of one of the era's greatest successes: *A esfinje* (1911), a fashionable romance between an idealistic artist and a lady of fashion. Broca's analysis of the book's peculiar and dramatic triumph speaks directly to the nature of the Carioca *belle époque*, particularly the elite anxieties and self-absorption central to the literature under discussion:

. . . no novel had been a high-society success among us before. And this certainly was because, until then, the novelists had not applied themselves, as Afrânio did, to making a minute painting of Carioca high society, of the aristocratic salons, of the diplomatic and political milieu, of the elegant society that summers in Petrópolis . . . the essential [element] of the novel consisted in its portraits of the worldly milieu of Rio, in that epoch in which the capital was modernizing and attempted to imitate Paris in everything.[111]

Essentially, Afrânio raised the columns of Figueiredo Pimentel to the level of bad literature, except that, in *A esfinje*, the tone is no longer didactic nor sensationalist; it is cool, distant. Like João do Rio or Elísio de Carvalho, Afrânio portrayed the Carioca elite as it desired to be. Unlike them, however, he displays less indulgence with the results. Through good fortune unrelated to his writing, Afrânio was already part of the *alto mundo*; thus he both knew it well and had no need to flatter its members. He displays a more authentic distance and irony, compared to the cloying affectation of the others. If his was a pose modeled after Anatole France's, it was well struck. Nevertheless, by focussing on the milieu he knew and playing down, romanticizing or isolating rural or artistic life, he effectively did much as the others had; he legitimized the elite's urbane life as the only real option. Afrânio merely daubed on the same cosmetics João do Rio, Figueiredo Pimentel, and Elísio de Carvalho smeared too energetically:

he was the most popular lad of the Petrópolis salons that season. He had recently arrived from Europe, accompanied by a dozen suitcases, bringing all the necessities of a style refined by the study of good international examples, who in Paris imitated the fashions of the English. It was said that he had experienced and enjoyed all the elegant [pleasures] of the boudoirs and bedrooms of the great *demi-monde*, of the theaters, salons, resorts and racecourse stands . . . In Vichy, in Montreaux, in Engadine, or Biarritz, wherever there might be something elegant consecrated by fashion, there he was, in a circle of English nobles and American parvenus, knowing how to live with liberality and tedium.[112]

Thus, however, surfeited by the *alto mundo*, Afrânio, too, effectively strengthened it. In *A esfinje*, he poses no real alternative to its decadence or the commercialization of art (one of the novel's sub-themes). If anything, the book demonstrates his willingness to profit from both, albeit with a studied, wholly *fin-de-siècle* irony. It seems fitting that it was this cynical physician who gave us the phrase, "literature is the smile of society", so often quoted since as characteristic of the era.[113]

I conclude this evocation of *belle-époque* high culture by turning to an author who, though typical in literary terms, is interesting to the modern reader for another reason, as well: her gender. I introduced Júlia [Valentina da Silveira] Lopes de Almeida (1862–1934)[114] earlier, as a measure of the change in elite women's status in the *belle époque*.[115] As was noted then, however, her merits as a period author require

7. D. Júlia Lopes de Almeida, *c.* 1907

attention, too. For D. Júlia was neither a dabbler nor a "token" woman. (See her portrait, illustraion 7.) As was the case with perhaps only one other woman, Carmem Dolores (pseudonym of Emília Moncorvo Bandeira de Melo, d. 1911), D. Júlia was recognized as a rightful member of the era's literary elite, only accidentally distinguished by her sex from almost all her colleagues. Although she did write feminine manuals, such as the one noted earlier, such work was apparently disregarded in contemporary appraisal. Instead, her colleagues dwelt on her post-Naturalist novels (*A viúva Simões*, 1897: *A falência*, 1902; *A intrusa*, 1908; *A Silveirinha*, 1914) often involving the traumatic decline of Carioca families, and since compared favorable with those of Eça de Queirós, the preeminent Portuguese Naturalist of the era.[116] As such, she suggests, like Coelho Neto, the way Naturalism or earlier French schools remained influential in Rio among the generation dominating the *belle époque*.

One's interest in D. Júlia lies not so much in her literature, perhaps, but in her odd place in the Republic of Letters. There were no noted women in the bohemia of the 1880s, and none in the Romantics' world save in the most passive or marginal roles. Women generally had simply lacked the opportunities or training for an active role in the creation of culture in Rio. The courageous feminist exceptions in the world of journalism which Hahner has recovered for us depressingly prove the rule.[117] Still, it is clear that, by the *belle époque*, for the most fortunate, the chance literature offered to move from a traditional, subordinate role to an active one had emerged for women in exceptional individual circumstances, much as it had earlier for men of color, who occasionally emerged throughout the century (e.g., Gonçalves Dias, Teixeira e Sousa, Machado de Assis, Cruz e Sousa[118]).

Broca has noted, for example, that certain provincial literary organizations were willing to admit women writers during this era.[119] It could be that, given the relative difficulty of finding writers of quality in the provinces, misogyny was laid aside. Not so in Rio, where the Academy denied women entrance, in conformity with French Academy strictures. In D. Júlia's case, the injustice was so keenly felt that it was clumsily addressed by the expedient of electing her husband, the Portuguese poet, Felinto de Almeida, in her stead.[120] (See group portrait, illustration 6.) When one considers the exceptional circumstances that made her entrance even a question, the situation for women is clearer still. D. Júlia was, after all, the daughter of a *titular*, and one who actively promoted her literary career (and presumably that of her sister, a published poet). Her marriage to Felinto was also quite exceptional; the dedication in her bridal manual and a joint interview they had with João do Rio make patent extraordinary mutual support and creativity, though D. Júlia still subordinated her literary interests to her role as a wife and mother.[121] Clearly, few other elite women born in the Rio of 1864 enjoyed such relatively fortuitous circumstances. Most important, how many authors would also have the extraordinary talent necessary to make use of such possibilities? In a small, competitive literary world limited by Rio's tiny market, D. Júlia was able not only to publish short stories and serial novels in the newspapers, but see them published in book form. Indeed, she created enough of a personal following to make her one of the few literati, along with Bilac, Coelho Neto, and João do Rio, celebrated enough to give fashionable public lectures.[122] D. Júlia's near solitary success as a woman and the obviously extraordinary talent that made it possible, like the odd case of Laurinda Santos Lobo in the salons of the era, thus bears mournful witness to the general lack of an active role for women in the culture of the Carioca *belle époque*. One should note, too, that this does not jar in comparison with the model culture of France. Though the role of salon hostesses was far more advanced for Frenchwomen, their position as writers was not so much better than that of their Brazilian sisters. One can point to an important woman poet, the Countess de Noailles, or to Colette, but, in general, is D. Júlia's exceptional case indicative of qualitative limitations special to Brazil?[123]

Here, then, in its most prominent exemplars, is the nature of the literary high culture of the Carioca *belle époque*. The limitations of the milieu in terms of career and readership, the relations between *alto mundo* and literati, French cultural influence, and the way in which Europhile commodity fetishism influenced cultural form and content are clear. The evocation of a Francophile high culture of elite fantasy and narcissism, however, must be tempered by an appreciation of conflict and paradox within the cultural milieu. The *belle époque* was not simple. Its complexity is suggested by the fact that this discussion has so far neglected the period's two great cultural critics, two great young authors, and the work of its literary titan. Their lives and work will be addressed now.

LITERARY CONFLICT AND PARADOX IN THE '*BELLE ÉPOQUE*'

10. Critics and rebels of the milieu

The literati's retreat from socio-political engagement, characteristic of the Carioca *belle époque*, was not a complete rout. Some remained on the field, and two new men charged onto it. If the Naturalism of the 1870s continued to influence writers like Coelho Neto and D. Júlia, its underlying notions of scientific social criticism were more explicit in the work of the critics Sílvio Romero and José Veríssimo and in the prose of Euclides [Rodrigues Pimenta] da Cunha (1866–1909), while the Realism of Flaubert had, in the young [Afonso Henriques de] Lima Barreto (1881–1922), a lonely but piercing voice.

Sílvio Romero had been one of the young literati of the Escola de Recife. Indeed, after 1880, he became its most celebrated champion in numerous volumes where he explained its origins, propagated its values, and continued to strop the edge of its critique. During the 1890s and early 1900s, when so many of his generation had reached some sort of accommodation with the elite society and values of the *belle époque*, he remained in opposition. The reasons for this singular stance are not only intellectual, but personal. As a youth, Sílvio perceived himself fighting behind Tobias Barreto's banner against the obscurantism and metaphysics of the Faculty of Law at Recife and the reigning Romanticism at the Côrte. As he aged, Sílvio continued in the role of provincial iconoclast, which had molded his critical work from its beginnings at the edge of Brazilian culture and now marked it deeply at its end in that culture's center. His intellectual combativity also owed something to his failure as a poet in the 1870s. Defeat as a poet seemingly strengthened his will to conquer as a critic, and strained acid into his passionate, defensive, and bitter attitude toward established Carioca literary cliques and such men as Machado de Assis and José Veríssimo. These, he felt, had denied Tobias Barreto his historical due and persisted in intellectual error and bad faith.[124]

Sílvio himself analyzed literature in historicist terms, believing its value lay in the authors' successes in exemplifying and exploring their epochs. Sílvio never considered himself a literary critic, but a critic of society who studied literature, a follower of Taine (at his most determinist) and the German and English materialist and evolutionist thinkers.[125] As their influence began to pale, and the *fin de siècle* flooded in, Sílvio necessarily became increasingly ferocious in vindicating his beliefs. It was probably no coincidence that he often dwelled outside Rio, citadel of the cosmopolitan urbanity he despised. He saw *fin-de-siècle* literature as a moment that was "simply *stationary*, not decadent."[126] He dismissed the Carioca elite and the Carioca literary milieu as parasitical and *literatice* (pedantic literary pretension), completely alien to Brazilian realities. The scandalous speech with which he once welcomed a new member of the Academy was characteristic. Sílvio described as an "extravagance" the contradiction between an elite of

> the intellectuals, weakened by foreign fads of all sorts, principally in the capital and the great cities, and the immense number of illiterates and ignorant people who make up the nation everywhere . . . The Brazilian problem *par excellence* consists precisely . . . in trying to do everything possible for such people . . . The greatest obstacle to this has been the literary pretensions of the writers and politicians, these men who enjoy public employment, social position, and the liberal professions, and who judge themselves the only genuine Brazilians, the soul and strength of the people.[127]

Sílvio's own self-appointed and enduring role as fulminating prophet of society and culture contrasts sharply with the shifts in his rival critic's career. José Veríssimo, like Sílvio, was a northerner and a member of the *geração de setenta* who had also become an established Carioca critic by the 1890s. (See group portrait, illustration 6.) Like Sílvio, he had, as a provincial novelist, editor, and essayist, shared a faith in materialist, scientific, and Naturalist truths as keys to the nation's regeneration. Unlike Sílvio, however, Veríssimo had become fundamentally disillusioned by the twisted, dwarfed successes of Abolition and the Republic. Like many other literati, he changed.[128]

Over the 1890s, the *engagé* provincial became a central figure in Rio's cosmopolitan literary world. This never meant becoming an *homme du monde* – Veríssimo remained a simple man of austere integrity – but it did mean a dramatic shift in his criticism. He had begun by judging literature along lines similar to those of Sílvio; now, he separated literature from social and economic concerns and criticized each by criteria he felt appropriate to each. Thus, like Sílvio, Veríssimo remained a perceptive, even bitter critic of social and political questions, maintaining the perspective (but not the activism) of the old days. But, unlike Sílvio, he began to criticize literature in what he thought were aesthetic terms, in which his personal taste, informed by an extraordinarily wide reading of national and foreign literature, was yoked to the views of contemporary French critics like Anatole France and Jules Lemaître. Contemplative aestheticism had succeeded literature as political engagement. The disappointments of the 1890s had driven the critic to the sanctuary of letters.

Veríssimo's decision to separate his cultural passions from his political preoccupations (and to distance himself from the latter) helps explain his focussed role in the *belle époque*. Veríssimo, it may be recalled, revived the respected *Revista Brasileira*, and thence, helped found the Academy. He also became the era's most respected and feared literary critic and the devoted admirer and friend of its preeminent author, Machado de Assis. In essence, Veríssimo attempted in the literary world and in his literary work to separate and strengthen this one last hope of his youthful aspirations from the detritus of the rest, to divide letters from the depressing realities of the nation, to which he now devoted an ironic, Anatolian criticism from a distance.[129]

Veríssimo, however, could not avoid the contradictions obvious in such an attempted separation. They eventually confronted him even in the Academy. Sílvio's position was easier: he damned both the elite who ran the nation and the literature that pleased them as one problem. Veríssimo's complexity was less fortunate. His attempt to separate national realities and national literature, to condemn the one and to promote and purify the other, had to founder. Since the literature and literary world of Rio were closely integrated with the values and social life of the *alto mundo*, such a separation was impossible. Veríssimo tried by distancing himself with a critical impartiality and a quiet, entirely literary social life, but the acid quality of the *alto mundo*'s claims on Carioca literature and literati was too corrosive.

After Machado's death, this quality became starkly obvious in one incident. The Academy's literary identity and integrity were shattered by the election of Lauro Müller, Rodrigues Alves' celebrated minister during Rio's great reforms.[130] The new academician had not even written a book. Until then, even the "engineered" elections (which Veríssimo had not shirked) had, at least, involved authors. Müller's political and national stature, however, made him too attractive a candidate for the Immortals to refuse him. Deeply disappointed, even enraged, Veríssimo cut his links to the Academy. Until his death, he maintained contact only with intimate friends and limited his other relations to his activities as a critic for prestigious periodicals. The phrase with which he parted from the Academy in which he had placed profound hope seems the epitaph of his literary generation: "Let us allow the Academy to make itself into the image of the society to which it belongs."[131]

Sílvio and Veríssimo, then, condemned the Carioca *belle époque* explicitly and implicitly. The explicit critiques were their writings, which, as the work of established figures, commanded respect, if not obedience and a following. The implicit critiques are perhaps more significant. Both writers, considered by contemporaries the preeminent critics of the epoch, were isolated from their fellows and their age, each in his own way. Sílvio was perceived with fear or annoyance as a loud and tactless figure too important to ignore, but too disturbing not to marginalize.[132] Veríssimo was perceived with fear and admiration as a personally modest but literarily aggressive purist, too important to ignore, but increasingly willing to marginalize himself.[133] Both men were praised, read, and noted; neither was typical. The age was not comfortable with social criticism or intellectual integrity.

The lives and works of two authors are painfully indicative of this. Euclides da Cunha and Lima Barreto were marginal to the *belle époque*, both socially and in terms of the purpose and circumstances of their writing. Yet both are now considered among the best Brazilian writers. Euclides' present stature was anticipated, albeit with surprise, by his contemporaries; Lima Barreto's work only knew largely posthumous acclaim.[134]

Euclides, though born too late (1866) to be a member of the *geração de setenta*, was certainly its heir. An engineer, trained in the Escola Militar, great bastion of the *geração*'s worldview, he emerged a militant, Positivist-influenced Republican. Like many others, the 1890s broke much of his faith in political and social regeneration, but not all. As his work indicates, he still believed in the importance of critical, engaged literature for national regeneration. He basically focussed his earlier Republican militancy into a more passive, though Comtean, faith in an elite of great men (the flower of the intellectuals and contemporary statesmen) who might be moved to act by writing engaged with social realities and crafted with science, patience, and skill. This was the great hope of his work.[135]

Os sertões (The Backlands) was created over the five years following the conflict it confronted – the messianic backlander rebellion in the Bahian hinterland at Canudos from 1895 to 1897. It was not the hasty work of a jaded journalist or bureaucrat producing another quick serial novel in his leisure time. Rather, it was an act of revolt and meditation by a timid idealist and patriot who dreamed of being a writer and needed to express the national trauma he had witnessed in Bahia. Euclides, a war correspondent during the Canudos campaign, had been shocked by the resistance and massacre of the *sertanejos* (backlanders). He had also been disturbed by the stark differences between the interior and the Europeanized urban civilization of the coast. The contradictions patent in that harsh and searing wilderness galvanized him. He stated matters passionately in the "Preliminary Note" to his masterpiece, where he pointed to the terrible logic of the massacre:

> we, sons of the same soil, have carried it out, because, ethnologically undefined, without common national traditions, living parasitically at the Atlantic's edge by civilizing principles elaborated in Europe, and armed by German industry – we had in the action the singular role of unconscious mercenaries. Moreover, poorly bound to those extraordinary fellow countrymen by a land we only partly know, a historical coordinate separates us from them completely – time.
>
> That campaign reminds one of a leap into the past. And it was, in the integral sense of the word, a crime.
>
> We denounce it.[136]

Euclides stole time to write *Os sertões* between a brief period of recuperation, various engineering duties, and three years building a bridge in the *paulista* hinterland. Happily, he did not struggle unaided. He began with field notes and the help of friends who, like himself, were deeply involved in private research on Brazil: men like Teodoro Sampaio, engineer and amateur regional historian, or Francisco Escobar, the provincial intellectual who provided the material and intellectual milieu which made Euclides' creation possible. In the end, however, it was Euclides' burden, an enormous work of research and critical thought, written in agonizing self-doubt.

Euclides, unable to publish the unusually long manuscript through his *paulista* newspaper editor, finally arranged matters with a Carioca publisher-bookseller, Laemmert, introduced to him by the academician, Lúcio de Mendonça. Terrified of the grammatical nit-picking modish on Ouvidor, new and virtually unprotected in the established

Carioca literary world, he spent the night before the book's appearance correcting, with penknife and pen, eighty errors he had found. When he finished with that first edition's thousand copies, he returned to the *paulista* hinterland, unable to face the response of the urbane readers his book implicitly condemned. *Os sertões*, however, was an immediate, unheard-of success.[137] The new author wrote to his father with excitement and pride that

> I received a letter from Laemmert stating that he is obliged to hasten the second edition of the "Backlands," already in process, in order to fill the orders that come to him even from Mato Grosso, and which he cannot satisfy because the first edition is already sold out. This in two months![138]

Later, he wrote of his enormous Carioca success in these terms:

> What satisfied me above all is the lucre of a moral sort obtained: the whole of national opinion which, through its best sons, is entirely on my side . . . I have conquered by myself alone, without advertisement, without patrons, without the Rua do Ouvidor, and without cliques.[139]

How is it that a man painfully uncomfortable in the *belle-époque* milieu and completely divorced from the Republic of Letters should triumph with a work unusual in style and subject and explicitly critical of much essential to the *belle époque*? The answers are complex and revealing.

For one, Canudos was still recent and had been deeply troubling. The *sertanejos*' supposed monarchist threat to the newly-established Republic; the extraordinary military defeats; the unknown, threatening messianic movement – all of this still piqued the interest of readers.[140]

For another, the sincerity, epic quality, and dramatic tension of Euclides' peculiar style captivated readers accustomed to entirely different prose; in Joaquim Nabuco's well-known phrase, Euclides "wrote with a liana." Even literati who were indifferent or hostile to the subject reported the seduction of the engineer's writing.[141]

For a third, the most important critics were members of the *geração de setenta*, steeped in its Romantic nationalism, Realism, Naturalism, and scientistic legacy. Though there was nothing in the European canon like *Os sertões*, its debts to the notions, preoccupations, and styles of respected masters were clear. Taine, Renan, Buckle, Spencer, Gumplowicz, Hugo, Musset, Eça, Zola – all leant strength to Euclides' hand as he molded a unique work about a uniquely Brazilian predicament.[142] Thus, critics like José Veríssimo, Sílvio Romero, and Araripe Júnior were prepared to recognize a masterpiece which spoke to the concerns (and in the language) of their youth. Indeed, there is a note of surprised, relished vindication in the critics' responses.[143] Sílvio, for example, stitched his public praise for Euclides with implied contempt for the contemporary literary milieu:

> Your book is not a product of facile writing or of discontented petty politics. It is a serious and deep social study of our people that has been the object of your constant research, your readings, you direct observations, your travels [and] your constant meditations.[144]

Finally, Euclides' conquest of such consecrated critics must have done much, in turn, to win the interest of the unprecedented thousands who quickly bought this unusual work by an unknown. Further accolades doubtless increased this effect. Within a year, for example, with the active promotion of such established figures, Euclides won membership in both the Academy and the Instituto Histórico e Geográfico Brasileiro. It was an ironic triumph in the *belle époque*, for it smacks of a rebuke to the era, and one administered by members of an older generation who seemingly gave vent here to their social and cultural frustrations. If old hopes had faded, and fashionable culture taken a new direction, here, at least, was one new author who had "fought the good fight" successfully. They rushed to press laurels on his brow, just as Euclides waited with a "schoolboy's" fears for their approval and greeted his triumph with profound gratitude and emotion.[145]

Matters were different with Lima Barreto. In an earlier chapter, I mention his background as an example of family patronage where, despite poverty and color, individuals could be "raised up" by powerful families.[146] Lima Barreto's story, however, ends somberly. Even with the unusual opportunities noted, which gave his parents, both mulattoes, the chance to marry, establish a household, give him an education, and see him enter a secondary school (again, like Euclides, in a Positivist citadel, Rio's Escola Politécnica), the weight of racism finally dragged Lima Barreto down. Blocked from graduation by the prejudices of a professor, he was fortunate to find "decent" employment as a petty ministerial bureaucrat. For Lima, the job was a kind of slow, mental death. Literary greatness became his private obsession, his only hope of personal vindication in a society whose Europhile pretenses, racism, and class prejudices he assimilated and suffered daily.[147] From 1909, the year he first published a novel, his diary records his despair and hope:

> As an undisciplined, incomprehensible and misunderstood mulatto, to be very very intelligent was the only thing that filled me with satisfaction! Humanity lives by intelligence, through intelligence, and for intelligence, and, being intelligent, I would enter into humanity by force, that is, into the great Humanity of which I wish to be a part.[148]

At his life's end, Lima's very European, bourgeois faith in mobility through intellectual achievement remained passionate:

man, through the intermediary of Art, does not remain bound to the prejudices and precepts of his time, of his birth, of his country, of his race, he goes beyond this . . . to reach the whole life of the Universe and to incorporate his life in that of the World.[149]

Like Euclides, Lima found his way in the European masters dear to the literati of past generations. His papers and library are replete with the French nineteenth century. He wished, especially, to emulate French Realism's analysis and insight. Indeed, it seems almost too symbolic that a volume of *La Revue des Deux Mondes* was in his hands at death. Even more than Euclides, however, Lima's capacity to adapt and discard is clear. Where, as Sevcenko shows, Euclides was driven by his scientism to accept the racist tenets of much contemporary European evolutionism, Lima, raw from the prejudice which blighted his life, put such theories aside with anger.[150] Indeed, unlike the great black poet, Cruz e Sousa – whose Symbolism and temperament responded to racism with compensatory visions and allusive defiance, hatred, and frustration[151] – Lima faced the racism of the Carioca elite and literati with acuity, ire, and scorn. Thus, in *Vida e morte de M.J. Gonzaga de Sá* (1919), Lima's protagonist, a descendant of Rio's founder, laughs at the social-column aristocracy of the *belle époque*:

Do you think that great noble families are being discussed [there]? Not at all. They are *parvenu* gentlemen, who naturally marry the daughters of newly-rich Portuguese. The grooms descend from bankrupt planters without any blue blood, and the grandparents of the bride are still at the plowhandle in the old fief of Minho . . . I have no superstitions about race, color, blood, caste, or anything else . . . I have avoided Petrópolis people because, for me, they are foreigners, invaders, generally without any culture and always rapacious, whether natives or foreigners. I am a Sá, I am of Rio de Janeiro, with its Tamoios, its blacks, its mulattoes, its *cafusos*, and its *gallegos*, too.[152]

So, while the Carioca literati subscribed to the French fashion of Latinity or the notion of Hellenism rather than confront Brazil's racial realities,[153] Lima identified with Brazil's people of color and ridiculed the Europhile pretensions of the *alto mundo*. The response of the Carioca readership and "respectable" literati to such an author could hardly be warm.

Indeed, Lima's novels, unlike *Os sertões*, enjoyed little success. They were brief, autobiographical, and simple, and their critical view of society did not recommend them in the era. *Os sertões*, too, had been critical, but, more so of the military and of general cultural and political problems.[154] Lima's acid was sprinkled on specific elite groups and individuals. Indeed, his first novel, *Recordações do escrivão Isaías Caminha* (which he published at his own expense after enormous difficulty), was a *roman-à-clef* attacking the literary and journalistic establishment.[155] Rather than introduce himself with an epic written in an impressive, grand style, as Euclides had, Lima announced his presence with a social and cultural satire of the very people who determined literary success, and he did this with a bitter, ironic phrasing that was as flexible and sharp as a rapier. Though José Veríssimo was privately both critical and impressed, and although the book sold, the public recognition was negligible.[156]

Subsequent novels – Lima published four and a book of stories – brought only uneven, grudging recognition; they never made him an accepted author of the first rank. Even *Policarpo Quaresma* (1915), an unqualified critical success, did not change his position as a writer kept at arm's length. Three times, Lima sought admission to the Academy; thrice, he was rejected. He attempted it because he believed as fervently as Flaubert in the transcendental value of Art and the consecrated character of the literary profession. Once, when a friend derided the term "literato," Lima wrote "I feel very honored with the title, and I have dedicated all my life to merit it."[157] He explained his thirst for the Academy himself by proclaiming: "I am a writer, and, whether great or mediocre, I have the right to demand the rewards that Brazil gives to those who distinguish themselves in her literature."[158]

Even if his novels had been more typical of the *belle époque*, Lima himself was not. Knowing the genteel pretensions of the literary establishment, Lima understood that his social marginality, too, denied him the Academy. He was cut off from it by his bohemian sprees in the *cidade velha* and by his lack of social position.

> I know well that I am not fit for the academy, and that the notoriety of my downtown life is not compatible with its respectability. I even stopped frequenting homes of any sort of gentility on my own – how could I hope for the academy? Certainly, I cannot.[159]

Lima's correspondent responded to these explanations with this forceful note on the Academy's hypocrisies:

> You cannot enter the academy because of the "impropriety of your downtown life"; nevertheless, the Academy admits the flagrant impertinence of a J[oão] do R[io]. The immortals, in Jupiter's case, always looked with indulgence on Ganymedes . . . After all, they are white, that is, immortals [and] they understand one another there.[160]

The enduring respect of a few literati over the years allowed Lima some pride, despite these disappointments. Moreover, his increasingly radical politics and regular articles in the emerging leftist press after 1915 brought him a new audience. These successes, however, left him better known without making him more acceptable, for obvious reasons. Still, by the 1920s, beyond the bohemian circle of old friends, others began to frequent his tables in various Carioca bars. He began to attract the interest of younger writers from Rio, the provinces, and São Paulo. It was pleasant but it was not compensation.

In the end, Lima's failure to achieve acceptance by the *belle-époque* literati, though he generally despised them as individuals, meant failure to achieve recognition for the only thing that mattered to him. Euclides met unexpected death in the full glory of literary triumph in 1909. Lima died slowly, dogged by madness and drink, a prematurely aged, ragged, bitter bohemian who never tasted the success essential to his personal sense of worth. He died in 1922, the year of his last attempt to enter the Academy. The academician whose place he failed to take was João do Rio, dead in 1921.[161]

Euclides' odd success and Lima Barreto's understandable failure, like the later careers of Sílvio Romero and José Veríssimo, tell one much about the complexity and limitations of the Carioca *belle époque*. And one must underscore, in concluding, the fact that the work of the two critics is connected to the creations of the two authors by the legacy of the literary and critical notions of the *geração de setenta*. Though no two of the four used this rich inheritance alike, each picked and chose from among its strands to weave together his particular work.

That might be expected; one would think some continuity usual from generation to generation. Indeed, in typical writers like Coelho Neto and Olavo Bilac, the Naturalism and Parnassianism of their youth continued to figure in the *belle-époque* writing. The main tendencies of *belle-époque* culture, however, were distinct. Coelho Neto, for example, subordinated his Naturalism to *fin-de-siècle* decadence. Nor did he or Bilac maintain their youthful opposition to the social or political structure of Brazil. Bilac did champion pet issues of progress, like literacy or Rio's urban reform, and both, like João do Rio (in his early phase), might occasionally demonstrate unease with some aspects of change or the loss of some old ideals and traditions.[162] For the most part, though, they accepted the *belle époque* on its own terms.

With the four writers selected here, however, acceptance of the *belle époque* was impossible. For them, a critical stance towards the modern era was *central* and bound up with their direct links to *geração de setenta* notions and positions which those more typical of the *belle époque* had abandoned. Here, it is especially interesting to note, for example, that Lima Barreto was obsessed with the concept of *bovarismo*, borrowed from a contemporary French critic, an idea he identified with his own perception of the era's self-illusion.[163] This gloss on Flaubert gave Lima one of his keys to the Rio of 1900; *bovarismo* pointed to the wishful fantasies central to the meaning of the Carioca *belle époque*. The old Frenchman still strengthened the young Brazilian's insight.

All of these four men, then, are distinct from other *belle-époque* writers because they employed what was useful in the European legacy to analyze the realities behind the façades of their Europhile, neo-colonial present. Because they did so, they reach across time to us, in works that still speak to Brazilian reality. Typical *belle-époque* authors, like Coelho Neto or the later João do Rio, generally spoke only to their era's elite: indeed, they helped to elaborate those expensive fantasies of theirs. They reach across time to us only as documents of the Brazilian fantasies of the era, the *bovarismo* Lima recognized in the anguished pages of his diary.

11. The triumph of Machado de Assis

The end came in mid-afternoon, on 29 September 1908. He had rejected the consolation of a Church long left behind and died surrounded by women drawn from his aristocratic social relations and men devoted to him. Ill for some time with a cancerous ulcer, he had endured great pain. The body borne out of the home on fashionable Cosme Velho was light enough to be carried by four women. Later, women would also strew the casket's path with rose petals, on its way to the cemetery. It was fitting. Women were his devoted readers. Three generations of Carioca women had enjoyed his fiction, and women were often the pivots on which his plots turned. Lying in state at the Academy and later, at the burial, he would be publicly mourned by men. Few of them were old enough to remember his beginnings; they lay a half-century in the past, in the Second Reign's palmy days, when even D. Pedro was young and Pereira Passos was watching Haussman remake Paris. All of the mourners, however, with all of Brazil's readers and readers elsewhere, in Latin America and even in Europe, all knew of him at his ending. For Machado de Assis had been long known as the great author of Brazil, the chief of its literati.[164]

Yet here is a signal paradox of the literary *belle époque*: its greatest author stood apart from it. Machado was of no era or school, nor did he leave one behind him. Coelho Neto, João do Rio, Olavo Bilac, Júlia

8. Machado de Assis, *c.* 1908

Lopes de Almeida, Afrânio Peixoto, Elísio de Carvalho – these are authors typical of the *belle époque*, just as Sílvio Romero, José Veríssimo, Euclides da Cunha, and Lima Barreto were its great critics and rebels. Machado was neither typical of the era nor explicitly critical of it; his work transcends literary fashions and periods. From beginning to mature creation, it lay outside canons; the eclectic influences which informed it were shaped to serve the taste and insight of an author quintessentially Carioca and triumphantly universal.[165]

The difficulties, triumphs, and compromises of Machado's career have been noted. One turns now to his literary persona and the development of his work. One might begin with a superficial comparison to João do Rio and Lima Barreto: For this mulatto, as for those, literature was the avenue of social ascent, one to which complete devotion was given. Very little else, however, is common between the three. Machado's long devotion included every aspect of Carioca letters. He began as a poet and writer of short stories, as well as a political journalist and reporter; in the 1860s, he added an enduring devotion to the *crônica*. He was an established poet by the 1870s as well as a dramatist and critic. By then, his French was good enough to write praiseworthy verse and to publish translations of current French literature. Over the next two decades, he reached beyond this common Francophile influence to English literature (especially Thackeray, Swift, Sterne, and Dickens) and an admiration for German philosophy (especially Schopenhauer). Between 1872 and 1881, the poet admired for his elegance and the critic acclaimed by José de Alencar also completed the first phase of his great prose fiction and established himself as a novelist. It was in this genre that he won his precedence among colleagues and posterity. The novels between 1891 and 1908 were masterpieces, each crafted secretly while Machado traced out his daily existence between ministry, Ouvidor, and home, and wrote the columns which, until 1901 when he quit, cast him in the role of Rio's chronicler.[166]

Indeed, in this season of his glory, Machado moved with simple majesty, political discretion, and bureaucratic regularity among the city's literary elite. One colleague recalled the *mestre*:

> His life, when I knew him, was monotonously regulated. He came every afternoon – at that time offices closed at three o'clock – from the Ministry of Transport toward Garnier's [bookstore]. There he installed himself in a small circle and talked about literature. If someone ventured into the burning questions of politics, into great social questions, he closed up. He did not express frank opinions [on such matters].[167]

A young poet remembered the same occasions this way:

> Machado de Assis never missed the regular hour at Garnier's, as he never [missed] that at the office where he worked . . . When he entered Garnier's, passing under the august arc of the "Sublime Porte," [as they called] the monumental arch of the bookshop's entrance, hats tipped in chorus, backs bent: – Mestre! And, then, faces at every side, turning to see the fragile little figure, ceremonious and agitated, distributing greetings, matching bows, his hat between his fingers, on his lips the frankest of smiles. He spoke discreetly, putting velvet into his voice, revealing his sincerity, goodness, timidity.[168]

Certain characteristics distinguish the man's presence among his colleagues. His youthful poverty and lack of schooling have been noted. Thence the quiet voracity of this autodidact, who, except for his wife's patient corrections and his friends' loans of books, depended on subscription libraries and the constant practice of his craft for his vast learning and celebrated style. His journalism and his public style were subtle and tactful. In a literary milieu torn by camps, vendettas, and marked social styles, Machado was noted for his calm, modesty, and abstention from questions of personality. He was quiet about his own writing but quite insistent in promotion of the literary profession. In private life, he treasured friendships and private contacts with the elite, but he abhorred any sign of high society flamboyance. A mulatto, a stutterer, and an epileptic, he avoided the *alto mundo*, preferring the quiet of his study, the "club" at Garnier's, and the sessions of the various ephemeral literary and musical associations he supported for over five decades. Born on one of the hills framing the *cidade velha*, he left Rio only four times, and never got further than its hinterland and Minas Gerais. Within the close frontiers of this life one maps out the terrain of his singularity. Two elements merit emphasis: a long, adaptive career, and a life spent traveling upward and, then, inward in the same place.

Antônio Cândido once remarked that Machado's unique quality lay in his learning from the successes and failures of each Brazilian literary generation, rather than only following European changes, as was common.[169] Thus, Machado built on the foundation of the two Romantic generations that came and went in his youth and then continued taking up and discarding or reshaping elements of the successive schools that washed ashore during the rest of his life. The length of this life and his characteristic rejection of the exclusivity of one school or another help to explain his development of an inimitable style, strained from his own meditations, disappointments, and understanding.[170]

Here the second element comes into play: Machado's voyages upward and inward in the same place. First, one notes Machado's link to the place. Others, following European schools to achieve a *Brazilian* novel, followed the Romantic dicta to Indianism and Regionalism, or the Naturalist or fin-de-siècle formulae to determinist decadence, and failed. Machado, with eyes on what he knew, used *elements* from these schools (as well as his reading in English literature, philosophy, the Portuguese classics, the Bible, and the classics) to probe the psychological aspects of dramas played out among Rio's elite and middle-sectors, and succeeded.[171] It was a triumph based on the comprehension and expression of the human beings around him; hence the authenticity and the basis for universal appeal. No Brazilian was so intimately rooted in the national reality as Machado, and, thus, no one else could realize its universal potential so masterfully. In this, Machado accomplished the task he set for literature when he began his novels; in 1873, he wrote of the "instinct of nationality," and challenged Romanticism in these terms:

> There is no doubt that a literature, above all a new-born literature, ought to nourish itself principally from the subjects offered by its region; but we should not establish doctrines so absolute that they impoverish. What one should demand of the writer, above all, is sure, intimate sentiment, that makes a man of his time and of his country, even when he treats of subjects remote in time and space.[172]

It was how Machado developed his "sure, intimate sentiment" that brings one to the upward and inward aspect. Upward – Machado's own extraordinary ascent in Second Reign society prepared him to be the superb portraitist of patronage. As Roberto Schwarz has shown, the petty quarrels and amorous gentility of even the most Romantic of Machado's novels reveal this. Machado displays the keen observations and edged implications of a meticulous registrar of favor. His novels pitilessly show how wealth and power work themselves into the most intimate relationships.[173]

Inward – as contemporary critics first noted, the greater phase of novels (1891–1908) represented the triumph of a subtle psychological sensitivity. Machado, increasingly ill and worn by the disillusionment of age, took an ironic, hard-won comprehension of human frailty to peel away the bandages of appearance to reveal raw flesh with an understanding smile and gentle, deft fingers. All his novels, depending on character interaction, with only the most telling, impressionistic dabs of descriptive or historical color to place them perfectly, necessarily focussed on the human experience from the interior. They could not work for readers unless weighted down with the authentic nuances readers could accept as their own. They did work because Machado had cultivated both authentic nuance and human experience slowly and surely as the chronicler of the city's life over four decades. Here is Machado's rootedness, his "sure, intimate sentiment." The *mestre*'s success meant, by its very nature, novels *Brazilian* in their very essence and universal in what that essence revealed – the humanity of the Cariocas whom he explored.[174]

Here, for example, is a minor character from Machado's first novel, *Ressurreição* (1872):

> Vianna was a consummate parasite, whose stomach had more capacity than prejudices, less sensibility than desire. One should not suppose, however, that poverty obliged him to the office; he possessed something that he inherited

from his mother . . . But these contrasts between fortune and character are not rare. Vianna was an example of this. He was born a parasite as others are born dwarves. He was a parasite by divine right.[175]

And here is the experience of first love, given us by Bento, whose fateful love for Capitu was the inner spring of Machado's greatest work, *Dom Casmurro* (1899):

I turned to her; Capitu had her eyes on the ground. We stood straight then, slowly, and stood looking at one another . . . We did not move, it was our hands that extended themselves little by little, all four, touching, pressing, joining. I did not note the exact hour of that gesture. I should have noted it; I regret the lack of a note written that very night . . . I would put it here with any spelling errors it might have; but it would not have one, so different were the student and the young boy in me. I knew the rules of writing, without suspecting those of loving: I had orgies with Latin and was a virgin with women.[176]

And here, last, from *Memorial de Aires* (1908), is the poverty of a couple's first years together:

Poverty was the lot of the marriage's first years. Aguiar worked hard at other jobs to supplement his small salary. D. Carmo directed the domestic servants, working with them to give the home the comforts possible without added expense. She knew how to save what was necessary and simple; but things were so ordered, so perfected by the lady of the house's hands that they captivated the eyes of husband and visitors. Everything had something of her spirit, which linked all of them and joined, with rare skill, necessity and grace in each object. Tablecloths and doormats, curtains and still more work that came over the years, all bore the mark of her labor, the intimate note of her person. She would have invented, if it were necessary, elegant poverty.[177]

With such sketches, from his first novel to his best and his last, the master's pen shapes living beings with quick, sure strokes, beings as familiar to his Carioca contemporaries as they are to us.

By this domination of technique and substance, Machado thus represents a culmination, a classic, and a contradiction. A culmination, by virtue of his studied mastery of the Brazilian tradition and his assured adaptation of European innovations. A classic, in that Machado's own psychological realism was so true, and his use of the language so limpid, that he continues to speak to all of us with an authority transcending the Rio of 1850–1900. A contradiction, because his very grandeur was based on novels which find but one obvious point of contact with the literary world or elite sensibility over which he presided. Only his elegant irony, which reminded his contemporaries of Anatole France,[178] suggests period affinities and helps to explain his popularity. Otherwise, one might suggest that Machado lived and triumphed in the *belle époque*, but was not of it. As one young contemporary put it, in 1909, "One does not read him unscathed; he is a strange figure among us. Normally, Brazilian culture would not permit his appearance; he hovers in a sphere superior to his time and his people."[179]

12. Civilization and its discontents

The tragedy of the *geração de setenta* had been the failure of its hopes of national regeneration, a failure manifest by the 1890s. Although many intellectuals did remain proud of Abolition, far fewer were happy with the Republic. Its vaguer, more embracing promise inevitably left it prey to disillusion and cynicism. All this has been noted as the context of the *belle époque*, marked by the literary retreat from activism and literary *embourgeoisement* in the Academy and journalism of the era. Other comments can now be made, however, by way of conclusion.

In a way, the literary *belle époque* in Rio may also be seen as a kind of compensation for the disappointments just noted. If Brazil had not emerged as a "civilized" nation, comparable to the North Atlantic powers, at least her capital could. As Sílvio Romero put it then, and as Sevcenko has reminded us,[180] the era was one of an urbane façade, in which Rio attempted to fabricate a way of life conforming to the pattern of France, England, and other "civilized" nations. This is the most obvious example of the central fantasy of Civilization, one explored in chapter 1, and elaborated since throughout these pages. What I have tried to emphasize, however, is that this façade was neither recent nor entirely superficial. Such conclusions are too simple. I have shown here that the origins of the Carioca *belle époque* often reach back into the colonial period and that the fantasy of Civilization, the identification with the style of life and perspectives of a primarily Franco–English elite culture, was both adapted to the Carioca elite's needs and quite internalized. The period 1898–1914 represents the triumph, not the emergence of the phenomenon. Literature and the literati were especially sensitive registers of these trends. Both were always integrally involved in the tendency to assimilate foreign models, and their nature made a successful reproduction of the models seemingly necessary and clearly more facile. That is, literature, *per se*, was understood only in European terms, and its creation along such lines was a good deal simpler than that of industrial capitalism or national integration.

There are, however, aspects of the literature and literary life of the *belle époque* which distinguish it from earlier periods in these Eurocentric respects. Whatever the failures of Brazil's Romantic and Naturalist eras, for example, they still provided a basis for *Brazilian* literature. Their programmatic cultivation of Brazilian themes was not unfruitful. Schwarz has shown the final failure of Alencar's Romanticism to "fit" Brazilian realities, for example – but there is no doubt that Alencar's seminal work of internalization and adaptation made it possible for Machado, for instance, to gather a later harvest.[181]

Typical *belle-époque* literature, however, was nationally sterile. Its cosmopolitan European model fitted in too well with the era's façade itself. This model, turning on the narcissistic, cosmopolitan urban experience of the aristocracy and *grande bourgeoisie* was a literature matched to the common experience of urbane elites in the Europeanized world as a whole. The new degree of wealth and communication possible in the period fostered surfeit, sensuality, decadence, conspicuous consumption, and an international, aristocratic style of life centered on Paris.[182] Thus, for certain privileged enclaves in Brazil, *fin-de-siècle* high culture and the *belle-époque* literature derived from it fitted their way of life and their perspectives quite naturally. This literature's very superficiality, its precious quality, worked naturally into the *alto mundo*'s cultivated fantasy experience. However, precisely because it did so, it necessarily failed to plumb national realities of a more enduring sort (except the enduring reality of such *bovarismo*) which might have allowed such literature to survive.

This is another way of glossing Broca's dictum on the way in which literature and worldly literary life tended to reverse their logical order of importance and even to be confounded.[183] Essentially, they were collapsed together under the weight of the fantasy of Civilization. Typical *belle-époque* literature displays this in its form, substance, production, and ends. The pleasure in a sensual description of expensive material objects, the concentration on the author or on the individual, the passion for vicarious experience in scenes of decadence, the occult, wealth, and the exotic, the use of irony and a worldly tone of disillusion – all of this reflected the tastes of the gilded bohemia and their readers, presenting the world as they wanted it and as they enjoyed it in *palacetes*, the Club dos Diários, on Ouvidor, and strolling down the Avenida. Too often, the literature derived from and reflected the same milieu. Sensationalist newspapers and chic reviews fed the consumer light fare, entertainment meant for quick reading, that often competed with the even easier attractions of illustrations and photographs.

In all, it was literary production sharing the worst aspects of mass and elite culture: superficiality and an emphasis on expensive, status-oriented experience and materialism. Like the objects and experiences discussed in the previous chapter on consumer fetishism, typical *belle-époque* literary production was bought partly as a reinforcing element of the elite fantasy. One purchased *Kósmos* because its appearance and expense went with one's décor and one's *mundano* image, and because it provided agreeable "culture" (in the vulgar sense of something designed to provide a sense of superior refinement).[184] One attended a fashionable public lecture for the same reasons. While men of the elite might pass the afternoon in chic hotels with celebrated French cocottes, from whom they bought both sensual and cultural gratification, their womenfolk might do much the same thing. After buying sensual and cultural gratification in the Ouvidor and Avenida shops, they went on to edifying halls where they purchased use of a frenchified literary celebrity.

In just such ways, high culture and its makers folded into the Carioca *belle époque*, an extension of the life, pleasure, and perspectives of the elite. The insights, condemnation, and disdain of marginal or maverick literati, and the psychological penetration of Machado, made little difference – then. The Carioca *belle époque* rested on foundations too old and too strong not to rise as it did. It would take the cultural trauma of the Great War, economic dislocation, and European culture's post-war failure of nerve to bring about its collapse, one whose first tremors broke up the Brazilian cultural landscape in 1922. That year, between the premature deaths of two Cariocas, João do Rio and Lima Barreto, a new era began, that of Brazil's Modernismo. It was to be a movement born, fittingly enough, in a city inland from the coast, one that had gone beyond plantation coffee to take the lead in industrialization. The new era washed over the old port capital at Rio from beyond the Serra do Mar. It was an age born in São Paulo.

Conclusion

At times, these pages have suggested the experiences of a traveller, in this case not only to a distant city, but to a dead one. The Rio analyzed here has long since changed profoundly; its very geography has been swept away or reshaped, and only the poorest or most honored corners of the city offer the historian some buildings from the past century. The names of the *cidade velha* streets often remain the same, but *cidade velha* has been replaced by *centro* in the language of the modern metropolis, and these streetnames no longer have their original meaning, nor even the symbolic one given by old glories. Today, the Rua do Ouvidor is an alley, crushed by modern banks and bars at one end and pocked by tawdry shops at the other. The urban, industrial sprawl has been fatal to the Côrte and the Federal Capital.

It is from that dead and distant place, from nineteenth-century Rio, that I have tried to recreate the world of the Carioca elite. I have hoped, in the way I have taken the analysis from the most exterior to the most intimate and intellectual aspects of elite life, to take apart elite culture and society with as little damage as possible to its wholeness, to demonstrate the common factors that make it understandable. The central theme was inevitable, given the nature of the subject, and the analysis has thus turned on the role of a culture of Franco-English aristocratic derivation in Rio over the nineteenth century. In chapter after chapter, one finds that the culture served to maintain and promote the interests and perspective of the elite by helping to provide a common socialization, common legitimization, and common ground for the ongoing relations of the powerful in a neo-colonial context. One has seen how the paradigms from Europe, borrowed intact often enough, were inserted into traditional socio-economic relations, serving to support and strengthen the elite's position in local circumstances. And, finally, it has also been seen that, despite this obviously useful, instrumental function, the culture analyzed was more than pervasive. It was permeating on the most intimate and creative individual levels, at home, in public, and in literature, informing choices, attitudes and expression, affections and tastes, working its way into the very fiber of Carioca elite experience.

I have also, as an historian, tried to make clear the nature of this cultural confluence as something inextricably bound up with change over time, something that emerged in the *belle époque* as the florescence of trends with colonial roots, something whose value in terms of legitimization was partly owed to tradition, yet something which was new to the extent that it was realized with greater success as a function of increasingly strong socio-economic factors born of growing export trade, new markets, and new technology. Franco-English aristocratic models were important by the eighteenth century, but took on enormous new importance with the establishment of the Bragança court and the Opening of the Ports in 1808. They informed elite culture, to a limited extent, in every aspect of elite life by at least the 1820s, and gained immeasurably with the new *fluminense* wealth sprung from coffee, important as early as the 1830s, flourishing by the third quarter of the century. With the great shift from coffee port and imperial court to commercial and financial center and republican capital, with all the changes in the preoccupations, careers, and even origins of members of the elite, such foreign paradigms or their adaptations within the Carioca milieu continued as one of the few relatively unchanged aspects of elite culture and society, and, thus, helped to maintain continuity, so crucial an element to ongoing elite hegemony.

I have also tried here to demonstrate the essential nature of the paradigms, discussing them in their original context at times to show the distinctions necessary for understanding how the significance of this aristocratic culture varied in Europe and Brazil. A culture arising in nineteenth-century Europe as part of bourgeois and aristocratic adjustments to a world born of the French and Industrial Revolutions took on an entirely different meaning in the Carioca neo-colonial context. What had often been in Europe part of an attempt to capture or retain superior class positions through identification with past aristocratic traditions became, in Rio, part of a successful attempt to do the same thing through identification with a powerful congeries of metropolitan symbols, institutions, and usages. And all of this in the face of an evolution from a more traditional, planter-dominated, familiar society, to a society that was rapidly changing, urban, and strangely complex.

Yet, if I have been successful, part of what has been done here will have been to show how all of this worked in a whole, increasingly dense fashion. How each aspect of elite culture and society tended to reinforce others, so that, by 1900, a member of the Carioca elite was part of a profoundly Europhile culture that informed every aspect of his or her life as a member of the dominant stratum in the most natural, hegemonic fashion. The ways in which they were socialized, the ways in which they related to their traditional dependants and equals, the ways in which they dressed, behaved, thought, ate, made love, and arranged marriage and business and politics, the schools they attended, the clubs they joined, the entertainment they enjoyed or sought out, the homes and buildings they lived and worked in, the society they cultivated (and the way that they cultivated it), the literature they read – all of these delicate and crucial aspects of culture and society have been shown here to have been increasingly informed by the Franco-English aristocratic paradigms accepted by this tropical elite as Civilization.

Appendix – Defining the elite

Many readers will be curious as to the size of the elite of which I write. The difficulty here has partially to do with the broad definition of the elite I use. Most commonly, scholars discussing the elite fasten on those who hold political office.[1] The elite I have studied is drawn from carefully selected institutions, groups, and primary sources, and is identified with a broader definition of power – power derived from wealth, occupation and perceived social status, as well as from political position, and, most commonly, power derived from an integral combination of all of these factors. Thus, I have followed a pattern of research that is inclusive, rather than exclusive, in its definition of the target group.

Further, I am also interested in the qualitative nature of the elite as Society, and in the individual combinations of factors that singled out, and allowed in, its members. In doing so, I naturally make various generalizations that often have validity for the larger elite pool in which Society finds its place, as the amorphous, self-conscious elite with recognized leaders that sets the cultural tone for the elite pool and, to a greater or lesser extent, for the more fashionable, ambitious elements of the middle sectors below them.

This relationship suggests the complexity of trying to find a number for the size of the elite, since the elite as I define it is barely sealed off from another, larger, group of people. My target group is Society, the elite, properly speaking. The other makes up what I have called here the "elite pool", the larger group of wealthy or powerful or well-connected and/or educated people who lack the proper cumulation of factors to allow their emergence into the elite *per se* and thus fall, perforce, into the social limbo above the middle sectors' upper reaches. It is from here, of course, that many in the elite come, and it is to there, just as surely, that many of the elite depart, especially when wealth or connections fail them. The very nature of either the elite or these upper reaches above the middle sectors is so amorphous as to defy precise numbers, but, from early on in the research, I have used certain approximate numbers as working definitions.

The number of names that surfaced from my initial survey of social columns, reports of certain Society events, and memoirs ran to about five hundred, a number composed of both men and women, and including many people with the same family names. This "universe" seems reasonable enough from all the qualitative information my research had been yielding about the elite's nature, particularly the assumptions, patent in both memoirs and contemporary journalism, that Society's members made up so small a group of people that everyone knew one another.[2]

I should note how this group of people was developed and used, particularly for chapter 3. I compiled several lists of names in my research. The longest, including the five hundred or so noted, was made up of all those cited as being members of the *alto mundo* or other similar catch-phrase for what, in English, is called Society, or high society. These people were commonly described in this manner in columns reporting Society events. The columns from which I drew up my lists included such examples as: the first night of the opera, reported in *Rua do Ouvidor;*, 2 July 1898, p. 4; an event at the Casino Fluminense, reported in *Rua do Ouvidor*, 15 October 1898, p. 5; the first night of the opera, again, reported in *Rua do Ouvidor*, 6 August 1904, pp. 3–4; the Parque Fluminense garden party, reported in *Gazeta de Noticias*, 20 July 1908, p. 3; and similar high society get-togethers reported in *Gazeta de Noticias* for 17 July 1908 (p. 2) and 12 July 1914 (p. 10). Naturally, the events chosen were picked to be as inclusive as possible, without putting the exclusive quality central to the elite into question. I wanted more than a clique, and less than the merely educated, merely rich, or merely elected.

I took from this long list those names which appeared toward both ends of the period 1898–1914, assuming that such people were more likely to represent the stable core of Society (as opposed to those whose fortunes only allowed a more ephemeral presence in the world under discussion). I then made up a list of those key people remembered by da Costa – see Luíz Edmundo [da Costa], *O Rio de Janeiro do meu tempo*, 5 vols. (Rio de Janeiro: Conquista, 1957), 2:329–31 – a successful poet and journalist of the epoch; and those people noted by Broca, in his indispensable work on literary society in an era when literature and Society were closely interwoven – see Brito Broca, *A vida literária no Brasil – 1900* (Rio de Janeiro: José Olympio, 1960), pp. 24–30. I then selected from among those names which either appeared in two or more of these three lists or which I knew to be important from the extensive research I was doing in primary sources. This final list amounted to more than fifty names. Those which the reader finds in chapter 3, then, are those belonging to the individuals from this final list who seemed to represent best the trends of the epoch and the tone of Society. I should note that I showed the final list to the survivors and descendants of the *belle-époque* elite whom I interviewed, and, besides the anecdotes which help to inform my descriptions, received general approbation with regard to the choices made.

As part of the corroboration noted, during an interview with an especially well-placed descendant of members of the *belle-époque* elite,[3] I asked how many families made up the elite at century's turn. The response fell between three and five hundred households. If one assumes a household made up of, say, ten people, between the head of the household, his wife, and a maiden aunt or bachelor brother or so and the couple's surviving children, this gives one an elite of about three to five thousand, certainly a figure commensurate with the face-to-face kind of Society explicit in the literature.

How reasonable a figure, however, is this in terms of what "hard" data are available? One can say that it is fairly reasonable, but only with a good deal of qualification, because the "hard" data are of a problematic value for research on an elite of this sort, and one's results are very rough estimates. For one thing, the only criteria likely to be useful for such purposes are those of professional category or educational degree, and these are too broad and too narrow at the same time. Too broad, because the categories used in the census are not refined enough to allow one to select out the elite, too narrow in that they register only one or another of the criteria defining the elite in which one is interested.

One turns, for example, to the data for professions in the Rio de Janeiro of 1870, when the Côrte had roughly a quarter of a million in population.[4] Two categories in which the elite would be more likely to be found would be those living off capital profits and property-holders. The census tells us that these two groups were made up of the following:

capitalists	245 men and women (116 men)
property-holders	1,572 men and women (882 men).

This would give one an 1870 approximation of 1,817 candidates for the elite, with 998 of them being men, and, thus, probably heads of households. But, obviously, though it is possible that many capitalists and property-holders were members of the elite, mere wealth, or, rather, the *probability* of mere wealth, has no necessary connection to the kind of elite under consideration here. It only gives one a good idea of one part of the elite pool, at best.

Doubtless, too, there were many members of the elite among the soldiers, public employees, members of the *profissão litterária*, farmers, and merchants noted in the census, but these are categories whose numbers suggest how broadly cast their definition was. Farmers, *lavradores*, for instance, are put down on the list with no distinction between plantation owners and small farmers. Is it any surprise their number is as high as 13,560, and that many of them are women? Nor is it clear whether a merchant in the census is a great merchant prince, with enormous investments in banking and land, who still makes his capital from a thriving import/export trade, or a petty shopkeeper, holed up in some dank first-floor place, selling dry goods and cheap rum. Worse, one has no way to know how a marquis, with extensive plantations in a province, investments in a bank and a railroad, and a nice position in the upper administration, will register himself. Is he one of the public employees, a farmer, a capitalist, or a property-holder?

Nor do matters become necessarily easier with the improvements in the census of 1890.[5] Then, if one accepts the narrowest categories most likely to give one elite candidates to the exclusion of others, one still has categories too broad and a potential elite total of 5,528 men and women, with 5,191 being men, and likely head of households:

Directors [male] of teaching establishments	48
Judges	178
Lawyers	761
Solicitors [native-born]	170
Physicians	965
Engineers [native-born]	579
Bankers	44
Capitalists	517
Property-holders	2,266
TOTAL	5,528

If one subtracts the broadest categories (e.g., Directors of teaching establishments, judges, lawyers, solicitors, physicians, engineers) in order to cut away possible middle-sector infiltration, one also cuts away many of the categories in which one finds elite individuals in the qualitative research on high society undertaken in chapter 2 and chapter 3. And such surgery leaves one with the same plutocracy of 1870, again, with the addition of the category "banker" and a total of 2,827 (of which 2,490 are men). It is hardly a satisfying exercise.

In 1906, matters are, if anything, moving a step backward.[6] The distinctions made so carefully in 1890 have been collapsed into broader, more abstract categories. If one adopts the same exclusive route, this plutocracy, made up this time of a *mélange* of *rentiers*, bankers, financiers, brokers, factors, and so on give one 4,235 people, of which 2,893 are men:

People that live principally from rents	3,522
Banking, credit, exchange, insurance	76
Brokerage, commissions, consignments	637
TOTAL	4,235

The liberal professions, excluding religious, yield 1,814 people, of which 1,804 are men, and these figures only count the one category of the professions most likely to exclude middle-sector members, i.e., the judicial profession (a dubious proposition, in any case):

Judicial	1,814 (1,804 men)
Health	3,784 (3,476 men)
Teaching	2,842 (883 men)
Sciences, letters, and arts	2,988 (2,842 men)
TOTAL	11,428 (9,005 men)
Less Health, Teaching and Sciences, etc.	1,814 (1,804 men)

The best that can be said, then, for such awkward measures of status is that they give one some general idea of the numerical strength of the elite and the elite pool combined, though nothing like the elite itself. With all these caveats in mind, the results look something like this, in approximate numbers in the thousands and with percentages of the total population noted:

Year	Population	Elite/Elite Pool Adults	Households
1870	235	1.8 (0.76%)	1 (0.43%)
1890	523	2.8–5.5 (0.54–1.05%)	2.5–5.2 (0.48–0.99%)
1906	811	4.2–6.0 (0.51–0.74%)	2.9–4.7 (0.36–0.58%)

Even with all of these problems, there is the added one that the "Households" count is bound to be off because more than one adult man probably dwelt in each elite household (a bachelor brother or uncle, or grandfather), which would shrink the numbers noted by some considerable figure impossible for one to know.

Of course, as one would expect, such numbers, as they are, are far greater than those my informant and the memoirs suggest. Where the 1906 figure has a minimum of 2,900 households, mine would have a maximum of around 500. But it is that for which the caveats and the idea of an elite pool would prepare one.

That the lesser figures, at least, are more accurate approximations of an idea of the elite, of Society, is suggested by other "hard" data. These have to do with the highly select social institutions that are the subject of chapter 2. Rare as such data are, they seem a good deal more useful for these purposes than the haze generated by the censuses. The Jockey Club was founded, for example, by some 59 men in 1868, about 6% of the elite/elite pool figure for Households in 1870.[7] I could obtain no figure for membership in 1890 or 1906, but the figure for 1921 was only 715, a figure much closer to the 1900 figure of around 500 suggested here than the elite pool figures of 2,900 to 4,700 (Household counts for 1906). At about the same time (1922), the number of members in the Club dos Diários was only 324.[8] Earlier figures for the Diários' predecessor, the Casino Fluminense, argue for the same small elite. The figure for the General Assembly of shareholders in 1856 is 113.[9] In 1862, the shareholders numbered only 75.[10]

Even assuming the members present did not represent the sum total of the membership in 1856 or 1862, and that the membership did not include all male heads of households comprising Society, the small numbers are still, I would argue, a better indication of the size of the elite than the census calculations above. The latter, as already suggested, are perhaps only apposite for establishing that, even at its greatest probable limits, the Carioca elite was numerically negligible. Even the greatest number indicated by the 1906 census, for example, would still give us only 4,700 male heads of households. This would be about 0.58% of the total urban population, and a group which, if one considers it was made up of relatives, colleagues, and schoolmates, and had been so for two or three generations for much of the membership, is a very small world, indeed. It is to the nature of that world, beyond the small numerical quantity of its members, that this work is devoted.

Notes

Preface

1 *Latinoamérica: Las ciudades y las ideas* (Buenos Aires, 1976), ch. 6.

1 Rio de Janeiro: capital of the Brazilian nineteenth century

1 See Stanley J. Stein and Barbara H. Stein, *The Colonial Heritage of Latin America* (New York: Oxford, 1970), pp. 7–17, 32, 57–9; Celso Furtado, *The Economic Growth of Brazil* (Berkeley: California, 1968), pp. 130–3; Emília Viotti da Costa, *Da senzala à colônia* (São Paulo: DIFEL, 1966), pt. 1: ch. 1, *passim*; and Warren Dean, *Rio Claro* (Stanford 1976), ch. 1 and *passim*. Cf. Caio Prado Júnior, *The Colonial Background of Modern Brazil* (Berkeley: California, 1967), pt. 3: 1st sec., *passim*; and Stuart B. Schwartz, "Free labor in a slave economy" in Dauril Alden (ed.), *The Colonial Roots of Modern Brazil* (Berkeley: California, 1973), *passim*. On population, one might note that in 1798, nearly half of Brazil's population was slave; in 1823, more than a quarter; in 1850, nearly a third. In 1823, there were provinces in Brazil where there were as many (or more) enslaved as free (e.g., Maranhão and Espírito Santo), and the four most populous provinces had slave populations comprising about a third of their total populations; see Stein, pp. 294–6; Robert Conrad, *The Destruction of Brazilian Slavery 1850–1888* (Berkeley: California, 1972), p. 283.

2 See Richard M. Morse, *From Community to Metropolis* (Gainesville: Florida, 1958), ch. 10, *passim*; Furtado, *Economic Growth*, chs. 15–20, *passim*; Stein and Stein, ch. 1, *passim*; Caio Prado Júnior, *História económica do Brasil* (São Paulo: Brasiliense, 1967), ch. 16, *passim*; Viotti da Costa, *Da senzala*, pt. 1: ch. 1, *passim*; and cf. Dean, chs. 1 and 2, *passim*.

3 See Gilberto Freyre. *The Mansions and the Shanties* (New York: Knopf, 1963). See also Fernando de Azevedo, *Brazilian Culture* (New York: Macmillan, 1950), pt. 1: ch. 3, *passim*; Richard Graham, *Britain and the Onset of Modernization in Brazil 1850–1914* (Cambridge: 1972), ch. 4, *passim*; and José Murilo do Carvalho, "A composição social dos partidos políticos imperiais," *Cadernos do Departamento de Ciência Política* (Belo Horizonte: UFMG) 2 (Dec. 1974), pp. 7–8. NB that the population of the four largest cities in Brazil remained at about 6% of the total population over the nineteenth century. See Richard M. Morse and Michael L. Conniff and John Wibel, *The Urban Development of Latin America* (Stanford: Center for Latin American Studies: 1971), p. 37; see also p. 46 and *passim*. On political

activity in colonial and later urban history, see Prado, *Colonial Background*, pt. 3: sec. 3, *passim*; and C. H. Haring, *Empire in Brazil* (New York: Norton, 1968), chs. 2, 3, *passim*.

4 See Viotti da Costa, *Da senzala*; Conrad, *Destruction*; and Leslie Bethell, *The Abolition of the Brazilian Slave Trade* (Cambridge: 1970).

5 Joseph L. Love, *São Paulo in the Brazilian Federation, 1889–1937* (Stanford: 1978), pp. 102–13; Wilson Cano, *Raízes da concentração industrial em São Paulo* (São Paulo: DIFEL, 1977), ch. 1: pt. 1, *passim*; Morse, *From Community*, chs. 10–14, *passim*.

6 See Roderick Barman and Jean Barman, "The role of the law graduate in the political elite of Imperial Brazil," JISWA, 18:4 (Nov. 1976): 430, 437–8, 440–3; José Murilo de Carvalho. "Elite and state building in Imperial Brazil" (PhD diss., Stanford, 1974); and his "A composição social", p. 15. Regarding regional representation in the governing elite over time see Barman and Barman, pp. 430, 438.

7 Joaquim [Aureliano Barreto] Nabuco [de Araújo], *Um estadista do Imperio*, 3 vols. (Rio de Janeiro: H. Garnier, 1897), 3: bk. 5: ch. 4, *passim*. Cf. José Maria dos Santos, *A política geral do Brasil* (São Paulo: J. Magalhães, 1930), ch. 5; [Francisco José] Oliveira Vianna, *O occaso do Imperio* (São Paulo: Melhoramentos, 1925), pt. 1: chs. 3–4; Haring, pp. 95–6. Dos Santos stresses Abolition's role in the events (pp. 101–9); Nabuco stresses Caxias (3: 109–16).

8 See Nabuco, *Um estadista*, 3: bk. 5: chs. 4, 5 and 7; Oliveira Vianna, pt. 3; and Murilo de Carvalho, "A composição social," pp. 8–9; José Maria Bello, *A History of Modern Brazil 1889–1964* (Stanford: 1966), ch. 3; Haring, ch. 7, *passim*. See also José Maria dos Santos, *Os republicanos paulistas e a abolição* (Rio de Janeiro: Martins, 1942) and George C. A. Boehrer, *Da Monarchia à República* (Rio de Janeiro: MEC, 1954).

9 Emília Viotti da Costa, "A proclamação da República," *Anais do Museu Paulista* 20 (1965): 191–200; Murilo de Carvalho, "A composição social," pp. 8–9, 14–17; Love, *São Paulo*. pp. 102–13, *passim*.

10 Murilo de Carvalho, "A composição social," pp. 7–9, 14–17; Azevedo, pt. 1: ch. 3, *passim*; Graham, *Britain and the Onset*, chs. 4 and 7, *passim*; Bello, ch. 3; *passim* [Affonso Celso de Assis Filho, conde de] Affonso Celso, *Oito annos de parlamento* (São Paulo; Melhoramentos, 1928), ch. 15, *passim*; Viotti da Costa, "A proclamação," pp. 184–6; Anyda Marchant, *Viscount Mauá and the Empire of Brazil* (Berkeley: California, 1965), pts. 2 and 4; cf. Roderick J. Barman, "Business and government in Imperial Brazil," JLAS, 13:2: 269–74; André [Pinto] Rebouças, *Diário e notas autobiográficos* (Rio de Janeiro: José Olympio, 1938). The latter three are good for an idea of the urban entrepreneurial milieu; neither Mauá nor Rebouças, however, was a Republican. Good exemplars of the latter, in terms of urban-based professionals or students would be Rui Barbosa (see below), and, for the idealistic student–soldier, Innocêncio Serzedello Correa, see João Neves da Fontoura, "Serzedello Correa" in Innocêncio Serzedello Correa, *Uma figura da República* (Rio de Janeiro: Freitas Bastos, 1959). Cf. Freyre, *Mansions*, *passim*; and Luíz Martins, "O patriarcha e o bacharel," *Revista do Arquivo Municipal* (São Paulo) 83 (May–June 1942). See also João Cruz Costa, *A History of Ideas in Brazil* (Berkeley: California, 1964), chs. 4–6, *passim*; and Thomas E. Skidmore, *Black into White* (New York: Oxford, 1974), pp. 1–30, *passim*.

11 See n. 4, above and Furtado, *Economic Growth*, ch. 24; Dean; Robert Brent Toplin. *The Abolition of Slavery in Brazil* (New York: Atheneum, 1972) and "From slavery to

fettered freedom," *Luso-Brazilian Review* 7: 1 (1970); Graham, *Britain and the Onset*, ch. 6, and "Causes for the Abolition of negro slavery in Brazil," HAHR, 46:2 (May 1966): 124, 126–7, 128, 137; and "Brazilian slavery reexamined," *Journal of Social History* 3: 4 (Summer 1970); Michael M. Hall, "Reformadores de classe média no Império brasileiro," *Revista de Histôria* 53:103 (January–March 1976): 148, 149–50, 151, 152–5, 169–71, Nabuco, *Um estadista*, 1: bk. 2: ch. 5, *passim*; Joaquim [Aureliano Barreto] Nabuco [de Araújo], *Abolitionism* (Urbana: Chicago, 1977); and André [Pinto] Rebouças, *Agricultura nacional* (Rio de Janeiro: A. J. Lamoureux, 1883). See, also, Robert E. Conrad, "Suggestions for further reading" in Nabuco, *Abolitionism*; Conrad's *Slavery* (Boston: G. K. Hall, 1977), and his *Children of God's Fire* (Princeton: 1983).

12 See Nabuco, *Um estadista*, 3: 186, 193–4, 549n.5, 549–50; Affonso Celso, *Oito annos*, pp. 145, 147–58, and *passim*; Oliveira Vianna; Gilberto Amado, "As instituições políticas e o meio social no Brasil" in Antonio Carneiro Leão *et al. À margem da história da República* (Rio de Janeiro: Annuario do Brasil, 1924); Vicente Licinio Cardoso, *À margem da história do Brasil* (São Paulo: Nacional, 1933), and others. Cf. Stanley J. Stein's, "The historiography of Brazil 1808–1889" HAHR 40:2 (May 1960): 251–8, 268–78; and Emília Viotti da Costa, "Sobre as origens da República," *Annais do Museu Paulista* (São Paulo) (1964): 63–120; "A proclamação," pp. 169–83; George C. A. Boehrer, "The Brazilian Republican Revolution," LBR 3: 2 (December 1966): 43–57; John D. Wirth, "Brazil, the Republic" in Charles C. Griffin and J. Benedict Warren, eds., *Latin America* (Austin: Texas, 1971), pp. 607–18, *passim*, especially, 614–16; and Thomas E. Skidmore, "The historiography of Brazil, 1889–1964: Part 1," HAHR 55: 4 (November 1975): 721–30, especially 729–30.

13 See June E. Hahner, *Civilian–Military Relations in Brazil* (Columbia, SC: South Carolina, 1969), ch. 1, *passim*; José Murilo de Carvalho, "As forças armadas na Primeira República" in Boris Fausto, ed., *História geral de civilização brasileira*, tomo 3, vol. 2, pp. 186–9, 195–7, 209–11, 215–17. Cf. Rebouças, *Diário*, ch. 3; Serzedello Correa, pp. 46–7.

14 Cruz Costa, p. 187. See, too, the preliminary observations in chapter 2:1.

15 E.g., Rebouças, *Diário*, chs. 1, 4–7, *passim*; see, also, Hall, pp. 149–51; Mattoon, "The Companhia Paulista de Estradas de Ferro, 1868–1900," PhD diss., Yale, 1971, pp. 220–1; Murilo de Carvalho, "As forças armadas," pp. 195–6.

16 See Hahner, *Civilian–Military Relations*; Oliveira Vianna, pt. 4, *passim*.

17 Hahner, *Civilian–Military Relations*, pp. 20–5; Ernesto Senna, *Deodoro* (Brasilia, 1981), *passim*.

18 On the general crisis, see Ernesto Mattoso, *Cousas do meu tempo* (Bordeaux: Gounouilhou, 1916), pp. 11–41, 249–50; Oliveira Vianna, pt. 1: chs. 15, 16, pt. 2: chs. 4, 5, pt. 5: chs. 3, 5, 6; Affonso Celso, *Oito annos*, pp. 145, 149–50, 153–8, 216–20; Amado, "As instituições," pp. 64–6. Cf. the letters from Francisco da Gama Lobo to his cousin, Francisco Carlos da Luz in 1889, or those from Marcos Antônio de Araújo e Abreu, Barão de Itajuba, and João Saldanha da Gama to Salvador de Mendonça, in the late 1880s (Coleções Francisco Carlos da Luz and Salvador de Mendonça, respectively, Seção de Manuscritos, Biblioteca Nacional, Rio de Janeiro [hereafter BNSM]). On the reforms, see Rebouças, *Agricultura nacional*, pp. 1–9, 11, 14, 30, 165–6, 350–2, 353, 362, 408; and André [Pinto] Rebouças, *A questão do Brazil* (Lisbon: n.p., 1890), 13 December 1889, pp. 1–4; 17 December 1889, pp. 1–4; 20 December 1889, pp. 1–2, 4; 28 December 1889, pp. 1–4; 1 January

1890, pp. 2–3; Nabuco, *Abolitionism*, chs. 13–15, *passim*; Richard Graham, "Landowners and the overthrow of the Empire," LBR, 7 (Winter 1970): 44–56. On the economic and financial factors, see Joseph E. Sweigart, "Financing and marketing Brazilian export agriculture" (PhD. diss., Texas, 1980), chs. 5–6, *passim*; Frank Colson, "On expectations – perspectives on the crisis of 1889 in Brazil," JLAS 13: 2 (April 1982): 265–92.

19 See Senna, *passim*; Serzedello Correa, pp. 41–4; Oliveira Vianna, pp. 43–7, 181–8; Bello, *History*, pp. 43–57; Haring, pp. 141–3, 147–53; Hahner, *Civilian–Military Relations*, pp. 28–33; Viotti da Costa, "A proclamação," pp. 203–7.

20 See E. M. Lahmeyer Lobo, *História do Rio de Janeiro*, 1: 78–9, 81–3, 155–6, 157–8, 209–22; Sweigart, chs. 2, 4, 5, *passim*; Graham, *Britain and the Onset*, pp. 94–9; Marchant, ch. 9, *passim*; and Furtado, *Economic Growth*, chs. 27–8.

21 Sweigart, ch. 5, *passim*, and pp. 218–19; Stanley J. Stein, *Vassouras* (New York: Atheneum, 1970), ch. 9, *passim*; Bello, *History*, pp. 16–18; Lahmeyer Lobo, 1: 222.

22 Max Leclerc, *Lettres du Brésil* (Paris: Plon, 1890), ch. 9 *passim*; Bello, *History*, pp. 72–6; Lahmeyer Lobo, 2: 453–4; Afonso Arinos de Melo Franco, *Rodrigues Alves*, 2 vols. (Rio de Janeiro: José Olympio, 1973), pp. 92–4.

23 Cf. Francisco Pereira Passos to Visconde de Mauá, Rio, 1875 (Documentos Pereira Passos, Museu da República, Rio de Janeiro, [hereafter, DPP] uncatalogued, *copiador* [hereafter, cop.] 6), *passim*; to Conselheiro Manuel Francisco Correa, Rio, 15 Aug 1875 (DPP uncat. cop. 6), pp. 124–6; to Conselheiro Theodoro M. F. Pereira da Silva, Rio, 5 Nov. 1875 (DPP uncat. cop. 6) pp. 151–3; to Sr. Conselheiro Visconde do Rio Branco, Rio, 18 July 1876 (DPP uncat. cop. 6), pp. 267–70; and see Nícia Vilella Luz, *A luta pela industrialização do Brasil 1808–1930* (São Paulo: Alfa-Omega, 1975), pp. 51–5, 67–101, *passim*, 107, 113; Robert G. Nachman, "Positivism, modernization, and the middle class in Brazil," HAHR 57: 1 (February 1977), pp. 7, 11–13, 14–15; Lahmeyer Lobo, 2: 456; Raymundo Faoro, *Os donos do poder* (São Paulo: USP, 1975), 2: 509, 512–15, *passim*.

24 See Vilella Luz, pp. 51–5 and *passim*; Lahmeyer Lobo, 1: 155–8, 170–206, *passim*, 2: 453–4, 456, 469, 471–87, *passim*.

25 Leclerc, ch. 9, *passim*; Luíz Viana Filho, *A vida de Rui Barbosa* (São Paulo: Nacional, 1968), ch. 16, *passim*; Vilella Luz, p. 113; [João] Dunshee de Abranches [Moura,] *Actos e actas do Governo Provisorio* (Rio de Janeiro: Nacional, 1907), pt. 1: chs. 3 and 4, *passim*.

26 See Lahmeyer Lobo, 2: 456–66; Bello, *History*, pp. 74–6; R. Magalhães Júnior, *Rui, o homem e o mito* (Rio de Janeiro: Civilização Brasileira, 1965), pp. 47–91, *passim*; Boris Fausto, "Expansão do café e política cafeeira," in Fausto, (ed.), tomo 3: vol. 1: bk. 2: 204–5; Melo Franco, 1:92–4, 112, 126–9.

27 Alfredo Maria Adriano d'Escragnolle Taunay, visconde de Taunay [pseud. Heitor Malheiros], *O Encilhamento*. 2 vols. (Rio de Janeiro: Domingos de Magalhães, Moderna, 1894), 1: 3–4.

28 See ibid.; Carlos Maul, *O Rio da bela época* (Rio de Janeiro: São José, 1967), pp. 9–10; Melo Franco, 1: 94; Bello, *History*, pp. 74–5; Magalhães Júnior, *Rui*, pp. 74–91 and Graham, *Britain and the Onset*, pp. 40, 43.

29 See Bello, *History*, pp. 16–17; Melo Franco, 1: 92–3; Joel Rufino dos Santos *et al.*, *Abolição* (São Paulo: Brasiliense, 1964), pp. 103–18, *passim*; Lahmeyer Lobo, 2: 456–69, *passim*, especially, pp. 458–63.

30 Lahmeyer Lobo, 2: 503; Furtado, *Economic Growth*, pp. 182–3, 189, 190–1; June E. Hahner, "Jacobinos versus galegos," JISWA 18:2 (May 1976): 129–30.

31 See Dunshee de Abranches, *Actos*, pt. 2: ch. 671, pt. 3: "Conclusão," *passim*; Magalhães Júnior, *Rui*, pp. 89–90; Serzedello Correa, pp. 44–59, *passim*.

32 See Rebecca Baird Bergstresser, "The movement for the abolition of slavery in Rio de Janeiro, Brazil, 1880–9" (PhD diss., Stanford, 1973), chs. 1–3, *passim*; and Hahner, "Jacobinos." Cf. Sandra Lauderdale Graham "The Vintem riot and political culture," HAHR 60:3 (August 1980): 431–49; [Alexandre José de] Mello Moraes Filho, *Factos e memórias* (Rio de Janeiro: H. Garnier, 1904), pt. 4: ch. 10, *passim*, pt. 5: ch. 11, *passim*.

33 Hahner, "Jacobinos," pp. 126–9. Eugene W. Ridings, Jr. confirms something of the Brazilian perception in "Business, nationality and dependency in late nineteenth-century Brazil," JLAS, 14 (May 1982) 55–96.

34 Hahner, "Jacobinos," pp. 131–2, Cf. Nachman, pp. 7, 10–14.

35 See Bello, pp. 136–8. Luíz Edmundo [da Costa], *O Rio de Janeiro do meu tempo*, 5 vols. (Rio de Janeiro: Conquista, 1957) 5: ch. 37, *passim*; and his *De um livro de memórias*, 5 vols. (Rio de Janeiro: Nacional, 1958) 2: 355–438, *passim*; [João] Dunshee de Abranches [Moura], *Como se faziam presidentes* (Rio de Janeiro: José Olympio, 1973), pt. 1: chs. 5, 18, *passim*.

36 See Bello, *History*, chs. 7–10, *passim*; Serzedello Correa, pp. 44–75, *passim*.

37 See Bello, *History*, pp. 136–48, *passim*; Dunshee de Abranches, *Como se faziam presidentes*, pp. 72, 83, 87, 88–90, and *passim*; and Joseph L. Love, *Rio Grande do Sul and Brazilian Regionalism 1882–1930* (Stanford: 1971), pp. 52–3, 88–94, *passim*, 98–9.

38 See *Rua do Ouvidor* (Rio de Janeiro) 2 April 1898, p. 6 and 19 November 1898, p. 2; Rui Barbosa to [Luís Felipe] Saldanha da Gama, Teddington, England, 20 August, 1894, Casa de Rui Barbosa, Arquivo Histórico, Rio de Janeiro, Correspondência [hereafter, RBAHC]: Luís Felipe Saldanha da Gama; Bello, *History*, pp. 89–95; cf. dos Santos *et al.*, "O significado do florianismo," pp. 103–58.

39 Murilo de Carvalho, "A composição social," pp. 8–9, 14–17; Love, *São Paulo*, pp. 102–13, 117; Viotti da Costa, "A proclamação," pp. 191–200; cf. Love, *Rio Grande*, especially chs. 3 and 4, *passim*, and cf. John D. Wirth, *Minas Gerais in the Brazilian Federation 1880–1937* (Stanford: 1977), pp. 99–105, 151–2; Robert M. Levine, *Pernambuco in the Brazilian Federation 1889–1937* (Stanford: 1978), pp. 73–6, 112.

40 Love, *São Paulo*, pp. 178–9, 208–11; Hahner, *Civilian–Military Relations*, pp. 125–34; Melo Franco, 1: 73–109, *passim*.

41 Hahner, *Civilian–Military Relations*, ch. 7, *passim*, especially, pp. 140–4.

42 See Dunshee de Abranches, *Como se faziam presidentes*, pts. 1 and 2, *passim*; Hahner, *Civilian–Military Relations*, ch. 8, *passim*; and Bello, *History*, chs. 11 and 12, *passim*. The analysis here and to follow draws on these sources.

43 The struggle was the basis for Euclides da Cunha's *Os sertões* (1902) (see ch. 6.10), and it continues to excite interest – see, e.g., Ralph della Cava, "Brazilian messianism and national institutions," HAHR 48: 3 (August 1968): 402–20; Walnice Nogueira Galvão, *No calor da hora* (São Paulo: Atica, 1977); Mario Vargas Llosa, *La guerra del fin del mundo* (Madrid: Seix Barral, 1981).

44 See *Gazeta de Noticias* (Rio de Janeiro), 7 November 1897, p. 2; The *Rio News* (Rio de Janeiro), 18 January 1898, pp. 4–5, ibid.; 22 March 1898, p. 8, and 8 November 1898, p. 7; ibid., 8 March 1898, p. 5; ibid., 1 March 1898, p. 6; Dunshee de Abranches, *Como se faziam presidentes*, p. 261.

45 On Campos Sales, see Dunshee de Abranches, *Como se faziam presidentes*, pt. 3, *passim*; Bello, *History*, ch. 13, *passim*; Melo Franco, 1: 110–66, *passim*; Love, *Rio Grande*, chs. 4, 5, *passim*; Franciscos de Assis Barbosa, "A Presidência Campos Sales," LBR 5: 1 (June 1968): 3–26, *passim*; Lahmeyer Lobo, 2; 467–8, 493, 503–7; Wirth, p. 180; and Furtado, *Economic Growth*, 190–7.

46 *Rua do Ouvidor*, 14 May 1898, p. 2.

47 Ibid. 5 November 1898, p. 2. The references to 1893 and 1894 are to the naval revolt and the civil war in Rio Grande and to the florianista response.

48 On Pereira Passos, see n. 50. By "neo-colonialism," I mean the combination of formal political independence with informal economic and political dependence characteristic of Latin America after the 1820s and flourishing by the 1880s; see Tulio Halperín Donghi, *Historia contemporánea de América Latina* (Madrid: Alianza, 1972), chs. 4, 5; Celso Furtado, *Economic Development of Latin America* (Cambridge: 1976), chs. 3–5; Stein and Stein, chs. 5, 6.

49 Nabuco, *Um estadista*, 1: 27–33, 40–1; Murilo de Carvalho, "A composição social," pp. 23–5; Haring, ch. 3; Furtado, *Economic Growth*, p. 104.

50 [Francisco Pereira Passos,] "Francisco Pereira Passos," Rio, Nov. 1903 (DPP 1.11.1), p. 1; [Francisco Oliveira Passos,] [Addendum to Francisco Oliveira Passos to Dr. Euzébio Naylor, Rio, 21 Nov. 1950 (DPP 7.8.2)] (DPP 7.3.3), p. 1; Raymundo A. de Athayde, *Pereira Passos* (Rio de Janeiro: A Noite, n.d.), 11–24; Barão de Vasconcellos and Barão Smith de Vasconcellos, *Archivo nobiliarchico brasileiro* (Lausanne: La Concorde, 1918), s.v., "Mangaratiba"; cf. Stein, chs. 1, 2, 5.

51 See section 1, above, and the references in n. 3.

52 Slave population did not reproduce sufficiently, so purchase in Africa was constantly required; see Conrad, *Destruction*, pp. 24–7, 287. For Rio's population statistics, see Lahmeyer Lobo, 1: 122–3, 135–6, 225–6.

53 Lahmeyer Lobo, 1: chs. 1–3, *passim*; C. R. Boxer, *The Golden Age of Brazil* (Berkeley, 1969), 312–16; Prado, *Colonial Background*, pp. 77, 88–9, 167–8, 286–8.

54 Lahmeyer Lobo, 1: 100–1, 162–3, 166; Gastão Cruls, *Aparência do Rio de Janeiro*, 2 vols. (Rio de Janeiro: José Olympio, 1965) 1: 146, 221–2, 397; Adolfo Morales de Los Rios Filho, *O Rio de Janeiro imperial* (Rio de Janeiro: A Noite, 1946), pp. 8, 18, 312; Edmundo Canabrava Barreiros, *Atlas da evolucão urbana da cidade do Rio de Janeiro* (Rio de Janeiro: IHGB, 1965), figs. 8–14.

55 Barreiros, figs. 8–14; Estélio Emanuel de Alencar Roxo and Manoel Ferreira, "O saneamento do meio físico" in Fernando Nascimento Silva, dir., *Rio de Janeiro em seus cuatrocentos anos* (Rio de Janeiro: Distribuidora Record 65, 1965), pp. 285–8.

56 Roxo and Ferreira, pp. 285–90; Ruy Maurício de Lima e Silva, "Iluminação e gás," in F. N. Silva, pp. 357–8; Vivaldo Coaracy, *Memórias da cidade do Rio de Janeiro* (Rio de Janeiro: José Olympio, 1965), pp. 161, "Anexo," *passim*.

57 Joaquim Manuel de Macedo, *Memórias da rua do Ouvidor* (São Paulo: Nacional, 1952), pp. 156–7; Coaracy, *Memórias*, pp. 180–8; Cláudio Bardy, "O século XIX" in F. N. Silva, pp. 104–6.

58 [Pereira Passos,] "Francisco Pereira Passos," 1–2; Athayde, pp. 38–40; on the Escola Militar (later named the Escola Politécnica), see Francisco Pereira Passos. [Draft opinion on "Estatutos da Escola Polytechnica"], Rio de Janeiro, 21 April 1874 (DPP 4.16.1, cop. 4), pp. 426–38; Cruz Costa, pp. 83, 86; Hall, pp. 149–51; Mattoon, pp. 220–1; Murilo de Carvalho, "As forças armadas," 2: 195–6; cf. Rebouças, *Diário*, ch. 1.

59 See, e.g., Coaracy, *Memórias*, chs. 3, 4, *passim*; Bardy, pp. 116–18; Roxo and

Ferreira, pp. 291–2; Lima e Silva, *passim*; Nestor de Oliveira Neto, "A evolução dos transportes" in F. N. Silva, *passim*; Graham, *Britain and the Onset*, chs. 3, 4, 7, *passim*. A more positive review of matters is A. de Lyra Tavares, "A engenharia brasileira no Segundo Reinado," RIGHB, 338 (January–March 1983), 259–78.

60 See Prado, *História econômica*, ch. 16, *passim*, and 170–1; Stein, pp. 3–4, 24–6; Furtado, *Economic Growth*, pp. 104–5, 116–17, 119–20, 123–4; Graham, *Britain and the Onset*, chs. 1, 2, 3, 7, *passim*; Murilo de Carvalho, "A composição social," pp. 24–5; Lahmeyer Lobo, 1: 101–5, 133, 155–61; Sweigart, pp. 2–4, ch. 1, *passim*; Nabuco, *Um estadista*, 3: 580–3 n. 1; Pedro Calmon, *O marquez de Abrantes* (Rio de Janeiro: Guanabara, 1933), ch. 17, *passim*; [José] Wanderley [de Araújo] Pinho, *Salões e damas do Segundo Reinado* (São Paulo: Martins, 1970), chs. 5, 8, 9, 10, *passim*.

61 Coaracy, *Memórias*, pp. 147–9, 161, 174; Oliveira Neto, pp. 347–55; Lima e Silva, *passim*; Roxo and Ferreira, pp. 291–3; Bardy, pp. 116–18; Graham, *Britain and the Onset*, pp. 92, 116, 118.

62 Coaracy, *Memórias*, pp. 147–9; Oliveira Neto, pp. 349–52; Marchant, pp. 59; Henry Hilliard, *Politics and Penpictures at Home and Abroad* (New York: G. P. Putnam, 1892), pp. 375–6; [A. J. Lamoureux,] The Editors of the *Rio de Janeiro News*, *Handbook of Rio de Janeiro* (Rio de Janeiro: A. J. Lamoureux, 1887), pp. 143–50; Hastings Charles Dent, *A Year in Brazil* (London: Kegan Paul, French, 1886), pp. 235–7; Ferreira da Rosa, *Rio de Janeiro* (Rio de Janeiro, 1905), pp. 57–61; Cruls, 1: 349–57, 397–401, 2: 459–60, 507–17; Calmon, *O marquez*, 237–9; Rios Filho, *Rio imperial*, pp. 303, 312–16.

63 Morse, Conniff, and Wibel, pp. 37, 44–8; Graham, *Britain and the Onset*, pp. 9–19, 21–2; Furtado, *Economic Growth*, chs. 19, 25, *passim*; Lahmeyer Lobo, 1: 81–3, 162–6, 209–22, *passim*; Murilo de Carvalho, "A composição social," pp. 10–14, 23–5, Vilella Luz, pp. 50–5; Rebouças, *Diário*, pp. 169–73, and *passim*; Marchant, chs. 4, 9, *passim*; Eugene W. Ridings, Jr., "Class sector unity in an export economy," HAHR 58 (1978): 432–50 and "Interest groups and development," JLAS 9 (1978): 225–50; Sweigart, chs. 2, 4, 5, *passim*; Roberta Delson argues that early, progressive municipal legislation was thwarted by the interests of the great landholders in "Land use and urban planning," LBR, 16:2 (Winter 1979) 191–214. F. N. Silva (pp. 121–2) notes stillborn urban planning by precursors, especially Grandjean de Montigny of the French Artistic Mission of 1816; cf. Adolfo Morales de los Rios Filho, *Grandjean de Montigny e a evolução da arte brasileira* (Rio de Janeiro: A Noite, 1941). On the French Artistic Mission, see chapter 4.8.

64 See e.g. Graham, *Britain and the Onset*, pp. 9–19, 21–2, and cf. pp. 33–5; Marchant, pp. 60–1; Nabuco, *Um estadista*, 1:12, 17; Coelho Netto, *A conquista* (Rio de Janeiro: Chardron, 1921), pp. 60, 228, 300; visconde de Nogueira da Gama, *Minhas memórias* (Paris: H. Garnier, 1893), 1st sec., *passim*; Amélia de Rezende Martins, *Um idealista realizador* (São Paulo: Laemmert, 1939), chs. 6, 7, *passim*; Joaquim [Aureliano Barreto] Nabuco [de Araújo] *Minha formação* (Paris: H. Garnier, 1900), chs. 4, 5, 6, *passim*.

65 The general question of Franco–English influence is the burden of the following chapters. On English technological influence, see Graham, *Britain and the Onset*, pp. 136–40; cf. Gilberto Freyre, *Ingleses no Brasil* (Rio de Janeiro: José Olympio, 1948), pp. 56–8, 63–6, 81–3. On French technological influence, see Gilberto Freyre, *Um engenheiro francês no Brasil*, 2 vols. (Rio de Janeiro: José Olympio, 1960),

1: 219–59, *passim*; Adolfo Morales de Los Rios Filho, *Dois notáveis engenheiros* (Rio de Janeiro: A Noite, 1951), pp. 40–7, *passim*.

66 See the citations in Francisco Pereira Passos, *et al.*, "Melhoramentos da cidade do Rio de Janeiro," *Jornal do Commercio* (Rio de Janeiro), pp. 18 May, 22 May, 29 May, 5 June, 13 June, 19 June, 27 June, 16 July, 2 Aug., 3 Oct. 1875; cf. Francisco Pereira Passos to Consro. Dr. J. A. Correa d'Oliveira, Rio de Janeiro, 6 March 1875 (DPP uncat. cop. 6), pp. 39–40. See also Athayde, pp. 38–41, 43; Azevedo, pp. 174–5, 236–7; Rios Filho, *Dois notáveis engenheiros*, pp. 38–46, *passim*. On the Ecole Polytechnique, see n. 68 below.

67 [Pereira Passos,] "Francisco Pereira Passos," p. 3; Athayde, pp. 15–18, 36–9, 43–4, 107; cf. Azevedo, pp. 179–190; Barman and Barman, pp. 425–7.

68 On the Ecoles and their tradition, see [Pereira Passos] ["Estatutos da Escola Polytechnica"], 437–8; *La grande encyclopédie*, (Paris, n.d.), s.v., "Ecole des ponts et chausées," and E. J. Hobsbawm, *The Age of Revolution* (New York: NAL, 1962), pp. 47, 329; Joseph N. Moody, *French Education Since Napoleon* (Syracuse, NY: 1978), pp. 30–1; R. D. Anderson, *Education in France* (Oxford: 1975), pp. 11, 27–9, 58–9, 202–3; John W. Wigmore, ed., *Science and Learning in France* (n.p., 1917), pp. 97–104. On Pereira Passos in France, see [Pereira Passos,] "Francisco Pereira Passos", p. 3; Athayde, pp. 107–10. Cf. Rebouças, *Diário*, pp. 15–16, 225–6.

69 On the reforms, see David H. Pinkney, *Napoleon III and the Rebuilding of Paris* (Princeton: 1958) and J. M. Chapman and Brian Chapman, *The Life and Times of Baron Haussmann* (London: 1957).

70 On the general picture, see Leonard Benevelo, *The Origins of Modern Town Planning*, (Cambridge, Mass.: 1976), pp. 85–147, *passim*; on Paris, see Pinkney, pp. 29–31, 37–40; Chapman and Chapman, pp. 63, 68, 86–7, 195–6. N.B. in ibid., 4, 61, 79, that some elements in the plans (e.g. the Great Crossing) were modifications of the 1797 "Artists' Plan" – cf. Pinkney, 32–3. On the Emperor and Haussmann, and the famous issue of urbanism versus counter-revolutionary planning, see Pinkney, pp. 35–8, 40–5 and Chapman and Chapman, pp. 63–6, 71–4, 184–6.

71 Chapman and Chapman, pp. 78–82, 180–4; Pinkney, pp. 56–9, ch. 3, *passim*.

72 Pinkney, pp. 9–10, 12–13, 23–4, 34–6, 57–8, 67, ch. 6, *passim*; Chapman and Chapman, pp. 184–7, *passim*.

73 Chapman and Chapman, pp. 85–9, 189–97; Pinkney, pp. 19, 300, ch. 4, *passim*; for the English model, see Edward Hyams, *A History of Gardens and Gardening* (New York: Praeger, 1971), pp. 28–42.

74 See Carl E. Schorske, *Fin-de-Siècle Vienna* (New York: Vintage, 1981), pp. 24–46, *passim*, especially 31–6; cf. Chapman and Chapman, pp. 189–95, especially 194–5. In Schorske's terms, Haussmann would be "baroque" in his stress on focus and radial organization; so, too, would Pereira Passos.

75 On Pereira Passos' early career and collaboration with entrepreneur cum industrialist Viscount de Mauá, see [Pereira Passos] "Francisco Pereira Passos," pp. 14–19; Francisco Pereira Passos to Consro. Je. Agostino Mora. Guimes., London, 5 Nov. 1873 (DPP uncat. cop. 5), pp. 190–2; to Conselheiro Visconde do Rio Branco, Rio de Janeiro, 18 July 1876 (DPP uncat, cop. 6), pp. 267–70; on his and others' infrastructural work, see Athayde, chs. 10–14, *passim*; Sacramento Blake, *Diccionario bibliographico brazileiro*, 7 vols. (Rio de Janeiro: Nacional, 1888–1902), 3: 89–90. Luiz Dodsworth Martins, *Presença de Paulo de Frontin* (Rio de Janeiro: Freitas Bastos, 1966), pp. 29–32, 38, and *passim*; Rebouças, *Diário*; and André [Pinto] Rebouças,

Apontamentos para a biographia do engenheiro Antonio Pereira Rebouças Filho (Rio de Janeiro: Nacional, 1874).

76 On Carioca epidemics note that yellow fever, brought to Rio in the mid-nineteenth century, periodically compelled government attention. The 1870s exemplify the pattern; in 1873 an epidemic killed 5 per cent of Rio's population. See the summary in Commissão do Saneamento do Rio de Janeiro, *Relatorios apresentados ao Exm. Sr. Dr. Prefeito Municipal pelos drs. Manoel Victorino Pereira . . . e Nuno de Andrade . . . 31 de Agosto de 1896* (Rio de Janeiro: Nacional, 1896), pp. 13–20. On Pereira Passos' role, see Francisco Pereira Passos to Conselheiro Dr. João Alfred Correa d'Oliveira, Rio de Janeiro, 24 May 1874 (DPP 4.11.11, cop. 4), pp. 444–6; to Sr. Marcellino Ramos da Silva, Rio de Janeiro, 24 May 1874 (DPP 2.13.13, cop. 4), p. 447; to Conselheiro João Alfredo Correa d'Oliveira, Rio de Janeiro, 29 May 1874 (DPP 4.11.12, cop. 4), p. 450; [Draft of "Cargo da Commissão de Melhoramentos da Cidade do Rio de Janeiro"] (DPP 4.11.12a, cop. 4) pp. 451–3; to L. R. d'Oliveira, Rio de Janeiro, 4 June 1874 (DPP uncat. cop. 5), pp. 301–2; Athayde, pp. 172–6; Nabuco, *Um estadista*, 3: 180, 202–3, 423n. 2–4; Blake, 3: 89–90, 315; Coaracy, *Memórias*, pp. 206–7; Rios Filho, *Dois notáveis engenheiros*, 40–7; Oliveira Reis, "As administrações municipais e o desenvolvimento urbano" in F. N. Silva, p. 127. The planned reforms emerged in two *relatorios* (12 Jan. 1875 and 29 Feb. 1876); see Francisco Pereira Passos, Jeronymo Rodrigues de Moraes Jardim, e Marcellino Ramos da Silva, *Primeiro relatorio da Commissão de Melhoramentos da cidade do Rio de Janeiro* (Rio de Janeiro: Nacional, 1875) and *Segundo relatorio da Commissão de Melhoramentos da cidade do Rio de Janeiro* (Rio de Janeiro: Nacional, 1876). The *Primeiro relatorio* was criticized by Luís Rafael Vieira Souto, defended by Pereira Passos, then criticized once again by Vieira Souto; see [Luís Rafael Vieira Souto,] "O melhoramento da cidade do Rio de Janeiro," *Jornal do Commercio*, 23 Feb., 25 Feb., 28 Feb., 4 March, 7 March, 9 March, 13 March, 18 March, 20 March, 26 March, 27 March, 31 March, 3 April, 8 april, 14 April, 15 April, 1875; Francisco Pereira Passos to Consro. Dr. J. A. Correa d'Oliveira, Rio de Janeiro, 6 March 1875 (DPP uncat. cop. 6), pp. 39–40; Jardim to Francisco Pereira Passos, s.l., 26 May 1875 (DPP 1.9.1.); Anon., "Melhoramentos da cidade do Rio de Janeiro," *Jornal do Commercio*, 20 May 1875; Francisco Pereira Passos, Jeronymo Rodrigues de Moraes Jardim, e Marcellino Ramos da Silva, "Melhoramentos da cidade do Rio de Janeiro", *Jornal do Commercio*, 18 May, 22 May, 29 May, 5 June, 13 June, 19 June, 27 June, 16 July, 2 Aug., 3 Oct. 1875; Luíz Raphael Vieira Souto, *O melhoramento da cidade do Rio de Janeiro* (Rio de Janeiro: Luís C. Teixeira, 1875–6). On the panic's impact, see Vieira Souto, "Appendice" to *O melhoramento*, pp. 172–3; Francisco Pereira Passos to L. R. d'Oliveira, Rio de Janeiro, 4 July 1875 (DPP uncat. cop. 6), pp. 101–4; Roderick J. Barman, "Business and government," pp. 257–62. On Glaziou, see the Coaracy citation above, and cf. *Enciclopédia brasileira mérito*, s.v., "Glaziou," or *Enciclopédia delta universal*, s.v., "Glaziou". The Frenchman (1833–1906), invited to Brazil by Pedro II in 1858, had already worked on the Jardim Botânico, the Quinta da Boa Vista, and the Floresta da Tijuca before his Campo labors.

77 See, e.g., Francisco Pereira Passos to Conselheiro Theodoro Machado Freire Pereira da Silva, London, 17 Sept., 1873 (DPP uncat. cop. 5), pp. 90–3; to Consro. Je. Agostino Mora. Guimes., London, 5 Nov. 1873 (DPP uncat. cop. 5) 190–2; Commissão do Saneamento, *Relatorios*, 13–52; G[uiseppi] Fogliani, *Projecto de melhoramentos na cidade do Rio de Janeiro* (Rio de Janeiro: F. Borgonovo, 1903), pp. 3, 33–4; Francisco Belisario Soares de Souza, "Notas de um viajante brazileiro" in

ibid., 40–4; Antonio Martins de Azevedo Pimentel, *Subsidios para o estudo de hygiene do Rio de Janeiro* (Rio de Janeiro: Silva, 1890), chs. 3, 5; Carolina Nabuco, *Oito décadas* (Rio de Janeiro: José Olympio, 1973), pp. 10; Albino José Barbosa de Oliveira, *Memórias de um magistrado do Império* (São Paulo: Nacional, 1943), pp. 220–1; Costa, *De um livro de memórias*, 1, pp. 159–60; Miguel Cané, *En viaje* (Buenos Aires, 1949), pp. 23–9; Vicente G. Quesada, *Mis memórias diplomáticas*, 2 vols. (Buenos Aires: Coni Hermanos, 1907), 1: 104–5, 108, 118, 120; Ina von Binzer, *Os meus romanos* (Rio de Janeiro: Paz e Terra, 1980), pp. 53–4, 61–2, 71; Leclerc, pp. 39–41, 49–51; C. C. Andrews, *Brazil* (New York: D. Appleton, 1889), pp. 15, 25–9; Ulick Ralph Burke and Robert Staples, Jr., *Business and Pleasure in Brazil* (London: ye Leadenhalle, 1884), pp. 36–48; Roxo and Ferreira, pp. 291–2; Jaime Larry Benchimol, "Pereira Passos – Um Haussmann tropical" (MS diss., UFRJ, 1982), ch. 6, pp. 352–9; Samuel C. Adamo, "The broken promise" (PhD diss., New Mexico, 1983), pp. 111–42, *passim*. On the portworks' complications, see Martins, pp. 63–4, 65–8; see, also, the summary in [José Barboza Gonçalves] Ministerio da Viação e Obras Publicas, *Portos do Brazil* (Rio de Janeiro: Nacional, 1912), pp. 344–6, 351–60 and the account in Graham, *Britain and the Onset*, pp. 192–4. For more detail, see Jeffrey D. Needell, "Making the Carioca *Belle Epoque* concrete," *Journal of Urban History* 10:4 (Aug. 1984): 415–16 n. 32.

78 See Sweigart, ch. 5, 218–19; Stein, ch. 9; Lahmeyer Lobo, 1: 170–223, *passim*, 2: 443–509, *passim*; Cano, ch. 1.1, ch. 3, *passim*; Benchimol, ch. 10. On the Campos Sales watershed, see sections 5 and 6 above. On the socio-economic transitions of Rio between 1870 and 1906, see Jeffrey D. Needell, "The *Revolta Contra Vacina* of 1904," HAHR 67:2 (May 1987).

79 See Rodrigues Alves' speech at the Convenção Republicana in *Jornal do Commercio*, 24 Oct. 1901; cf. Fogliani, *Projecto de melhoramentos*, pp. 3, 44–9; N.B. the reaction to Pereira Passos' appointment in *Jornal do Commercio*, 29 Dec. 1902; *O Paiz*, 30 Dec. 1902; and in Amalio, "Chronica" in *O Malho*, 3 Jan. 1903, [2]. See also, Athayde, pp. 87–93; Melo Franco, 1: 168–71. 190–1, 307–12; Bello, *History*, pp. 174–7, 183–4, 190–1; Costa, *Rio* 1: 126–41. Melo Franco (1:170–1); notes the impetus to reform given by Buenos Aires; see Adrian Beccar Varela, *Torcuato de Alvear* (Buenos Aires; Kraft, 1926) or James R. Scobie, *Buenos Aires* (New York: Oxford, 1974); João de Barros, "Chronica," *Renascença*, 1 (June 1904): 124; Thomaz Lopes, "Buenos Aires," *Kósmos*, 5:3–4 (March–April, Aug. 1908), *passim*. On Oswaldo Cruz, see Nancy Stepan, *The Beginnings of Brazilian Science* (New York: Science History, 1981), ch. 5; Nilson do Rosário Costa, "Estado e políticas de saúde pública (1889–1930)." (MA thesis, IUPRJ, 1983), ch. 3; and Needell, "*Revolta Contra Vacina*."

80 The origins of Pereira Passos' 1903–6 reforms derive directly from the explicitly Parisian-style projects of the *Segundo relatorio* of 1875. See Passos, *et al.*, *Segundo relatorio*, 5–6, 12, 17, 25, 35–38; cf. *Jornal do Commercio*, 5 April 1903; *O Paiz*, 5 April 1903; *Correio da Manhã*, 5 April 1903; Alfredo Americo de Souza Rangel, "No. 30 – Comissão de Carta Cadastral do Districto Federal, em 13 de abril de 1903" in Francisco Pereira Passos, *Melhoramentos projectados* . . . (Rio de Janeiro, 1903); [Francisco Pereira Passos,] *Mensagem do Prefeito de Districto Federal . . . 1 de Setembro de 1903* (Rio de Janeiro: *Gazeta de Noticias*, 1903), 11–14. The *Segundo relatorio*'s origins are less clear; Pereira Passos had access to numerous Carioca reform proposals (most of which were explicitly Parisian in orientation), all the revelvant

published regulations and reforms from Europe, Vieira Souto's critique of the *Primeiro relatorio*; and Rebouças' proposal: see, e.g., Francisco Pereira Passos to Conselheiro Dr. José Bento de Cunha e Figueiredo, Rio de Janeiro, 5 July 1876 (DPP uncat. cop. 8), pp. 249–54; to L. R. d'Oliveira, Rio de Janeiro, 4 June 1874 (DPP uncat. cop. 9), p. 301; to L. R. d'Oliveira, Rio de Janeiro, 17 Aug. 1874 (DPP uncat. cop. 6), p. 350; [Vieira Souto,] "O melhoramento da cidade . . . VI" 9 March 1875; Passos, *et al.*, *Segundo relatorio*, p. 17; Vieira Souto, "Apendice," 169–70; A. R. [Aarão Reis?] "Avenida à beira mar – Commentario" in [*Gazeta de Noticias*,] *Questões municipais* (Rio de Janeiro: *Gazeta de Noticias*, 1905), pp. 229–30; Pereira Passos, *Mensagem . . . 1 de Setembro*, p. 12; cf. Rebouças, *Apontamentos*, p. 8; Rebouças, *Diário*, pp. 201, 271–2, 275–6; [Francisco Pereira Passos] Commissão de Melhoramentos da Cidade do Rio de Janeiro to Consero. José Bento da Cunha Figueiredo, Rio de Janeiro, 8 April 1876 (DPP 4.11.6), pp. 1–2, 9–10. For more detail, see Needell, "Making the Carioca *Belle Epoque* concrete," p. 417 n. 35. See, also, Athayde, pp. 174–6; Martins, pp. 76–7; Coaracy, *Memórias*, pp. 206–7; Oliveira Reis, p. 127; Melo Franco, 1: 313–15; Costa, *Rio*, 1: 30, 41; Paulo F. Santos, "Arquitetura e urbanismo na Avenida Central" in Marc Ferrez, *O álbum da Avenida Central* (Rio de Janeiro: Ex Libris, 1982), pp. 27–8; Benchimol, ch. 8, *passim*. On the breadth of Brazilian engineers' European references, see Passos *et al.*, *Segundo relatorio*, pp. 6–7, 15; Souza Rangel, "Os melhoramentos do Rio de Janeiro," *Renascença*, 5 (July 1904), pp. 181–2; and Alfredo Lisboa, "A Avenida Central," *Kósmos* 1:11 (Nov. 1904), pp. [1–7].

81 The continuity between the 1876 *Segundo relatorio* and the *belle-époque* reforms is patent, as is their Parisian derivation (see n. 80). Cf. *Segundo relatorio*, 12–13, 16–17, 25, 35–8 to the program in Rangel, "Commissão da Carta Cadastral" and in [Pereira Passos] *Mensagem . . . de 1903*, pp. 11–14. For detail on the role and interests of the Müller/Frontin group and the Club de Engenharia, see Needell, "Making the Carioca *Belle Epoque* concrete," p. 418 n. 36, *passim*. On Haussmann and the general question of the plans see, also, Athayde, pp. 92–3, 174–6, 201–2, 215, 244–5, 248; Martins, pp. 75–8, 83–4; Melo Franco, 1:316–19, 332–5, 344–6, 350–1; Oliveira Reis, pp. 127–8; Benchimol, chs. 13, 14; Prefeitura do Districto Federal, *Planta dos melhoramentos projectados pelo prefeito Dr. F. P. Passos incluindo os melhoramentos projectados pelo Governo Federal: 1903* (Rio de Janeiro: E. Bevilacqua, 1903).

82 [Pereira Passos,] *Mensagem do Prefeito . . .* 1903, pp. 7–8; [Francisco Pereira Passos,] *Mensagem do Prefeito do Districto Federal . . . 2 de Abril de 1904* (Rio de Janeiro: *Gazeta de Noticias*, 1904), p. 75; "Impressões de um 'ex-dictador' " in [*Gazeta de Noticias*] *Questões municipals*, p. 9; "Uma entrevista com o Prefeito" in ibid., p. 109; *Jornal do Commercio*, 13 Feb. 1904: *O Paiz*, 9 Feb. 1904; Rangel, "Commissão de Carta Cadastral," *passim*; Benchimol, ch. 14, *passim*; Athayde, ch. 13, *passim*; Melo Franco, 1: 319–28; Rios Filho, "O Rio de Janeiro da Primeira República," pp. 10–15; Oliveira Reis, pp. 128–33.

83 On the aesthetic styles and attention to public parks, see Santos, "Arquitetura," pp. 32–47; Melo Franco, 1: 324, 345, 350; Martins, pp. 82–3; Athayde, pp. 243–4; Oliveira Reis, pp. 232–3. Melo Franco terms the architectural style *belle époque*; it is better known as Beaux-Arts or Eclectic. See section 10, below.

84 Melo Franco, 1:351; Martins, p. 163; Lisboa, [p. 1]; *O Malho*, 14 March 1903, [p. 2]; *Jornal do Commercio*, 5 April, 21 May 1903; *O Paiz*, 4, 5 April 1903; *Correio da Manhã*, 9 Jan., 5 April 1903; Paulo H. and Luíz Carlos de Paranaguá, interview,

15 July 1980, Rio de Janeiro: Passos, *et al.*, *Segundo relatorio*, pp. 5–6, 12, 17, 25, 35–8; Francisco Pereira Passos to Conselheiro Dr. José Bento da Cunha e Figueiredo, Rio de Janeiro, 5 July 1878 (DPP uncat. cop. 8), pp. 249–54.

85 "Porto do Rio de Janeiro," *Correio da Manhã*, 9 Jan. 1903; *O Paiz*, 4 April 1904; Rangel, "Commissão de Carta Cadastral," and "Melhoramentos da Cidade," *Renascença*, Sept. 1904, p. 75; and "Melhoramentos da Cidada," ibid., Nov. 1904, pp. 131–2; "O Porto do Rio de Janeiro," *Jornal do Commercio*, 21 May 1903.

86 Rangel, "Melhoramentos," Sept. 1904, pp. 75–80; and Nov. 1904, pp. 131–2; "Echos e factos," *Rua do Ouvidor*, 1 March 1904, p. 6; "Drs. Lauro Müller e Paulo Frontin," ibid., 2 April 1904, pp. 1–3; "A Avenida Central," ibid., 10 Sept. 1904, pp. 1–2; Ferreira da Rosa, "Avenida Central," *Kósmos*, 2:11 (Nov. 1905), *passim*.

87 The best contemporary iconography in published form is to be found in *Kósmos*; see, e.g., Ferreira da Rosa, *passim*. On postcards, see Paulo Berger, *O Rio de Janeiro de ontem no cartão postal* (Rio de Janeiro: Rio de JaneiroArte, 1983), *passim*.

88 Marc Ferrez, *Avenida Central* (Rio de Janeiro: E. Bevilecqua, 1905), now reproduced as Marc Ferrez, *O álbum da Avenida Central* (Rio de Janeiro: Ex Libris, 1982). See Gilberto Ferrez, "A Avenida Central e Seu Album," in ibid., pp. 18–23.

89 Rangel, "Melhoramentos," Nov. 1904, pp. 131–2; M. Ferrez (1982), pp. 197–231; Benchimol, pp. 461–5, 498–503; O. P. Rocha, "A era das demolições," (MA thesis, UFF, 1983), pp. 79–81; "Concurso de Fachadas para a Avenida Central," *Renascença*, April 1904, pp.66–8; Chapman and Chapman, pp. 183, 189, 250–1; Schorske, pp. 46–7, 49–50, 60; Richard Chafee, "The teaching of architecture at the Ecole des Beaux-Arts," in Arthur Drexler, ed., *The Architecture of the Ecole des Beaux-Arts* (New York: MOMA, 1977), p. 97; Claude Mignot, *Architecture of the 19th Century in Europe* (New York: Rizzoli, 1984), pp. 18–19, 100–2; see, also, P. F. Santos, pp. 32–4.

90 Chafee, pp. 65–82, 96, 106–7; Mignot, pp. 248–58; David Van Zanten, "Architectural composition at the Ecole des Beaux-Arts from Charles Percier to Charles Garnier" in Drexler, pp. 232, 252–4; Chapman and Chapman, pp. 190–1.

91 See Van Zanten, pp. 219–23, 230, 232, 242, 253, 286; Mignot, pp. 94–9, 100–11, 137–67.

92 Van Zanten, pp. 152, 159–63, 185, 191, 281–6; Mignot, pp. 99, 102, 104, 148, 154–5, 187.

93 "Concurso de Fachadas," p. 67; Chafee, pp. 95, 106–7; Mignot, pp. 148–58; P. F. Santos, pp. 33–4. NB, the absence of Art Nouveau, in ibid., p. 34 (cf. Melo Franco, 1:324, 345, 352).

94 P. F. Santos, p. 46.

95 On Morales de los Rios, see Adolfo Morales de los Rios Filho, *Adolfo Morales de los Rios* (Rio de Janeiro: Borsoi, 1959), especially pp. 42–8, 183–8; P. F. Santos, pp. 32–3, 37–8. For his façades, see M. Ferrez (1982), pp. 68–9 ("das Águias"), pp. 84–5 (Mourisco), pp. 92–3 (Equitativa), p. 116 (Escola), p. 120 (Archi episcopal), p. 166 (Empregados), pp. 170–1 (O Paiz).

96 P. F. Santos, pp. 38–9.

97 On the Biblioteca Nacional, see, e.g., "Bibliotheca Nacional, O futuro edificio," *Renascença*, Oct. 1905, pp. 143–7; Brito Broca, *A vida literária no Brasil – 1900* (Rio de Janeiro: José Olympio, 1975), pp. 150–5; P. F. Santos, pp. 38–9.

98 Cf. Garnier's and Oliveira Passos' plans and elevations in Van Zanten, pp. 262–7, 269 and Gil Seabra, "Teatro Municipal," *Renascença*, June 1906, pp. 270, 273, 275. See, also, ibid., pp. 270–1, 274, 276; P. F. Santos, pp. 34–7, 186, 188. The

fact that the competition for the theater's plan was won by the son of the city's prefect, who presided over the selection, did not go without indignant, and often acid, comment in the opposition press.

99 See P. F. Santos, p. 32. The result can be seen in Marc Ferrez's contemporary photographs (see, ibid., pp. 31, 50, 51), in which the tile-roofed buildings in the foreground often seem to have the façades merely attached to them.

100 Van Zanten, p. 286.

101 This "slogan" for the era was coined by Figueiredo Pimental; see Broca, *A vida literária*, p. 4, ch. 1, *passim*.

102 These were officially sponsored get-togethers for Rio's high society. The latter came to the Campo de Santana to watch floral floats compete and to eat a French meal to music; see *Rua do Ouvidor*, 1 Oct. 1904.

103 João de Barros, "Chronica," *Renascença* 1 (May 1904), p. 85. See also Lage and Cia. "Apresentação" in Fogliani, p. 3, and Fogliani and Ferreira Araújo, "Considerações" in ibid., p. 12; *O Paiz*,, 29 Dec. 1901; *Gazeta de Noticias*, 24 Sept. 1901; *O Malho*, 14 March 1903, [2].

104 "A Avenida Central," *Rua do Ouvidor*, 10 Sept. 1904. NB that Frontin and Müller were explicitly interested in the "civilizing" impact of the Avenida, and that this figured in the decision to drive it deeper south into the *cidade velha* than existing commerce required: see *Jornal do Commercio*, 21 May 1903 and *O Paiz*, 27 May 1903.

105 J. C. de Mariz Carvalho, "Pulcherrima Rerum," *Kósmos*, 1:9 (Sept. 1904): 4. See also the accounts of Paul Latteux, *A travers le Brésil au pays de l'or et des diamants* (Paris: Aillaud, Alves, 1910), p. 135; Alured Gray Bell, *The Beautiful Rio de Janeiro* (London: Heinemann, 1914), p. 192; Gilberto Amado, *Mocidade no Rio e primeira viagem à Europa* (Rio de Janeiro: José Olympio, 1956), 20–1; Maul, pp. 115–17.

106 "Drs. Lauro Müller e Paulo Frontin," *Rua do Ouvidor*, 2 April 1904. On the underlying assumptions, see Rodrigues Alves' speech in *Jornal do Commercio*, 24 Oct. 1901; Joaquim Murtinho, "Relatório da Industria, Viação e Obras Públicas," rpt. in *Revista do Instituto Histórico e Geográfico Brasileiro* 219 (1953), pp. 239–66; F. A. Barbosa, pp. 3–4, 14–16, 25; Vilella Luz, pp. 180–9, and chs. 3–5, *passim*; Heitor Ferreira Lima, *História do pensamento econômico no Brasil* (São Paulo: Nacional, 1978), chs. 9–11, *passim*; Steven Topik, "State interventionism in a liberal regime," HAHR, 50 (1980), pp. 593–616. Although elite and middle-sector factions struggled over means, the end of government intervention in the economy, to achieve Civilization and Progress, was assumed. The debates centered on the extent of intervention and Brazil's role in the world economy. Rodrigues Alves, like Campos Sales, presumed that Brazil was fundamentally agricultural, and the government's role was the relatively limited one of indirect support via provision of infrastructure and the facilitation of foreign capital and immigrant labor.

107 Olavo Bilac, "Chronica," *Kósmos* 1:3 (March 1904), p. [2]: see also "Drs. Lauro Müller," *passim*; "Avenida Central," *passim*; Olavo Bilac, "Chronica," *Kośmos* 3:8 (Aug. 1906), p. [2]; Olavo Bilac, "Chronica," *Kósmos*, 2:11 (Nov. 1905), pp. [1–2].

108 Olavo Bilac, "Chronica," *Kósmos*, 1:3 (March 1904), p. [1]; Pereira Passos attempted restraint by licencing requirements: see *Jornal do Commercio*, 13 Feb. 1904.

109 João do Rio, *A alma encantadora das ruas* (Rio de Janeiro: Simões, 1951), pp. 126–7.

110 Ibid., p. 130.

111 Costa, *Rio*, 4: 771, 773–4; cf. *Jornal do Commercio*, 18 Feb. 1904. On *Carnaval*, see Costa, ibid., 4: 767–74, 800–5, ch. 25, *passim*; Rio, pp. 123–34, especially 129–32. Not all of the traditions of Carioca *Carnaval* were African in origin; Costa (4: 767–71), for example, notes its Portuguese elements, and members of the middle sectors and even of the elite celebrated a more genteel version of clubs, pranks, and disguise. See ibid., 4: ch. 25, *passim*; "Echos e factos," *Rua do Ouvidor*, 30 Jan. 1904; ibid., 12 Feb. 1904; von Binzer, pp. 67–71; Dent, p. 239; Andrews, p. 41; *The Rio de Janeiro News*, 1 March 1898, pp. 5–6.

112 On Afro-Brazilians and the elite, see chapter 4.5, below, and the references in n. 92 there. Working-class, black neighborhoods at the turn of the century are clear in Ministerio de Industria, Viação e Obras Publicas. Directoria Geral de Estatistica, *Rescenseamento geral de República . . . do Brazil . . . 1890: Districto Federal . . .* (Rio de Janeiro, 1895), pp. 404–21; see also F. N. Silva, p. 123; Costa, *Rio*, 2: chs. 8, 11, 12, passim; Costa, *De um livro de memórias*, 1: 198–9; Rio, *A alma encantadora*, p. 126; Lahmeyer Lobo, 1: 237–59, 2: 504–5; Benchimol, ch. 10; Adamo, pp. 4–40, 229–58; Rocha, pp. 97–107, 116–24. On Pereira Passos' long-lived interest in state intervention in workers' housing, see Needell, "Making the Carioca *Belle Epoque* concrete," pp. 421–2n. 51. On working-class housing and its demolition see Everardo Backheuser, "Onde moram os pobres," *Renascença*, 2 (March 1905) pp. 89–94 and 2 (May 1905), pp. 185–9; Benchimol, ch. 10, *passim*, and 592–609; Rocha, ch. 4, *passim*; Adamo, pp. 31–40. The limited nature of Pereira Passos' intervention to provide housing could not assuage the impact of the demolition, in which approximately one tenth of the *cidade velha*'s population was forcibly ejected. The demolition played a role in the urban revolt of 1904, the so-called *Quebra-Lampiões* riots or *Revolta Contra Vacina*; see Benchimol, pp. 610–41; José Murilo de Carvalho, "A Revolta Contra Vacina" (Prelim. draft, Seminário Rio Republicano, 4 Oct. 1984); Needell, "*Revolta Contra Vacina*."

113 Costa, *De um livro de memórias*, 1:162.

114 Skidmore, pp. 27–32 and ch. 2, *passim*.

115 Costa, *De um livro de memórias*, 1: 181–2.

116 Ibid., 1: 162–3.

117 Rocha, ch. 7, reaches similar conclusions coming from an entirely different direction – that of popular Carioca culture.

2 Formal institutions of the elite

1 See Azevedo, pp. 365–6, 385, 389–90. Regarding the military and the Church as sole avenues for non-elite education, see Cruz Costa, pp. 82–3, 187. The quotation is from Azevedo, p. 393.

2 See Azevedo, pp. 377–8; interview with Américo Jacobina Lacombe, Rio de Janeiro, 15 September 1980; interview with Alceu Amoroso Lima, Rio de Janeiro, 3 October 1980. Cf. Carolina Nabuco, *A vida de Joaquim Nabuco* (Rio de Janeiro: Nacional, 1928), chs 1–2, *passim*; Emília G. de la Rocque, *Gente da minha vida* (Petrópolis: Vozes, 1977), pp. 95–7; and Camilla Barbosa de Oliveira, *Águas passadas*. (São Paulo: Edanec, 1956), p. 109. The quotation is from J[oão] B[aptista]

Mello e Sousa, *Estudantes do meu tempo* (Rio de Janeiro: Internato do Colégio Pedro II, 1958), pp. 132–3.

3 E.g., [Imperial Collegio de Pedro II,] *Programma do Ensino . . . 1862* (Rio de Janeiro: Nacional, 1862), pp. 8, 10, 13, 15–16, 22, 23, 26, 30. See Azevedo, pp. 365–7, 370, 382, 385, 390. Cf. Emília Nogueira, "Alguns aspectos da influência francesa em São Paulo ne segunda metade do século XIX," in *Revista de História*, 4: 7 (1953): 319–20, 330–3, 335.

4 See [Eugénio de Barros] Raja Gabaglia, "O Collegio Pedro II," in [Collegio Pedro II,] *Annuario do Collegio Pedro II . . . 1 Anno*. (Rio de Janeiro: Revista dos Tribunaes, 1914), p. 50; and cf. Nogueira, pp. 330–31; Leclerc, pp. 218, 253; and Delso Renault, *O Rio antigo nos anúncios de jornais*. (Rio de Janeiro: José Olympio, 1969), pp. 42–4, 57–8, 64, 65–6, and *passim*.

5 Azevedo, pp. 374, 382; Leclerc, pp. 213–14; Amoroso Lima interview; Nair de Tefé, "Sou francamente pelo sorriso em matéria de caricatura," in Francisco de Assis Barbosa, *Testamento de Mário de Andrade e outras reportagens* (Rio de Janeiro: MEC, 1954), pp. 33–6; C. Nabuco, *Oito décadas*, pp. 32–4; C. Barbosa de Oliveira, p. 109; Rocque, pp. 95–7; Vera Roxo Delgado de Carvalho, "Sob a proteção de Santa Cecília . . ." in *Reminiscencias* (Petrópolis: Vozes, 1938), p. 33. The *alunas* in the Rio of 1865 numbered 666 out of a total 2,555: see Primitivo Moacyr, *A instrução e o Imperio*, 3 vols. (São Paulo: Nacional, 1936–38), 3: 47. However, these girls were probably from the middle sectors, and were being given basic public-school training in order to become teachers themselves. As the figures are official, one doubts they are drawn from the kind of elite private schools teaching French, manners, literature, and piano that Renault cities (see n. 4 above). Nor is it likely that the figure includes students in the earliest nuns' school, Imaculada Conceição, in Botafogo, which had a curriculum of greater scope; see C. Nabuco, *Oito décadas*, pp. 61, 68).

6 See Azevedo, pp. 382, 385, 389–90. Cf. the ideal in the descriptions of the winners of the "Concursos de Belleza" sponsored annually by the *Rua do Ouvidor* (Rio de Janeiro) beginning in 1900. The quotation is from *Rua do Ouvidor*, 4 June 1898, p. 3.

7 Gabaglia, pp. 44–5; [Luís Gastão d'] Escragnolle Dória, *Memoria historica commemorativa do 1 centenario do Collégio Pedro II*. (Rio de Janeiro: MEC, 1937); Moacyr, *passim*; Azevedo, pp. 379–81; "Gymnasio Nacional," in *Rua do Ouvidor*, 10 December 1898, p. 2 (NB the Colégio's name was republicanized briefly to Gymnasio Nacional after the Emperor's fall); [Colégio Pedro II], *Anuário de Colégio Pedro II*. (Rio de Janeiro: Nacional, 1944).

8 Amoroso Lima interview; interview with Paulo Braga de Menezes, Rio de Janeiro, 4 July 1980; interview with Irmã Carmem Maria, Rio de Janeiro, 22 September 1980; cf. Mello e Sousa, pp. 175–6.

9 See, e.g., Azevedo, pp. 367–9.

10 Quoted in Paulo José Pires Brandão, "Dois bacharéis do Pedro II" in *Anuário* [*1944*], pp. 221–2. See the program of study cited in Gabaglia, pp. 47–8, for 1838, and those in [Imperial Collegio Pedro II,] *Programa . . . 1862*, and *Plano e programa . . . 1876*. (Rio de Janeiro: Nacional, 1882); and cf. the programs in [Gymnasio Nacional,] *Programa de ensino . . . 1892*. (Rio de Janeiro: Nacional, 1892); Collegio Pedro II, *Regulamento do Collegio Pedro II* [*1911*], reprinted in *Annuario . . . 1 anno*, pp. 179–86. In defense of the classical curriculum, see Alfredo Alexander, *Gymnasio Nacional: Memoria historica do anno de 1906*. (Rio de Janeiro: Nacional, 1908),

pp. 37–8; and C. R. de Lessa, "Recordações do antigo Internato Pedro II," cited in [Colegio Pedro II,] *Anuario do Colegio Pedro II, vol. 9, 1935–36.* (Rio de Janeiro: Rua da Misericordia, 86, 1939), pp. 241–2.

11 The 1865 figure is from Moacyr, 3: 47. The sum of all students in Rio at the time, as noted in n.5 above, was 2,555. Regarding scholarship boys, note that the Colégio's *externato*, as well as its tradition, owed something to the earlier Escola de São Joaquim, which had stood on the *externato* site, and had been a charitable institution for orphans. This heritage endured in a stipulated number of scholarship students. I was unable to determine the actual number of *alunos gratuitos*. As late as 1888 the largest number of scholarship boys *possible* was 125 out of a student population ranging around 500 to 750. One should also bear in mind that those deemed eligible were hardly the randomly chosen, deserving poor. Preference was given to Colégio staff children and the sons of government bureaucrats. See Gabaglia, p. 45, 92; and cf. [Colégio Pedro II,] "Indice dos processos de matrículas de: 1838 . . . a: 1930," 3 vols. [Rio de Janeiro: MS, Biblioteca do Colégio Pedro II, São Cristóvão c., 1930].

12 See Ignesil Marinho and Luis Inneco, *O Colegio Pedro II cem anos depois* (Rio de Janeiro: Villas Boas, 1938), pp. 17–19; Collegio Pedro II. Ministerio da Justiça e Negocios Interiores. [Octacilio A. Pereira, comp.,] *Almanack do pessoal docente e administrativo até 30 de junho de 1924*, no. 2 (Rio de Janeiro: Revista dos Tribunães, 1925), *passim*. The quotations are from Marinho and Inneco, p. 66 and Lessa, p. 240, respectively.

13 Lessa, pp. 26, 238.

14 Raul Pederneiras, "A vida do estudante do Collegio Pedro II em 1884" in Marinho and Inneco, p. 50. See, also, Pires Brandão, pp. 218–19; and J[oão] B[aptistal] Paranhos da Silva, "Reminiscências do Internato" in *Anuário* . . . [*1944*], p. 208. Note that one of the imperial princes attended the Colégio, and that it is said that, by chance, Pedro II's last official act before the 15 November coup was that of presiding over a Colégio examination.

15 See *Programma* . . . 1862, passim. In the 1880s, though the sciences gained ground, the humanities still dominated – see [Imperial Colegio Pedro II,] "Horario das aulas do Imperial Collegio de Pedro II para o anno de 1882" attached to *Programma . . . 1881*.

16 [Luís Gastão d'Escragnolle Dória] 'Discurso do orador official do collegio: Prof. Luíz d'Escragnolle Dória" in Marinho and Inneco, p. 79.

17 Pederneiras, p. 50; da Silva, "Reminiscencias," p. 208 and, Mello Sousa (*passim*). The latter was of a later and, if anything, more liberal period in the Colégio's history (i.e., *c.* 1904), yet it is obvious that many of the same regulations quoted below were in force. Cf. Moacyr, 1: 280–4 and 3: 25.

18 Drawn from Moacyr's compilation, 1: 280–1.

19 Cf. Dória p. 79; *Annuario* . . . *1935–36, passim; Anuário* . . . [*1944*], *passim*; Marinho and Inneco, *passim*; C. Nabuco, *Joaquim Nabuco*, pp. 25–6; Tristão de Ataíde [pseud. of Alceu de Amoroso Lima], "O Ginásio Nacional," reprinted in *Anuário* . . . [*1944*], pp. 172–3; and Vivaldo Coaracy, "Gymnasio Nacional" reprinted in Marinho and Inneco, p. 46.

20 Brandão, pp. 218–19.

21 *Conselheiro*: meaning councillor, a prestigious title referring to membership of the Council of State or the honorary Council of the Emperor. *Titular*: literally, titleholder; a reference to someone granted a title of nobility, something which, in Brazil, could not generally be inherited.

22 See the two *anuários* cited in n.19; Marinho and Inneco; Azevedo, pp. 379–81; and

Os bacharéis em lettras pelo Imperial Collegio de Pedro II e Gymnasio Nacional. (Rio de Janeiro: n.p., 1896). Among the family names of obvious importance among the Brazilian elite mentioned in the "Indice dos processos de matrículas" are: Soares Ribeiro (commerce), Rodrigues Torres (coffee, finance, politics), Paes Leme (*), Betim Paes Leme (*) Saldanha da Gama (*), Dias Paes Leme (*), Albuquerque Diniz (*), Nabuco de Araújo (politics), Rodrigues Alves (coffee, politics), Delamare (navy), Calmon Nogueira Valle da Gama (coffee, State), Silva Prado (coffee), Suckow (commerce?), Albuquerque Cavalcanti (*), Escragnolle Taunay (army, State), Calmon du Pin e Almeida (planting, commerce, State), Duque Estrada (*), Silva Paranhos (State), Mayrinck (finance), Jacobina (politics), Vieira Souto (entrepreneur, professions), Niemeyer (entrepreneur, professions, commerce), Gracie (commerce?), Mendes de Almeida (liberal professions), Chagas Dória (army, entrepreneur, professions), Lustosa da Cunha Paranaguá (State, politics), Rego Barros (*), Bulhões Carvalho (liberal professions), Ottoni (politics) Furquim Joppert (coffee, commerce), Araújo Vianna (liberal professions), Cochrane de Alencar (*), Chapot Prévost (liberal professions). NB I indicate parenthetically the basis for the elite position of each family named, as best I know it. (*)indicates an extensive, traditional family, whose basis is too diverse to note briefly.

23 See, e.g., Coaracy, "Gymnasio Nacional" p. 46; Sousa p. 20; and Brandão, p. 219.

24 See Brandão, p. 219; and *Os bacharéis*, p. 13.

25 Amoroso Lima interview. The newer *colégios* included Santo Inácio, Salesianos *et al.* Jacobina Lacombe, in our interview, also emphasized the growing importance of "American" schools (i.e., schools run by Americans in a more liberal, progressive spirit, and generally located in Botafogo) toward the turn of the century. Another "progressive" school, perhaps the most famous, is the Colégio Abílio, run by a pedagogue made a baron for his efforts, and the factual background for the fictional school in Raul Pompéia's celebrated *O ateneu*. All the indications are, however, that such "progressive" education was a subordinate trend in elite secondary education at the time.

26 See, e.g., La Rocque, pp. 38, 49, 54–5, 67–8, 94–5.

27 See Tefé, "Son francamente pelo sorriso em matéria de caricatura" in F. de A. Barbosa, Testamento de Mário de Andrade e antras reportagens, pp. 33–6; C. Nabuco, *Oito décadas*, pp. 32–4; La Rocque, p. 54.

28 Carmem Maria interview; Delgado de Carvalho, "Sob a proteção," p. 33.

29 See Delgado de Carvalho, pp. 33–6.

30 See Sylvia Nioac M. de Souza Prates, "Cincoenta anos de dedicação" in *Reminiscencias*, pp. 24–32; and "Origens da congregação" in ibid., pp. 5, 12–15.

31 Irmã Carmem Maria, MS given the author at interview, pp. 1–6, *passim*; Carmem Maria interview; Carmem de Faro Lacerda, "Nossa formação sionense" in *Reminiscencias*, pp. 130–2.

32 Sophia A. Lyria, *Rosas de neve* (Rio de Janeiro: Cátedra, 1974), p. 103.

33 Carmem Maria MS, *passim*. See also Magdalena Lacerda Bicalho, "Notre mére Angelina" in *Reminiscencias*, pp. 50–1, 55–6.

34 Ibid., and Delgado de Carvalho, "Sob a proteção" p. 37; Prates, pp. 25–9; Bicalho, p. 48; Carmem Maria interview.

35 Lacerda, p. 131. Also, Jacobina Lacombe interview; Luíz Carlos de Paranaguá, interview, Rio de Janeiro, 1 September 1980; Carmem Maria interview.

36 Carmem Maria interview; Jacobina Lacombe interview.

37 The incident with the Parisian in 1855 was recalled by Gama, p. 37 – see, also,

pp. 37–9, 45–6. The journalist was Max Leclerc (see Leclerc, p. 204, and cf. pp. 203–10, *passim*). Mme de Caillavet is quoted in George Painter, *Marcel Proust: A Biography*, 2 vols. (New York: Vintage Books, 1978), 2: 155–6.

38 See Leclerc, p. 218: in a note more telling than intended, Leclerc states that the best of the Brazilians would match the members of the best Parisian salons. Why the Brazilians should care to do so is a question that probably occurred to neither Leclerc, his Parisian readers, nor his Brazilian subjects.

39 Nabuco, *Minha formação*, pp. 40–1, 42–3.

40 See J. Galante de Souza, *O teatro no Brasil* (Rio de Janeiro: MEC, 1960), pp. 277–308, *passim*; *Gazeta de Noticias* (Rio de Janeiro) is very good for this sort of thing, and *Rua do Ouvidor* often published pertinent profiles and historical accounts.

41 "Ribaltas e bastidores" in *Rua do Ouvidor*, 9 April 1904, p. 7.

42 "Echos e factos" in *Ruo do Ouvidor*, 4 June 1904, p. 6.

43 Mario Pederneiras, "A vida do hoje" in *Kósmos* (Rio de Janeiro) 5 (May 1908): [1].

44 Marcos Carneiro de Mendonça, interview, Rio de Janeiro, 10 July 1980; Carolina Nabuco, interview, Rio de Janeiro, 9 June 1980; *et al*. See the next two chapters.

45 See Casa de Rui Barbosa, Arquivo Histórico: Correspondência [hereafter: RBAHC]: Clubs: Club-Beethoven, Rio de Janeiro, 12 March 1886; Clubs: Club-Beethoven, Carta de Sócio [1886]; Wanderley Pinho, pp. 296–8; and "Local Notes," in *The Rio News* 5 January 1885, 24 July 1885, 15 April 1885, and 24 March 1885.

46 Burke and Staples, p. 64; Wanderley Pinho, ch. 18; Deodato C[ezino] Vilella dos Santos, "Cassino Fluminense (Sua história)" (Rio de Janeiro, 1909, MS in the Arquivo do Automóvel Club do Brasil [hereafter: AACB], based on the Casino's old archive, much of which has been destroyed). pp. 23–4; RBAHC: Clubs: Club-Beethoven: Carta do Sócio [1886]; Biblioteca Nacional, Seção de Manuscritos [hereafter: BNSM]: Coleção Ramos Paz, I–4, 2, 44: Machado de Assis to Paz, Rio de Janeiro, 1 April 1883; BNSM: Coleção Ernesto Senna, I–5, 22, 41: Dr. José de Saldanha da Gama to unknown, 14 November 1902.

47 Early sample names come from AACB "Documentos de valor histórico," vol. 1: 1856/1967: "Documento 6 de Fevereiro de 1856," *passim*; "Sócios accionistas do Casino Fluminense de 1862", *passim*. Information regarding the members drawn from these two documents derives, in order of utility, from: Vasconcellos and Vasconcellos; Sacramento Blake; and Joaquim Manoel de Macedo, *Anno biographico brasileiro*, 3 vols. (Rio de Janeiro: Imperial Instituto Artistico, 1876). Later sample names come from [AACB,] "Diretorias do Fluminense: 1845–1902," (MS, Typescript, 1962, based on Casino archives material). Member information comes from Vasconcellos and Sacramento supplemented by *Almanak administrativo, mercantil e industrial do Rio de Janeiro* [*Almanak Laemmert*] (Rio de Janeiro: Laemmert, 1895, 1900); *The Rio News*; and *Gazeta de Noticias*. Additional information on Quartim was found in Sweigart, pp. 91–2. The generalizations about period elites are drawn from these same sources

48 Vilella dos Santos, "Cassino," pp. 4–6, 7–8, 16–17, *et seq*.

49 See chapter 1. 1, 3.

50 See Vilella dos Santos, "Cassino," pp. 18–19.

51 See La Rocque, p. 54; and C. Nabuco, *Oito décadas*, pp. 21–2, *passim*.

52 Vilella dos Santos, "Cassino," pp. 19–24.

53 See, also, the traditional elite names in [AACB,] "Diretorias do Casino," *passim*. The generalizations noted here and below are drawn from the sources cited in n. 47, above.

54 On the nature and importance of the urban shift for elite careers, see Barman and Barman, *passim*; Stein chs. 1, 5, 9–11; Sweigart chs. 3–4; Lahmeyer Lobo 2: ch. 4, *passim*; Freyre, *Mansions* and Azevedo's chapter on the city; on families and the pattern of adaptation, see e.g., La Rocque, *passim*; Barbosa de Oliveira Aguas, Ridings, "Class." Dean, ch. 1, and *passim*; Colson. Descendants of the elite proved conscious of how fortunes were made and lost in the agro-export and urban-based economy in interviews (e.g., the Carneiro de Mendonça, Braga de Menezes, and Amoroso Lima interviews).

Urban rents played an important role during this era of uncertainty (Paranaguá interview). See, e.g., the family names in the attachments "Terrenos vendidos" and "Relação geral dos prédios desapropriados para Avenida Central mediante indemnisação em dinheiro" in Ferrez, *Avenida Central*. Family adaptation to mutable economic circumstances is discussed in ch. 4 below.

55 "Ribaltas e Bastidores" in *Rua do Ouvidor*, 10 December 1904. See also the commentary of Olavo Bilac in the "Chronica" for *Kósmos* 3: 12 (December 1906): [1–2]; and La Rocque, pp. 98–9, 101–3; (Amoroso Lima interview).

56 La Rocque (101–2); Maul, pp. 9–10.

57 See Wanderley Pinho pp. 145–7. I discuss Petrópolis at greater length in chapter 4.9 below.

58 RBAHC: Clubes: Cartão dos Diários, 1 August 1900.

59 [AACB,] "Diretorias do Club dos Diários: 1895–1924", MS, Typescript, 1962; Nelson Pinto, *Historia da fusão do Automovel Club com o Club dos Diarios*. (Rio de Janeiro: Automóvel Club do Brasil, 1938), pp. 7, 37; La Rocque p. 102; on the Count de Figueiredo see Vasconcellos and Vasconcellos; on Sousa Leão, see Wanderley Pinho, p. 309; on José Carlos de Figueiredo and his wife see C. Nabuco, *Oito décadas*, p. 58; Costa, *Rio*, 2: 332, 334, 337; Ambassador Eiras recalled them, too, as did Gilberto Trompowsky (Carlos da Ponte Ribeiro Eiras, interview, Rio de Janeiro, 25 July 1980; Gilberto Trompowsky, interview, Rio de Janeiro, 13 June 1980); on Buarque de Macedo see the advertising and company information in *Almanak Laemmert*; on the Baron de Santa Margarida, see Vasconcellos and Vasconcellos and de La Rocque, pp. 102–3; on Rocha Miranda see Vasconcellos and Vasconcellos – the two Rocha Mirandas are in AACB "Documentos de valor histórico . . .; 6 de Fevereiro de 1956"; on Rego Barros see *Rua do Ouvidor* for the 1898 season; his family was mentioned to me by José Thomáz Nabuco (interview, Rio de Janeiro, 2 June 1980); on Chaves see *Rua do Ouvidor* 28 May 1910; on Azeredo's role as a journalist and relations with Rui Barbosa see RBAHC: Azeredo, Antonio Francisco de; on Januzzi see *Rua do Ouvidor*, 16 April 1904 and de la Rocque, pp. 36–37; on Vilella dos Santos see the clipping in his member's dossier in the AACB; Hime advertised in *Almanak Laemmert* and the major *jornais* of the period and appears in the later Casino directories cited above; on Pereira Passos and his son, see chapter 1: 5–10 and chapter 3.1; on Teixeira Leite Guimarães, see La Rocque pp. 65–9.

60 Vilella dos Santos, "Cassino,"pp. 23–4.

61 On the Jockey membership, see the ubiquitous [Deodato Cezino] Vilella dos Santos, "Socios fundadores," "Relação dos socios que tem exercido cargos de administração de 1868 a 1922," "Administração do Jockey Club em março de 1922," and "Socios effectivos em 1921" in his *Jockey-Club* (Rio de Janeiro: Fluminense, 1922). Names which are common to the other clubs include: Eduardo Pellew Wilson, Francisco Pereira Passos, Count d'Eu, Antônio Francisco de Azeredo, Jacinto Alves Barbosa,

Leopoldo Augusto de Camara Lima, Baron de Canindé, Elkim Hime, Baron de Drummond, Viscount de Nogueira da Gama, Count de São Clemente, Count da Estrela, Baron de Ibirocaí, Fernando Mendes de Almeida, José Carlos de Figueiredo, Harold Hime, Otávio da Rocha Miranda, Guilherme Guinle, Luís Betim Paes Leme, Francisco de Oliveira Passos, Carlos Guinle, João Borges, Luís Felipe de Souza Leão, Luís da Rocha Miranda, and Otávio Guinle.

62 See *La grande encyclopédie*, vol. 13, s.v. "Course." On the Paris Jockey and its milieu see Albert Dresden Vandam, *An Englishman in Paris* (New York: D. Appleton, 1893), pp. 37–8; [Rees Howell] Gronow, *The Reminiscences and Recollections of Captain Gronow* (New York: Viking, 1964), *passim*. Ellen Moers, *The Dandy* (New York: Viking, 1960), pp. 64, 117–20, and *passim*, discusses the English and French Jockey Clubs.

63 Burke and Staples, pp. 60–1.

64 Vilella dos Santos, *Jockey Club*, pp. 1, 342–6, *passim*; government support came later – Vilella dos Santos notes 1914 aid (p. 346); and in 1880, "Councilor [João Luís Vieira Cansansão de] Sinimbú and Dr. [Francisco Pereira] Passos have been made honorary members of the Jockey Club. These gentlemen, when government officials, caused an imperial premium to be paid at the Club's races." See "Local Notes" *The Rio News*, 15 August 1880, p. 2.

65 Vilella dos Santos, *Jockey-Club*, pp. 243, 247, 345–6.

66 See, e.g., "Sport: Turf," in *Rua do Ouvidor*, 21 May 1910, p. 6.

67 The account of 1851 is cited in Vilella dos Santos, *Jockey-Club*, pp. 342–3. See the photographs in the *Jornal do Brazil*'s *Revista da Semana* and *A Illustração Brazileira*.

68 Trompowsky interview.

69 "Sport: Turf," in *Rua do Ouvidor*, 27 August 1910, p. 6 [*] "turfmen" was in English in the original.

70 The Derby (founded 1885) was the creature of Paulo de Frontin, and never achieved the status of the Jockey, which was thought more exclusive. The Derby was absorbed after Frontin's death in the 1930s, and its building and capital went to the Jockey, which coveted both (each being considered more handsome than those of the Jockey itself). The foundation of the Derby is celebrated in "Derby Club," in *Rua do Ouvidor*, 30 July 1910, pp. 1–2 and "Gazeta dos Sports: Turf: O Derby-Club festeja mais um anniversario de sua fundação" in *Gazeta de Noticias*, 2 August 1914, p. 8. My information on the rivalry and relative status of the clubs comes from interviews (e.g., Eiras interview, José Thomáz Nabuco interview).

71 Trompowsky mentioned the loss of elegance and refinement as increasingly clear in Society after the Great War, until the final step in the Revolution of 1930 and its aftermath. He emphasised the loss of the milieu associated with the *chá dançante*: refined gatherings of brilliance, wit, and flirtation. Eiras suggested that the absorption of the Derby was a blow to the Jockey's exclusivity – but this also points to the Jockey's elasticity, which helps to explain its survival. In comparing the Diários and the Jockey, it is interesting that Carolina Nabuco noted that very few aspects of the Jockey actually promoted active social intercourse (interview, Rio de Janeiro, 9 June 1980), which suggests how incidental those aspects were to the nature and attractions of the club.

72 See Souza, *O teatro no Brasil*, pp. 277–308, *passim*. Note that the Teatro Lírico was called the Imperial Theatro Dom Pedro II until 1890. Only the Real Teatro de São João, founded in 1813, might claim a longer history by virtue of the various theaters on its old site. See Galante de Souza, pp. 284–8.

73 See Coaracy, *Memórias* pp. 140–4. Marcos Carneiro de Mendonca mentioned this in a discussion of my research at the Instituto Histórico e Geográfico Brasileiro (Rio de Janeiro, 25 June 1980); Trompowsky confirmed it (Trompowsky interview).
74 "Local Notes," in *The Rio News*, 24 July 1885, p. 5.
75 Quoted in Costa, 2: 429; cf. Costa, 2: 340–5. Réjane was half-accurate: Coaracy, *Memórias*, pp. 140–1, notes that the theater was originally constructed to serve as a circus, too.
76 "Binoculo de um dilettante" in *Rua do Ouvidor*, 28 May 1910, p. 3.
77 *Rua do Ouvidor*, 14 May 1898, p. 7.
78 "Local Notes" in *The Rio News*, 5 July 1885, p. 5. Cf. Coaracy *Memórias*, pp. 141–2; and da Costa, 2: 444–7; "A Marthe Regnier" in *Rua do Ouvidor*, 27 August 1910, p. 4. I write of the special place of French actresses in the elite male sexual imagination in chapter 5.3. Both Trompowsky and Mendonça confirmed the high quality of visiting performers, as does Coaracy (*Memórias*, pp. 142, 144), and Barbosa de Oliveira, *Águas* (pp. 114–15). C. Nabuco, though she makes clear the quality and social importance of the opera at the Lírico, argues for the greater value attached to the French theater to be had at the Teatro Municipal (*Oito décadas*, pp. 63–4). Coaracy argued, loc. cit., that the eclipse of the Lírico began only with the new-built (1910) Municipal's increasing prestige and comparative splendor. As these are social and cosmetic values – it was probably the Municipal as a better showplace, rather than French theater *per se*, which secured Carioca preference.
79 "Binoculo de um dilettante" in *Rua do Ouvidor*, 28 May 1910, p. 3.
80 Trompowsky interview.
81 Lyra, p. 67.
82 On this paradigm, cf., e.g., the magnificent scene in which Proust describes Mme. de Guermantes at the Opéra in *Remembrance of Things Past*, 7 vols., (New York: Vintage 1970), 3: 35–9, complete with the "demi-gods of the Jockey Club". See also the original from which Proust worked, in Painter, 2: 177–8.
83 Frank Bennett, see *Forty years in Brazil* (London: Mills and Born, 1914), p. 73; cf. [Alfredo Maria Adriano d'Escragnolle Taunay, visconde de Taunay,] *Memórias do Visconde de Taunay*, (São Paulo: Instituto Progresso 1948) p. 579. The old Teatro São Pedro had served the same purpose earlier; See Oliveira, *Memórias*, p. 262.
84 Delgado de Carvalho (interview, Rio de Janeiro, 14 May 1980). Yet, cf. Lyra, p. 67.
85 RBAHC: Azeredo, Antônio Francisco de: Antônio de Azeredo to Ruy Barbosa, Rio de Janeiro, October 1903.

3 The salon and the emergence of high society

1 See the Appendix.
2 See chapter 1.5–10, for Pereira Passos' professional career and the urban reforms of 1902–5. Otherwise, on Pereira Passos see *Almanak Laemmert*, [hereafter *AL*], *1895*, pp. 709, 1273, 1410–11, and "Indicador," p. 192; *AL* 1906, "Indicador," p. 2436; Eli Bahar, *Vultos do Brasil* (São Paulo: Exposição do Livro, 1967); Sacramento Blake, [hereafter *SB*]; Vasconcellos and Vasconcellos, [hereafter *VSV*], s.v. "Mangaratiba"; Athayde, *passim*, especially pp. 11–25, 75–86, 107–10; Graham, *Britain and the Onset*, pp. 196–7; [Deodato Cezino] Vilella dos Santos, *Jockey-Club*, p. 440; and Nelson Pinto, *Historia da fusão do Automovel Club com o Club dos Diarios* (Rio de Janeiro: Automovel Club do Brasil, 1938), p. 7.
3 See Athayde, pp. 76–8, 80; cf. Costa, *Rio*, 1: 34–41; and [José Joaquim de Campos

da Costa de] Madeiros e Albuquerque, *Minha vida* (Rio de Janeiro: Calvino Filho, 1934), 2: 89–96, *passim*.

4 Costa, *Rio*, 2: 329, 331–2, 335, 346–9; see, also, Athayde, pp. 79–80; and *Rua do Ouvidor*, 3 September 1904, pp. 4–5.

5 Costa, *Rio*, 2: 332; "Dr. F. de Oliveira Passos" in *Rua do Ouvidor*, 26 November 1904, pp. 1–2; *AL 1905*, "Indicador," p. 2436; Marcos Carneiro de Mendonça, interview, Rio de Janeiro, 15 July 1980.

6 Alceu Amorosa Lima, interview, Rio de Janeiro, 2 October 1980 (Lima lived up the street from the old engineer as a child).

7 Athayde, p. 79.

8 Albuquerque, 2: 95.

9 On Rui Barbosa see *SB*; Behar, *AL 1905*, "Indicador," p. 2274; Graham, *Britain and the Onset*, pp. 264–76; Magalhães Júnior, *Rui*; Viana Filho, *Rui Barbosa*; [Francisco Clementino de] San Tiago Dantas, *Dois momentos de Rui Barbosa* (Rio de Janeiro: Casa de Rui Barbosa, 1951); Barbosa de Oliveira, *Águas*; Maria Augusta [Viana Bandeira Rui Barbosa] and Maria Adélia [Rui Barbosa], "Rui Barbosa" in Francisco de Assis Barbosa, *Retratos de família* (Rio de Janeiro: José Olympio, 1968), pp. 27–36; Costa, *Rio*, 2: 330, 335; [João] Dunshee de Abranches [Moura], *Governos e congressos da Republica dos Estados Unidos do Brazil . . . 1889–1917*, 2 vols. (São Paulo: Abranches, 1918), 1: 11.

10 See Barbosa de Oliveira, *Águas*; de La Rocque; and Rezende Martins. Rui was related to the Teixeira Leite family of Minas Gerais and Rio de Janeiro, and to the Sousa Queirós and Ribeiro de Rezende families of São Paulo and Rio de Janeiro, families which included at least ten titles – see *VSV*; the first two sections of chapter 4, below; and Oliveira, *Memórias* ch. 1 and nn., *passim*.

11 See chapter 1.3.

12 See Melo Franco, 2: bk. 7, *passim*, bk. 8, ch. 3, *passim*; and Bello, *History*, pp. 169, 193–5, 203–7. See, also, chapter 1.4, 7.

13 See, e.g., *Diario de Noticias* (Rio de Janeiro) 30 November 1907; *Rua do Ouvidor*, 26 February 1910, p. 6. See also Casa de Rui Barbosa, Arquivo Histórico: Correspondência (hereafter RBAHC]. Antônio de Azeredo to Rui Barbosa, Rio de Janeiro, 15 July 1907. See Melo Franco (2: 600–3 and 2: bk. 8, ch. 3, *passim*, on the schism between Rui and the *bloco*, Bello, *History*, (pp. 11–15) or Viana Filho, *Rui Barbosa*, pp. 242–9. Rui, of course, would put himself forward for the presidency on another occasion, in 1919, again without success. NB that Rui's Hague reputation was a piece of calculated self-promotion – he bought, with funds supplied by the Baron do Rio Branco, a journalist's time and space; see Magalhães Júnior, *Rui*, pp. 310–11, 314–20.

14 See Magalhães Júnior, *Rui*, pp. 248–66; Graham, *Britain and the Onset*, p. 268; and Viana Filho, *Rui Barbosa*, pp. 199–201.

15 Leclerc, pp. 164–5.

16 Martín Garcia Mérou, *El Brazil intellectual* (Buenos Aires: Félix Lajouane, 1900), pp. 326–7.

17 José Gomes Pinheiro Machado (1851–1915) chief of the *bloco*, was the senator from Rio Grande do Sul and the vice-president of the Senate who, representing the highly disciplined political party of his state, played a central role in Federal politics during the *belle époque*. After a bloody apprenticeship in the war-torn *gaúcho* state, he became prominent in the era inaugurated by Campos Sales' famous *política dos governadores* in 1898, moving into the vacuum left in the national partisan scene after the

radical/military débâcles of 1897 and the fall of Francisco Glicério. He represented elements of the radical and military strains of Republicanism, which combined well with the positivist, military traditions of the state he represented in Rio. On the strength of this electoral and ideological basis, which gave him permanence coupled with national prestige and connections, Pinheiro Machado arranged a *modus vivendi* with the *paulista* Republicans – loyalty to the new status quo in exchange for sensitivity to Rio Grande's interests. He also moved into crucial committee positions in the Congress which gave him enormous power over the elected representatives of the less powerful states. He thus became the broker at the center of the era's political dealing. His power reached its acme with the 1910 election of his creature, General Hermes da Fonseca. See Dunshee de Abranches, 1: 264–71 and Amado, *Mocidade*, pp. 107–32, 395–404. The references cited in n. 11 above put the *gaúcho* in context. See also Love, *Rio Grande*. Again, for a sense of these trends see chapter 1.3, 4.

18 On Pinheiro Machado and Rui, see Viana Filho, *Rui Barbosa*, pp. 209–11; on the bookstores, see Costa, *Rio*, 4: 728–31; on the cinema, see M. A. V. B. and M. A. Rui Barbosa, pp. 29, 34. Gilberto Ferrez, whose father was a pioneer of the Brazilian cinema, noted Rui's penchant for the *cinematógrafo* (interview, Rio de Janeiro, 11 July 1980).

19 M. A. V. B. and M. A. Rui Barbosa, p. 33. See, also, Viana Filho, *Rui Barbosa*, pp. 199–211 and Costa, *Rio*, 2: 330, 335.

20 See Viana Filho, *Rui Barbosa*, p. 211, and cf. example cited at the end of chapter 2.

21 On Francisco de Figueiredo, see Lery Santos, *Pantheon fluminense* (Rio de Janeiro: G. Leuzinger e Filhos, 1880), pp. 383–5; *SB*; *VSV*; Dunshee de Abranches, 1:343, *AL 1895*, pp. 635, 1119, 1125, 1318, 1428, "Indicador," p. 133; *AL 1905*, pp. 656, 903, 924, 1905, "Indicador," p. 2313; Magalhães Júnior, *Rui*, pp. 47–91, *passim*; Graham, *Britain and the Onset*, pp. 198–9, 225. On Figueiredo in Second Reign high society, see Wanderley Pinho, pp. 78, 182, 309–10. Figueiredo was the first president of the Diários; see [Arquivo do Automóvel Club do Brasil (hereafter AACB),] "Diretorias do Club dos Diários: 1895–1924," (MS, Typescript, Rio de Janeiro, 1962, based on primary source-material of the AACB).

22 *SB*, 2: 446.

23 Lery Santos, *Pantheon*, p. 385.

24 See C. Nabuco, *Oito décadas*, p. 58; [Manuel de] Oliveira Lima, *Memorias* (Rio de Janeiro: José Olympio 1937), p. 82; Bello, *History*, pp. 17, 74; *AL 1895*, p. 1125; Serzedello Correa, pp. 44–75, *passim*; Magalhães Júnior, *Rui*, pp. 47–91, *passim*; the *roman-à-clef* by Taunay *O encilhamento*. Information on Mayrink's part appears in Magalhães Júnior and Taunay (where the financier appears as Mayermayer). See, also, Dunshee de Abranches, 1: 339–41. On Figueiredo's venture into politics see ibid. 1: 343.

25 Wanderley Pinho (p. 309) notes that Figueiredo's daughters married into the Gudin, Sousa Leão, and Braga families.

26 Costa, *Rio*, 2: 330.

27 The portrait is in Wanderley Pinho (between pp. 352 and 353).

28 On José Carlos see C. Nabuco, *Oito décadas*, p. 58; Vilella dos Santos, p. 443; and the [AACB] "Diretorias."

29 On Frontin's role in Rio's 1902–6 reforms, see chapter 1.8, 9. On Paulo de Frontin's life and social position, I relied on *Rua do Ouvidor*, 25 March 1899, pp. 1–2 and 30 July 1910, pp. 1–2; *AL 1895*, pp. 706, 1419–21, 1457 and "Indicador," p. 29;

AL 1905, pp. 803, 929, 936, 2763; Dunshee de Abranches, 2: 446–9; Luíz Carlos de Paranaguá and P. H. de Paranaguá, interview, Rio de Janeiro, 15 July 1980; José Thomáz Nabuco, interview, Rio de Janeiro, 2 June 1980; Ferrez interview; Marcos Carneiro de Mendonça, interview, Rio de Janeiro, 15 July 1980; Gilberto Trompowsky, interview, Rio de Janeiro, 13 June 1980; Américo Jacobina Lacombe, MS in author's files, written in response to author's questions and given 24 September 1980 in Rio de Janeiro; Carlos da Ponte Ribeiro Eiras, interview, Rio de Janeiro, 25 July 1980; Martins, *Presença*.

30 See Dunshee de Abranches, 2: 446–9.

31 See, e.g., *Rua do Ouvidor* 25 March 1899; Dunshee de Abranches, loc. cit.; this feat was remembered by many interviewed (e.g., Carneiro de Mendonça, Eiras, Ferrez, Jacobina Lacombe, and the Paranaguá brothers, whose grand-uncle was an associate of Frontin's in the enterprise), as oral history – each was born after the event.

32 See chapter 1.9, 10.

33 See *Rua do Ouvidor*, 30 July 1910, pp. 1–2; *Gazeta de Noticias*, 2 August 1914, p. 8; Dodsworth Martins, pp. 40–1, 190–1.

34 See Needell "Making the Carioca *Belle Epoque* concrete," 416–19 n. 36, for a glimpse of the Club's role and Frontin's clique within it.

35 See, e.g., *AL 1895*, p. 1457.

38 Jacobina Lacombe MS.

37 Trompowsky interview.

38 Ibid., and Carneiro de Mendonça interview. See also *Rua do Ouvidor*, 24 September 1904, pp. 5–6.

39 On Quartim, see *AL 1895*, pp. 766, 1123, 1125, 1131, 1428, "Indicador," pp. 85, 407; *AL 1905*, "Indicador," p. 2449; *VSV*; *IFS*; da Costa, 2: 330; Sweigart, pp. 291–2; Arquivo do Instituto Histórico e Georgráfico Brasileiro [hereafter AIHGB]: Coleção do Instituto Histórico, 573/19, Max Fleiuss to João Lira Filho, Rio de Janeiro, 23 December 1932.

40 See chapter 2.2.

41 See Sweigart, pp. 291–2. On the Rodrigues Torres family, one might begin with *VSV* s.v. Barão de Itamby or, Visconde de Itaboray. The family's importance is obvious in the marriages it made; see chapter 4.2.

42 See Sweigart, ch. 5, *passim*; Lahmeyer Lobo, 1: ch. 3, 2: ch. 4, *passim*; Stein, *Vassouras*, p. 64, and *passim*.

43 See *IFS* s. v. Quartim.

44 See Sweigart, *passim*, especially ch. 3, and Ridings, "Class," 432–50. The lusophobia of the Brazilian urban masses and middle sectors is mentioned in chapter 1.3.

45 One of them married into the Simonsen banking family (J. T. Nabuco interview) and C. Nabuco (p. 154) mentions Zizi and Beatriz Quartin [*sic*] as regulars of Petrópolis' Tennis Club.

46 Costa, *Rio*, 2: 330, 346–7; the Rua do Riachuelo had, as the Rua de Matacavalos, been associated earlier with the villas of wealthy Cariocas, as readers of Machado de Assis may recall. See Rios Filho, *O Rio de Janeiro imperial*, pp. 209–10, 315.

47 For Antônio de Azeredo, I rely on *AL 1895*, "Indicador," p. 2269; da Costa, 2: 335, 5: 975–6; Oliveira Lima, *Memórias*, pp. 150, 156–7; Argeu Guimarães, *Diccionario bio-bibliographico brasileiro de diplomacia, politica externa e direito internacional*. (Rio de Janeiro: Irmãos Pongetti, 1937) [hereafter, *AG*]; Jacobina Lacombe MS; J. T. Nabuco interview; Carneiro de Mendonça interview; Eiras interview; Trompowsky interview; Broca, *A vida literária*, p. 25.

48 See the *anúncio* in *AL 1895*, p. 1447. As we shall see below, this *faculdade*, (founded 1882) whose advertisement suggests the Carioca attempt to institutionalize a rival to the traditional provincial faculties of the older elites, would come to employ as professors many of the most important lawyers and legally-trained intellectuals in the capital.

49 Viana Filho, *Rui Barbosa*, pp. 115–16; *AG*.

50 Melo Franco, 1: 156–8, 2: 503, *et seq.*. See also Azeredo's correspondence with Rui on the federal role in Mato Grosso political violence during the Campos Sales regime in RBAHC.

51 See chapter 1.4.

52 Amado, *Mocidade*, p. 120.

53 Oliveira Lima, *Memórias*, p. 150; see, also, pp. 156–7. Cf. Melo Franco, 2: 510, 510 n. 8; and Costa, *Rio*, 5: 975–6.

54 See "Binoculo," *Gazeta de Noticias*, 24 July 1908, 24 August 1908. See, also, C. Nabuco, *Oito décadas*, p. 82; Viana Filho, *Rui Barbosa*, p. 115; and Broca, p. 25. The salon was also mentioned in the Trompowsky, J. T. Nabuco, Eiras, and Carneiro de Mendonça interviews, as well as in the Jacobina Lacombe MS.

55 See RBAHC: Azeredo, Antônio Francisco de, *passim*; Viana Filho, p. 211. *Rua do Ouvidor*, 2 July 1898, p. 4; ibid., 13 August 1898, p.6; *Gazeta de Noticias*, 20 July 1908, p. 3; note the Azeredos at the Lírico, the Rego Barros musical salon, and the Parque Fluminense garden party, respectively.

56 On Inglês de Sousa, see Paulo Inglês de Sousa, "Inglês de Sousa" in Barbosa, *Retratos*, pp. 105–17; *AL 1895*, p. 1451, "Indicador," p. 216; *AL 1905*, pp. 926, 932; Raimundo de Menezes, *Dicionário literário brasileiro*, 5 vols. (São Paulo: Sarvaiva, 1969); *SB*; Otto Maria Carpeaux, *Pequena bibliografia crítica da literatura brasileira* (Rio de Janeiro: Artes e Letras, 1964); Broca, *A vida literária*, pp. 28, 29.

57 That is, Antônio Carlos de Andrada, son and namesake of one of the famous Andrada brothers so important in the political questions of Independence, and the First Reign, Regency, and early Second Reign. Antônio Carlos was one of the great Liberals of the Second Reign, and enjoyed immense prestige among the faculty students.

58 Other novels (*O cacaulista*, 1876, and *O coronel Sangrado*, 1877) preceded *O missionário* and, incidentally, antedate the naturalist works of Aluísio de Azevedo, thus making Inglês de Sousa "the first Brazilian Naturalist." See Carpeaux, p. 172. On Azevedo and Naturalism, see chapter 6.3, 6.

59 [Herculano Marcos] Inglês de Sousa, "Diário" quoted in P. Inglês de Sousa, pp. 109–10.

60 P. Inglês de Sousa, p. 110.

61 See chapter 6.7

62 Ibid., p. 117.

63 See Costa, *Rio*, 4: 742.

64 Broca, *A vida literária*, pp. 28, 29; P. Inglês de Sousa, pp. 116–17.

65 On Escragnolle Dória, see: *Rua do Ouvidor*, 22 October 1898, pp. 1–2; *AL 1895*, "Indicador," p. 161; *AL 1905*, "Indicador," p. 2330; *SB*, *AG*.

66 See Escragnolle Dória's profiles (as well as *VSV* s.v. "Escragnolle", "Taunay") in *Rua do Ouvidor*, 1 April 1899 and 25 May 1899. See *AL 1895*, p. 1279 and *AL 1905*, pp. 656, 929 (for Francisco Manoel das Chagas Dória, Escragnolle Dória's paternal grandfather) and *AL 1895*, pp. 711, 1334 (for Luíz Goffredo de Escragnolle Taunay, his maternal cousin or uncle).

67 Alfredo Maria Adriano d'Escragnolle Taunay, Viscount de Taunay (1843–99), was a soldier, engineer, professor, senator, provincial president, Abolitionist, monarchist, founding member of the Academia Brasileira de Letras, descendant of three aristocratic French families, and was connected by marriage to the *titular* Brazilian family of Teixeira Leite. Taunay wrote, among other works, *Retirada da Laguna*, *Innocência*, *O encilhamento* (noted earlier), and numerous historical essays, as well as the memoirs cited in various places in these pages. See Menezes, *SB*, and *VSV*.

68 *Rua do Ouvidor*, 22 October 1898, p. 1. The importance of French literature in the *alto mundo* is central to the analysis in chapter 6.

69 E.g., "Stéphane Malarmé" [*sic*] and "Pierre Loti" in *Rua do Ouvidor*, 17 September 1898, p. 5 and 24 September 1898, p. 5, respectively.

70 Escragnolle Dória was not alone in this, as is shown in chapter 6.9.

71 These skills were traditional by 1900; cf. Wanderley Pinho, *passim*. I discuss the expectations regarding elite women in chapter 4.5, below.

72 On Bebê Lima e Castro, see the information on João da Costa Lima e Castro in: *SB*, *AL 1895*, p. 1385, and "Indicador," p. 241; *AL 1905*, pp. 904, 927, "Indicador," p. 2302. Bebê is mentioned in Costa, *Rio*, 2: 333, and Broca, pp. 29–30. I also draw on my interviews with L. C. de Paranaguá, Carneiro de Mendonça, and Eiras.

73 Gouveia, a son-in-law of Conselheiro Nabuco de Araújo, the noted statesman was one of the foremost physicians of Rio, being distinguished for his European training. The preferred doctor in the Parisian colony of the Brazilian elite in the 1890s, he enjoyed prestige not only because of his skills, but because of his monarchism. See *Rua do Ouvidor*, 13 May 1898, p. 1; and Joaquim Nabuco, *Cartas a amigos*, 2 vols. (São Paulo: Progresso, 1949), 1: 68.

74 See RBAHC: Castro, Violeta Lima e; and A. J. Barbosa de Oliveira, pp. 175 n. 51, 252 n. 9. Cf., also, RBAHC: Pasta 19 October 1889, Baile da Ilha Fiscal: Convite.

75 See Viana Filho, *Rui Barbosa*, p. 211 and *Rua do Ouvidor*, 2 July 1898, p. 4; ibid., 27 August 1898, p. 6; *Gazeta de Noticias*, 12 August 1908, p. 4.

76 E.g., Carneiro de Mendonça interview; Jacobina Lacombe MS.

77 Personal communication from Sra. Maria Celina do Amarante.

78 Broca, *A vida literéria*, pp. 29–30, 29n. 16; Costa, *Rio*, 2: 333.

79 See *Rua do Ouvidor*, 27 August 1898, p. 6; Broca, pp. 29–30.

80 For D. Laurinda, I relied on: the interviews with Trompowsky, Carneiro de Mendonça, Eiras, J. T. Nabuco; the Jacobina Lacombe MS; C. Nabuco, *Oito décadas*, pp. 82–4; Broca, pp. 24–5. In general, as da Costa's list makes clear (2: 333–5), women were crucial to Society for their "elegance and beauty," their "high distinction," their "wit," and their "great personal gifts." The salons, however, are the instruments of men and the extensions of their positions in Society. When da Costa lists the hosts of the "great salons of Rio," they are, except two widows, D. Adelaide Muniz de Sousa and D. Germana Barbosa, all men. Broca's list reveals the same characteristic. Cf. the French case, where salons were often expression of the social ambition and/or artistic taste of women, in Painter, 1: 7, 10, and *passim* or the salons remembered by Paul Morand, *1900 A.D.* (New York: Wm. Farquhar Payson, 1931), pp. 187–90. Again, I discuss elite women's position at length in chapter 4.5, below.

81 Murtinho made his fortune in businesses started in the *Encilhamento*. He criticized the financial policies of the era when he left the Senate to take up the portfolio of Minister of Finance under Campos Sales, in 1898. Murtinho promoted deflation and

the retreat of government intervention, which broke the back of many Carioca enterprises and encouraged renewed financial penetration from Europe. See Murtinho; chapter 1.4; Dunshee de Abranches, 1: 109–12; Graham, *Britain and the Onset*, pp. 238–9; Magalhães Júnior, *Rui*, p. 71; Barbosa, "A presidência."

82 Trompowsky interview.

83 C. Nabuco, *Oito décadas*, pp. 83–4.

84 E.g.: João Borges (son of a Portuguese retailer who became enriched supplying the armed services), the Viscount de Schmidt (despite the name, a wealthy Portuguese merchant), Ildefonso Dutra (brother-in-law of Borges, and seemingly of the same immigrant/merchant background), *et al.* (information on these less well-known men was drawn from the Eiras, J. T. Nabuco, and Carneiro de Mendonça interviews, as well as the Jacobina Lacombe MS).

85 On the Guinle family, I relied on: *AL 1895*, pp. 777, 1311, 1410–11, "Indicador," p. 153; *AL 1905*, pp. 910, 929, "Indicador," p. 2368; British Chamber of Commerce of São Paulo and Southern Brazil, *Personalidades no Brasil* (São Paulo: Chamber of Commerce of São Paulo and Southern Brazil, 1932), p. 342; Costa, *Rio*, 2: 332; Jacobina Lacombe MS; Carneiro de Mendonça, Eiras, Ferrez, J. T. Nabuco, Paranaguás, L. C. de Paranguá interviews; Vilella dos Santos, appendices, *passim*.

86 Bell, p. 139. Newspaper advertising shows Guinle interests as do the entries in the *Almanak Laemmert*. Bell, pp. 139–41, clarifies Guinle interests in energy development and utilization, noting the foreign firms which the Guinles represented: The General Electric Company, American Locomotive Company, Babcock and Wilcox, Otis Elevator Company, Chloride Electrical Storage Company, Jones and Colver (high speed steels), Swan and Finch (oils and lubricants), Herring-Hall-Marvin Safe Company, J. G. Bril (electric cars), Underwood Typewriter Company, Hothert and Pitt (cranes and hoisting apparatus), Fairbanks, Morse and Company (railroad material), Sherwin Williams Company (paints and varnishes). The Guinles, Bell continues, were involved in steam power and hydro-electric installations and headed utilities in the states of Rio de Janeiro, São Paulo, Minas Gerais, and Bahia – often through their Companhia Brasileira de Energia Elétrica, (founded in 1909 with capital worth two million pounds). The fortune rested on the Companhia de Docas de Santos, which Bell states had a capital worth eight million pounds. The Guinles were also heavily involved in real estate and construction, especially on the Avenida Central, including an enormous hotel and a theater, as well as the magnificent Docas de Santos office building; see the illustrations in Bell, the announcement in *Rua do Ouvidor*, 7 May 1910, p. 6; and the appendices to Marc Ferrez, *Avenida Central*, *passim*. Guinle may well have had confidence in Frontin's project, as the two men had long known one another in the Club de Engenharia.

Besides the partnership with Gaffrée, the elder Guinle had had one with Adolfo Aschoff (1864–1904). Aschoff, a native of Alagoas and a *bacharel* of the Escola Politécnica, had been a pioneer in the Rio telephone system of the late 1870s, using experience gained in the U.S. (and possibly the aid of an American partner, one James Mitchell). See *Rua do Ouvidor*, 13 February 1904, p. 6. Aschoff helped point Guinle in the direction of urban-based infrastructure and electricity.

87 See, e.g., *Gazeta de Noticias*, 20 July 1908, p. 3; ibid., 17 July 1908, p. 2; British Chamber of Commerce, note 86 above; Pinto, *passim*; and Vilella dos Santos, appendices, *passim*.

88 C. Nabuco, *Oito décadas*, p. 80.

89 On Ataúlfo de Paiva I relied on: *AL 1895*, "Indicador," p. 72; *AL 1905*,

"Indicador," p. 2435; Costa, *passim*; *AG*, Jacobina Lacombe MS; and the J. T. Nabuco, Eiras, and Carneiro de Mendonça interviews.

90 De La Rocque, p. 111.

91 Jacobina Lacombe, Eiras, and J. T. Nabuco interviews; Jacobina Lacombe MS.

92 Costa, *Rio*, 3: 505, and *passim*.

93 See chapter 5.3.

94 See the Appendix.

95 Carvalho, pp. 238–40. Cf. Wanderley Pinho, pp. 7–8; Carvalho, chs. 1, 15, *passim*.

96 See chapter 2.2.

97 See Wanderley Pinho, chs. 8–10, 12, 15, *passim*. The generalization about salon activity is drawn from ibid., pp. 181–5, 349–50, and *passim*.

98 See Wanderley Pinho, chs. 8–10, 12, *passim*, and pp. 265–6. Carvalho, stresses the *salões* of Abrantes and Nabuco de Araújo (see especially, pp. 240–2). Cf. Calmon, *O marquez*, ch. 17, *passim*; and Vicente Quesada on the São Clemente, Haritoff and Cotegipe salons in *Mis memórias diplomáticas*, 1: 189–93, 296–7.

99 See Wanderley Pinho, pp. 12–13, 265–6; Calmon, *O marquez*, pp. 240–3. Cf. Nabuco, *Um estadista*, 3: 580–3n. 1.

100 E.g., Wanderley Pinho, pp. 117–18 (cf. Carvalho, p. 240). Cf. Frédéric Loliée, *Women of the Second Empire* (London: John Lane, 1907).

101 A "cronista da época" quoted by Wanderley Pinho (pp. 117–18). The impact of French culture will be discussed at length in chapters 4, 5 and 6, below.

102 See Wanderley Pinho, *passim*, but cf., ibid., see pp. 250–3. The contemporary French salon was similar. Graña distinguishes, in fact, between the salon, as the meeting place of the powerful and the talented, and the *cénacle*, the meeting place of "the intellectuals themselves." See César Graña, *Bohemian Versus Bourgeois* (New York: Basic Books, 1964), pp. 30–1. See, also, Painter, 1: chs. 7 and 10.

103 E.g., see Broca, *A vida literária*, pp. 24–5, 28–9.

104 Examples are from Costa, *Rio*, 2: 329–31; Occupations are from *AL 1895* and *AL 1905*, in the "Indicador" sections.

105 See chapter 2.2

106 See chapter 1.4.

107 On the Paranaguá family I relied on interviews with the Marquis de Paranaguá's great-grandsons, Paulo and Luíz Carlos de Paranaguá. On the Marquis, see, the entries in *VSV*, *SB*, and *AG*; *AL 1895*, pp. 1382, 1451, 1457, 1474, "Indicador," p. 373; *AL 1905*, pp. 934, 935, 937, "Indicador," p. 2436. Another example of the same kind of familial transition is that of the Nabucos; see chapter 4.2.

108 Olinda, once site of a post-Enlightenment, reformed school, was the first site of the region's Faculty of Law, before its final establishment in Recife.

109 See R. Magalhães Júnior, *A vida vertiginosa do João do Rio* (Rio de Janeiro: José Olympio, 1978), p. 261.

110 See the Appendix.

111 Nabuco, *Um estadista*, 3: 580–3n.1.

112 See Calmon, *O marquez*, pp. 242–3.

113 C. Nabuco, *Oito décadas*, p. 58.

114 See the Appendix.

115 On Maciel Monteiro, see Macedo, *Anno biographico*, 3: 96 *et seq.*; *SB*, *VSV*; Carvalho, ch. 9, *passim*; Wanderley Pinho, pp. 161–2.

116 *SB*.
117 Macedo, *Anno biographico*, 3: 96.
118 Ibid.
119 See the portrait in Carvalho, p. 143, and the description of his style, pp. 245–6.
120 Ibid., p. 148.
121 See the bibliography in *SB*.
122 See Wanderley Pinho, pp. 162–4. On Joaquim Nabuco I relied on: Nabuco, *Minha formação*; C. Nabuco, *Joaquim Nabuco*; C. Nabuco, *Oito décadas*, *passim*; Luíz Viana Filho, *A vida de Joaquim Nabuco* (São Paulo: Nacional, 1952); *SB*; *Rua do Ouvidor*, 22 January 1910, pp. 1–2; José Maria Bello, *Intelligencia do Brasil* (São Paulo: Nacional, 1935), pp. 65–142.
123 J. T. Nabuco interview. Nabuco had his first diplomatic post in England. On the impact of English aristocratic prejudices on Nabuco's political attitudes, see *Minha formação*, chs. 12–13.
124 On French influence, see *Minha formação*, pp. 5–9, chs. 4–8, *passim*. On his repartee see C. Nabuco, *Oito décadas*, p. 43; and Oliveira Lima, p. 193.
125 Ibid., pp. 204–5. See also ibid., pp. 174, *et seq*., but cf. Broca, pp. 191–4.
126 Elysio de Carvalho, "Diplomatas extrangeiros" *Kósmos*, 6 (March 1909) [p. 3]; cf. *Rua do Ouvidor* 22 January 1910, pp. 1–2.
127 Nabuco was Brazil's first ambassador to the United States (1905–10). In the years just before 1899, he had withdrawn from the public as a monarchist. That period of intense intellectual activity and relative poverty came to an end with the *belle époque*, when Nabuco decided to serve his country as a diplomat abroad. For these reasons, Nabuco was not present in Rio during the *belle époque*, and thus, could not play an active role in its *alto mundo*. However, he remains an example of many of its socio-cultural characteristics, as will be shown here repeatedly.
128 One might note, as the exception that proves the rule, the host and meetings at the Morro da Graça. Pinheiro Machado's "receptions" were reflexes of a man whose background was completely removed from that of a Nabuco, a Pereira Passos, or a Rui Barbosa. Pinheiro Machado was always respected, feared, and admired as a man of charismatic physical presence, virile dignity, tested courage, and a natural capacity for command. He was never described as a well-bred man of polished refinement or social grace.

Thus, the meetings at his home were political cabals in the most obvious sense, the meals and billiards, relaxations and a kind of reward shared among friends and creatures, where the pecking order was made clear and adulation was common; see, e.g., Amado, pp. 123–4. Naturally, the same thing often went on in the salons – that is one of my points, after all – but the *way* it went on was quite different, and, as I have shown and will emphasize again here, that was crucial to the meaning of the salon. This contrast may help to explain something of the distaste the *gaúcho* inspired in many of his more Europeanized contemporaries. Certainly, what Pinheiro actually *did* was only partially the issue – Rui and Azeredo, after all, helped him to do it to their mutual benefit, without either ever inspiring the same kind of reaction. See Costa, *Rio*, 5: 1032; and Alburquerque, 1: p. 265.
129 Costa, *Rio*, 4: 701.
130 Ibid., 2: 331.
131 Afrânio Peixoto, *A esfinje* (Rio de Janeiro: Francisco Alves, 1911) pp. 210–11.
132 Broca, pp. 25–8.

133 See, e.g., Morand, pp. 188–90; Painter, 1: chs. 7, 10, *passim*.
134 Paulo Braga de Menezes interview (Rio de Janeiro, 4 July 1980); and, e.g., Wanderley Pinho, ch. 10, *passim*; Peixoto, pt. 1: chs. 5, 6, *passim*; pt. 2; ch. 2, *passim*.

4 Domestic institutions of the elite

1 For travellers, see, e.g., Paul Adam, *Les visages du Brésil* (Paris: Pierre Lafitte, 1914), pp. 92–4. For scholars, see Gilberto Freyre, *The Masters and the Slaves* (New York: Knopf, 1971), pp. 3–4, 24–7, and *passim*; Pedro Calmon, *História social do Brasil*, 2 vols. (São Paulo: Nacional, 1935), *passim*; Azevedo, pp. 89–94, *et seq.*; Prado, *Colonial Background* pp. 333–8 and *passim*; Antônio Cândido [de Mello e Sousa], "The Brazilian Family" in T. Lynn Smith and Alexander Marchant, (eds), *Brazil* (New York: Dryden, 1950), pp. 291–312. On colonial context, see C. R. Boxer, *The Portuguese Seaborne Empire* (New York: Knopf, 1969), pp. 86–8 and ch. 12; and A[fonso] H[enriques] de Oliveira Marquês, *History of Portugal*, 2 vols. (New York: Columbia, 1972 & 1976), 1: 431–48, *passim*. See, also, Diana Balmori, "A course in Latin American family history" in *The History Teacher*, 14: 3 (May 1981), pp. 401–41.
2 See Chapter 3.1. In terms of regional and economic change and the elite family, cf., e.g., Darrell E. Levi, *A família Prado* (São Paulo: Cultura 70, 1977); on the family and politics, see Linda Lewin, "Politics and *parentela* in Paraíba" (PhD diss., Columbia, 1975). On the family at the rural municipal level in late colonial times, see Alida Metcalf, "Families of planters, peasants and slaves," (PhD diss., Texas, 1982); the broadest study, albeit with specific regional focus, may well be Dain E. Borges, "The family in Bahia, Brazil, 1870–1945," (PhD diss., Stanford, 1986). A recent piece with excellent references to the current literature is Alida Metcalf, "Fathers and sons," HAHR, 66, 3 (August 1986).
3 Marcos Carneiro de Mendonça, interview, Rio de Janeiro, 10 July 1980; Paulo Braga de Menezes, interview, Rio de Janeiro, 4 July 1980; Carlos da Ponte Ribeiro Eiras, interview, Rio de Janeiro, 25 July 1980; de La Rocque, p. 113. On economic instability, see Prado and Furtado, *Economic Growth*.
4 See Oliveira, *Memórias passim*, especially notes; Barbosa de Oliveira, *Águas passim*; Rezende Martins, *Um idealista realizador* ch. 12.
5 De La Rocque, chs. 1 and 2; Stein, *Vassouras*, pp. 17–20, and *passim*. See also Vasconcellos and Vasconcellos, [hereafter *VSV*], s.v. Vassouras, Itambé, and Ayuruóca.
6 See the sketch of Luís Gastão d'Escragnolle Taunay in chapter 3.1. See also Taunay, *Memórias*, la.pt., *passim*.
7 Rezende Martins, ch. 4 and *passim*; *VSV*, s.v. Valença, Rezende, and Lorena.
8 A. J. Barbosa de Oliveira, ch. 6, nota 1 and *passim*; Rezende Martins, ch. 5; and *VSV*, s.v. Sousa Queiroz and Limeira.
9 See chapter 2.2.
10 De La Rocque, pp. 33–45, 51–64; *VSV*, s.v. Rio Negro, Amparo, and Barra Mansa. Cf. such families as Estrela, Rio Bonito, and Nova Friburgo, chapter 2.2. For comparable *paulista* examples see Elizabeth A. Kuznesof, "The role of merchants in the economic development of São Paulo," HAHR, 60:4 (November 1980) 571–92.
11 On family, property, and politics, see Linda Lewin's "Some historical implications of family-based politics in the Brazilian Northeast" in *Comparative Studies in Society*

and History 21:2 (April 1979): 271–4, 283–6, 288. On endogamy, see, e.g., de La Rocque, p. 42 and chs. 1 and 2, *passim*; Barbosa de Oliveira, *Aguas*, *passim*; Lyra, *passim*; Levi, pp. 71–5. Gilberto Freyre suggests endogamy was a safeguard against racial mixture – see *Mansions*, pp. 97, 101. Cf. the importance of the frontier as an element in elite exogamy in western São Paulo; see Metcalf, "Fathers and sons."

12 C. Nabuco, *Joaquim Nabuco* pp. 15–17.

13 See Nabuco, *Cartas*, 1: 146–7. Cf. Viana Filho, *Joaquim Nabuco* ch. 4, *passim*; C. Nabuco, *Oito décadas*, pp. 198–203: cf. Viana Filho, pp. 167–9.

14 Carolina Nabuco, [notes to] José Thomáz Nabuco, "Núpcias" in MS biography of the first Nabuco in Brazil (Rio de Janeiro, 1980, author's photocopy), *passim*, see *VSV*, s.v. Inohan, Itambí, Vasconcellos de Drummond, Estrella, Jaguarão, Itaborahy, and Paraná.

15 A. J. Barbosa de Oliveira, p. 170.

16 Ibid., pp. 167–70, 173–5.

17 Viana Filho, pp. 55–6 and C. Nabuco, [notes to] Nabuco, *Cartas*, 1: 146–7.

18 C. Nabuco, *Oita décades*, p. 200; cf. Viana Filho, pp. 167–9.

19 A. J. Barbosa de Oliveira, pp. 181–3.

20 Ibid., p. 200 (see pp. 199–200).

21 Viana Filho, pp. 165–6 (see also pp. 47, 49–50).

22 Viana Filho, p. 47–8; C. Nabuco, [notes to] Nabuco, *Cartas*, 1: 146–7.

23 Ibid., p. 201; C. Nabuco, *Joaquim Nabuco*, pp. 48–9; C. Nabuco, *Oito décadas*, pp. 201–3; José Thomáz Nabuco, interview, Rio de Janeiro, 2 June 1980; cf. Oliveira Lima, *Mémorias* pp. 200–1.

24 See [Joaquim José de] França Júnior, *Folhetins*, (Rio de Janeiro: *Gazeta de Noticias*, 1878), pp. 181–6; Bennett, pp. 231–2. *Rua do Ouvidor* (Rio de Janeiro); and *Gazeta de Noticias* (Rio de Janeiro) often carried descriptions of elite weddings, at times including gift lists. See, e.g, Nabuco's wedding in *Gazeta de Noticias*, 24 April 1889; or the one covered in *Rua do Ouvidor*, 11 June 1898, p. 3; cf. "Normas de Polidez" in *Rua do Ouvidor*, 17 September 1898, pp. 6–7.

25 On bondsmen, see Barbosa de Oliveira, *Aguas*, p. 98; confirmed by D. Yolanda Penteado (interview, Stanford, 16 September 1981). Though Abolition (1888) changed their formal status, the custom of taking servants along to start a new household continued well into the twentieth century; C. Nabuco, *Oito décadas*, pp. 166–7; confirmed, interview with Delgado de Carvalho's oldest servant, Rio de Janeiro, 14 May 1980.

26 See Levi, pp. 74–5; Mello e Sousa, "Brazilian family" p. 298.

27 See chapter 3.2.

28 Such gatherings punctuate Machado de Assis' contemporary novels, *Ressurreição, Helena, A mão e a luva*, etc. See, also, A. J. Barbosa de Oliveira, pp. 242, 296, 301, 304–5. For the earlier period, cf. Maria Graham [Lady Callcott], *Journal of a Voyage to Brazil* (London: Longman, Hurst, Rees, Orme, Brown and Green and J. Murray, 1824), pp. 224, 264, 266, 272–3; Maria Beatriz Nizza da Silva, *Cultura e sociedade no Rio de Janeiro (1808–1821)* (São Paulo: Nacional, 1978), pp. 57–80, *passim*; Freyre, *Masters*, pp. 467–8; and *Mansions*, pp. 160–2, 227; von Binzer, pp. 24–5; Lyra, pp. 234–5. The quotation is from Carneiro de Mendonça's interview.

29 See chapters 2.2 and 3.1.

30 Magalhães Júnior, *João do Rio* p. 260, notes earlier society columns, e.g., José Maria da Silva Paranhos, "Cartas ao amigo ausente" in the *Jornal do Commercio* at mid-century and José de Alencar, "Ao correr de pena" in the *Diário Mercantil* later

on. It seems clear, however, that these ran more in the direction of gossip, literary observation, and description – what we discuss here is clearly different. In the earlier period, the more limited need for the advice discussed here was often met with a translation of one of the classic French manuals – the renowned *Código do bom tom* (Paris: n.p., 1845) cited by Freyre (see *Masters*, p. 416).

31 See, e.g., Rezende Martins, chs. 6 and 7; de La Rocque, chs. 2 and 3, *passim*; Barbosa de Oliveira, *Aguas*, pp. 100–1; C. Nabuco, *Oito décades*, pp. 21–2, 50–1, 198, 199–200.

32 "Binoculo," *Gazeta de Noticias*, 1 August 1908, p. 2.

33 Maul, pp. 25–7. Cf. Magalhães Júnior, p. 260; C. Nabuco *Oito décadas*, p. 58; Costa, *Rio* 5: 924–6; Broca, *A vida literária*, pp. 3–5; Amado, *Mocidade*, p. 89.

34 "Binoculo," *Gazeta de Noticias*, 5 August 1914, p. 5.

35 Ibid., 20 July 1914, p. 4.

36 See *Rua do Ouvidor*, 13 May 1898, p. 1.

37 Internal evidence (e.g., the reader is often addressed as "*leitora*") suggests the assumed gender. The biographies were of public bureaucrats and statesmen, representatives from the arts and letters, noted professionals, merchants, and industrialists. The title, *Rua do Ouvidor* (the traditional locale for the purchase of luxury imports, conversation, and *flânerie*) suggests that the readership was both restricted and elite-oriented. Indicative of this is a quiz published from time to time in which a nameless "regular" of the Rua do Ouvidor would be described, and the reader invited to guess the person's identity.

38 She is introduced as "One of our most distinguished countrywomen but recently arrived from Europe . . . the Countess S.D." See "Indicações Úteis," *Rua do Ouvidor*, 11 June 1898, p. 5.

39 J. T. Nabuco interview; Carneiro de Mendonça interview; Ferrez interview; Penteado interview; Lyra, pp. 62, 73, 128–9, 136; Nabuco, *Oito décades*, pp. 48, 62, 108, 110; [Francisco de Paula] Rodrigues Alves Filho, "Rodrigues Alves" in Barbosa, *Retratos*, p. 16; M. A. V. B. and M. A. Barbosa, in F. A. Barbosa, *Retratos*, pp. 32, 33; Lizeta Osvaldo Cruz Vidal, "Osvaldo Cruz" in F. A. Barbosa, p. 45; Paulo Inglês de Sousa, "Inglês de Sousa" in F. A. Barbosa, p. 106.

40 The Seção de Manuscritos da Biblioteca Nacional, the Arquivo Histórico do Instituto Histórico e Geográfico Brasileiro, and the Arquivo Histórico of the Casa de Rui Barbosa [hereafter, referred to as BNSM, AHIHGB, and RBAHC, respectively] are replete with examples. See, on the importance of the card itself, the letter from Antônio Fontoura Xavier to Max Fleiuss, New York, 19 April, 1901, AHIHGB Coleção Max Fleuiss, 474/79/11.

41 E.g., Peixoto; França; João do Rio [pseud. of Paulo Barreto], *Cinematographo* (Porto: Chardron, 1909); cf. Amado, p. 98. See chapter 6.9.

42 "Normas de Polidez" in *Rua do Ouvidor*, 27 August 1898, p. 6. Cf. the clear distinction made for invitations to get-togethers of the traditional sort, described as invitations to "a cup of tea," a gathering "without ceremony" or "luxury of any sort," and "*muito em família*"; see Max Fleiuss to Leitão, Rio de Janeiro, 15 March 1901, BNSM Coleção Ernesto Senna, 1–5, 16, 7; Júlia Lopes de Almeida to Viscount de Morais, Rio de Janeiro, 18 June 1910, BNSM Coleção Ramos Paz; J. Maurity to Ernesto Senna, Rio de Janeiro, 12 January 1900, BNSM Coleção Ernesto Senna 1–5, 17, 89.

43 "Normas de Polidez" in *Rua do Ouvidor*, 3 September 1898, pp. 5–6.

44 Ibid., 30 July 1898, pp. 5–6.

45 Ibid., 1 Oct. 1898, p. 6.
46 Ibid., 26 Nov. 1898, p. 6.
47 See Proust, especially vols. 1–3; see also Morand, chs. 5 and 6; Barbara W. Tuchman, *The Proud Tower* (New York: Bantam, 1964), ch. 1; Lenore Davidoff, *The Best Circles* (Totowa, NJ: Rowman and Littlefield, 1973), chs. 1–3; Kate Caffrey, *The 1900 Lady* (London: Gordon Cremonesi, 1976), chs. 1, 4, and *passim*; Philippe Julian, "Can-can and flappers" in E. Bairati *et al.*, *La belle époque* (New York: William Morrow, 1978), *passim*; Theodore Zeldin, *France*, 2 vols. (Oxford: Oxford, 1977), 1: ch. 1, *passim* and 2: 666–73, *passim*.
48 Davidoff, pp. 14–15, 17.
49 Julian, pp. 98–100; cf. Morand, p. 194.
50 See the next section and cf. chapters 2 and 3.
51 See, e.g., Davidoff, pp. 42, 49 on the French visiting card and the English "at home" with tea, and Proust, 2: pt. 1, *passim*.
52 Beyond those noted in the text, a particularly nice example (especially *vis-à-vis* the examples in the note above), is [Joaquim Maria] Machado de Assis, *A semana*, 3 vols. (Rio de Janeiro: W. M. Jackson, 1944), 3:22–3.
53 See Mello e Sousa, "Brazilian Family" p. 294, 298–9; Azevedo, p. 129n.; Prado, pp. 333–9, *passim*.
54 [Joaquim Maria] Machado de Assis, *A mão e a luva* (São Paulo: W. M. Jackson, 1942); see pp. 30, 67, 70, 111, 170–1. Cf. Roberto Schwarz, *Ao vencedor as batatas* (São Paulo: Duas Cidades, 1977), pt. 3, *passim*.
55 The case described concerns Lima Barreto; see Francisco de Assis Barbosa, *A vida de Lima Barreto (1881–1922)* (Rio de Janeiro: José Olympio, 1975), pp. 3–17, 94–9. On Lima Barreto, see chapter 6.10.
56 The case described concerns Max Fleuiss and Rui Barbosa; see RBAHC Correspondência Max Fleiuss, *passim*.
57 The case described concerns Pinheiro Machado, Carlos Vianna Bandeira, and Rui Barbosa (see chapter 3.1); R. Magalhães Júnior, *Rui, o homem e o mito* (Rio de Janeiro: Civilização Brasileira, 1965), pp. 252–60. For other interesting exchanges of favors, see Ruy Barbosa to Francisco de Paula Mayrink, Rio de Janeiro, 4 April 1892, RBAHC, Correspondência Francisco de Paula Mayrink; the visiting card note of Antônio de Azeredo to Ruy [Barbosa], [Rio de Janeiro,] n.d., RBAHC, Correspondência Antônio Francisco de Azeredo; Francisco Glicerio to Jaguaribe, Rio de Janeiro, 7 November 1902, BNSM, Coleção Jaguaribe, 1–5, 4, 76.
58 E.g., José Augusto Vinhais to Ernesto Senna, Rio de Janeiro, 25 June 1903, BNSM, Coleção Ernesto Senna 1–5, 4, 35; and José do Patrocínio to Ernesto Senna, [Rio de Janeiro,], n.d., BNSM, Coleção Ernesto Senna 1–5, 18, 89, cf. França, pp. 90–1.
59 For the once wealthy, see RBAHC, Correspondência Mauricio Haritoff; Wanderley Pinho, ch. 12; or Joaquim Nabuco to Salvador de Mendonça, London, 10 February 1882, BNSM, Coleção Salvador de Mendonça 1–4, 20, 48. For the sons of fathers prematurely dead, see the example of Maurício Nabuco's rescue through José Carlos Rodrigues, Cândido Gaffrée, and Jorge Street, in Mauricio Nabuco, *Reminiscências sérias e frívolas* (Rio de Janeiro: Pogetti), 1969, pp. 11–12, 16; cf. Gilberto Amado, *Presença na política* (Rio de Janeiro: José Olympio, 1960), pp. 28–9 on J. C. Rodrigues.
60 Julian, p. 98.
61 The historiography of women in Brazil (and in Latin America generally) is still at the

pioneering stage. Much of the work that *has* been done is concerned with women in political movements, industrial labor, or with feminists {e.g., June Hahner, "Feminism, women's rights, and the suffrage movement in Brazil, 1850–1932" in *Latin American Research Review* (hereafter, LARR) 15:1 (1980): 65–111; her "Women and work in Brazil , 1850–1920" in Dauril Alden and Warren Dean, eds. *Essays Concerning the Socioeconomic History of Brazil and Portuguese India* (Gainesville: Florida, 1977), pp. 87–117; cf. her "Recent research on women in Brazil" in LARR, 20:3 (1985): 163–79.} Recent research in which women play a focal role includes dissertations by Linda Lewin, "Politics and *parentela*"; Sandra Lauderdale Graham, "Protection and obedience." (PhD diss., Texas, 1982); Metcalf, "Families," and Borges; see also Fúlvia Rosemberg *et al.*, "Suplemento bibliográfico: 1: Levantamento preliminar sobre a situação da mulher brasileira: março 1976" in *Cadernos de Pesquisa* (São Paulo: Carlos Chagas, 1979); Miriam Lifschitz Moreira Leite, Maria Lúcia de Barros Mott, and Bertha Kauffman Appenzeller, *A mulher no Rio de Janeiro no século XIX* (São Paulo: Chagas, 1982); Asunción Lavrin, (ed.) *Latin American Women* (Westport, Connecticut: Greenwood, 1978), especially the "Introduction" and its endnotes; and "Women in Latin American history" in *The History Teacher*, 14:3 (May 1981) 7–399.

62 Lyra, pp. 57–8, 61, 130; C. Nabuco, *Oito décadas*, pp. 168–9; Nabuco, *Minha formação*, pp. 218–19; Barbosa de Oliveira, *Aguas*, p. 111; de La Rocque, pp. 45–6, 49–50, 52, 91, 93, 96–8; Binzer, pp. 97–8; Yolanda Penteado, *Tudo em cor-de-rosa* (São Paulo: Ed. da Autora, 1977), pp. 38, 43–4, 46–7; Costa, *De um livro de memórias*, 1: 57–60, 200–1; James C. Fletcher and D. P. Kidder, *Brazil and the Brazilians Portrayed in Historical and Descriptive Sketches* (Boston: Little, Brown, 1866), pp. 166–75, *passim*; Charles Expilly, *Mulheres e costumes do Brasil* (São Paulo: Nacional, 1935) pp. 401, 405; Andrews, pp. 17–20, *passim*; Leclerc, pp. 213–14. Cf. "A mulher no lar" in *Rua do Ouvidor*, 24 December 1898, p. 4; Júlia Lopes de Almeida, *Livro das noivas* (Rio de Janeiro: n.p., 1896). Secondary sources include Freyre, *Masters*, pp. 350–2; Freyre, *Mansions*, pp. 85–7, 98; Levi, pp. 79–80, 89, 91, 98–9, 114, 118, 152, 155–6; Mello e Sousa, "Brazilian Family," pp. 295–6.

63 See, e.g., chapter 3.1, 2.

64 See Wanderley Pinho, chs. 2 and 4, *passim*; Rezende Martins, *passim*; Penteado, C. Barbosa de Oliveira, and Levi, all *passim*. On São Paulo's metamorphosis over the century see Morse's *From Community*; and Love's *São Paulo*.

65 See chapter 3.2.

66 Burke and Staples, p. 72; cf. p. 64; Binzer, p. 61; Wanderley Pinho, ch. 7 *passim*. See the initial references in n. 28 above; Fletcher, pp. 175–6; Freyre, *Mansions*, p. 87.

67 Calmon, *O marquez*, ch. 17; cf. Wanderley Pinho, ch. 8.

68 Wanderley Pinho makes the most of the exceptions to this rule. Cf., however, Marie Robinson Wright, *The New Brazil* (Philadelphia: George Barrie and Son, 1901), pp. 444–2; Bell, p. 188; the classic condemnation of Second Reign high society is [José Duarte] Ramalho Ortigão – "O quadro social da revolução brazileira" in *Revista de Portugal*, 2 (1890): 79–102, pp. 99–100; and cf. Gilberto Freyre, *Order and Progress* (New York: Knopf, 1970), pp. 62–5. Cf., however, Quesada, 1: ch. 3, *passim*.

69 Graham, p. 224; França, pp. 15–16; Professor and Mrs. Louis Agassiz {Agassiz, Louis and Agassiz, Elizabeth Cabot Cary}, *A Journey in Brazil* (Boston: Felds,

Osgood, 1871), pp. 478–80; Fletcher, pp. 164–5; Andrews, p. 34, 67; Binzer, pp. 21, 26; Expilly, p. 405; Edouard Montet, *Brésil et Argentine* (Geneva: Ch. Eggimann, 1890s?), p. 104; Alice R. Humphrey, *A Summer Journey to Brazil* (New York: Bonnell, Silver, 1900), p. 55; Leclerc, pp. 213–14; Lopes de Almeida, *Livro das noivas*, pp. 204–6; Lyra, pp. 28, 57–8, 126; C. Barbosa de Oliveira, p. 97; de La Rocque, pp. 32–3, 42, 47. See also Freyre, *Mansions*, pp. 85–7, 90–1, 92–3, 25; Freyre, *Masters*, pp. 354, 360–3, 418, 419.

70 On education see chapter 2.1. On the general situation of women sketched, see: Francisco Pereira Passos, to L. R. d'Oliveira, Rio, 4 July 1875 (Documentos Pereira Passos: Uncatalogued document in *Copiador* 6), pp. 101–2 [this citation refers to a document in the Pereira Passos archive of the Museu da República, Rio de Janeiro; hereafter, such documents will be referred to by DPP, by their catalogue number or the designation "uncat." and by "cop." for copiador, with its respective number]; to William Lloyd, Nictheroy, 15 March 1875 (DPP: Uncat. Cop.6) 49; Lyra, pp. 27–8; de La Rocque, chs. 1–3, *passim*; Wright, p. 441; E. R. Pearce Edgcumbe, *Zephyrus* (London: Chatto and Windus, 1887), p. 50; Leclerc, pp. 211–14; Humphrey, pp. 46–7; Etienne de Rancourt, *Fazendas et estancias* (Paris: Plon, 1901), pp. 58–9; Expilly, pp. 400–5; Costa, *Memórias*, 1: 57–6, 200–1; Gustave Aimard quoted in Afonso de E[scragnolle] Taunay, *No Rio de Janeiro de Dom Pedro II* (Rio de Janeiro: Agir, 1947), p. 142; Binzer, pp. 63, 66–7, 87; Joaquim Manuel Macedo quoted in Andrews, pp. 34–5; Bell, pp. 187–8, 192; Agassiz, pp. 478–80; Fletcher, pp. 165–6; Taunay, *Memórias*, pp. 70–1, 149. See also Freyre, *Masters*, pp. 363–5, 379; Levi, pp. 78–9, 152, 155, 156. I also benefited from the interviews with Jacobina Lacombe and Carneiro Mendonça here.

71 Burke and Staples, p. 120. Cf. Lopes de Almeida, p. 189; Fletcher, pp. 164–5; Andrews, p. 34, Expilly, pp. 400–7; Agassiz, pp. 478–80.

72 See Rios Filho, *O Rio de Janeiro imperial* (Rio de Janeiro: A Noite, 1946), pp. 292–4, 296.

73 Fletcher, pp. 175–6.

74 Freyre, *Mansions*, p. 187.

75 On gluttony, diet and results, see Lyra pp. 129–36; Fletcher, pp. 165–6; Binzer pp. 24, 25; Edgcumbe, p. 50. On the window sill, see Bennett, pp. 236–7; Leclerc, pp. 57–8; Rancourt, pp. 548–9; *et al.* Los Rios, pp. 292–3, notes the tradition was undermined by Pereira Passos' reforms in 1902, but does not specify how. On *cafuné*, see Expilly pp. 366–8; Freyre, *Masters*, pp. 354–5, 397 (who notes that boys indulged, too).

76 The only people who went about on foot were the poor. Before *bonds*, the elite used litters, sedan chairs, or several types of carriages (see Calmon, *Historia social*, 2: 239–42; Los Rios, pp. 110–18). On the *bond*, and its impact, see França, pp. 6, 144–6; Aimard in Afonso Taunay, p. 143; Macedo, *Memórias* p. 258; Burke p. 35; Andrews, pp. 30–2; Wright, p. 116; Alfonso Lomonaco quoted in Afonso Taunay, p. 207. On the development of the system, initiated by the Viscount de Mauá and one Greenough, see Marchant, p. 58; Hilliard, pp. 375–6; Cruls, 2: 459–60; Lamoureux pp. 143–50; Dent, *A Year in Brazil*, pp. 235–7; Rosa, *Rio*, pp. 57–61; Bell, ch. 3, *passim*. The origin of the word "*bond*" is in Macedo, p. 258: the issuing of bonds in 1868 was associated in the public mind with the other topical issue of the day, the new streetcars and their tickets. The latter were soon called *bonds* and, in time, so were the streetcars.

77 Elysio de Carvalho, *Esplendor e decadência da sociedade brasileira* (Rio de Janeiro:

pp. 228–9. Paquin, Redfern, and Doucet were three of the most fashionable Parisian couturiers.

78 On the kind of educational experience women had by the *belle époque*, see chapter 2.1. See also Tefé, pp. 33–6; C. Nabuco, *Oito décadas*, pp. 32–4; C. Barbosa de Oliveira, p. 109; de La Rocque, pp. 54, 95–8; Lyra, ch.9, *passim*. *Belle-époque* travellers were impressed – see Wright, pp. 439–40, 441; Humphrey, pp. 46–7; Bell, pp. 188–9. On walking, see "Normas de Polidez" in *Rua do Ouvidor*, 22 October 1898, p. 6; see also C. Nabuco, *Oito décadas*, p. 59; Binzer, pp. 66–7. The greatest claims made for the breadth of education and circle of activity are in Carvalho, pp. 228–9; cf. Costa, *Rio*, 2: 327–8. Regarding French marriages, these occasionally happened even earlier, in diplomats' families; see the famous 1830 case of the Countess de Barral in Wanderley Pinho, pp. 203–4. The phenomenon noted here is, rather, exemplified by the trend suggested in Rezende Martins, p. 93 and chs. 6 and 7, *passim*. See also, Levi, p. 131; Ortigão, pp. 99–100; and Freyre, *Order*, pp. 62, 64–5. The fiction cited is Peixoto, *A esfinje* (whose reflection of reality is suggested by Brito Broca, pp. 148–9), and João do Rio, "Laurinda Belfort" in *Dentro da noite*, (Rio de Janeiro: H. Garnier, 1910).

79 On Lopes de Almeida, see chapter 6.9. D. Laurinda and Bebê, two exceptional lights of the salon world of the era, have been discussed in chapter 3.1; Penteado, in the interview cited, suggested that both women were "advanced" for their era. Cf. Amado, *Mocidade*, pp. 208–9.

80 Cited in n. 62 above. Dedicated to Lopes de Almeida's husband, the manual is prefaced by an open letter to him, graced with one of his poems.

81 Lopes de Almeida, pp. 76–7.

82 Lopes de Almeida, pp. 28–9; cf. pp. 75–8. [*] Lopes de Almeida took the advanced position that women (read *white* women – most people of color could not afford a choice) ought to nurse their children themselves. See pp. 189–92.

83 Ibid., pp. 35–9, 41–9, 130–1, 204–5.

84 Ibid., pp. 55–9, 66–7, 81–7.

85 C. Nabuco, *Oito décadas*, pp. 39, 47–8, 51, 62; Penteado, pp. 52–3, 56–7; de La Rocque, pp. 100, 106, 109–10, 113; Lyra, pp. 31, 32, 57–8, 62, 72, 105–6, 109, 110; Bell, pp. 188–9; Humphreys, p. 55.

86 See Zeldin, 1: chs. 1, 11, 13, *passim*, and 2: 666–72; Davidoff, chs. 1–3, *passim*; Caffrey, chs. 2 and 3, *passim*.

87 C. Nabuco, *Oito décadas*, p. 31. See also pp. 29–30, 48.

88 The bibliography in Balmori does not raise the issue of children *per se*. I rely on Freyre, Mello e Sousa, and Levi, the study of education, travellers' accounts, memoirs, and interviews with period survivors.

89 Freyre, *Mansions*, p. 58, cites two early nineteenth-century travellers' accounts to this effect.

90 A. J. Barbosa, p. 220. The mention of innocence refers to the belief that children went direct to heaven, having avoided the sins common to those who had the natural opportunities longer life brought.

91 Ibid., p. 252; Francisco Pereira Passos to Conselheiro Theodoro Machado Freire Pereira da Silva, London, 4 Nov. 1873 (DPP uncat. cop.5), p. 183; Lopes de Almeida, e.g., pp. 19–26, 175–6, 179–97, 181–2; Lyra, pp. 29, 60, 76, 112; de La Rocque, chs. 1–5 *passim*; Levi, pp. 78–9.

92 A. J. Barbosa de Oliveira, p. 252; Binzer, ppo. 22, 24; Fletcher, p. 163; Agassiz, pp. 481–2; Taunay, *Memórias*, pp. 5–6, 12, 15, 22, 44, 120–2; Lopes de Almeida,

p. 190; Costa, *Memórias*, 1: 64; C. Nabuco, *Oito décadas*, pp. 166–7; Lyra, p. 61; C. Barbosa de Oliveira, pp. 102, 109, 111–12; de La Rocque, pp. 92, 96. Nabuco, *Minha formação*, ch. 20; Gilberto Amado, *História da minha infância* (Rio de Janeiro: José Olympio, 1966), pp. 34–5, 80–2, 88–9, 90–1. Freyre, *Masters*, pp. 278, 342, 354–5, 367–8, 369–72 (see n. 264), 379, 398–9, 418, 460–7; Freyre, *Order*, pp. 512–2; Calmon, *Historia social*, 2: ch. 7. The impact of African cultures on elite Brazilians is hard to recover in memoirs (though, the memory of black nurses etc. implies much, especially then, when direct African influence on Brazilian culture was very vital) and in interviews (though both Jacobina Lacombe, Ferrez, and Penteado affirmed its importance in terms of stories, "superstition," etc). Afro-Brazilian culture in its organized form and in its more threatening variety (*capoeira*, *macumba*, etc.) was officially repressed, and one doubts Afro-Brazilian religion was openly taught in elite homes, considering the associated public opprobrium. Still, participation of elite whites in such folk culture surfaces in sensationalist reporting and period fiction, a *caveat* about generalizations: see João do Rio, *As religiões no Rio* (Rio de Janeiro: Francisco Alves, 1904) and [Joaquim Maria] Machado de Assis, *Essaú e Jacób*. A good beginning for considering the African role in Rio is Arthur Ramos, "The Negro in Brazil" in Marchant. More recent work for the nineteenth and early twentieth centuries includes Adamo; Rocha; the recent doctoral dissertation of Alison Raphael, "Samba and social control" (PhD diss., Columbia, 1981); and Mary C. Karasch, *Slave Life and Culture in Rio de Janeiro, 1808–1850* (Princeton: 1987).

NB Ramos (pp. 130–2) shows that in 1872 around half the population was black or mulatto (14.6 and 32.4% respectively) and blacks alone were 26.8% of Rio de Janeiro Province. Conrad, *Destruction* p. 287, shows that in 1872 Rio and Rio de Janeiro Province alone had about 70,000 slaves of African *birth*. In Rio, there were nearly 11,000 African-born slaves in a population of about 235,381 (see, also, Lahmeyer Lobo, 2: 469). The impact of African culture on the Carioca world can hardly be doubted.

93 See chapter 2.1. On the educational experience, see: Francisco Pereira Passos to Madame Kerr, London, 15 Aug. 1873 (DPP 6.2 cop. 5), pp. 31–2; to L. R. d'Oliveira, Rio, 8 Nov. 1874 (DPP uncat. cop.5), pp. 440–1; to same, Niteroy, 8 Aug. 1875 (DPP uncat. cop.6), p. 123; C. Nabuco, *Oito décadas*, pp. 6, 8–9; Lyra, pp. 102–3; C. Barbosa de Oliveira, pp. 107–10, *passim*; de La Rocque, pp. 94–9, *passim*, 64; Amado, p. 42–50, *passim*; Taunay, *Memórias*, pp. 12–13, 18–19; cf. Binzer and Costa, *Rio*, 2: 327. Freyre draws attention to the racism implied in the dolls, literature, and fashion illustrations of the period in *Order*, pp. 55–6. The influence of French governesses was confirmed in the Jacobinas Lacombe and Penteado interviews.

94 See chapter 2.1. Also, see C. Nabuco, *Oito décadas*, pp. 39–40, 47–8, 108–9; Lyra, pp. 30–1; de La Rocque, pp. 100, 103, 105, 106, 109–10, 111–12; C. Barbosa de Oliveira, pp. 113–16; Taunay, *Memórias*, p. 71; Amado, *Infância*, pp. 187–8; Fletcher, pp. 176–7, 180–1; Expilly, pp. 375–8. NB Lopes de Almeida's attack on the pressure on children to be small adults (cf. Fletcher and Expilly), p. 201, or prodigies, p. 204. See also Levi, pp. 79–80, 82; Freyre, *Masters*, pp. 404–5, 416–17; Freyre, *Mansions*, pp. 58–61, 68; Freyre, *Order*, ch. 4, *passim*.

95 Rodrigues Alves Filho in F. A. Barbosa, *Retratos*, p. 9; C. Nabuco, *Oito décadas*, pp. 108–9, 169; Binzer, pp. 17–18, 82, 84–5; Lyra, pp. 31, 63. Cf. Freyre, *Masters*, p. 417. The formal usages were also corroborated in interviews (e.g.,

Jacobina Lacombe, Penteado interviews, and Alceu Amoroso Lima, Rio de Janeiro, 2 October 1980). Freyre notes the slaves Africanized the honorifics in *Masters*, "Glossary of the Brazilian terms used," e.g. *iaiá, ioiô*, (young mistress, young master, respectively). Some of these became the names used in the family, and enter into correspondence and memoirs; see C. Nabuco's *Oito décadas*, p. 169); Rodrigues Alves Filho (in F. A. Barbosa, *Retratos;*, p. 13); Freyre, *Masters*, p. 418 where the Africanized honorific implying a subordinate, affectionate position was used, coupled with self-references to "your Negro" or "your humble little Negro". The *beija-mão* was used not only in formal greeting, but as a sign of subordinate gratitude (see, e.g., Machado de Assis, *A mão e a luva*, pp. 12, 69).

96 C. Nabuco, *Oito décadas*, pp. 8–9, 37–43, *passim*, 62, 168–70, 204, 209–10; Lyra, pp. 58, 62–3, 72, 105–6, 109; de La Rocque, pp. 66–7, 96–7, 108, 113, 114; C. Barbosa de Oliveira, pp. 107, 110–11; Luiz Viana Filho, *A vida do barão do Rio Branco* (Rio de Janeiro: José Olympio, 1959), p. 16; Viana Filho, *Rui Barbosa*, pp. 6–11, *passim*; Nabuco, *Minha formação*, pp. 196–7, 198; C. Nabuco, *Joaquim Nabuco*, pp. 23, 26; Viana Filho, *Joaquim Nabuco*, pp. 19–21; Levi, pp. 79–80; Freyre, *Masters*, pp. 416–18; Amoroso Lima, Jacobina Lacombe, and Penteado interviews.

97 Zeldin, 1: ch. 12, *passim*, especially pp. 318–20; Caffrey, ch. 2, *passim*.

98 Edgcumbe, p. 47.

99 "Binoculo" in *Gazeta de Noticias*, 25 July 1914, p. 6. See also Burke, p. 60; Bennett, p. 238; A. J. Barbosa de Oliveira, p. 175. Joaquim Nabuco, *Minha formação*, pp. 196–7, Viana Filho, *Joaquim Nabuco*, p. 24 or Carlos Süsekind de Mendonça, *Salvador de Mendonça* (Rio de Janeiro: MEC, 1960), p. 18.

100 A. J. Barbosa de Oliveira, *passim*; see the correspondence cited in Viana Filho, *Joaquim Nabuco*, chs. 2–5, *passim*.

101 Paulino José Soares de Souza Jr. to Papai, Petropolis, 9 November 1907, BNSM, Cartas Avulsas. See also Rui's letter cited in M. A. V. B. and M. A. Barbosa, pp. 34–5; as well as C. Nabuco, *Oito décadas*, pp. 9–10, 39–43; P. Inglês de Sousa pp. 116–17; Lyra, p. 73; de La Rocque, pp. 68–9, 102–3; C. Barbosa de Oliveira, pp. 107, 114.

102 Nabuco, *Minha formação*, ch. 8, *passim*. See also Viana Filho, *Joaquim Nabuco*, chs. 2–5, *passim*; C. Nabuco, *Joaquim Nabuco*, [Part] 1, chs. 2–4, *passim*; cf. Viana Filho, *Rui Barbosa*, p. 7; and Francisco Pereira Passos to L. R. d'Oliveira, Rio, 4 July 1875 (DPP uncat. cop.6), p. 102; same, (DPP uncat. cop.6), pp. 122–3.

103 All memoirs cited in this chapter confirm the extended nature of the family living together. On the number of servants see Lyra, p. 61 – her "poor" father maintained five – cook, nurse, cleaning woman/maid, and washerwoman; da Costa counts twenty-two for Rui Barbosa's staff (see *Rio de Janeiro*, 2: 327). See Binzer, p. 34, on resident dependants on a *fazenda* in the state of Rio, *c.*1882; also, note A. J. Barbosa de Oliveira's reference to his household as an inclusive unit of "masters and slaves" (p. 221).

104 Dr. Luíz Corrêa de Azevedo, address to the Royal Academy of Medicine, quoted in Freyre, *Mansions*, p. 157.

105 See Fletcher, p. 162; Los Rios, *Rio imperial*, ch. 3, section 1; Rios Filho, *Grandjean de Montigny*, pp. 190–1; Nestor Goulart Reis Filho, *Quadro da arquitetura no Brasil* (São Paulo: Perspectiva, 1970), ch. 2; Freyre, *Mansions*, pp. 150–8. Cf. Binzer p. 66. See, also, the illustrations in Los Rios, *Rio imperial*; Cruls; Gilberto Ferrez, *Aquarelas de Richard Bate* (Rio de Janeiro: Galeria Brasiliana, 1965).

106 See Rodrigo Octavio [de Langgaard Meneses] *Minhas memorias de outros*, (Rio de Janeiro: José Olympio, 1935), pp. 29–30, 82–3.

107 The older *solar* or *mansão*, was a grander version of the *sobrado de moradia*, distinct from the newer, neo-classical *solar* (cf. de Los Rios, *Rio imperial*, illustrations between pp. 160 and 161). See the older *solar* Los Rios discusses in *Grandjean do Montigny*, pp. 194–9. Goulart Reis Filho analyzes the differences on pp. 34–8, 43–4, 46, 48, 50, 61–2. Cf. Louis Hautecoeur, *Histoire de l'architecture classique en France*, vol. 6: Paris: A. et J. Picard, 1955), pp. 50–1 (figs. 37 and 38), 193–9 (figs. 158–72).

108 Fletcher, pp. 162–3. See also [Visconde de Taunay,] *Mémorias*, pp. 4–5, 7; Lomonaco in Afonso Taunay, *Rio de Pedro II*, p. 207; Dent, pp. 182–3, 185; Humphrey, p. 41; Quesada, pp. 156–8; cf. Graham, pp. 162–3. On the neo-classical *solares per se*, see Los Rios, *Grandjean de Montigny*, p. 196; Los Rios, *Rio imperial*, pp. 133–8; cf. Freyre, *Mansions*, pp. 152–4 (traditional gardens) and pp. 105–6 (impact of European aristocratic taste); Goulart Reis Filho, pp. 40–2, 46, 48, 171–2. The elite during the *belle époque* still used many; see Costa, *Rio de Janeiro*, 2: 323–5).

109 This period sees the triumph of European motif, construction, materials, and finishing (Goulart Reis Filho, pp. 43–4, 61–2, 171–4, 178). The paradigms are in Hautecoeur, pp. 253–77. The Avenida Central and the Eclectic are discussed in chapter 1.10. Antônio Januzzi, an important contractor and architect of the eclectic, built in that style for over forty years, from the Avenida's Companhia Docas de Santos and *Jornal do Commercio* building to several hundred private residences, among them the Palácio Rio Negro in Petrópolis (later summer residence of the President of the Republic); see Bell, pp. 97–100. See, also, the illustrations in ibid. and Reginald Lloyd, dir. principal, *Impressões do Brasil no século vinte* (London: Lloyds Greater Britain 1913), especially pp. 484, 487, 488, 492, 493, 505, 520, 526, 533, 539–40, 546, 588, 612. Descriptions are in Quesada, 1: 190–3; Lyra, p. 75, and C. Nabuco, *Oito décadas*, p. 57.

110 Freyre, *Mansions*, pp. 158–9, 162–3, 204–5; Los Rios, *Rio imperial*, pp. 304–5; Los Rios, *Grandjean de Montigny*, pp. 80–1, 93, 94–5.

111 Los Rios, *Grandjean de Montigny*, pp. 79, 80–1, 90, 92, 93; Freyre, *Mansions*, pp. 226–7.

112 See Hautecoeur, pp. 365–8, 370–82; Egon Friedell, *A Cultural History of the Modern Age*, 3 vols. (New York: Knopf, 1932), 3: 298–301, 302–3; Arnold Hauser, *The Social History of Art*, 4 vols. (New York: Vintage, n.d.), 4: 62–4, 89–90; Zeldin, 2: 420–31. For illustrations see Gabriel Heuriot, *Les beaux meubles des collections privées* (Paris; Ch. Massin, n.d.); Gaston Lefol, dir., *Hôtels particuliers* (Paris; Ch. Massin, n.d.); Hector Saint-Sauveur, *La décoration intérieure en France* (Paris: Ch. Massin, n.d.); Berenice Abbott, *The World of Atget* (New York: Berkley, 1977), *passim*; Arthur Trottenberg, ed. and intro., *A Vision of Paris* (New York: Macmillan, 1963), *passim*.

113 C. Nabuco, *Oito décadas*, pp. 162–4; Costa, *Rio de Janeiro*, 2: 325–6; Bennett, pp. 230–1, 236–7; Adam, pp. 88–9; Lyra, p. 75; de La Rocque, pp. 39–40; Quesada, 1: 190–3. See, also Los Rios, "O Rio de Janeiro da Primeira República", 121–6, especially 125; Goulart Reis Filho, p. 178; and, for photographs, see Lloyd, pp. 497, 504. I visited the home of D. Carolina Nabuco, the Casa de Rui Barbosa, and the Palácio do Catete.

114 See Nikolaus Pevsner, *Academies of Art Part and Present* (New York: De Capo,

1973), pp. 82–9, 132–3. NB Colbert assumed craftsmen would follow academic taste without government direction (pp. 158–60). The exception, however, is crucial – Colbert, organized (1667) the minor arts and luxury crafts involved in interior décor in the Manufacture des Meubles de la Couronne (with Lebrun, head of the Académie Royale de Peinture et de Sculpture, 1655, made director) with *académiciens* giving lessons to the artisans (pp. 243–4). State patronage of commercial artisanship came in 1767 with the Ecole Gratuite de Dessin; again with royal monies and classes for copying designs associated with the Royal Academy (pp. 161–2). On the emulation of the royal academies throughout the Continent, generally undertaken by the French-trained, see pp. 165–6.

115 On *estilo* João V, see Los Rios, *Grandjean de Montigny*, p. 79; cf. José Mariannio (Filho), "Acerca do mobiliário chamado D. João V e o seu processo de nacionalização no Brazil" in *Estudos de arte brasileira* (Rio de Janeiro: n.p., 1942?). On the tradition and survival of French artisanship, see Pevsner, pp. 165–6, 246–8; cf. Hauser's general comment: "As a result of the far-reaching participation of the middle class in artistic life long before the Revolution, there was a certain continuity of development . . ." (see 3: 158–63). That continuity helps explain the strength of Classical elements in France after 1830; see below.

116 Oliveira Marquês, 1: 406–17, 420 and Boxer, pp. 355–66 give the context. French impact on Brazil was less institutional (e.g. academies) and more in terms of elite consumption and taste. See Cruls, 1, illustrations *passim*, for dress, portraiture, monuments and statuary – particularly the work of "Mestre Valentim," Valentim da Fonseca e Silva (*c.*1740–1812), who was trained in Enlightenment Portugal (Cruls, 1: 207–13). See also Marianno: "Mestre Valentim," "A propósito da Escola de Arte de Vila Rica," "Acerca do mobiliáro chamado D. João V e o seu processo de nacionalizacão no Brasil." Boxer quotes a French traveller of 1748 who remarked on the ostentation of the elite, accustomed to "Marchandises de goût, tirées pour la plus grade [sic] partie des Manufactures de France." See Boxer, *Golden Age*, p. 314.

117 Oliveira Marquês, 1: 406–7, 409–11.

118 See Afonso de E [scragnolle]) Taunay, *A Missão Artística de 1816* (Rio de Janeiro: MEC, 1956), pp. 8–9; Marianno, "Uma linda aventura. A missão artística Lebreton"; de Los Rios, *Grandjean de Montigny*, pp. 28–33; Gean Maria Bittencourt *A Missão Artística Francesa de 1816* (Petrópolis: Ferreira da Cunha, 1967), pp. 5–10. The connections were effected in Paris, where Portuguese diplomats, through the kind offices of Alexander von Humboldt, met with Joachim Lebreton, recently dismissed from the academic establishment for Bonapartist sympathies. Lebreton helped recruit the others.

119 See Nizza da Silva, pp. 32–40, 50–6, 147–53; Freyre, *Mansions*, pp. 226–7; Freyre, *Um engenheiro francês no Brasil*, 1: 219–59, *passim*. For the impact of French luxury goods see Macedo, pp. 164–5, 176–7, 184–6; Cruls 1: 298, 300; and Renault, pp. 24–7.

120 Los Rios, *Rio imperial*, p. 300; Cruls, 2: 511; cf. Calmon, *O marquez*, pp. 37–8, 39–40.

121 The Missão's architect, Grandjean de Montigny, left the Académie d'Architecture just before it united with the Académie de Peinture et de Sculpture to form the celebrated Ecole des Beaux-Arts (1819), guardian of classicism and arbiter of art and architecture throughout the nineteenth century. See Chafee, and van Zanten,

in Drexler. See Grandjean de Montigny's part in Carioca neo-classicism in Los Rios, *Grandjean de Montigny*, pp. 261–3; Goulart Reis Filho, pp. 34–7; and Bittencourt.

122 Calmon, *O marquez*, ch. 17, *passim*; Hautecoeur, p. 371.

123 Hautecoeur, pp. 371–82; Hauser, 4: 62–4.

124 Hautecoeur, pp. 365–8, 370–1, 382; Hauser, 3: 159–60, 4: 62–3, 89–90; Friedell, 3: 298–301, 302–3; Carlton J. H. Hayes, *A Generation of Materialism* (New York: Harper Torchbooks, 1963), pp. 163–4; Zeldin, 2: ch. 10, *passim*; Renato Poggioli, *The Theory of the Avant Garde* (Cambridge, MA: Belknap, 1968), chs. 5 and 6.

125 Hautecoeur, pp. 253–5, 382; Hauser, 4: 62–3, 89–90; see also Alfred Cobban, *A History of Modern France*, 3 vols. (Baltimore: Penguin, 1965), 2: 96–8, 114–17, 121, 170–1.

126 Goulart Reis Filho, pp. 178, 180, 183–4.

127 Ibid., pp. 182–3, 185–6. Goulart Reis Filho's reference is to Cruz Costa, *A History of Ideas in Brazil*, pp. 53–9. See, also, chapter 1.1.

128 See Goulart Reis Filho, pp. 140–2, 184–5.

129 Burke, p. 48.

130 Edgcumbe, p. 45. See also Leclerc, pp. 62–6; Quesada, 1: 129, 150; Lomonaco in Afonso Taunay, *Rio de Dom Pedro II*, p. 225; Hastings, pp. 220–1; França, pp. 203–13; M. Nabuco, pp. 28–9; de La Rocque, pp. 36–7, 98–9; 101–2; C. Nabuco, *Oito décadas*, pp. 47–56, *passim*; Wanderley Pinho, pp. 145–7.

131 See Martins, *Presença* p. 18; Cruls, 2: 519. Cf. Quesada, 1: 104–5, 108, 118, 120; Viscount de Taunay, *Memórias*, p. 8; and C. Nabuco, *Oito décadas*, p. 10.

132 Goulart Reis Filho, pp. 34–7, *passim*. See Bittencourt plates; and Gilberto Ferrez, *A fotografia no Brazil* (Separata of *Revista do Patrimônio Histórico e Artístico Nacional*, 10 (1953), plate 5.

133 See chapter 2.2.

134 Foreign diplomats and men of affairs antedated the 1890s there, but that era was the town's watershed. See A. J. Barbosa de Oliveira, pp. 259–60, for Petrópolis in 1860; Quesada, 1: 129–30, for Petrópolis in 1882; Maul, pp. 9–10, for Petrópolis c. 1900; and M. Nabuco, pp. 28–9, for Petrópolis of c. 1910.

135 Elysio de Carvalho, "Diplomatas Extrangeiros." [*] Redfern, with Doucet, Worth and Poiret, dominated *belle-époque haute couture*. **honors Laurinda Santos Lobo, the niece of the villa's owner, Joaquim Murtinho; see chapter 3.1.

136 See Goulart Reis Filho, pp. 118–19, 173–4; C. Nabuco, *Oito décadas*, pp. 163–4; Costa, *Rio de Janeiro*, 2: 325; Los Rios, *Rio imperial*, p. 304; and Los Rios, "Rio da Primeira República," [pt. 1:] 121–6.

137 C. Nabuco, *Oito décadas*, pp. 164–5; Costa, *Rio de Janeiro*, 2: 325–6; Los Rios, *Rio imperial*, pp. 304–5; Goulart Reis Filho, pp. 57, 176–8.

138 C. Nabuco, *Oito décadas*, pp. 58–9; and de La Rocque, p. 36.

139 C. Nabuco, *Oito décadas*, p. 165.

140 Cruls, 1: 146, 221–2, 397; Los Rios, *Rio imperial*, pp. 8, 312. The *cidade velha* proper, de Los Rios states (p. 18), stretched between the Campo de Santana and the Bay, as of 1808. See Barreiros, plates 8–14. See, also, chapter 1.6.

141 Cruls, 1: 349–57; Nizza da Silva, pp. 41–3; Los Rios, *Rio imperial*, pp. 303, 312–16; Demosthenes de Oliveira Dias, *O solar da marquesa de Santos* (Rio de Janeiro: Carlos Ribeiro, 1972), p. 20; Taunay, *Memórias*, pp. 4–5; Graham,

pp. 161–3, *passim*; Calmon, *O marquez*, pp. 237–9. Contemporary illustrations are in Cruls, 1: 90, 216–17, 220, 224, 284; and Ferrez, *Aquarelas*, pp. 56–7, 58–9, 64–5, 66–7, 70–1, 76–7.

142 Anonymous, "Rua do Ouvidor" in *Rua do Ouvidor*, 22 October 1898, p. 3. On the Southern Zone shift, see: Calmon, *O marquez*, pp. 238–9 and Cruls, 2: 507–17. Regarding the *cidade velha* fringe, one finds A. J. Barbosa de Oliveira's mansion on Rua dos Inválidos (see A. J. Barbosa de Oliveira, pp. 314–18). See Cruls on the elite status of the old city area including Inválidos, Lavradio, Riachuelo, etc. (Cruls, 1: 397–401).

Cruls argues (loc. cit.) that this status survived for lack of urban transportation to alternative areas, and claims no change for this fringe until around 1900. This is misleading. The impact of the *bond* system (after 1868) would have made the fringe obsolete much earlier. New elite housing in fact preceded the *bond* in the south and simply increased with it. What Cruls assumes is continued fringe practicality was probably an older elite district that now survived as elite because its aging inhabitants preferred established residences to the new frontier. The examples Cruls musters are older people who established their importance by the mid-Second Reign. The major exception, the Count de Figueiredo (see chapters 2.2 and 3.2), may have maintained his residence on Rua da Constituição because his demanding concerns were headquartered only blocks away. The Baron de Quartim, unmentioned by Cruls, continued at his Riachuelo address, too – with concerns like Figueiredo's, his reasons may have been the same. On the southern districts preeminence, see: C. Nabuco, *Oito décadas*, , p. 56; Costa, *Rio de Janeiro*, 2: 324–5; Quesada, 1: 181, 189; França, pp. 146–50; Dent, pp. 182–3, 199, 204–5; Lomonaco in Afonso Taunay, *Rio de Dom Pedro II*, p. 207; Adam, p. 95; Fletcher, pp. 162–3; Andrews, p. 14; Binzer, p. 61; Costa, *Memórias*, 1: 180–1.

143 Cruls, 2: 459, notes that the first connection was from Gonçlaves Dias and Ouvidor to Largo do Machado, where the Rua das Laranjeiras begins in Flamengo district. The next lines reached through Botafogo to Jardim Botânico and up Laranjeiras.

144 Cruls, 1: 349–53; Dias, p. 20; Paulo de Paranaguá and Luíz Carlos de Paranaguá, interview, Rio de Janeiro, 15 July 1980; see also Ferrez, *Aquarelas*, notes cited in n. 140 above.

145 This has been discussed in section 7. See specific examples in Cruls, 2: 507–17, *passim*.

146 Freyre, *Mansions*, pp. 105, 206–8, 217–18, 224–7. Cf. Levi, pp. 135–6.

147 We noted material and aesthetic influences earlier. For the intellectual, see Cruz Costa, pp. 30–5; E. Bradford Burns, "The intellectuals as agents of change and the independence of Brazil, 1724–1822" in A. J. R. Russell-Wood, *From Colony to Nation* (Baltimore: Johns Hopkins, 1975); E. Bradford Burns, "The role of Azeredo Coutinho in the enlightenment of Brazil" in *Hispanic American Historical Review*, 44: 2 (May 1964), 145–60; Jacques Godeschot, "Independência do Brazil e a revolução do Occidente" in Carlos Guilherme Mota, ed., *1822: Dimensões* (São Paulo: Perspectiva, 1972); and, most especially Kenneth R. Maxwell, *Conflicts and Conspiracies* (Cambridge: 1973)

148 On the emergence of the neo-colonial order, see Celso Furtado, *Economic Development* ch. 3; Stein and Stein, Parts 2 and 3, *passim*; Halperín Dongi, chs. 2 and 3; on the Anglo-French role, see, e.g., Alan K. Manchester, *British Preeminence in Brazil* (Chapel Hill: North Carolina, 1933); Carlos Guilherme Mota, "O processo de

independência no Nordeste," in Mota; Freyre, *Um engenheiro francês*, 1: 219–59, *passim*.

149 The phrase is Halperín Donghi's – see chs. 4 and 5. See also Manchester; Graham, *Britain and the Onset* chs. 1–5; Celso Furtado, [Part] 4, *passim*.

150 De La Rocque, p. 35.

5 The Rise of consumer fetishism

1 On the evolution of *ancien régime* fashion, see Anny Latour, *Kings of Fashion* (New York: Coward-McCann, 1958), pp. 4–5, 20; Norah Waugh, *The Cut of Men's Clothes* (London: Faber & Faber, 1964), pp. 52–4, 56, 103, 104; Anne Hollander, *Seeing Through Clothes* (New York: Viking 1978), p. 118; James Laver, *Taste and Fashion* (London: George G. Harrap, 1948), pp. 13–15. On the impact of the Revolution and Napoleonic era, see Waugh, pp. 110, 112; Latour, pp. 20, 25–6, 28–9, 35–42; Hollander, pp. 225–6; Laver, pp. 15–25, *passim*. On the early nineteenth century, see ibid., and Latour, pp. 62, 78; Alison Adburgham, *Shops and Shopping* (London: George Allen & Unwin, 1964), pp. 10, 29, 37, 39–40; Hollander, pp. 352–3.

2 See Honoré de Balzac, "Traite de la vie élégante" in *Oeuvres diverses*, 2 vols. (Paris: Conard, 1938), 2: 157–61; Latour, pp. 70–1; Waugh, pp. 116–17; Hollander, p. 360; John C. Prévost, *Le dandysme en France (1817–1839)* (Paris: Minard, 1957), pp. 65–7, 165–71; Moers, pp. 61, 121–22.

3 Cf. chapter 4.8 and, especially, Poggioli, chs. 5 and 6, which essentially sets up the pattern elaborated here.

4 On the centrality of aristocratic taste, see Prévost, pp. 43–4, 65; Moers, pp. 108–14; Latour, pp. 70–1, 72–3; Laver, ch. 2; on the social domination of the aristocracy, see Gronow, pp. 56–7, 98–9, 356; Vandam pp. 37–8; and Moers, pp. 41–5, 60, 119–20. On the role of the dandy as trendsetter, see Moers, pp. 61–2, 132, or Prévost, p. 30; or note the attack on the extreme types, in ibid. pp. 65, 67–8, in the cartoons in Moers; and Balzac, pp. 177, 183–4. The importance of anxiety and higher social status informs Thorstein Veblen's celebrated "The theory of the leisure class" (see *The Portable Veblen*, [New York: Viking 1948], pp. 53–214), and such followers as Quentin Bell, *On Human Finery* (New York: Schocken, 1976). After reading Veblen, however, I left Bell for the more useful pointers in Balzac, Latour, pp. 88–9; Moers, pp. 61, 121–2; Hollander, pp. 357, 362; and Poggioli, ch. 6. NB that the direction of fashionable change (if not the motor, whose sociology I set out here) conforms to aesthetic modulations less easily tied to precise social impulses (see Hollander, pp. 357, 360, 364–5; Latour, p. 96). On clothing, fashion, and industrialization, see Hobsbawm, *The Age of Revolution*, p. 51 and chs. 2, 9, *passim*; his *Industry and Empire* (Baltimore: Penguin Books, 1969), chs. 2, 3, *passim*; and Dorothy Davis, *Fairs, Shops and Supermarkets* (Toronto: 1966), pp. 289–92; Latour, pp. 35–42; and Michael B. Miller, *The Bon Marché* (Princeton: 1981), ch. 2, *passim*, especially pp. 31–9. Cf. the "invention" of ready-made clothing for men, and gradually, clothing for women, in Latour, pp. 59–62. Another correlate was the rise of the popular press (and the first generation of *feuilletonistes*, e.g. Balzac), which often found both its subject and its advertisers in fashion – see Moers pp. 126–38; Latour, pp. 79–80; Zeldin, 2: 492–7; and cf. Latour, ch. 1, for elite predecessors. For the larger socio-literary questions raised, see Graña, chs. 3, 4.

5 The formulation of the commodity and commodity fetishism here and throughout the chapter derives ultimately from Marx; see "The Fetishism of Commodities and the Secret Thereof" from *Capital*, in [Karl Marx and Friedrich Engels,] *The Marx-Engels Reader* (New York: Norton 1972), pp. 215–25. My sense of both, however, owes much more to my reading of Walter Benjamin's "Paris, the capital of the nineteenth century" and "The Paris of the Second Empire in Baudelaire" (and the latter's "Addendum"), included in *Charles Baudelaire* (London: NLB, 1973).

6 See Miller, ch. 1; Adburgham, pp. 1–21, 96–7; Davis, pp. 187–96, 289–92; Benjamin, especially "Paris, Capital," pts. 1–3; and Bernard Marrey, *Les grands magasins* (Paris: Lib. Picard, 1979), [chs.] 2–3. On the chronology of the evolution, see Marrey, chs. 2–3; Adburgham, pp. 18–20, ch. 13; Miller, pp. 25–7, ch. 5. Miller claims precedence for Bon Marché, and is contradicted by Marrey (see, especially, p. 69) and Adburgham.

7 Balzac, pp. 156, 170.

8 Albert Wolff, quoted in Joanna Richardson, *The Courtesans* (New York: World, 1967), p. 228.

9 The historical importance for fashion of both figures is recognized in, e.g., Balzac, pp. 183–4; Zeldin, 2:432, 435; Laver, pp. 24–5, 55; Latour, pp. 68, 84–90, 101–4; Prévost, p. 30; Waugh, p. 112; Hollander, p. 228.

10 On Brummell see Willard Connely, *The Reign of Beau Brummell* (London: Cassal, 1940), chs. 1, 5–7; Moers, pp. 45, 62; Waugh, p. 112; Laver, pp. 24–5; Latour, p. 68; Hollander, p. 228; and Gronow, pp. 49–50. The origins of the business suit derive from the white-tie-and-tails, whose story may be reconstructed in Moers, pp. 68, 82; Herbert Norris and Oswald Curtis, *Costume and Fashion*, 7 vols. [London: J. M. Dent, 1933], 6; pp. 13–14; Gronow, p. 191; and Edward George Earle Lytton Bulwer Bulwer-Lytton's, novel, *Pelham* (1828), a "manual of dandyism" to both the English and the French that "set" the final combination. Brummell, long retired to a debt-ridden exile in France, was supposed to have disliked the final version, and told a friend dressed in it: "My dear Jesse, I am sadly afraid you have been reading 'Pelham'; but excuse me, you look very much like a magpie." (see Connely, p. 45). On the fashion role of the dandy, see n. 4, above. On Brummell's social ascent, see Gronow, pp. 49–50; Harriette Wilson, *The Memoirs of Harriette Wilson Written by Herself*, 2 vols. (London: Navarre, 1924), pp. 47–8; Connely, chs. 5–7, Moers, pp. 41–5, 62; Waugh, p. 112; Hollander, p. 228; Laver, pp. 24–5. On the impact of fashionable London, see Prévost, pp. 27–30, 45–50, 60–7, 82–94; Moers, pp. 41–5, 68, 108–23; Margery E. Elkington, *Les rélations de société entre l'Angleterre et la France sous la Réstauration (1814–1830)* (Paris: Honoré Champion, 1929), pp. 172–4 and *passim*; Hollander, p. 376. Brummell's influence is exemplified by Balzac, op. cit., and Jules Barbey d'Aurevilly: *L'amour impossible suivi de pensées détachées et du Dandysme [et de G. Brummell]*, in *Les oeuvres complètes*, v. 9 (Paris: François Bernourard, 1927).

11 Cf. Latour, p. 68; Hollander, p. 228; Bell, pp. 225–6. In these analyses' focus on the process from a bourgeois individual's style to an aristocratic fashion and a bourgeois convention, the use of the word "bourgeois" is often confused and obscures Brummell's reality and significance. Hollander (see pp. 374–80) suggests the question in distinguishing between the moment when the dark suit is the badge of the Romantic individual (e.g., Byron) from the moment when it is the badge of the respectable, because conventional, bourgeois. She notes that the moments are related; the fashion is adopted from the Romantic and aristocratic type by the

bourgeoisie, which adds its own values to it (e.g. black as a "sober" color). Poggioli, however, brings us to the problem, correctly suggesting that both moments are "bourgeois" in a different way: the first, in terms of the individualism associated with bourgeois culture (the individual has a distinct merit and potential, the sort of thing Romanticism celebrates) as opposed to the values associated with aristocratic culture, in which the individual's value is assigned by estate. The second, in terms of the conventional values associated with the nineteenth-century bourgeoisie, a class suffused with aristocratic values, desires for individual mobility, and a general anxiety about social position allayed by a conformist style of life guaranteeing "respectability" by its aristocratic derivation. "Bourgeois" may thus be used both for the style established by the Romantic individual, and the mass-marketed commodity derived from it. I point to the usage associated with the latter to avoid confusing the issues involved in Brummell's case: the aristocratic values and the class-based anxiety central to fashion in the bourgeois era (cf., too, Zeldin, 2:432–3; Laver, p. 188; Benjamin makes a suggestive connection between snobs in art, dandies in fashion, and the anxiety over novelty in "Paris, Capital," pt. 5).

12 On bourgeois attitudes, see Cobban, 2: 218–19 and Zeldin, 1: ch. 1; on Brummell's social position, see Gronow, pp. 49–50; Wilson, pp. 47–8; Hollander, p. 228. Nor was Brummell unaware of his singular position: he did not devote "his talents to a higher purpose" because "I know human nature well. I have adopted the only course which can place me in a prominent light, and separate me from the society of the herd. If I were to do [otherwise]. . . , do you think I could stand in the middle of the pit at the opera, and beckon [the Marquis of] Lorne on one side, and [Lord] Villiers on the other, *and see them come to me?*" (quoted in Connely, pp. 44–5, italics original). On the qualities of an *homme du monde*, see Balzac, *passim*, and Prévost, pp. 67–8, 94.

13 Cf. Madame Carette, *Recollections of the Court of the Tuileries* (New York: D. Appleton, 1890), pp. 52, 133–4, 156–7; and Harold Kurtz, *The Empress Eugénie: 1826–1920* (Boston: Houghton-Mifflin, 1964), pp. 32–3, 61, 84, 181–2; and Loliée; Gronow, p. 242; Vandam, pp. 288–97; Latour, pp. 100–4.

14 Edith Saunders' *The Age of Worth* (London: Longmans, Green, 1954) is informative; but Latour, pp. 59–65, 80–90, 96; and Hollander, pp. 352–7 are analytic.

15 The word chic achieved its first definition in this century. See *Trésor de la langue française* (Paris: Centre Nationale de Récherche Scientifique, 1977), s.v. One of the couturier Worth's clients once defined the word in a letter: "This M. Worth is a very amiable man, and he assures me that I have 'chic', a word you have probably never heard, and which means that I have a certain personal elegance." (quoted in Latour, p. 120).

16 On Worth's success with Eugénie, see Gronow, p. 242. On his impact on fashion and the subsequent use of models, see Latour pp. 59–65, 128–59; Hollander, pp. 353–4; cf. Brigitte Scart [ed. and complier], *L'atelier Nadar et la mode* (Paris: Direction des Museés de France?, n.d.). The importance of Napoleon III's industrial politics and Lyon textiles is noteworthy; see Latour, pp. 81, 84–5; Zeldin, 21: 435–6; and Kurtz, pp. 181–2. Actresses were important earlier as very visible trendsetters, too – the difference is that the fashions established were associated with them, primarily, and not their tailors, and that their clothes were not reproduced for a mass market, but imitated. The contradiction between actresses and the idea that the fashions were aristocratic is only apparent. It must be remembered that the actresses in both periods had success representing figures embodying precisely such

values. Further, these women were a part of the aristocratic world – they generally mixed socially and sexually with its men. The Scart collection shows that actresses and aristocrats would be used interchangeably by the fashion houses, so long as the women in question looked "aristocratic" – the point was the successful placement of the fantasy, not the accurate placement of the model, e.g. see, Norris and Curtis, pp. 16–17, 51–2, 99–104. On the use of celebrated prostitutes, see Anne Manson, "Quand les trois grandes régnaient sur Paris" in Gilbert Guilleminault, *La belle époque* (Paris: Denoël, 1957), pp. 163, 172–3; Latour, pp. 121–2, 124, 126.

17 On the stage and prostitution, see Gronow, pp. 102–7, 158–62; Vandam, pp. 128–40, *passim*; [Marie Paul Ernest Boniface de Castellane,] Marquis de Castellane, *Confessions of the Marquis de Castellane* (Strand: Thornton Butterworth, 1924), pp. 60–1; Norris and Curtis, pp. 16–17; Ian Dunlop, *Degas* (New York: Harper & Row, 1979), pp. 131–7, 140–51; Morand, pp. 185–6, 193–4. On the locale, evolution, and gradation of prostitution, see F. Carlier, *Les deux prostitutions (1860–1870)* (Paris: Société des Gens de Lettres, 1889), ch. 2, especially, pp. 133–4; Alain Corbin, *Les filles de noce* (Paris: Aubier Montaigne, 1978), pp. 197–206; Richardson, *passim*; Latour, pp. 121–2, 129; Castellane, pp. 73–4; Manson, pp. 173–4. The origins and the success of Dumas fils' work are given in Vandam (pp. 110–15), with a notice of Alphonsine Plessis, the original of Marguerite Gautier. On the phantasmagoria of Parisian commodities, see Benjamin, especially "Paris, Capital," pt. 3.

18 On the *horizontales* and fashion, see Manson, pp. 163, 172–3; Latour, pp. 121–2, 124, 126; on the *cocodettes*, see Gronow, p. 242; Latour, p. 123.

19 See e.g., Manson, pp. 163–82; Richardson, *passim*; and her *La Vie Parisienne* (New York: Viking 1971), pp. 67–75.

20 Perhaps the earliest department store prototype was Notre Dame de Paris, founded mid-century on the Ouvidor, flourishing by the late 1870s into different departments selling French material, confections, and dresses; see Macedo, pp. 294, 297–8, 301. Notices of 1913 department stores mention none going back further than the 1870s; see Lloyd, pp. 578–626, *passim*. Their history of successive mergers, stores and store architecture, on Quitanda, Ouvidor, and the Avenida Central, exhibits explicit references to Parisian precedents (cf. illustrations in ibid. and Marrey).

21 On Ouvidor and its shop windows, see Macedo, pp. 160, 176–7, 183–6, 217–32, 46–7. See Benjamin's analysis in "Paris, Capital," pts. 1–3, and in "Paris of the Second Empire," pp. 33–8, 50, 53–6 and cf. his predecessors – João do Rio, on the impact of shop windows on the fantasies of the passers-by in "As mariposas do luxo" in *A alma encantadora das ruas* and, Ezequiel Martínez Estrada, on Buenos Aires' calle Florida, in *X-Ray of the Pampa* (Austin: Texas, 1971), pp. 245–53. I take "interiorization" from Benjamin's discussion of Paris' commercial arcades and the *intérieur* which includes the transformation of a public space into a private one in which one loses oneself in commodity objects in an aimless, leisurely exploration. ("Paris of the Second Empire," pp. 50, 54–5).

22 Lloyd, loc. cit. and Macedo, loc. cit. European visitors noted the relative expense; see, e.g. Binzer, pp. 61, 72; Montet, pp. 72–4.

23 On Cariocas' pursuit of European fashion, see Francisco Pereira Passos, Rio, to L. R. d'Oliveira, Paris, 4 June 1875 (DPP uncat.: cop. 6) pp. 10, 364; and 13 Nov. 1875 (DPP uncat.: 6) p. 155; C. Nabuco, *Oito décadas* pp. 6–7; de La Rocque, pp. 111–12; Gustavo Aimard, in Afonso de Taunay, *Rio de Dom Pedro II*, p. 142; Binzer, p. 42;

Macedo, pp. 183, 186, 246; João do Rio, "Cinematographo" in *Gazeta de Noticias* (Rio de Janeiro) 12 July 1908, p. 1; "Rua do Ouvidor," in *Rua do Ouvidor* (Rio de Janeiro) 24 December 1898, p. 3; Adam, pp. 22–3; Joseph Burnichon, S. J., *Le Brésil d'aujourd'hui* (Paris: Académique, Perrin, 1910), pp. 127–8; França, pp. 3–4, 128–30; Burke and Staples, p. 64; Moraes Filho, pp. 249, 258–61; Costa, *De um livro de memórias*, 1: 81, 195–6; Wright, *The New Brazil*, pp. 439–40; Taunay, *Memórias* p. 71; Fletcher pp. 180–1; and the photographs illustrating Wanderley Pinho, *passim*. On Figueiredo Pimentel, see chapter 4.3; and, e.g., "Binoculo," *Gazeta de Noticias*, 6 July 1908, or 27 August 1914, p. 3.

24 On the shopgirls and D. Pedro, see e.g., Mello Moraes; pp. 250–1; cf. Pereira Passos' impatience with such women, quoted in Athayde, pp. 50–1. The best source for Carioca prostitution is Pires de Almeida, who may have emulated Carlier; see Dr. [José Ricardo] Pires de Almeida, *Hygiene moral* (Rio de Janeiro: Laemmert, 1906), pp. 48–9, 73. The Alcazar, doubtless named after the noted *café cantante* of Paris (see Dunlop, p. 151), supposedly revolutionized Rio's moral climate for reasons discussed below – see Macedo, pp. 258–9; Mattoso, pp. 271–3; Mello Moraes, pp. 284–5; Aimard, in Taunay, pp. 149–50; França, p. 186; Costa, 1: 203–8; Expilly, pp. 146–7; Taunay, *Memórias*, pp. 125–8. The general assumption about even operatic stars is implicit in the memoirs of our old friend Albino José Barbosa de Oliveira, who noted their reputations – see *Memórias de um magistrado do império* pp. 227, 243.

25 Mattoso, pp. 286–7, 333–5; Lomonaco, in Taunay, p. 212; João do Rio, "Historia de gente alegre" in *Dentro da noite*.

26 Cobban, 2: 219; cf. Zeldin, 1: ch. 1.

27 Amado, *Mocidade*, pp. 20–1 indicates a shift by 1910. On the Avenida, see chapter 1.10.

28 See chapter 4.5.

29 Mattoso, pp. 269–70.

30 It is difficult *not* to find the Ouvidor in the primary sources. See, e.g., Mello Moraes, "Rua do Ouvidor," in *Factos e memórias*; Aimard, in Taunay, p. 147; Lomonaco Taunay, pp. 206–7; Binzer, pp. 60–1; França, pp. 3–6; Maul, pp. 127–9, 173–4; Costa, pp. 191–3, 200–1; Latteux, pp. 130–3; Andrews, pp. 32–4; Burnichon, pp. 127–8; Leclerc, pp. 56–7; Rancourt, pp. 58–9; Wright, pp. 105–6; Humphrey, pp. 45–6; Quesada, 1: 182; Costa, *Rio*, 1: ch. 2, 3: *passim*, 4: chs. 23–4. The most useful are Mello Moraes and Macedo.

31 See, e.g., Prévost, pp. 61–5, 67–8, 90, 94,; Elkington, pp. 95–8, 193–4; Moers, pp. 41, 60, 109–10, 116–20; Richardson, *La Vie*, ch. 6, *passim*.

32 Costa, *Memórias*, 1: 198–9; see also ibid., 1: 191–3, for the contrast between the Ouvidor and the surrounding streets. "Cabrocha" derives from the Portuguese "she-goat" and refers to mulattos; "Capoeira" is a word for an Afro–Brazilian martial art; then, it also referred to the street toughs who practised it. See, e.g. Lomonaco, in Taunay, p. 213. Saúde and Saco do Alferes were traditional districts of the working poor; cf. chapter 1.11. On the conflict with Afro–Brazilian Rio, see, also, Needell, "*Revolta Contra Vacina*."

33 Mattoso, pp. 285–7; cf. Richardson, *La Vie*, *passim*; and Morand, *passim*.

34 Quoted in Levi, p. 143.

35 See Waugh; Norris and Curtis; James Laver, *The Concise History of Costume and Fashion* (New York: Harry N. Abrams, 1969); and Alison Gernsheim, *Fashion and Reality* (London: Faber and Faber, 1963).

36 See Norris and Curtis; Hollander; Latour; Laver, *Concise History*; and Gernsheim.

37 A. L. Kroeber, "On the Principal of Order in Civilization as Exemplified by Changes in Fashion" in *American Anthropologist*, s. 21 (1919), pp. 253–4. Kroeber based his system on mouth-to-floor measure, and arrived at a ratio of 7 to 9% variation in the waist diameter over the period. Using this, one has 3.92″ and 5.04″ for a mouth/floor measure of 56″. Kroeber's findings stem from the study of fashion plates. The mouth-to-floor base arose in attempting to rule coiffures out of the calculation. The toilettes examined were evening dresses. Norris and Curtis report (pp. 44, 65) that in the 1820s and 1830s men sometimes forced themselves into corsets, too, to manage the natty line of the mode.

38 See Gernsheim, p. 45; Worth is credited with launching the crinoline in developed form (see Latour, p. 88).

39 Carette, pp. 156–7.

40 Figueiredo Pimentel, "Binoculo" in *Gazeta de Noticias*, 10 July 1908, p. 3. A survey of the winter of 1884 shows a low of 46°F. and a high of about 86°F. Generally, temperatures ran from the low 50s° (apparently at night) to the low 70s°F. See Dent, pp. 341–4, whose readings are lows taken in Botafogo and highs taken on Morro do Castelo, from 30 May to 27 July. That hill and Botafogo would enjoy the effects of breezes from the sea lacking in the *cidade velha*.

41 Leclerc, pp. 54–5. Cf. Lomonaco, in Taunay, p. 243.

42 F. P. Passos to Viscount de Mauá, Rio, 10 Jan. 1876 (DPP uncat., cop. 6), p. 93.

43 See João do Rio, "Cinematographo" in *Gazeta de Noticias*, 12 July 1908, p. 1; von Binzer, pp. 61, 72; and Montet, pp. 72–4.

44 Figueiredo Pimentel, "Binoculo" in *Gazeta de Noticias*, 5 August 1914, p. 5.

45 See chapter 4.3.

46 Costa, *Rio*, 1: 74–7; cf. França, pp. 22, 221–4; Amado, *Infância*, pp. 23–4; Costa, *Memórias*. 1: 196–7. The women made up a ritual parade of fashion on the Ouvidor each day by century's end; see Costa, *Memórias*, 1: 200–1 and the regular column, "Rua do Ouvidor" in *Rua do Ouvidor*. Lomonaco, in Taunay, p. 213, attacked this *desfile*'s audience: "the indiscreet and impertinent multitude that seems inebriated and ecstatic on contemplating the parade of these walking mannequins." Yet, cf. the crowds Latour cites (p. 124) applauding the return of the well-dressed *horizontales* from Longchamp and the Bois.

47 Costa, *Memórias*, 1: 196–7.

48 Amado, pp. 23–4.

49 Costa, *Memórias*, 1: 196–7.

50 See Freyre, *Masters*, pp. 279, 323–5, 335–6, 394–5, 455–6; Pires de Almeida, *Hygiene moral*, pp. 46, 51, 54, 64–5, 66, 69–70, 74–5; and Expilly, pp. 142–3, 144–5, 147–8, 416–17.

51 Pires de Almeida, pp. 48, 50. Almeida tells us that they "sought in public prostitution an easy and quick means for acquiring money and perhaps fortune." The moralist seems a bit sanguine.

52 I assume here that Pedro I was not alone among elite men in finding his way to the Ouvidor. See Mello Moraes, pp. 250–1.

53 Rachel, a great name in French theater, was notorious for her mercenary love-life (see Gronow, pp. 161–2). Blanche d'Antigny could not really act, and only used the stage to appear scantily clad and attract a proper clientele; see Richardson, *Courtesans*, ch. 1.

54 Pires de Almeida, pp. 50–3, 56; Corbin, pp. 412–23.

55 Pires de Almeida, pp. 48–9, 56; Amado, *Mocidade*, pp. 21–3; interviews with

Américo Jacobina Lacombe, Rio de Janeiro, 15 September 1980; with Alceu Amoroso Lima, Rio de Janeiro, 3 October 1980; and with Paulo Braga de Menezes, Rio de Janeiro, 4 July 1980.

56 Pires de Almeida, p. 56; Corbin, pp. 413, 417–19, 421, 421 n. 134. Perhaps the popular Carioca word for procurer and pimp, *cáften*, comes from the traditional caftan worn by Eastern European Jews. Corbin, p. 413, notes the role of the era's anti-semitic waves in the exodus of Eastern European Jewry. For the Carioca Jewish colony, and the prostitution within it, see João do Rio *As religiões no Rio*, pp. 169–74. The Argentine variant is in Francis Korn, *et al.*, *Buenos Aires, los huéspedes del* 20 (Buenos Aires: Sudamérica, 1974).

57 Reports of 1889–1906 state that Frenchwomen "are always very prized and bring in double or triple what the other women do" (Corbin, p. 423).

58 Lomonaco, in Taunay, p. 212; Amado, *Mocidade*, pp. 21–3; Amado, *Prescença*, p. 25; Macedo, pp. 210–11, 258, 275–7; Mattoso, pp. 271–3, 285–7; França, pp. 153, 186; Costa, *Memórias*, 1: 203–4; Costa, *Rio*, 3: 605–7, and *passim*; Mello Moraes, pp. 284–5; Pires de Almeida, pp. 71–2, 88; Lamoureux, pp. 141–2; do Rio, "Gente alegre"; interviews with Jacobina Lacombe, Amoroso Lima, and Braga de Menezes.

59 Gronow, p. 242; Latour, p. 123 were cited earlier – for later eras see Proust's first three volumes, Painter, and Morand.

60 See chapter 4.

61 "Indicações úteis" in *Rua do Ouvidor*, 25 June 1898, p. 3.

62 Pires de Almeida, pp. 70–1 and, especially, Mello Moraes, pp. 312–15. See, e.g., Peixoto, *A esfinje*, pp. 459–61; João do Rio, *Dentro da noite*, pp. 183–4, 185; Costa, *Rio*, 2: 350–3.

63 An Italian, Boldini (1842–1931) made his home in Paris from 1871, where he became well-known in Society and mixed with fashionable painters such as Jacques-Emile Blanche. Boldini was celebrated as a portraitist of Society figures and the beautiful women of the stage and the *demi-monde*.

64 Hollander, chs. 2–3, makes a helpful observation regarding the erotic in art and clothing. She notes the eroticism in "nakedness", the painted statement that a "real" woman has removed clothing, as opposed to "nudity," an ideal, as in a Greek nude. This has direct application to the paintings by Boldini cited.

65 [Giovanni] Boldini, *L'opera completa di Boldini* (Milan: Rizzoli, 1970), e.g., pp. 99, no. 107; 100, no. 120; 101, no. 129; 104, no. 166; 108 nos. 218–20; 124, no. 449; 126, no. 488; 129, nos. 530a, 530b, 532; 130, nos. 546a, 546b, bis 547a, bis 547b, 548.

66 Ibid., e.g., plate 27, "Ritratto de Emiliana Concha de Ossa," plate 33, "Ritratto della Contessa de Leusse."

67 Ibid., e.g., plate 45, 'L'espagnole del "Moulin Rouge" '; pp. 115, nos. 325a, 325b [Cléo de Mérode, the noted dancer and well-known siren, mistress of famous men]; 120, no. 390, "Ritratto de Mme. Marthe Regnier" [the celebrated actress, mistress of Gabriele d'Annunzio].

68 An interesting example is the postcards popularly collected in Rio around 1900 – many were illustrated by the most celebrated actresses and cocottes of France – Sarah Bernhardt, Cléo de Mérode, *La Belle* Otero, *et al.* (see Costa, *Rio*, 4: 716–17; and the notices regarding collecting in *Rua do Ouvidor* during the era).

69 Mattoso, pp. 272–3. Note that *paio*, figuratively a tolerant fool, literally refers to a pork sausage – perhaps a rather unkind allusion.

70 This is a point of Freyre's; see *Order*, pp. 57–9; my interviews with Jacobina

Lacombe, Braga de Menezes, and Amorosa Lima, as well as with Luíz Carlos de Paranaguá (Rio de Janeiro, 1 September 1980), tended to support the contention, though Jacobina Lacombe thought Freyre might have been exaggerating.

6 The literary *belle époque* in Rio: the end of the Brazilian nineteenth century

1 On the popular and European influence, see José Ramos Tinhorão, *Pequena história da música popular* (Petrópolis, Vozes, 1974), chs. 1–6, *passim*, especially chs. 4–6. On elite music, see Gerald Martin. "The literature, music and art of Latin America: 1870–1930" in Leslie Bethell, (ed.), *Cambridge History of Latin America*, vol. 4 (Cambridge: 1985), pp. 470, 471–2, 493–4. My reference to Villa Lobos' first work is from Judith Robinson's notes to "Julian Bream plays Villa-Lobos" LSC–3231 (New York: RCA, 1971). On the Alcazar Lyrique's more earthy contributions to Carioca culture see chapter 5; Tinhorão's analysis of its role is on pp. 48, 87. I am indebted to Gérard Béhague for suggesting Tinhorão. On the Teatro Lírico and the Club-Beethoven, see chapter 2. On elite attitudes towards salon music, see, e.g. [Affonso Celso de Assis Filho, conde de] Affonso Celso, "Chronica Musical," *Renascença* 2:9 (Nov. 1904); "Chronica Musical," ibid., 3:12 (Feb. 1905); Olavo Bilac, "Chronica," *Kósmos*, 4:5 (May 1907); "Echos e factos," *Rua do Ouvidor*, 3 Dec. 1910, pp. 5–6. A fixture of Carioca salon musical culture was the Portuguese pianist, Artur Napoleão; see [Sanches de Frias, visconde de] Sanches de Frias, *Arthur Napoleão* (Lisbon: n.p., 1913).

2 On the milieu and painters, see Martin, pp. 473–4; Carlos Lemos, José Roberto Teixeira Leite, and Pedro Manuel Gismonti, *The Art of Brazil* (New York: Harper & Row, 1983), ch. 5, especially pp. 176, 188–9, 190–3. On Almeida Júnior, see Martin, p. 475. On elite responses to such painting and the salons of the period, see, e.g., Olavo Bilac, "Chronica", *Kósmos*, 3:6 (June 1906); [Luís de] Gonzaga Duque [Estrada], "Paisagens", ibid., 4:6 (1907); "A Exposição de 1905," *Renascença*, 4:20 (Oct. 1905); João de Barros, "Pedro Americo," ibid., 4:21 (Nov. 1905).

3 On the appeal of Rio, cf. Nabuco *Um estadista*, 1:12, 17; Coelho Netto, *A conquista*, pp. 60, 228, 300; Gilberto Amado, *Minha formação no Recife* (Rio de Janeiro: José Olympio, 1955), pp. 357–63. On the specific appeal to literati, cf. Broca, *A vida literária*, ch. 6, *passim*; Antônio Luís Machado Neto, *Estrutura social da república das letras* (São Paulo: Grijalbo/USP, 1973), pp. 62–5.

4 On elite education, see chapter 2.1. On literary culture and the elite, see ibid. and Azevedo, *Brazilian Culture*, pp. 187–9.

5 See Antônio Cândido [de Mello e Sousa], *Formação da literatura brasileira*, 2 vols. (São Paulo: Martins, 1964), 2:42–4; and Azevedo, pp. 149, 212–13.

6 Oliveira Marquês, *A History of Portugal*, 1: ch. 8 *passim*, 2: ch. 10, *passim*; Maxwell, chs. 1, 2, *passim*; Mello e Sousa, 1: chs. 7, 8, *passim*, Burns, "Intellectuals," and "Azeredo Coutinho;" Viotti da Costa, "José Bonifácio" in Carlos Guilherme Mota, *1822*, *passim*.

7 See Afonso de Taunay, *A Missão Artística*, chs. 1–4, *passim*; Mello e Sousa, 1: 285–92; Nizza da Silva, *Cultura*, (Part) 2, *passim*; Taunay, *Memórias*, pp. 4–5, 21.

8 On Romanticism, see André Lagarde and Laurent Michard, *Les évolutions du XIXe siècle* (Paris: Bordas et Laffond, 197), pp. 10–11, 23–4, 32–9, 232–41; A. K. Thorlby, "The concept of Romanticism," and M. G. Hutt and Christophe Campos, "Romanticism and history," both in John Cruickshank, ed., *French Literature and its Background*, 6 vols. (Oxford: 1969), 4. On Romanticism in Brazil, see Mello e

Sousa, 1:285–92, 310–11, 334, 2: ch. 1, *passim*, and pp. 322–4; Afrânio Coutinho, *An Introduction to Literature in Brazil* (New York: Columbia, 1969), pp. 119–39, *passim*: Alfredo Bosi, *História concisa da literature brasileira* (São Paulo: Cultrix, 1970), pp. 99–108, *passim*; Ferdinand Denis, *Résumé de l'histoire littéraire du Brésil* (Paris: Lecointe et Durey, 1826), ch. 1, especially pp. 515–21. Mello e Sousa, Coutinho, and Bosi also note the importance of Almeida Garrett, the Portuguese Romantic, in promoting Romanticism among the Brazilians in Paris, and in writing of Brazilian literature in his "*Bosquejo da história da poesia e língua portuguesa*," in *Parnaso lusitano* (Paris: Aillaud, 1826–7); see Mello e Sousa, 2:12; Coutinho, p. 138; Bosi, p. 107; and António José Saraiva and Óscar Lopes, *História da literatura portuguesa* (Porto: Porto, s.d.), pp. 624–8.

9 Mello e Sousa, 2: 11–13.

10 Mello e Sousa, 2: chs. 1–3, 8, *passim*. Cf. Bosi, pp. 116–19; Coutinho, pp. 131–51, *passim*.

11 Mello e Sousa, 2:81–96, 218–32, 263–78; Coutinho, pp. 140, 143–8; Bosi, pp. 148–54; Schwarz, ch. 2; David T. Haberly, *Three Sad Races* (Cambridge: 1983), ch. 3.

12 On the origins and nature of the milieu drastically simplified here, see Lagarde and Michard, pp. 313–14, 316–26, 337–41, 351–2, 427–38, 442–4, 509–20; D. G. Charlton, "Positivism and its aftermath," B. L. Nicholas, "Poetry and pure art," Cecil Jenkins, "Realism and reality in the novel," and S. B. John and H. R. Kedward, "Literature and ideology," all in John Cruickshank, (ed.), vol. 5; D. G. Charlton, *Positivist Thought in France During the Second Empire* (Oxford: 1959), chs. 2, 3, 6, 7, and pp. 190–9 (but cf. pp. 160–4); Claude Digeon, *La crise allemande de la pensée française (1870–1914)* (Paris: Presses Univ. de France, 1959), chs. 4, 5, *passim*; Richard M. Chadbourne, *Ernest Renan as an Essayist* (Ithaca: Cornell, 1957), chs. 4–6, *passim*; Carter Jefferson, *Anatole France* (New Brunswick, N.J.: Rutgers, 1965), pp. 8–10; Georg Lukács, *Studies in European Realism* (New York: Grosset and Dunlap, 1964), ch. 4; Hauser, 4: 60–8, *passim*.

13 Coutinho, pp. 152–70, *passim*; Bosi, pp. 181–92, 209–17, 246–57; Alexander Coleman, *Eça de Queirós and European Realism* (New York, 1980), ch. 1, Cf. Jean Franco, *An Introduction to Spanish-American Literature* (Cambridge: 1969), ch. 4, *passim*. On Inglês de Sousa, see chapter 3.1.

14 See Antônio Cândido [de Mello e Sousa], "O método crítico de Sílvio Romero" in *Teoria literária e literatura comparada* (São Paulo) 26:1 (1963), chs. 1, 2, 6, *passim*; João Alexandre Barbosa, *A tradição do impasse* (São Paulo: Atica, 1974), ch. 2, *passim*; Cruz Costa, chs. 4–5 *passim*; Ivan Lins, *História do positivismo no Brasil* (São Paulo: Nacional, 1967), chs. 37–44, 3a. pt., 4a. pt. 7a. pt., *passim*, especially pp. 133–9, 243–8, 453–7, 469–75, 489–94; Skidmore, *Black into White*, ch. 1, *passim*. Cf. similar movements in contemporary Portugal and Spain in Coleman, ch. 1, *passim*; Oliveira Marquês, 2: 39–40; Juan López-Morillas, *The Krausist Movement and Ideological Change in Spain, 1854–1874* (Cambridge: 1981), pp. 57–62, 81–3. In Spanish America, the influence of movements like Positivism and Social Darwinism (except, perhaps, in Chile) generally emerged out of a triumphant Liberalism, and thus did not have the same, combative quality. See the suggestive, classic discussion in Leopoldo Zea, *Positivism in Mexico* (Austin: Texas, 1974) and *The Latin American Mind* (Norman: Oklahoma, 1963); William R. Crawford, *A Century of Latin American Thought* (Cambridge, Mass.: Harvard, 1961), chs. 5, 9, *passim*.

15 Antônio Cândido [de Mello e Sousa], *Literatura e sociedade* (São Paulo: Nacional,

1976), pp. 112–14; Coutinho, pp. 176, 186, 187, 188, 193–4; Bosi, 219–21; Alfredo Bosi, *O pré-modernismo* (São Paulo: Cultrix, s.d.), pp. 11–12, 19–20, 75–7, 85, 115–18, 120; cf. Broca, pp. 272–3, and his "Coelho Netto, Romancista" in *Ensaios da mão canhestra* (São Paulo: Polis, 1981).

16 Broca, *A vida literária*, pp. 3–4, 20, 272.

17 Lima Barreto to Monteiro Lobato, Rio de Janeiro, 4 Jan. 1919, in [Afonso Henriques de] Lima Barreto, *Correspondência*, 2 vols. (São Paulo: Brasiliense, 1961), 2:56–7.

18 On French domination of *belle-époque* Carioca literary taste, see Broca, *A vida literária*, chs. 11, 19; Costa, *Rio*, 4:701–2; José Maria Bello, "O que se lê entre nós" in his *Novos estudos criticos* (Rio de Janeiro: Revista dos Tribunaes, 1914); Raul de Azevedo, *Meu livro de saudades* (Rio de Janeiro: Freitas Bastos, 1938), pp. 223–4; Fortunat Strowski, "O livro francês na biblioteca de Rui Barbosa" and Broca, "A literatura na biblioteca de Rui Barbosa," both in Fundação Casa de Rui Barbosa, *Rui* (Rio de Janeiro: FCRB/MED, 1980). The emphasis on current French authors was also confirmed in conversation with period survivors: Irmã Carmem Maria, Cosme Velho, 22 Sept. 1980; Gilberto Ferrez, Flamengo, 11 July 1980; Alceu Amoroso Lima, Flamengo, 3 Oct. 1980; Marcos Carneiro de Mendonça, Cosme Velho, 10 July 1980; Paulo Braga de Menezes, Centro, 4 July 1980; Carolina Nabuco, Botafogo, 9 June 1980; Gilberto Trompowsky, Tijuca, 13 June 1980. The impact of French models on period literature is discussed in Coutinho, pp. 1.76–95 and Broca, *A vida literária*, chs. 3, 9, *passim*. On this period of French literature, see Lagarde and Michard, pp. 466–52, 463–7, 560–610, *passim*; André Lagarde and Laurent Michard, *Les métamorphoses du XXe siècle* (Paris: Bordas et Laffond, 197), ch. 2 and p. 43–5; John and Kedward, *passim*; C. L. Campos, "Symbolism and Mallarmé" in Cruickshank, vol. 5, *passim*; Jean Pierrot, *The Decadent Imagination, 1880–1900* (Chicago: 1981), pt. 1, *passim*, especially ch. 1; Hauser, 4: 166–206; Edmund Wilson, *Axel's Castle* (New York: Charles Scribner's Sons, 1934), chs. 1, 8, *passim*.

19 Amado, *Mocidade*, p. 98.

20 See the excellent biographical synopses in Mello e Sousa, *Formação*, 2:376–86; and the anecdotal detail in Broca, *Românticos, pré-românticos, ultra-românticos* (São Paulo: Polis, 1979), *passim*, especially pp. 55–62, 80–2, 117–21, 151–8, 185–9, 233–4, 301–4. On Maciel Monteiro, see chapter 3.3.

21 Mello e Sousa, *Formação*, 2:367–86, *passim*; Broca, *Românticos*, pp. 147–50, 196–9, 227–7.

22 See chapters 1.5, 3.4.5.

23 Wanderley Pinho, ch. 16; cf. chapter 3.3, 5.3.

24 On São Paulo and the Romantics, see Mello e Sousa, *Literatura e sociedade* pp. 147–57; Broca, *Românticos*, pp. 206–15; Morse, *From Community* pt. 2, *passim*, especially chs. 7–8; Wanderley Pinho, ch. 4, *passim*; Nabuco, *Minha formação*, pp. 4–8. On the literati, the Rua do Ouvidor, the newspapers, the cafés and *confeitarias*, the bookshops and presses, see chapter 5.3; Macedo, *Memórias*, pp. 196–7, 205, 252–3, 309–10; Moraes Filho, pp. 139, 148–50, 287–91; Brasil Gerson, *História das ruas do Rio* (Rio de Janeiro: Brasiliana, 1964), pp. 66, 67–8, 69, 72, 74; Wanderley Pinho, ch. 16, *passim*; Broca, *Românticos*, pp. 52–4, 63–8; Eunice Ribeiro Gondim, *Vida e obra de Paula Brito* (Rio de Janeiro: Brasiliana, 1965), pp. 15–18, chs. 3, 4, *passim*; Elmano Cardim, *Justiniano José da Rocha* (São Paulo: Nacional, 1964), chs. 1–2, *passim*; Nelson Werneck Sodré, *História da*

imprensa no Brasil (Rio de Janeiro: Civilização Brasileira, 1966), pp. 22–6, 40–2, 45–6, 58–9, 115–17, 122–7, 208–11, 217–25, 226–8, 232–9; Coutinho, pp. 135–6. The French dominated bookselling from the late eighteenth century, ceding to the Portuguese (e.g. Francisco Alves) by the end of the nineteenth. Even then, the firm Baptiste Louis Garnier (brother to the Parisian Garnier) had established the greatest prestige. The French were also among the earliest involved in printing, lithography, and newspapers. The prestigious and venerable paper, the *Jornal do Commercio*, was founded by a Frenchman in 1827 (on these matters, see Sodré, above, *passim*). The French mix of literature and journalism also served as a model. For example, the *feuilleton-roman*, crucial to nineteenth-century literature, was introduced to Brazil in 1842 by the Parisian-educated political journalist, Justiniano José da Rocha (1811–62), who used it when he also established the tradition of translating popular French novelists. The Brazilian Romantic novelists followed suit; their major works first appeared in that format, perhaps starting with the first Brazilian novel, Teixeira e Sousa's *O filho do pescador*, which may have appeared in Paula Brito's *Marmota* before Brito published it as a book in 1843. See Hauser, 4:14–19; Campos, pp. 58–9; Mello e Sousa, *Formação* 2:127–35, *passim*; Broca, *Românticos* pp. 174–8; Gondim, pp. 44–5; Cardim, pp. 26–7.

25 E.g., the careers of Alencar, Teixeira e Sousa, Macedo, Almeida, J. J. da Rocha, Francisco Otaviano, Torres Homem, Quintino Bocaiuva, *et al.* in Mello e Sousa, *Formação* 2:367–86, *passim*; Broca, *Românticos* pp. 196–9, 222–7, 233–5, 268–70; Cardim, chs. 2, 4, 5, *passim*; Sodré, pp. 217, 221, 224; Sacramento Blake, s.v. "Quintino de Souza Bocayuva."

26 Machado de Assis is the greatest name in Brazilian letters; seemingly every author and critic of note since the late nineteenth century has discussed his life and work. The biography appended to his *obra completa* takes up more than three double-columned pages of fine print: see [Joaquim Maria] Machado de Assis, *Obra completa*, 3 vols. (Rio de Janeiro: José Aguilar, 1962), 3:1182–5. Most of my biographical information derives from the account of Machado's painstaking biographer, R[aimundo] Magalhães Júnior, *Vida e obra de Machado de Assis*, 4 vols. (Rio de Janeiro: Civilização Brasileira, 1981). The latter is a critical, cumulative, and documentary summation. For interpretation and analysis of Machado's work, I have relied on varied sources, as will be seen below. For the paragraph noted here, see Lúcia Miguel-Pereira, *Machado de Assis* (São Paulo: Nacional, 1939), pp. 32–9; Magalhães Júnior, 1; chs. 1–6, 9–10, 12, 16, 20, 25, 2:31–9, 45, *passim*; Gondim, pp. 31, 61–2; Melo e Sousa, *Formação*, 2:370–2, 375; Broca, *Românticos*, pp. 196–9, 222–4, 233–5, 268–70. Machado first published in the *Periódico dos Pobres* in 1854 (see Magalhães Júnior, 1:17–18).

27 See the Bosi and Coutinho citations in n. 12, above, and the citations made in the first section of n. 13 for background. For Castro Alves and the transition, see Mello e Sousa, *Formação* 2: ch.6, *passim*. The most often quoted contemporary analysis is Sílvio Romero's, repeated in his speech receiving Euclides da Cunha (see section 10, below) into the Academy of Letters: see "Resposta do Sr. Sylvio Romero" in "Discursos Proferidos na Academia Brazileira," *Revista da Academia Brazileira de Letras* (hereafter, RABL) 2(1911):467–9. The intellectual and literary aspects at issue here must be understood in the context of the larger political and socio-economic shifts I trace in chapter 1.1, 2.

28 Urbano Duarte to [Lopes] Trovão, s.l., 10 March 1894. Biblioteca Nacional, Seção

de Manuscritos, Rio de Janeiro [hereafter, BNSM], Coleção Ernesto Sena: 1–5, 15, 58.

29 Pedro do Couto, "Sylvio Romero" in [Colegio Pedro II,] *Anuario do Colégio Pedro II vol. IX, 1935–36.* (Rio de Janeiro: Rua da Misericordia, 1939), pp. 219–22.

30 In 1821, the population of urban and suburban Rio was about 113,000; in 1849, about 186,000; in 1870, about 235,000: see Republica dos Estados Unidos do Brazil. [Directoria Geral do Estatistica], *Recenseamento do Rio de Janeiro (Districto Federal)* (Rio de Janeiro: Officina de Estatistica, 1906), p. 100, and Lahmeyer Lobo, 1:122, 135, 226. Regarding a potential reading public, NB the few comparable figures for the growth in the liberal professions between 1857 and 1870 in ibid., 1:229–32: physicians and surgeons, from 412 to 438; pharmacists, from 79 to 369; lawyers, from 108 to 242; professors and "men of letters," from 129 to 897. Other potential readers were the public employees (in 1872, 2,498), *capitalistas* (in 1870, 245), *comerciantes* (in 1870, 21,583), and *proprietários* (in 1870, 1,562), for which neither Lobo nor the censuses previous to that of 1870 have figures for comparison (see the comments in the census cited above, p. 100). On the great shift in literary periodicals and journalism, see José Veríssimo [Dias de Matos], "A imprensa" in Associação do Quarto Centenario do Descobrimento do Brasil, *Livro do centenario*, 4 vols. (Rio de Janeiro: Nacional, 1900), 1:41–2, 43–6; "Antônio P. Leitão," *Rua do Ouvidor* 25 June 1910; "Henrique Chaves," ibid., 28 May 1910; interview with Felinto de Almeida in João do Rio, *O momento literario* (Rio de Janeiro: H. Garnier, s.d.), pp. 29–30; interview with Sylvio Romero, in ibid., p. 49; interview with Coelho Netto, ibid., pp. 56, 60; interview with Osorio Duque Estrada, ibid., p. 204; interview with Mario Pederneiras, ibid., pp. 225–6; Olavo Bilac, "Prefacio," *Ironia e piedade* (Rio de Janeiro: Francisco Alves, 1916) and cited in Machado Neto, p. 128; Broca, *A vida literária* p. 218; Sodré, pp. 256–86, *passim.*

31 See, e.g. [Antônio] Valentim [da Costa] Magalhães, quoted in Eloy Pontes, *A Vida exuberante do Olavo Bilac*, 2 vols. (Rio de Janeiro: José Olympio, 1944), 2:486–90; Amadeu Amaral, quoted in ibid., 1:108–9; Olavo Bilac, quoted in ibid., 1:97–107, *passim*; Euclides da Cunha, "Discurso de Euclydes da Cunha" in "Discursos proferidos na Academia Brazileira" in RABL, 2 (1911): 439–41. On the earlier phase, see the citations in n. 21, above.

32 Henri Murger, *Scènes de la vie de bohème* (Paris: Michel Levy Frères, 1874). Murger's fictionalized memoir was tremendously successful; many readers will recall it as the source for Puccini's opera – it provided the greatest paradigm of Paris' nineteenth-century bohemian milieu. See, e.g., Graña, pt. 1, *passim*, especially pp. 22–7, 35–6, 71–82; Hauser, 4:66–7, 190–3. The self-conscious quality of the Carioca bohemia is evident: see, e.g., Raul Pompéia and Olavo Bilac, quoted in Pontes, 1:69–70.

33 The classic fictional memoir of the Carioca bohemia is Coelho Netto, *A conquista* (1897), and its sequel, *Fogo fátuo* (1929). Less familiar accounts are [Luíz de] Gonzaga Duque [Estrada], *Mocidade morta* (1899), and Leoncio Correia, *A bohemia do meu tempo.* Pontes, 1:299–352, *passim*, gives an excellent evocation, drawing on Bilac's dispersed journalistic accounts of the era, as well as other hard-to-find materials. See, also, the serial memoir of Gonzaga Duque in *Kósmos* 5:9, 10, 11 (Sept., Oct., Nov., 1908). See, also, Machado Neto, pp. 91–8.

34 See the comprehensive group analysis in ibid., pp. 98–104, *quadros* 3, 9, 10; in which the sociologist shows that 58.6 per cent of his sample came from the *classes dominantes* and 34.9 from the *classe média*, and in which 52.5 were *bacharéis* (or, at

least, had been law students), 14.5 were physicians (or, at least, had been medical students), and 8.5 were engineers (or, at least, had been students in the military schools), etc. He counts 86 per cent of his sample as thus having had an education *em cursos superiores* (p. 103). The sample is qualitative and includes all the relevant literary figures, and then some – 200 literati from the generations flourishing between 1870 and 1930 (see ch. 1 and *quadro* 10). The bohemians of which I write were drawn from two of the generations Machado Neto defines (i.e., those born between 1848 and 1862 and between 1863 and 1877); only three of the well-known bohemians charted had less than a secondary education (Aluisio Azevedo, B. Lopes, and Guimarães Passos).

35 See the memoirs in Pontes, 1:63–96, 299–352, *passim*; Coelho Netto, *A conquista*, pp. 37–60, 66–7, 87–8; Duque, "No tempo de 'Gazetinha' " *Kósmos* 5:9 (Sept. 1908): 1–4; Blake, s.v., "João Alexandre Passos," "Sebastião Guimarães Passos"; Machado Neto, *quadro* 10. On Patrocínio, see, also, Oswaldo Orico, *O tigre da Abolição* (Rio de Janeiro: Civilização Brasileira, 1977), *passim*, especially, pp. 109–23.

36 *A conquista* pp. 66–7.

37 On Patrocínio, see Bilac, *et al.* quoted in Pontes, 1:305–22; Nabuco, *Minha formação*, pp. 243–4; Orico; Conrad, *Destruction*, ch. 10, *passim*; on Aluisio Azevedo, see [Tristão de Alencar] Araripe Júnior, *Obra crítica de Araripe Júnior*, 2 vols. (Rio de Janeiro: MEC/Casa de Rui Barbosa, 1960), 2:63–90; and Juan Armando Epple, "Aluisio Azevedo y el naturalismo en Brasil," *Revista de Crítica Literaria Latinoamericana* (Lima) 6:11 (1980): 29–46; on Paula Nei, see Pontes, 1:83, 144–5, 327–30, and Coelho Netto, *Fogo fátuo* (where Nei is the central figure, under the pseudonym "Neiva"); on Guimarães Passos, see João do Rio, "Discurso de Recepção" in *Psychologia urbana* (Rio de Janeiro: H. Garnier, 1911), pp. 190–218; Coelho Netto, "Discurso do sr. Coelho Netto" in "Discursos Proferidos na Academia Brazileira," RABL, 3 (1912): 417–23; Pontes, 1:330–3. Olavo Bilac and Coelho Neto are dealt with at greater length in section 2, below.

38 See the biographical synopses in Mello e Sousa, *Formação*. 1:367–86. See, also, the mention of literati in Wanderley Pinho, chs. 9, 10, 17, *passim*.

39 On the careers of Rui Barbosa and Joaquim Nabuco, see chapters 1.3, 3.1.3, 4.2; those of Sílvio Romero and José Verissimo are analyzed in section 10, below. NB that Nabuco, although an Abolitionist and a Liberal reformist, remained faithful to the monarchy itself, however much he wished to change it.

40 "Resposta do Sr. José Veríssimo" in "Discursos Proferidos na Academia Brazileira de Letras," RABL 1 (1910): 186.

41 Humberto de Campos, quoted in Machado Neto, pp. 95–6; Pontes, 1:160–89, ch. 5, 332–52, *passim*; T[ristão de] Alencar Araripe Júnior, "Recordações do Club Rabelais," RABL 2 (1911): 265, 269, 271–5; Rodrigo Octávio [de Langgaard Meneses], *Minhas memorias dos outros* (Rio de Janeiro: José Olympio, 1936), pp. 45–6, 72; his *Minhas memórias dos outros* (Rio de Janeiro: Civilização Brasileira/ MEC, 1979), ch. 4, *passim*; and his *Minhas memorias dos outros* (Rio de Janeiro: José Olympio, 1934), pp. 296–305; J. A. Barbosa, pp. 128–46; Nicolău Sevcenko, *Literatura como missão* (Rio de Janeiro: Brasiliense, 1983), pp. 86–93.

42 Mello e Sousa, *Formação*, 2:12n. 4; B. Mossé [agent for José Maria da Silva Paranhos Júnior, *barão* do Rio Branco], *Dom Pedro II* (Paris: Fermin-Didot, 1889), pp. 329–30n.1; Magalhães Júnior, 1: chs. 6, 14, 3: chs. 55, 63.

43 See the characteristically modest acknowledgment with which Machado opened the

Academy's first session: "Discurso de Machado de Assis, presidente" in "Discursos Proferidos na Academia Brazileira," RABL 1 (1910): 165–6. See, for contemporaries' evaluation of the man: José Veríssimo, "Machado de Assis" in *Estudos de literatura brasileira*, 6 vols. (Belo Horizonte: Itatiaia, 1977), 6:103 and *passim*; Sylvio [Vasconcelos de Silveira Ramos] Romero, "A litteratura" in Associação do Quarto Centenario, 1:74–5, 116–17; García Mérou, pp. 418–21; Magalhães Júnior, 3:233–4, 235–6, 249–50, ch. 72, *passim*, 4: ch. 74, *passim*.

44 On the critique of Machado, contemporary and posthumous, see Broca, *A vida literária*, pp. 212–15; and his *Machado de Assis e a política* (São Paulo: Polis, 1983), pp. 28–30; Magalhães Júnior, 2: chs. 59, 78, 79; Machado's defense is made in Broca, *Machado de Assis*, pp. 27–89, 177–93, *passim*; Magalhães Júnior, 1: ch. 12, 15, 18, 22–5, 29, 3: ch. 60, *passim*. On the question of age, illness, career, and disillusion, see Broca, *Machado de Assis*, pp. 37–40, 54–61; Magalhães Júnior, 2: chs. 45, 48, 50, 3: chs. 51–3, 61, 68, *passim*; Miguel-Pereira, pp. 154–5, 158, ch. 10, *passim*, 180–5, 192–9, ch. 14, *passim*; Afrânio Coutinho, "Machado de Assis na Literatura Brasileira" in Machado de Assis, *Obra completa*, 1:25–6, 39–42.

45 José Verissimo, "A Instrucção," pp. 44–5; Langgaard Meneses, *Minhas memorias*, (1934) pp. 323–4; *Minhas memórias*, (1979) pp. 59–61, 64.

46 Ibid., pp. 64–8; Josué Montello, *O presidente Machado de Assis* (São Paulo: Martins, 1961), pp. 24–5, 26–9, 31–40; Magalhães Júnior, 3: ch. 72, 4: chs. 73–5, 82, *passim*.

47 Ibid., 4: chs. 77, 83, 91, *passim*; Montello, pp. 40–52; José Veríssimo, "A Academia Brasileira" in *Estudos*, 6; Machado de Assis, "Discurso", and Joaquim Nabuco, "Discurso de Joaquim Nabuco, secretario geral" in "Discursos Proferidos . . ." RABL 1 (1910): 166–76.

48 Ibid., p. 166.

49 Ibid., p. 171.

50 Ibid., pp. 174–5.

51 J. Nabuco, "Discurso" in ibid., pp. 172–3; cf. Machado de Assis, in ibid., p. 176.

52 "Resposta do Sr. José Verissimo" in ibid., p. 193. See the parliamentary maneuvers for recognition and financial support in Magalhães Júnior, 4: ch. 82; Montello, pp. 36–40.

53 Jean-Jacques Brousson, *Itinéraire de Paris a Buenos-Ayres* (Paris: Crès, 1927), p. 193.

54 The noted example is that of Emílio de Meneses. See Pontes, 2:394–401; Langgaard Meneses, *Minhas memórias*, (1979) pp. 53–5; cf. Broca, *A vida literária*, pp. 8–9; Montello, pp. 24–9; Antônio Cândido [de Mello e Sousa], *Vários escritos* (São Paulo: Duas Cidades, 1977), p. 16.

55 *A vida literária*, pp. 7–10.

56 On Symbolists, see sections 8, 9, below. On the established literati, see Machado Neto, ch. 5, *passim*, especially pp. 81, 83–5; almost all of the 1900 literati Machado Neto cites were professionals who, while writing literature (generally in periodicals), earned a living in bureaucratic or other government employment (e.g., teaching at the Colégio Pedro II, diplomacy, the judicial apparatus).

57 See chapter 1.8–11.

58 See the introductions to João do Rio, *Cinematographo* and *O momento literario*; Broca, *A vida literária*, ch. 19; Sodré, ch. 6, *passim*, especially pp. 303–8, 313–15, 321–46; Costa, 4: chs. 29–30, 5: chs. 31–3, 39; Antônio Dimas, *Tempos eufóricos* (São Paulo: Atica, 1983), 1a. pt., *passim*, especially chs. 1, 6.

59 See the comments on the impact of journalism from the literati interviewed by João

do Rio in *O momento literario*, especially Olavo Bilac, Coelho Netto, Guimarães Passos, Sylvio Romero, Osorio Duque Estrada, Mario Pederneiras, Inglês de Sousa, and Sousa Bandeira; da Costa, 4: 702; Broca, *A vida literária*, chs. 14, 19, *passim*; Sodré, pp. 330–50, *passim*; Mello e Sousa, *Literatura e sociedade*, pp. 85–8; Machado Neto, pp. 77–83, 88–91, 118–22; *Literatura e sociedade*, pp. 85–8; Machado Neto, pp. 77–83, 88–91, 118–22; Sevenko, pp. 100–4. Bilac (in do Rio, *O momento literario*, p. 11) claimed that all of the papers of Rio combined sold only 150,000 copies daily; elsewhere, he commented that Garnier had only had two books that had ever exhausted their first edition in little more than a year, and Garnier's editions were commonly between 2,000 and 2,200 copies (quoted in Machado Neto, p. 120). In Brazil, according to the 1890 census, only 18.5 per cent of the nation's 11,444,891 people could read; according to the 1900 census, only 33.1 per cent of 13, 422, 259, (ibid.).

60 *História* da minha infância (Rio de Janeiro: José Olympio, 1958), p. 237.

61 On the *colégio* Francophile tendencies, see Chapter 2.1; on the overwhelmingly French influence in literary taste, see n. 18, above; on the pervasive quality of the French language among the Brazilian literati by 1900, see, e.g., Joaquim Vianna, "A reacção contra a influencia intellectual francesa," *Kósmos* 5:12 (Dec. 1908): 1–3; Bilac, quoted in do Rio, *O momento literario*, pp. 6–7; Nabuco, *Minha formação*, ch. 7, *passim*, especially pp. 67–8; C. Nabuco, *a Joaquim Nabuco*, pp. 315–18; Wilson Martins, *História da inteligência brasileira*, 5 vols. (São Paulo: Cultrix, 1977–78), vol.5: 5–6. The translation of French works is cited in the last references in n. 21 above – see the case of Machado de Assis: Magalhães Júnior, 1:91–2, 94, 133, 139, 2:83, 86–9, 118–19; and *passim*; cf. Broca, *Machado de Assis*, pp. 216–19, 275–7.

62 See Bello, "O que se lê . . .," *passim*; Costa, 4: chs. 23, 24; Costa, *De um livro de memórias*, 2:539–40; note the importance of *La Revue des Deux Mondes* for Brazilian literati in Broca, *Machado de Assis*, pp. 216–17, and the centrality of current French periodicals for João do Rio, section 9, below.

63 On the earlier periods, see the J. Nabuco, Magalhães Júnior, and Broca citations noted in n. 61, above; on the *belle époque*, see Bello, pp. 96–102.

64 General background for the French *fin de siècle* is cited in n.18, above. On Anatole France, see Jefferson, chs. 1–3, especially ch. 2; Haakon M. Chevalier, *The Ironic Temper* (New York: Oxford, 1932), *passim*, especially ch. 3; on Bourget and Huysmans, see Pierrot, especially pp. 11–16, 60–3; on Loti, see Alec G. Hargreaves, *The Colonial Experience in French Fiction* (London: Macmillan, 1981), pt.1, especially ch.3; on Prévost, see Jules Bertaut, "Marcel Prévost" in *Les célébrités d'aujourd'hui*, 5 vols. (Paris: E. Sansot, 1904), 4:14–30; Emilien Carassus, *Le snobisme et les lettres françaises* (Paris: Armand Colin, 1966), pp. 470–1; Carassus has a good deal to say about France, Bourget, and Huysmans, too.

65 See the background references in nn. 12 and 17, especially Hauser, Digeon, Pierrot, and Charlton. See, also H. Stuart Hughes, *Consciousness and Society* (New York: Vintage, 1961), ch. 2 and pp. 336–58, *passim*. Cf. Roger Shattuck, *The Banquet Years* (New York: Vintage, 1968), pp. 3–28, *passim*.

66 On Symbolism and the *novos* see Bello, pp. 96–102, *passim*; do Rio, *O momento literario*, interviews with Nestor Victor, Júlio Afranio [Afranio Peixoto], and Elysio de Carvalho; Elysio de Carvalho, "Raros e impassivos," *passim*, in *As modernas correntes estheticas na literatura brazileira* (Rio de Janeiro: H. Garnier, 1907), and pp. 191–216; and his *Five o'clock* (Rio de Janeiro: H. Garnier, 1909); Duque, *Mocidade morta*; Costa, *Rio* 3:ch. 22, 4:ch. 23, *passim*; and his *Memorias*, 2:503–58;

Coutinho, pp. 176–81, 186–87, 193–5; Broca, *A vida literária*, ch. 12. NB that the newer generation not only often embraced French Symbolism, but other modish elements of the cosmopolitan culture established in *fin-de-siècle* Paris, e.g., Nietzsche, Oscar Wilde, *et al.* see, ibid., ch. 11, and the Bello and the Carvalho citations above.

67 My information on Bilac is generally drawn from: do Rio, *O momento literario* s.v. Olavo Bilac; Bilac's *crônicas* in *Kósmos*; Pontes; Costa, *Rio* 3:ch. 21; and his *memórias*, 2:605–16; [José Joaquim de Campos da] Albuquerque, 2:173–87;Dimas, ch. 3.

68 Costa, *Rio*, 3:620–1.

69 Albuquerque, 2:180–1. On the *conferências*, see ibid.; Broca, *A vida literária*, ch. 13; Olava Bilac, *Conferências literarias* (Rio de Janeiro: Francisco Alves, 1912); João do Rio, *Psychologia urbana* (Rio de Janeiro: H. Garnier, 1911).

70 Digeon, *passim*; John Leddy Phelan, "Pan-Latinism, French intervention in Mexico (1861–1867) and the genesis of the idea of Latin America," *Conciencia y autenticidad históricas* (Mexico: UNAM, 1968): 279–98.

71 Broca, *A vida literária*, ch. 10.

72 On Parnassian poetry in Brazil, see Coutinho, Bosi, Mello e Sousa, and Broca, as cited in n. 15, above; and José Veríssimo, *Estudos*, 2: ch. 13; on Bilac as a poet, see ibid., 5: ch. 1; Pontes, 1: chs. 3, 4, *passim*, 2:chs. 1, 3, *passim*; on the lack of response to Symbolism, see Coutinho, pp. 176–7, 186–7; Broca, *A vida literária*, pp. 126–30; J. A. Barbosa, pp. 176–81; Dimas, pp. 90–4; on the Symbolist milieu, see Costa, *Memórias* 2: 539–57.

73 (Rio de Janeiro: Francisco Alves, 1916).

74 Quoted in Costa, *Memórias*, 1:162.

75 "Chronica," *Kósmos* 1:3 (March 1904):2.

76 Ibid.

77 Cf. Bilac, *Ironia e piedade*; Pontes, 1:181–9; 2:432–82, *passim*; Dimas, p. 53 and ch. 3, *passim*.

78 See Broca, "Coelho Neto, Romancista" in *Ensaios*, and Bosi, *História*, pp. 219–29. My information on Coelho Neto is generally drawn from: do Rio, *O momento literario*, s.v. Coelho Netto; Paulo Coelho Netto, "Imagem de Uma Vida" in Coelho Netto, *Obra seleta*, 2 vols. (Rio de Janeiro: José Aguilar, 1958) 1: LXXXIII–CX, *passim*; Zita Coelho Netto, *Coelho Netto* (Rio de Janeiro: Simões, 1961), *passim*.

79 Coelho Neto, quoted in P. Coelho Netto, p. LXXXIV.

80 On his vocabulary, see the introduction to the Coelho Neto interview in do Rio's *O momento literario*; Barbosa Lima Sobrinho, *A língua portuguesa e a unidade do Brasil* (Rio de Janeiro: José Olympio, 1958), p. 127; on the vocabulary and the volumes, see P. Coelho Netto, pp. XCIX, CIV–CVI.

81 All these men figure in Coelho Neto's *romans-à-clef*, *A conquista* and *Fogo fátuo*.

82 See chapter 3.1.

83 "*Padrinho*" refers either to a godfather or a sort of "best man" at a wedding; the female equivalent is "*madrinha*."

84 P. Coelho Netto recalls the praise of Machado de Assis for his father (pp. LXXIX–LXXX), and notes the official apotheosis of Coelho Neto as elected Prince of Brazilian Prose writers in 1928 (p. CX). R. de Azevedo, pp. 223–4, recalls the writer's national prestige in the era, and Broca confirms it in "Coelho Neto, Romancista" in *Ensaios* and in his *A vida literária*, pp. 26–7, and *passim*. Cf. Bosi, *História*, pp. 222–9.

85 Benedito Costa, quoted in Broca, *A vida literária*, pp. 26–7.

86 Broca, ibid., pp. 27–8.

87 Bilac, quoted in do Rio, *O momento literario*, pp. 11–12.

88 See the contemporary critique in J. Verissimo, *Estudos*, 4: ch. 1; cf. his *Estudos*, 1: ch. 5, especially, pp. 87, 92–4, 97–8. See, also, João do Rio, "Conferencias Literarias" in *Almanaque Brasileiro Garnier* 4 (1907): 311–13.

89 Coelho Netto, quoted in do Rio, *O momento literario*, pp. 55–6.

90 Ibid.

91 Broca, "Coelho Netto, Romancista," pp. 180–2, 196–8; Bosi, *História*, pp. 228–9, cf. p. 346. NB Veríssimo's anticipation in *Estudos*, 4:11–13, 16–20.

92 Bosi, *História*, pp. 223, 225.

93 *Tormenta* (Porto: Chardron, de Lello & Irmão, 1915), p. 12.

94 José Veríssimo, *Estudos*, 4:13.

95 See the descriptions and analysis of décor in chapter 4.7. An excellent example of both the style and the pleasure in consumption is given, in an understandable coincidence, in João do Rio's description of Coelho Neto (or Olavo Bilac) at home: see *O momento literario*, pp. 1–2, 50–2. See, also, the observations of Martins, 5: 104–6.

96 My information on Paulo Barreto is generally drawn from: Amado *Mocidade*, ch. 5, *passim*; Costa, *Rio* 3: ch. 19, 5: ch. 31, *passim*; *Memórias*, 2:559–68; Constáncio Alves, "Discurso de recepção do sr. Constáncio Alves" in RABL 12 (1922): 137–54; Coelho Netto, "Discurso do sr. Coelho Netto" in RABL 4 (1912): 417–27; Broca, *A vida literária*, pp. 247–51; Luís Martins, "Introdução" in João do Rio, *João do Rio* (Rio de Janeiro: Sabiá, 1971), *passim*; R[aimundo] Magalhães Júnior, *João do Rio*; Freyre, *Order* pp. 148–9, 151–2, 305–9, 352; Skidmore, pp. 94–8; Gentil Luíz de Faria, "A recepção e a influência do Oscar Wilde na '*belle époque*' literária brasileira" (PhD diss., USP, 1979), pp. 55–9, 74–81, and *passim*.

97 See, e.g., the reminiscences in J[oão] B[aptista] de Mello e Sousa, *Estudantes do meu tempo passim*, and Magalhães Júnior, *João do Rio*, pp. 12–17; Amado, *Mocidade*, pp. 60, 68–9; C. Alves, p. 15; and Freyre, p. 319.

98 Amado, *Mocidade*, pp. 60–1, 68–9; Magalhães Júnior, *João do Rio*, p. 12; Lima Barreto, *Correspondência*, 2:55–7.

99 Paulo's homosexuality was never noted directly by contemporary biographers, but later writers take it for the common knowledge it was in Society (see, e.g., Freyre, p. 352, and Magalhães Júnior, *João do Rio*, p. 117). Contemporary enemies were more direct (Costa, *Rio*, 3:384); see, e.g., Lima Barreto, *Recordações do escrivão Isaías Caminha* (São Paulo: Brasiliense, 1968), in which João do Rio is the character Raul Gusmão (e.g., pp. 67–70, 138–9, 185).

100 See Martins; C. Alves; Costa, *Memórias* p. 561; and Broca, *A vida literária*, pp. 247–51. As Costa and Broca suggest, the influence on his innovations was definitely Parisian. On this aspect of João do Rio's writing, see Faria, who argues again the plagiarism with which others have charged him (see Faria, pp. 56, 76–8). A suggestive analysis of João do Rio's *Dentro da noite* has been made by Carmen Lúcia Tindó Secco: *Morte e prazer em João do Rio* (Rio de Janeiro: Francisco Alves, 1978); her arguments about João do Rio's style and the values of the *belle époque* parallel much analyzed at length here (cf., e.g., Secco, pp. 25–9, 33–61). The best early pieces are collected in *As religiões no Rio* (1904), *O momento literario* (1908), *Vida vertiginosa* (1911), *Psychologia urbana* (1911), and *Cinematographo* (1911).

101 Amado, *Mocidade* p. 59. The portrait described is the fashionable Abreu e

Companhia photograph used as the frontispiece to *Cinematographo* (Porto: Chardron, 1911); the reference to monocle and style is from Costa, *Rio* 3:510; the note on do Rio's status as a dandy is from one of his rivals – Paulo Hasslocher, "Fui elegante por amor ao Brasil" in Francisco de Assis Barbosa, *Testamento de Mário de Andrade e outras reportagens*, p. 49.

102 Amado, *Mocidade* pp. 67–70. Amado, in discussing the second phase, makes reference to a collection of the 1916 *crônicas* João do Rio wrote for his society column, "Pall-Mall Rio" in *O Paiz*, the successor of Figueiredo Pimentel's "Binoculo" in the *Gazeta de Noticias* (on Figueiredo Pimentel, see chapter 4.3); see Magalhães Júnior, *João do Rio*, chs. 25–26.

103 In this, of course, he recalls Escragnolle Dória, whom I analyzed in the context of the salon, rather than literature, partly for this reason.

104 "Discurso de recepção," pp. 224, 225–6.

105 On Figueiredo Pimentel's place in Society consumerism, see chapters 4.3, 5.2. My information on the columnist is generally drawn from: Costa, *Rio* 3:642, 663, 670, 672, 673; Broca, *A vida literária*, pp. 20, 22, 44, 47, 143–4, 255, 256; and Maúl, pp. 25–9. In this context, it is apposite to recall that it was Figueiredo Pimentel who coined the era's motif: "o Rio civiliza-se."

106 Archivo Nacional, Rio de Janeiro, Seção de Arquivos Particulares, cod. 978, No. 84.

107 "Binoculo," *Gazeta de Noticias*, 9 Aug. 1914.

108 My information on Elísio de Carvalho is drawn from: Elysio de Carvalho, *As modernas correntes*, pp. 191–216, *passim*; *Five o'clock*, *passim*; *Esplendor*; "Diplomatas extrangeiros," *Kósmos* 6:3, 5 (March, May 1909); Elysio de Carvalho, quoted in do Rio, *O momento literario*, pp. 256–73; da Costa, *Rio de Janeiro*, 3:363, 4:742, 761–3; Broca, *A vida literária*, pp. 21–2, 111, 112, 119; Fabio Luz, "Elysio Carvalho," *Almanaque Brazileiro Garnier* 4 (1907): 295–6.

109 *Five o'clock*, p. 5.

110 Ibid., pp. 56–7.

111 Broca, *A vida literária* p. 149.

112 *A esfinje*, pp. 70–1.

113 See ibid., pp. 474–82, for Afrânio's dim views of contemporary Brazil, the prostitution of art, and the proper perspective on matters by the man of the world. On the phrase "a literatura é o sorriso da sociedade," see Broca, *A vida literaria*, p. 3; Bosi, *História* p. 220; he apparently meant literature was a reflection of its milieu, not its frivolous expression. For our purposes, there is little difference.

114 My information on D. Júlia is generally drawn from: do Rio, *O momento literario*, pp. 23–34; José Veríssimo, *Estudos*, 5:79–34; Sacramento Blake, s.v. "D. Júlia Lopes de Almeida"; for more on D. Júlia's place in the era, see Lucio Mendonça, "As tres Júlias" in *Almanaque Brasileiro Garnier* 4 (1907): 246–9; and Broca, *A vida literária* p. 252. See ibid. for Carmem Dolores, too.

115 See chapter 4.5

116 Martins, pp. 111–12, 195, 384.

117 See Hahner, "Feminism," 70–95, especially 86–95.

118 João da Cruz e Sousa (1861–98), perhaps the preeminent Brazilian Symbolist; see Costa, *Memórias* 2:547–58; Gonzaga Duque, "O poeta negro," *Kósmos* 6:2 (Feb. 1909); Bosi, *História*, pp. 302–10; Martins, pp. 50–4; Haberly, ch. 6.

119 Broca, *A vida literaria*, p. 57.

120 See Felinto de Almeida, quoted in do Rio, *O momento literario*, p. 29, and the

speculation of Machado Neto, p. 193. Cf. Mendonça, p. 249, and Lúcio Mendonça quoted in Magalhães Júnior, *Machado de Assis*, 3:287–8.

121 Do Rio, *O momento literario*, pp. 23–4 (suggestively entitled "An Artists' Home"). The first several pages suggest how unusual her vocation seemed to D. Júlia as a girl and the singular help her father was, arranging for her first published piece in a newspaper. Her attitude towards feminism is implicitly negative in the interview (p. 33). Cf. Mendonça, p. 247.

122 On D. Júlia's works, see Blake and the Martins citation in n. 116 above; on her *conferência*, see do Rio, *Psychologia urbana*, p. 9.

123 On women, salons, and Society in Rio, see chapters 3, 4.5; Veríssimo, *Estudos*, 3:46–7; Broca, *Românticos*, pp. 76–9; Mendonça, *passim*. On the contemporary situation in France, see Gordon Wright, *France in Modern Times* (New York: Norton, 1981), pp. 293–5; and the authors and special circumstances (so parallel to those of D. Júlia's and D. Carmem's) in Pierre-Olivier Walzer, *Le xxe siècle* (Paris: Arthaud, 1975), ch. 6 and pp. 376, 393.

124 My information on Sílvio Romero is drawn from: Mello e Sousa, *O método crítico*; Cruz Costa, pp. 187–97; Carlos Süsekind de Mendonça, *Sílvio Romero* (São Paulo: Nacional, 1938), chs. 2, 3; do Rio, *O momento literario*, pp. 35–49; Veríssimo, *Estudos*, 1:ch. 3; 6:ch. 1; García Mérou, chs. 6–8; Magalhães Júnior, *Machado de Assis*, 2:ch.49, 44:chs. 78, 79; Broca, *A vida literária*, pp. 66–7, 199–204.

125 See the analysis of Taine's enduring determinist metaphysics in Charlton, pp. 130–1, 132–3, 134, 139–54. Cf. Mello e Sousa, *O método crítico*, pp. 38–9, 46, 51–8, 72–5, 108–16; Sílvio's position is made clear in the methodological introduction to his greatest work – see *História da literatura brasileira*, 5 vols. (Rio de Janeiro: José Olympio, 1949) 1: pt.1, chs. 3–6, pt.3, pt.4, and, pp. 331–7.

126 Romero quoted in Rio, *O momento literario*, p. 47.

127 "Discurso do Sr. Sylvio Romero," RABL 2 (1911): 484, 485. His self-conception as champion of the "real" Brazil derived from his provincial, rural past; see his deposition in do Rio, *O momento literario*, pp. 39, 43.

128 My information on José Verissimo is drawn from: J. A. Barbosa; João Alexandre Barbosa, "Introdução" in Veríssimo, *Estudos*, 1; García Mérou, pp. 90–6, chs. 9–12; Broca, *A vida literária*, pp. 63–6, 199–204; Magalhães Júnior, *Machado de Assis* 3: 178–9, 192–5, 276–9, 4: ch. 83, *passim*.

129 See J. A. Barbosa, *A tradição do impasse*, chs. 3, 4; Magalhães Júnior, *Machado de Assis* as cited in n.43 above. For examples of his *belle-époque* work, see the six volumes of *Estudos de literatura brasileira* cited here and his *Historia da literatura brasileira* (Rio de Janeiro: Francisco Alves, 1929). On his models, Anatole France and Jules Lemaître, see Chevalier, ch. 3; Raymond Pouilliart, *Le romantisme* (Paris), pp. 162–3, 263.

130 See chapter 1.9, 10.

131 Quoted in Broca, *A vida literária*, p. 65.

132 See ibid., pp. 66–7, 199; Albuquerque, 2: 156–7; Ronald D. Dennis, "Brazilian literary nationalism among the critics, 1870–1900." (PhD diss., Wisconsin, 1972), pp. 140–2.

133 See Broca, *A vida literária*, pp. 63–5, 199–200; J. A. Barbosa, *A tradição do impasse*, pp. 63–7, 75–6, 161–8, ch. 5, *passim*.

134 My information on Euclides da Cunha and Lima Barreto is drawn from (for Euclides) Sílvio Romero, "Discurso de recepção" and *História*, 5:402–22; Veríssimo, *Estudos*, 5:ch.6; Francisco Venancio Filho, *Euclydes da Cunha a seus amigos* (São

Paulo: Nacional, 1938); Gilberto Freyre, *Perfil de Euclides e outros perfis* (Rio de Janeiro: José Olympio, 1944), pp. 21–63; Sylvio Rabello, *Euclides da Cunha* (Rio de Janeiro: Civilização Brasileira, 1966); Sevcenko, chs. 3, 4, *passim*; Martins, *História*, pp. 3–6, 203–17; Bosi, *História*, pp. 344–53; Euclides [Rodrigues Pimenta] da Cunha, *Rebellion in the Backlands* (Chicago: 1944); and Walnice Nogueira Galvão's critical edition of *Os sertões* (São Paulo: Brasiliense, 1985); (for Lima Barreto) Lima Barreto, *Correspondência*, 2 vols.; [Afonso Henriques de] Lima Barreto, *Diário íntimo* (São Paulo: Brasiliense, 1961); Francisco de Assis Barbosa, *Lima Barreto*; Sevcenko, chs. 3, 5, *passim*; Bosi, *História*, pp. 355–65; see also Maria Luisa Nunes, *Lima Barreto* (Boston: G. K. Hall, 1979).

135 See Euclides' letters of the mid-1890s, e.g. to the *Gazeta de Noticias*, Rio, 18 Feb. 1894 and 20 Feb. 1894; to Gen. Solon Ribeiro, São Paulo, 10 Jan. 1895, and his letters concerning *Os sertões*: to José Veríssimo, Lorena, 3 Dec. 1903; to Meu Pai [i.e., My Father (Manuel Rodrigues Pimenta da Cunha)], Lorena, 25 Feb. 1903; and, Lorena, 12 June 1903; to Dr. Affonso Celso, Lorena, 17 July 1903; to [Francisco] Escobar, Lorena, 24 July 1903; to Meu Pai, Lorena, 22 Sept. 1903; to Machado de Assis, Lorena, 22 Sept. 1903; to Lucio de Mondonça, s.l., s.d. [1904?]; to Coelho Neto, Rio, 22 April 1904 (all letters from the collection in Venancio Filho, pp. 56–122; *passim*). See, also, Freyre, *Perfil de Euclides*, pp. 25–6; and, most especially, Sevcenko, pp. 146–54.

136 Da Cunha, *Os sertões*, p. 86.

137 Euclydes [da Cunha], to [Francisco] Escobar, Lorena, 10 Aug. 1902; to Escobar, Lorena, 19 Oct. 1902; to Meu Pai, Lorena, 19 Feb. 1903 (in Venancio Filho, pp. 74–83, *passim*); Rabello, pp. 87–91, 137–70; Freyre, *Perfil de Euclides*, pp. 46–7.

138 Quoted in Venancio Filho, p. 83.

139 Ibid. p. 85.

140 See Martins, pp. 3–6 (but cf. Rabello, p. 171); and the thorough reconstruction of the coverage of the Canudos campaign in Walnice Nogueira Galvão, *No calor da hora*.

141 See Romero, *História*, 5:402; even Verissimo, who censured Euclides' "technical terms," "archaisms," and "neologisms," was exceptionally impressed (*Estudos*, 5:45–7, 53); see the résumé of critical response in Rabello, pp. 181–7; Olímpio de Sousa Andrade, *História e interpretação de "Os sertões*," (São Paulo: Edart, 1966), pp. 299–303. See also Freyre's apt comments in *Perfil de Euclides*, pp. 22–4; and Sevcenko, pp. 133–6. Cf. Martins' study of the links between Euclides' style and that of his contemporaries (pp. 204–14).

142 See the summary analysis in Sevcenko, pp. 133–4.

143 See, e.g., Romero, "Discurso de recepção," pp. 468–9 and *História*, 5:417–21; Veríssimo, *Estudos*, 5:45, 46–7, 50, 51; Araripe Júnior, quoted in Sousa Andrade, pp. 301–2.

144 Romero, "Discurso de recepção," p. 469.

145 See Euclydes da Cunha to José Verissimo, Lorena, 3 Dec. 1902 and to [Francisco] Escobar, Lorena, 27 Nov. 1903, in Venancio Filho, pp. 79–80, 113.

146 See chapter 4.4.

147 Lima Barreto's understanding of Carioca elite fantasy and race and class prejudice is clear in his published fiction (see below); in his private writings race and class issues are naturally even more harshly voiced: see, e.g., on racism, *Diário íntimo*, pp. 61–2, 76, 81–2, 84, 88, 109–10, 130–2.

148 Lima Barreto, ibid., p. 135.
149 Lima Barreto, Rio Preto conferência, quoted in Francisco de Assis Barbosa, "Prefácio" to *Recordações . . . Isaías Caminha*, pp. 19–20.
150 On his literary influences, see, e.g., *Diário íntimo*, pp. 36, 44, 57, 94, 145, 146, 147; F. de A. Barbosa, "Prefácio," pp. 11, 13, 20; and his *A vida de Lima Barreto*, pp. 138–9 (and the appended library inventory); Sevcenko, pp. 164–7. On his greater discrimination *vis-à-vis* Euclides, see ibid., pp. 123–4, and, specifically, on his views of scientific racism, *Diário íntimo*, pp. 110–12.
151 See Martins, pp. 52–3; Bosi, *História*, pp. 302–10; and, especially, Haberly, ch. 6.
152 *Morte e vida de M. J. Gonzaga de Sá* (São Paulo: Estante Panorama, 1943), pp. 57, 59. Lima Barreto's reference to Sá refers to Rio's founder, Martim Afonso de Sá; a *cafuso* was a person of mixed Amerindian and African and European descent; a "gallego" is a pejorative term for a poor Portuguese immigrant. See, also, ibid., pp. 57–60, 121–2, 122–3, 138; Sevcenko, pp. 123–4.
153 See ibid. and Broca, *A vida literária*, ch. 10.
154 See Romero, *História*, 5:417–18.
155 On the publication and character of *Isaías Caminha* see F. de A. Barbosa, *A vida de Lima Barreto*, 3a. pt.: chs. 5, 6, *passim*. On the personal and critical aspects, see *Isaías Caminha*, pp. 67–70 (attack on João do Rio), 119–20 (attack on literati and literature in Rio), 134–8, 185 (attack on fashionable revolutionary pretensions), 138–9 (allusions to João do Rio's homosexuality and its usefulness in terms of public attention), (attack on Edmundo Bittencourt, editor of the *Correio da Manhã*), 174, 178, 182 (fashionable, frivolous character of the Carioca), 190 (journalistic collusion with the politically powerful), etc.
156 Veríssimo did review the first chapters in passing, in a more general notice of an ephemeral review edited by Lima Barreto (*Floreal*); he wrote a letter of criticism to the author on later receipt of the completed book. Only two critics, Madeiros e Albuquerque and Alcides Maia, reviewed the work as such, criticizing its personalist nature. See José Veríssimo to Lima Barreto, Riachuelo, 5 March 1910, in Lima Barreto, *Correspondência*, 1:203–5 and *Diário íntimo*, pp. 125–6; F. de A. Barbosa, *Lima Barreto*, 3a. pt.: ch. 6, *passim*. On the question of style, see Lima Barreto quoted in ibid., pp. 240–2, 247; *Diário íntimo*, pp. 133–4; Veríssimo to Lima Barreto, Riachuelo, 5 March 1910 *Correspondência*, 1:205; Lima Barreto to Gonzaga Duque, Todos os Santos, 7 Feb. 1909, ibid. 2:169; Sevcenko, pp. 164–9.
157 Lima Barreto to Monteiro Lobato, s.l., 4 Jan. 1919, in *Correspondência*, 2:56.
158 Quoted in F. de A. Barbosa, *Lima Barreto*, p. 277.
159 Lima Barreto to Monteiro Lobato, s.l., s.d., ibid. 2:69
160 Monteiro Lobato to Lima Barreto, s.l., 25 April 1919, ibid. 2:70.
161 On Lima Barreto's bohemianism, illness, and literary following, which actually extended to the first Modernists, see F. de A. Barbosa,, *Lima Barreto*, 4a, pt.: chs. 2, 3, *passim*, 5a, pt.: chs. 3, 4, 6a. pt.; pp. 353–9; and "Epílogo," *passim*. His *Diário íntimo* details his personal agony at decline: see, pp. 32, 41, 51, 57, 76–7, 81, 84, 88, 91, 94, 135–6. On his leftism and the leftist press, see F. de A. Barbosa, *Lima Barreto*, 5a. pt.: ch. 2 and, pp. 266–9; Sodré, pp. 350–70, *passim*; Sevcenko, pp. 189–92.
162 See, e.g., Coelho Netto, "Discurso de Coelho Netto," RABL 4 (1912); O. B. [Olavo Bilac], "Chronica," *Kósmos*, 2:5 (May 1905); João do Rio, "O Chá e as

visitas," or "A era do automóvel" in *Vida vertiginosa* (Rio de Janeiro: H. Garnier, 1911).

163 *Diário íntimo*, pp. 92–4. The word derives from Jules de Gaultier's celebrated *Le bovarysme*, which Lima Barreto read closely, with the satisfaction that came from reviewing arguments already formulated in his own thinking. See F. de A. Barbosa, *Lima Barreto*, pp. 139–40; Sevcenko, pp. 177–8. Sevcenko observes how important the concept was to *Policarpo Quaresma*.

164 On the circumstances of Machado's death, see Langgaard Meneses, *Minhas memórias*, (1979), p. 85; Euclydes da Cunha, "A última visita," *Renascença*, 5:55 (Sept. 1908): 98; Carlos Magalhães de Azeredo to Fabio Ramos Paz, Rome, 21 Oct. 1908, BNSM, Col. Ramos Paz: I–4, 7, 41; Miguel-Pereira, ch. 20. On Machado's status, see the citations in n. 43, above.

165 This opinion of Machado as essentially apart and superior has become a commonplace. Veríssimo changed what he meant by it but not the characterization, and Antônio Cândido has put the matter before us lately with his usual mastery: see Veríssimo, *Estudos*, 3:25, 26–7, 29–30; ibid., 5:80; ibid., 6:105–7; *Historia*, pp. 41, 419–20, 422–8, 430–1; Mello e Sousa, *Vários escritos*, pp. 17, 21–3. See, also, the Magalhães Júnior citations in n. 43, above.

166 Except where noted, I rely on Magalhães Júnior, *Machado de Assis* for my account of Machado's career.

167 Quoted in Montello, p. 29.

168 Costa, *Rio* 4:708. On the special role of Garnier's, see ibid. 4:ch. 23; João Luso, "Typos e symbolos," *Kósmos*, 5:11 (Nov. 1908); Broca, *A vida literária*, ch. 4.

169 Mello e Sousa, *Formação*, 2:118–19.

170 Ibid. and Coutinho, "Estudo crítico," pp. 29–33, 43–4.

171 Veríssimo, *Estudos*, 3:29; ibid., 6:105–6; *História*, pp. 422–4; Broca, *Machado de Assis*, pp. 204–8; Mello e Sousa, *Formação*, 2:109–19; Coutinho, "Estudo crítico," pp. 34–9.

172 "Notícia da Atual Literatura Brasileira" in *Obra completa*, 3:804.

173 Schwarz, pt. 3; cf. Haberly, ch. 5, *passim*. The great study of Second Reign society in the work of Machado is Faoro's *Machado de Assis*.

174 See Veríssimo, *Estudos*, 3:29; ibid., 6:105–6; *História*, pp. 422–4; Olavo Bilac, quoted in Magalhães Júnior, *Machado de Assis*, 4:212–13; Mello e Sousa, *Formação*, 2:115; *Vários escritos*, pp. 17–18; Coutinho, "Estudo crítico," pp. 31–2, 34.

175 *Ressurreição*, in *Obra completa*, 1:118.

176 *Dom Casmurro*, in ibid., 1:821.

177 *Memorial de Aires*, in ibid., 1:1105.

178 See, e.g., José Maria de A. Bello, "Machado de Assis" in *Kósmos* 6:4 (April 1909) and Mello e Sousa, *Vários escritos*, pp. 18–20.

179 Bello, "Machado de Assis," p. 44.

180 Romero, "Discurso do Sr. Sylvio Romero", RABL 2:490–97; Sevcenko, pp. 96, 25–41, 93–108, *passim*. See, also, Chapter 1.10, 11; Jeffrey D. Needell, "Rio de Janeiro at the turn of the century," *Journal of Interamerican studies and World Affairs* 25:1 (Feb. 1983).

181 Schwarz, ch. 2. On Machado as Alencar's heir, see, e.g., Mello e Sousa, *Formação*, 2:118.

182 See, e.g., Pierrot, pp. 170–1; Shattuck, ch. 1, *passim*; Hauser, 4:166–8, 175–88, *passim*.

183 Broca, *A vida literária*, pp. 3–4, 272; cf. Machado Neto, pp. 214–31.

184 In this sense, Dimas' link between the Avenida Central and *Kósmos* in the symbolic sense (in that they both celebrated Civilization and Progress), complete with photographs of the new boulevard's façades and Parisian perspective, is to the point (see pp. 133–6).

Appendix – Defining the elite

1 See the three joint studies of regional elites integral to the work of Levine, Love, and Wirth, cited in Chapter 1.4. Each discusses their joint methodology regarding the elite in an appendix. See, e.g., John Wirth, *Minas Gerais in the Brazilian Federation*, Appendix A, pp. 237–41. Another example is Barman and Barman, pp. 424–6, in which the political position of the elite is explicitly assumed. If political office is understood broadly to mean state bureaucratic position, still another example is José Murilo de Carvalho's work; see his "Elite"; *A construção da ordem* (Rio de Janeiro: Campus, 1980); and "Political elites and state building," *Comparative Studies in Society and History*, 24:3 (July 1982) 378–99.

2 See e.g. C. Nabuco, *Oito décadas* p. 58, or "Binoculo" in *Gazeta de Noticias*, 24 August 1908. A sophisticated review of the literature and the question of definition is Joseph L. Love and Berk J. Barickman, "Rulers and owners," HAHR, 66, 4 (November 1986).

3 The person with whom I spoke was Luíz Carlos de Paranaguá (interview, Rio de Janeiro, 1 September 1980), great-great grandson of the Marquis de Montserate, great-grandson of the Marquis de Paranaguá (whose sister was a favorite of the Imperial Heiress), grandson of the Conde de Paranaguá, son of a career diplomat.

4 To be precise, 235,381. The figures and other information are drawn from the extract published in the 1906 census. See Republica dos Estados Unidos do Brazil. [Directoria Geral do Estatística], on *Recenseamento do Rio de Janeiro (Districto Federal) . . . 1906*. (Rio de Janeiro: Officina de Estatística, 1907), p. 100. For discussion of such material and its problematic nature, see Lahmeyer Lobo.

5 See Ministerio da Industria, Viação e Obras Publicas. *Recenseamento geral . . . 1890*, pp. 408–15.

6 See Republica, *Recenseamento . . . 1906*, pp. 388–9.

7 See the list in Vilella dos Santos, *Jockey-Club* pp. 437–8.

8 See Eugênio Gudin [pai], quoted in Nelson Pinto, *Historia de fusão do Automovel Club com o Club dos Diarios* (Rio de Janiero: Automóvel Club do Brasil, 1938), p. 9.

9 See "Documento 6 de Fevereiro de 1856" in Arquivo do Automóvel Club do Brasil, "Documentos de valor histórico," Vol. 1: 1856–1907.

10 See "Sócios accionistas do Cassino Fluminense 1862" in ibid.

Bibliography

Abbreviations

HAHR = *Hispanic American Historical Review*
JISWA = *Journal of Interamerican Studies and World Affairs*
JLAS = *Journal of Latin American Studies*
LARR = *Latin American Research Review*
LBR = *Luso-Brazilian Review*
RABL = *Revista da Academia Brasileira de Letras*
RIHBG = *Revista do Instituto Histórico e Geográfico Brasileiro*

Interview sources

Carlos Miguel Delgado de Carvalho, Copacabana, Rio de Janeiro, 14 May 1980.
Carlos da Ponte Ribeiro Eiras, Flamengo, Rio de Janeiro, 25 July 1980.
Gilberto Ferrez and Mary Ferrez, Largo de Leões, Rio de Janeiro, 11 July 1980.
Américo Jacobina Lacombe, Botafogo, Rio de Janeiro, 15 September 1980.
Alceu Amoroso Lima, Centro and Flamengo, Rio de Janeiro, 2 and 3 October 1980.
Irmã Carmem Maria, Cosme Velho, Rio de Janeiro, 22 September 1980.
Marcos Carneiro de Mendonça, Cosme Velho, Rio de Janeiro 10 and 15 July 1980.
Paulo Braga de Menezes, Centro, Rio de Janeiro, 4 July 1980.
Carolina Nabuco, Botafogo, Rio de Janeiro, 9, 11, and 19 June 1980.
José Thomaz Nabuco, Centro, Rio de Janeiro, 2 June 1980.
Luíz Carlos de Paranaguá, Lagôa Rodrigo de Freitas, Rio de Janeiro, 1 September 1980.
Luíz Carlos de Paranaguá and Paulo H. de Paranaguá, Centro, Rio de Janeiro, 15 July 1986.
Yolanda Penteado, Stanford University, Stanford, California, 16 September 1981.
Gilberto Trompowsky, Tijuca, Rio de Janeiro, 13 June 1980.

Archival sources

All archival sources noted are in the city of Rio de Janeiro. The abbreviations noted in brackets refer to those used in the text.
Arquivo do Automóvel Club do Brasil (AACB).
Arquivo do Colégio Pedro II. (NB, unless otherwise noted, references to the school archive refer to the one located at the old Externato, rather than the São Cristóvão branch).

Arquivo Geral da Cidade do Rio de Janeiro.
Arquivo Histórico do Instituto Histórico e Geográfico Brasileiro (AHIHGB). Coleção do Instituto Histórico. Coleção Max Fleuiss.
Biblioteca Nacional, Seção de Manuscritos (BNSM). Cartas Avulsas. Coleção Jaguaribe. Coleção Francisco Carlos da Luz. Coleção Salvador de Mendonça. Coleção Ramos Paz. Coleção Ernesto Senna.
Casa de Rui Barbosa, Arquivo Histórico, Correspondência (RBAHC): Azeredo, Antônio Francisco de; Castro, Violeta Lima e; Clubes; Gama, Saldanha da; Haritoff, Mauricio; Mayrink, Francisco de Paula.
Documentos Pereira Passos, Museu da República, Palácio do Catete. (DPP).

Contemporary Carioca periodical sources

Correio da Manhã
Gazeta de Noticias
A Illustração Brasileira
Jornal do Commercio
Kósmos
O Malho
O Paiz
A Renascença
A Revista da Semana (Jornal do Brasil)
The Rio News
Rua do Ouvidor

Primary sources

Abranches [Moura,] [J.] D. de., *Actos e actas do Governo Provisorio*. Rio de Janeiro: Nacional, 1907.
Como se faziam presidentes. Rio de Janeiro: José Olympio, 1973.
Adam, P. *Les visages du Brésil*, Paris: Pierre Lafitte, 1914.
Agassiz, L. and Agassiz, [E. C. C.] *A Journey in Brazil*. (Boston: Felds, Osgood, 1871.
Albuquerque [J. J. de C. da C.], M. e. *Minha vida*, 2 vols. Rio de Janeiro: Calvino Filho, 1933–4.
Alexander, A., *Gymnasio Nacional*. Rio de Janeiro: Nacional, 1908.
Almanak administrativo, mercantil e industrial do Rio de Janeiro (*Almanak Laemmert*). Rio de Janeiro: Laemmert, 1895, 1900, 1905.
Almanaque brazileiro Garnier para o anno 1904. Rio de Janeiro: Garnier, 1907.
Almeida, J. L. de. *Livro das noivas*. Rio de Janeiro: n.p., 1896.
Almeida [J. R.], P. de. *Hygiene moral*. Rio de Janeiro: Laemmert, 1906.
Alves Filho [F. de P.] R. "Rodrigues Alves" in F. de A. Barbosa, *Retratos de família*.
Alves, C., "Discurso de recepção do sr. Constáncio Alves," *RABL*, 12 (1922).
Amado, G. "As instituições políticas e o meio social no Brasil" in A. C. Leão et. al. *À margem da história da República*.
História da minha infância. Rio de Janeiro: José Olympio, 1958.
Minha formação no Recife. Rio de Janeiro: José Olympio, 1955.
Mocidade no Rio e primeira viagem à Europa, Rio de Janeiro: José Olympio, 1956.
Presença na política. Rio de Janeiro: José Olympio, 1960.
Andrews, C. C. *Brazil*. New York: D. Appleton, 1889.

Araripe Júnior [T. de A.], "Recordações do Club Rabelais," *RABL*, 2 (1911).
Obra crítica de Araripe Júnior, 2 vols. Rio de Janeiro: MEC/Casa de Rui Barbosa, 1960.
Arquivo do Automóvel Club. "Documentos de valor histórico," 2 vols (MSS) Rio de Janeiro: 1856–1907, 1908–76.
Assis, [J. M.] M. de. "Discurso de Machado de Assis, presidente" in "Discursos proferidos na Academia Brazileira," *RABL*, 1 (1910).
"Notícia da atual literatura brasileira" in [J. M.] M. de Assis, *Obra completa*.
Chronicas, 4 vols. São Paulo: Wm. Jackson, 1942.
Chronicas – Crítica – Poesia – Teatro. São Paulo: Cultrix, 1964.
Esaú e Jacob, São Paulo: Wm. Jackson, 1942.
A mão e a luva. São Paulo: Wm. Jackson, 1942.
Obra completa, 3 vols. Rio de Janeiro: José Aguilar, 1962.
A Semana, 3 vols. Rio de Janeiro: Wm. Jackson, 1944.
Associação do Quarto Centenario do Descobrimento do Brasil, *Livro do centenario*, 4 vols. Rio de Janeiro: Nacional, 1900.
Aurevilly, J. B. d'. *Les oeuvres complètes de Jules Barbey d'Aurevilly*, vol. 9. Paris: François Bernourard, 1927.
Azevedo, R. de, *Meu livro de saudades*. Rio de Janeiro: Freitas Bastos, 1938.
Bacharéis em lettras pelo Imperial Collegio de Pedro II e Gymnasio Nacional. Rio de Janeiro: n.p., *c*. 1896.
Backheuser, E., "Onde moram os pobres," *Renascença*, nos. 1, 3 (March, May 1904).
Balzac, H. de, *Oeuvres diverses*, 2 vols. Paris: Louis Conrad, 1938.
Barbosa, F. de A. *Retratos de família*. Rio de Janeiro: José Olympio, 1956.
Testamento de Mário de Andrade e outras reportagens. Rio de Janeiro: MEC, 1954.
Barbosa, M. A. [V. B. R.] and Barbosa, M. A. [R.]. "Rui Barbosa," in F. de A. Barbosa, *Retratos de família*.
Barreto, [A. H. de] L. *Correspondência*, 2 vols. São Paulo: Brasiliense, 1961.
Diário íntimo. São Paulo: Brasiliense, 1961.
Morte e vida de M. J. Gonzaga de Sá. São Paulo: Estante Panorama, 1943.
Recordações do escrivão Isaías Caminha. São Paulo: Brasiliense, 1968.
Barros, J. de. "Chronica," *Renascença*, 1, no. 3 (May 1904).
"Chronica," *Renascença*, 1, no. 4 (June 1904).
"Pedro Americo," *Renascença*, 4, no. 21 (Nov. 1905).
Bell, A. G., *The Beautiful Rio de Janeiro*. London, Heinemann, 1914?.
Bello, J. M. de A., "Machado de Assis" in *Kósmos*, 6, no. 4 (April 1909).
"O que se lê entre nós" in J. M. Bello, *Novos estudos críticos*.
Novos estudos críticos. Rio de Janeiro: Revista dos Tribunaes, 1914.
Bennet, F. *Forty Years in Brazil*. London: Mills and Born, 1914.
Bertaut, J. "Marcel Prévost" in *Les célébritiés d'aujourd'hui*, vol. 4.
"Bibliotheca Nacional, o futuro edifício," *Renascença*, 2, no. 8 (Oct. 1905).
Bicalho, M. L. "Notre mère Angelina" in Collège de Sion, *Reminiscencias*.
Bilac, O. [B. M. dos G.] "Chronica," *Kósmos*, 1, no.3 (March 1904).
"Chronica," *Kósmos*, 2, no.5 (May 1905).
"Chronica," *Kósmos*, 2, no.11 (November 1905).
"Chronica," *Kósmos*, 3, no.6 (June 1906).
"Chronica," *Kósmos*, 3, no.8 (August 1906).
"Chronica," *Kósmos*, 4, no.5 (May 1907).
Conferencias literarias. Rio de Janeiro: Francisco Alves, 1912.
Ironia e piedade. Rio de Janeiro: Francisco Alves, 1916.

Binzer, I. von. *Os meus romanos*. Rio de Janeiro: Paz e Terra, 1980.
Blake, S., *Diccionario bibliographico brazileiro*, 7 vols. Rio de Janeiro: Nacional, 1888–1902.
Brousson, J.-J. *Itinéraire de Paris a Buenos-Ayres*. Paris: Crès, 1927.
Burke, U. R. and Staples, Jr., R. *Business and Pleasure in Brazil*. London: ye Leadenhalle, 1884.
Burnichon, J., S. J. *Le Brésil d'aujourd'hui*. Paris: Académique, Perrin, 1910.
Cané, M. *En viaje*. Buenos Aires: n.p., 1949.
Cardoso, V. L. (ed.), see Leão.
Carette, Mme. *Recollections of the Court of the Tuileries*. New York: Appleton, 1890.
Carvalho, E. de. "Diplomatas extrangeiros," *Kósmos*, 6, nos. 3, 5 (March, May 1909).
"Raros e impassivos" in E. de Carvalho, *As modernas correntes esthéticas na literatura brazileira*.
Esplendor e decadencia da sociedade brazileira. Rio de Janeiro: Garnier Irmãos, 1911.
Five o'clock. Rio de Janeiro: H. Garnier, 1909.
As modernas correntes esthéticas na literatura brazileira. Rio de Janeiro: H. Garnier, 1907.
Carvalho, J. C. de M. "Pulcherrima Rerum," *Kósmos*, 1, no.9 (Sept. 1904).
Carvalho, V. R. D. de. "Sob a proteção de Santa Cecília . . ." in Collège de Sion, *Reminiscencias*.
Castellane [M. P. E. B. de C.], Marquis de. *Confessions of the Marquis de Castellane*. London: Thornton Butterworth, 1926.
Les célébrités d'aujourd'hui, 5 vols. Paris: E. Sansot, 1904.
Celso [A. C. de A. F., conde de] A. "Chronica musical," *Renascença*, 3, no.12 (February 1905).
Oito annos de parlamento São Paulo: Melhoramentos, 1928.
"Chronica Musical," *Renascença*, 2, no.9 (November 1904).
Coaracy, V. "Gymnasio Nacional," rpt. in I. Marinho and L. Inneco, *O Colegio Pedro II cem anos depois*.
Anuário do Colégio Pedro II. Rio de Janeiro: Nacional, 1944.
Collège de Sion. *Reminiscencias*. Petrópolis: Vozes, 1938.
Colégio Pedro II. *Anuário do Colégio Pedro II, vol. IX, 1935–36*. Rio de Janeiro: Rua da Misericórdia, 1939.
Anuario do Collegio Pedro II . . . 1° anno. Rio de Janeiro: Revista dos Tribunaes, 1914.
Collegio Pedro II. "Regulamento do Collegio Pedro II (1911)," rpt. in Collegio Pedro II, *Annuario do Collegio Pedro II . . . 1° anno*.
Commissão do Saneamento do Rio de Janeiro. *Relatorios apresentados ao Exm. Sr. Dr. Prefeito Municipal pelos drs. Manoel Victorino Pereira . . . e Nuno de Andrade . . . 31 de Agosto de 1896*. Rio de Janeiro: Nacional, 1896.
"Concurso de fachadas para a Avenida Central," *Renascença*, no.2 (April 1904).
"Copiada ata da Assembléia Geral Extraordinária do Club dos Diários, 27 de Setembro de 1924" (MS) in Arquivo do Automóvel Club do Brazil, "Documentos de Valor Histórico", vol. 2.
Correa, I. S. *Uma figura da República*. Rio de Janeiro: Freitas Bastos, 1959.
Correia, L. *A bohemia do meu tempo*. Rio de Janeiro: Estado do Paraná, 1955.
Costa, F. A. P. da, *Dicionario biographico de pernambucanos celebres*. Recife: Universal, 1882.
Costa, L. E. da. *O Rio de Janeiro do meu tempo*, 5 vols. Rio de Janeiro: Conquista, 1957.
De um livro de memórias, 5 vols. Rio de Janeiro: Nacional, 1958.

Couto, P. do, "Sylvio Romero" in Colégio Pedro II, *Anúario do Colégio Pedro II vol. IX, 1935–36.*

Cunha, E. [R. P.] da. "Discurso de Euclydes da Cunha" in "Discursos Proferidos na Academia Brazileira," *RABL*, 2 (1911).

"A última visita," *Renascença*, 5, no.55 (September 1908).

Rebellion in the Backlands. Chicago: 1944.

Os sertões. São Paulo: Brasiliense, 1985.

Denis, F. *Résumé de l'histoire littéraire du Brésil*. Paris: Lecointe et Durey, 1826.

Dent, H. C. *A Year in Brazil*. London: Kegan Paul, French, 1886.

"Documento 6 de Fevereiro de 1856" in Arquivo do Automóvel Club do Brasil, "Documentos de Valor Histórico," vol. 1.

Dória [L. G.], d'E. "Discurso do orador official do collegio: Prof. Luíz d'Escragnolle Dória" in I. Marinho and L. Inneco, *O Colégio Pedro II cem anos depois*.

Memória histórica commemorativa do 1° centenário do Colégio Pedro II. Rio de Janeiro: Educação, 1937.

Duque [Estrada], [L. de] G. "O cabaret de Yvonne: (Recordação de um tempo)," *Kósmos*, 5, no.11 (November 1908).

"Chronica de saudade," *Kòsmos*, 5, no.10 (October 1908).

"Paisagens," *Kósmos*, 4, no.6 (June 1907).

"No tempo de 'Gazetinha'," *Kósmos*, 5, no.9 (September 1908).

"O poeta negro," *Kósmos*, 6, no.2 (February 1909).

Mocidade morta. (Rio de Janeiro: Moderna, 1899).

Edgcumbe, P. *Zephyrus*. London: Chatto and Windus, 1887.

Expilly, C. *Mulheres e costumes do Brasil*. São Paulo: Nacional, 1935.

"A Exposição de 1905," *Renascença*, 4, no.20 (October 1905).

Ferrez, M. *O álbum da Avenida Central*. Rio de Janeiro: Ex Libris, 1982.

Avenida Central. Rio de Janeiro: E. Bevilacqua, 1906.

Fletcher, J. C. and Kidder, D. P. *Brazil and the Brazilians Portrayed in Historical and Descriptive Sketches*. Boston: Little Brown, 1866.

Fogliani, G. *Projecto de melhoramentos na cidade do Rio de Janeiro*. Rio de Janeiro: F. Borgonovo, 1903.

Fogliani, G. and Araujo, F. "Considerações" in G. Fogliani, *Projecto de melhoramentos na cidade do Rio de Janeiro*.

França Júnior, [J. J. de]. *Folhetins*. Rio de Janeiro: *Gazeta de Noticias*, 1878.

Frias [S de F, visconde de] S. de. *Arthur Napoleão*. Lisbon: n.p., 1913.

Gama [N. A. N. V. da G.], Visconde de N. da. *Minhas memórias*. (Paris: Garnier, 1893).

García Mérou, M. *El Brasil intelectual*. Buenos Aires: Félix Lajouane, 1900.

Garrett, A. "Bosquejo da história da poesia e língua portuguesa" in A. Garrett, *Parnaso lusitano*.

Parnaso lusitano. Paris: Aillaud, 1826–7.

Gaultier, J. de. *Le bovarysme*. Paris: Cerf, 1892.

Gazeta de Noticias. *Questões municipais*. Rio de Janeiro: *Gazeta de Noticias*, 1905.

Gonçalves, J. B., Ministério da Viação e Obras Públicas, *Portos do Brazil*. Rio de Janeiro: Nacional, 1912.

Graham, M. [Lady Calcott], *Journal of a Voyage to Brazil and Residence There*. London: Longman, Hurst, Rees, Orme, Brown, and Green and J. Murray, 1824.

La grande encyclopédie. Paris; Lamirault, n.d.

Gronow, (R. H.) *The Reminiscences and Recollections of Captain Gronow*. New York, Viking, 1964.

Gymnasio Nacional. *Programa de ensino . . . 1892*. Rio de Janeiro: Nacional, 1892.
Hasslocher, P. "Fui elegante por amor ao Brasil" in F. de A. Barbosa, *Testamento de Mário de Andrade e outras reportagens*.
Hilliard, H. *Politics and Penpictures at Home and Abroad*. New York: G. P. Putnam, 1892.
Humphrey, A. R. *A Summer Journey to Brazil*. New York: Bonnell, Silver, 1900.
Imperial Collegio de Pedro II. "Horario das aulas do Imperial Collegio de Pedro II para o anno de 1882," attached to Imperial Collegio de Pedro II, *Programa do ensino . . . 1881*.
Plano e programa . . . 1876. Rio de Janeiro: Nacional, 1877.
Programa do ensino . . . 1862. Rio de Janeiro: Nacional, 1862.
Programa do ensino . . . 1881. Rio de Janeiro: Nacional, 1882.
Lacerda, C. de F. "Nossa formação sionense" in Collège de Sion, *Reminiscencias*. Petrópolis: Vozes, 1938.
Lacombe, A. J. Carioca elite roster 1900 (MS). Rio de Janeiro: *c*. 24 September 1980, author's possession.
Lage and Cia. "Apresentação" in G. Fogliani, *Projecto de melhoramentos na cidade do Rio de Janeiro*.
Lamoureux, A. J. The Editors of *The Rio de Janeiro News, Handbook of Rio de Janeiro*. Rio de Janeiro: A. J. Lamoureux, 1887.
Latteux, P. *A travers le Brésil au pays de l'or et des diamants*. Paris: Aillaud, Alves, 1910.
Leclerc, M. *Lettres du Brésil*. Paris: Plon, 1890.
Lessa, C. R. de. "Recordações do antigo Internato Pedro II" in [Colégio Pedro II] *Anuário de Colégio Pedro II, vol. IX, 1935–36*.
Lima, A. de A. [pseud. Tristão de Ataíde]. "O Ginásio Nacional," rpt. in Colégio Pedro II, *Anuário do Colégio Pedro II*.
Lima [M. de], O. *Memorias*, Rio de Janeiro: José Olympio, 1937.
Lisboa, A. "A Avenida Central," *Kósmos*, 1, no. 11 (November 1904).
Lloyd, R. *et al*. (eds.) *Impressões do Brasil no século vinte*. London: Lloyd's Greater Britain, 1913.
Loliée, F. *Women of the Second Empire*. London: John Lane, 1907.
Lopes, T. "Buenos Aires," *Kósmos*, 5, nos. 3, 4, 8 (March–April, August 1908).
Luso, J. "Typos e symbolos," *Kósmos*, 5, no. 11 (November 1908).
Luz, F.[C.] "Elysio Carvalho," in *Almanaque Brazileiro Garnier para o anno 1904*.
Lyra, S. A. *Rosas de neve*. Rio de Janeiro: Cátedra, 1977.
Macedo, J. M. de. *Anno biographico brazileiro*, 3 vols. Rio de Janeiro: Imperial Instituto Artístico, 1876.
Memórias da rua do Ouvidor. São Paulo: Nacional, 1952.
Maria, Irmã Carmem. Memoir of the Collège de Sion (MS) (Rio de Janeiro, June 1980, in author's possession).
Marinho, I. and Inneco, L. *O Colegio Pedro II cem anos depois*. Rio de Janeiro: Villa Boas, 1938.
Martins, A. de R. *Um idealista realizador*. São Paulo: Laemmert, 1939.
Mattoso, E. *Cousas do meu tempo*. Bordeaux: Gounouilhou, 1916.
Maul, C. *O Rio da bela época*. Rio de Janeiro: São José, 1967.
Mendonça, L. "As tres Júlias" in *Almanaque Brasileiro Garnier para o anno 1904*.
Meneses, R. O. de L. *Minhas memorias dos outros*. Rio de Janeiro: José Olympio, 1934.
Minhas memorias dos outros. Rio de Janeiro: José Olympio, 1936.
Minhas memorias dos outros. Rio de Janeiro: Civilização Brasileira/MEC, 1979.
Ministerio da Industria, Viação e Obras Públicas. Directoria Geral de Estatistica,

Recenseamento geral da Republica dos Estados Unidos do Brazil . . . 1890. Rio de Janeiro: Leuzinger, 1895.
Montet, E. *Brésil et Argentine*. Geneva: Eggimann, *c*. 1890s?.
Moraes Filho [A. J. de], M. *Factos e memorias*. Rio de Janeiro, Garnier, 1904.
Morand, P. *1900 A. D*. New York: Farqhuar Payson, 1931.
Mossé, B. [agent for J. M. da S. Paranhos, baron do Rio Branco]. *Dom Pedro II*. Paris: Fermin-Didot, 1889.
Murger, H. *Scènes de la vie de bohème*. Paris: Michel Levy Frères, 1874.
Murtinho, J. "Relatório da indústria, viação e obras públicas," rpt. in *RIHGB*, no. 219 (1953).
Nabuco [de Araújo], J. [A. B.] "Discurso de Joaquim Nabuco, secretario geral" in "Discursos Proferidos . . .," *RABL* 1 (1910).
Abolitionism. Urbana: Chicago, 1977.
Cartas a amigos, 2 vols. São Paulo: Progresso, 1949.
Um estadista do Imperio, 3 vols. Rio de Janeiro: H. Garnier, 1897.
Minha formação. Paris: H. Garnier, 1900.
Nabuco, C. *Oito décadas*. Rio de Janeiro: José Olympio, 1973.
Nabuco, M. *Reminiscências sérias e frívolas*. Rio de Janeiro: Pongetti, 1969.
Netto [H. M.], C. "Discurso do sr. Coelho Netto" in "Discursos proferidos na Academia Brazileira," *RABL* 4 (1912),.
A conquista. Rio de Janeiro: Chardron, 1921.
Fogo fátuo. Porto: Chardron, 1929.
Obra seleta, 2 vols. Rio de Janeiro: José Aguilar, 1958.
Tormenta. Porto: Chardron, de Lello & Irmão, 1915.
Netto, Z. C. *Coelho Netto*. Rio de Janeiro: Simões, 1961.
Oliveira, C. B. de, *Águas passadas*. São Paulo: Edanec, 1956.
Oliveira, J. A. B. de. *Memorias de um magistrado do Império*. São Paulo: Nacional, 1943.
"Origens da congregação" in Collège de Sion, *Reminiscencias*.
Ortigão [J. D.], R. "O quadro social da revolução brazileira," *Revista de Portugal*, 2 (1890).
Passos, F. O. (Addendum to) Francisco Oliveira Passos to Dr. Euzébio Naylor, Rio, 21 Nov., 1950 (*Documentos Pereira Passos*, 7.8.2) in *Documentos Pereira Passos*, 7.3.3.
Passos, F. P. (Draft of "Cargo da Commissão de Melhoramentos da Cidade do Rio de Janeiro") in *Documentos Pereira Passos*, 4.11.12a.
(Draft opinion on "Estatutos da Escola Polytéchnica") Rio de Janeiro, 21 April 1874 in *Documentos Pereira Passos*, 4.16.1.
"Francisco Pereira Passos," Rio, November 1903, in *Documentos Pereira Passos*, 1.11.1.
"Uma entrevista com o Prefeito" in *Gazeta de Noticias, Questões municipais*.
"Impressões de um 'ex-dictador'" in *Gazeta de Noticias, Questões municipais*.
Melhoramentos projectados . . . Rio de Janeiro: Nacional?, 1903.
Mensagem do Prefeito . . . 1 de Setembro de 1903. Rio de Janeiro: *Gazeta de Noticias*, 1903.
Mensagem do Prefeito . . . 2 de Abril de 1904. Rio de Janeiro: *Gazeta de Noticias*, 1904.
Jardim, J. R. de M. and Silva, M. R. da. *Primeiro relatorio da Commissão de Melhoramentos da cidade do Rio de Janeiro*. Rio de Janeiro: Nacional, 1875.
Jardim, J. R. de M., and Silva, M. R. da. *Segundo relatorio da Commissão de Melhoramentos da cidade do Rio de Janeiro*. Rio de Janeiro: Nacional, 1876.
Pederneiras, M. "A vida de hoje," *Kósmos*, 5, no. 5 (May 1908).

Pederneiras, R. "A vida do estudante do Collegio Pedro II em 1884" in I. Marinho and L. Inneco, *O Colégio Pedro II cem anos depois*.
Peixoto, A. *A esfinje*. Rio de Janeiro: Francisco Alves, 1911.
Penteado, Y. *Tudo em cor-de-rosa*. São Paulo: ed. da autora, 1977.
Pimentel, A. M. de A. *Subsidios para o estudo de hygiene do Rio de Janeiro*. Rio de Janeiro: Silva, 1890.
Prates, S. N. M. de S. "Cincoenta anos de dedicação" in Collège de Sion, *Reminiscencias*.
Proust, M. *Remembrance of Things Past*, 7 vols. New York: Vintage, 1978.
Quesada, V. G. *Mis memórias diplomáticas*, 2 vols. Buenos Aires: Coni, 1907.
R., A. [Aarão Reis?] "Avenida à beira mar – Commentario" in *Gazeta de Noticias, Questões municipais*.
Rancourt, E. de. *Fazendas et estancias*. Paris: Plon, 1901.
Rangel, [A. A. de] S. "Os melhoramentos do Rio de Janeiro," *Renascença*, 1, no. 5 (July 1904).
"Melhoramentos da Cidade," *Renascença*, 1, no. 7 (September 1904).
"Melhoramentos da Cidade," *Renascença*, 1, no. 9 (November 1904).
"No. 30 – Commissão da Carta Cadastral do Districto Federal, em 13 de abril de 1903" in F. P. Passos, *Melhoramentos projectados* . . . Rio de Janeiro: Nacional 1903.
Rebouças, A. [P.] *Agricultura nacional*. Rio de Janeiro: A. J. Lamoureux, 1883.
Apontamentos para a biographia do engenheiro Antonio Pereira Rebouças Filho, Rio de Janeiro: Nacional, 1874.
Diário e notas autobiográficos. Rio de Janeiro: José Olympio, 1938.
A questão do Brazil. Lisbon: n.p., 1890.
Republica dos Estados Unidos do Brazil. (Directoria Geral da Estatistica), *Recenseamento do Rio de Janeiro (Districto Federal)*. Rio de Janeiro: Officina de Estatistica, 1906.
Rio, J. do [pseud. for Paulo Barreto]. "Conferencias Literarias" in *Almanaque Brasileiro Garnier para o anno 1904*.
"Discurso de Recepção " in J. do Rio, *Psychologia urbana*.
A alma encantadora das ruas. Rio de Janeiro: Simões, 1951.
Cinematographo. Rio de Janeiro: H. Garnier, 1911.
Dentro da noite. Rio de Janeiro: Garnier, 1910.
João do Rio. Rio de Janeiro: Sabiá, 1971.
O momento literario. Rio de Janeiro: H. Garnier, s.d.
Psychologia urbana. Rio de Janeiro: H. Garnier, 1911.
As religiões no Rio. Rio de Janeiro: Garnier, 1904.
Vida vertiginosa. Rio de Janeiro: Garnier, 1911.
Rocque, E. G. de La. *Gente da minha vida*. Petrópolis: Vozes, 1977.
Romero, S. [V. da S. R.], "Discurso do Sr. Sylvio Romero," *RABL*, 2 (1911).
"A litteratura" in Associação do Quarto Centenario, *Livro do centenario*, vol. 1.
"Resposta do Sr. Sylvio Romero" in "Discursos proferidos na Academia Brazileira," *RABL*, 2 (1911).
História da literatura brasileira, 5 vols. Rio de Janeiro: José Olympio, 1949.
Rosa, [F.] F. da, "Avenida Central," *Kósmos*, 2, no. 11 (November 1905).
Rio de Janeiro. Rio de Janeiro: Schmidt, 1905.
Santos, D. C. V. dos. "Cassino Fluminense," (MS in Arquivo do Automóvel Club do Brasil). Rio de Janeiro: 1909.
Jockey Club. Rio de Janeiro: Fluminense, 1922.
Santos, L. *Pantheon fluminense*. Rio de Janeiro: Leuzinger, 1880.
Seabra, G. "Teatro Municipal," *Renascença*, 5, no. 28 (June 1906).

Senna, E. *Deodoro*. Brasília: 1977.

Silva, J. B. P. da. "Reminiscências do Internato" in Colégio Pedro II, *Anuário do Colégio Pedro II*.

"Socios accionistas do Cassino Fluminense de 1862" in Arquivo do Automóvel Club, "Documentos de valor histórico," vol. 1.

Sousa, J. B. de M. e. *Estudantes do meu tempo*. Rio de Janeiro: Colégio Pedro II, 1958.

Sousa, P. I. de. "Inglês de Sousa" in F. de A. Barbosa, *Retratos de família*.

Souto, L. R. V. *O melhoramento da cidade do Rio de Janeiro*. Rio de Janeiro: Teixeira, 1875–6.

Souza, F. B. S. de. "Notas de um viajante brazileiro" in G. Fogliani, *Projecto de melhoramentos na cidade do Rio de Janeiro*.

Taunay, A. de E. *No Rio de Janeiro de Dom Pedro II*. Rio de Janeiro: Agir, 1947.

Taunay, A. M. A. d'E. T., visconde de, [pseud. Heitor Malheiros]. *O Encilhamento*, 2 vols. Rio de Janeiro: Domingos de Magalhães, Moderna, 1894.

Memórias do visconde de Taunay. São Paulo: Progresso, 1948.

Tefé, N. de. "Sou francamente pelo sorriso em matéria de caricatura" in F. de A. Barbosa, *Testamento de Mário de Andrade e outras reportagens*.

Vandam, A. D. *An Englishman in Paris*. New York: Appleton, 1898.

Vasconcellos, Barão de, and Vasconcellos, Barão S. de. *Archivo nobiliarchico brasileiro*. Lausanne: La Concorde, 1918.

Venancio Filho, F. *Euclydes da Cunha e seus amigos*. São Paulo: Nacional, 1938.

Veríssimo [Dias de Mattos], J. "A Academia Brasileira" in J. Veríssimo [Dias de Matos], *Estudos de literatura brasileira*, vol.6.

"A imprensa" in Associação do Quarto Centenario do Descobrimento do Brasil, *Livro do centenario*, vol.1.

"Machado de Assis" in J. Veríssimo [Dias de Matos], *Estudos de literatura brasileira*, vol.6.

"Resposta do Sr. José Veríssimo" in "Discursos proferidos na Academia Brazileira de Letras," *RABL*, 1 (1910).

Estudos de literatura brasileira, 6 vols. Belo Horizonte: Itatiaia, 1977.

Historia da literatura brasileira. Rio de Janeiro: Francisco Alves, 1929.

Vianna, J. "A reacção contra a influencia intellectual francesa," *Kósmos*, 5, no. 12 (Dec. 1908).

Vidal, L. O. C. "Osvaldo Cruz" in F. de A. Barbosa, *Retratos de família*.

Wigmore, J. W. (ed.) *Science and Learning in France*. n.p., 1917.

Wilson, H. *The Memoirs of Harriette Wilson Written by Herself*, 2 vols. London: Navarre, 1924.

Wright, M. R. *The New Brazil*. Philadelphia; Barrie, 1901.

Secondary Sources

Abbot, B. *The World of Atget*. New York: Berkley, 1977.

Adamo, S. C., "The broken promise," PhD diss., New Mexico, 1983.

Adburgham, A. *Shops and Shopping*. London: Allen & Unwin, 1964.

Alden, D. (ed.) *The Colonial Roots of Modern Brazil*. Berkeley: California, 1973.

Anderson, R. D. *Education in France*. Oxford: Clarendon, 1975.

Andrade, O. de S. *História e interpretação de "Os sertões"*. São Paulo: Edart, 1966.

Arquivo do Automóvel Club do Brasil, "Directorias do Club dos Diários" (MS). Rio de Janeiro: 1962.
"Directorias do Casino Fluminense" (MS). Rio de Janeiro: 1962.
Athayde, R. A. de. *Pereira Passos*. Rio de Janeiro: A Noite, n.d.
Azevedo, F. de, *Brazilian Culture*. New York: Macmillan, 1950.
Bairati, E. *et al*. *La Belle Epoque*. New York: Morrow, 1978.
Balmori, D. "A course in Latin American family history," *The History Teacher*, 14, no.3 (May 1981).
Barbosa, F. de A. "Prefácio" in [A. H. de] L. Barreto, *Isaías Caminha*.
"A Presidência Campos Sales," *LBR*, 5, no.1 (June 1968).
A vida de Lima Barreto (1881–1922). Rio de Janeiro: José Olympio/MEC/INL, 1975.
Barbosa, J. A. "Introdução" in J. Veríssimo [Dias de Matos], *Estudos de literatura brasileira*, vol. 1.
A tradição do impasse. São Paulo: Ática, 1974.
Bardy, C. "O século XIX" in F. N. Silva, *Rio de Janeiro em seus cuatrocentos anos*.
Barman, R. J. "Business and government in Imperial Brazil," *JLAS*, 13, no.2 (1982).
and Barman, J. "The role of the law graduate in the political elite of Imperial Brazil," *JISWA*, 18, no.4 (November 1976).
Barreiros, E. C. *Atlas da evolução urbana da cidade do Rio de Janeiro*. Rio de Janeiro: IHGB, 1965.
Beccar Varela, A. *Torcuato de Alvear*. Buenos Aires: Kraft, 1926.
Behar, E. *Vultos do Brasil*. São Paulo: Exposição do Livro, 1967.
Bell, Q. *On Human Finery*. New York: Schocken, 1976.
Bello, J. M. [de A.] *A History of Modern Brazil* Stanford: 1966.
Intelligencia do Brasil. São Paulo: Nacional, 1935.
Benchimol, J. L. "Pereira Passos – um Haussmann tropical," MS diss., UFRJ 1982.
Benevelo, L. *The Origins of Modern Town Planning*. Cambridge, Mass.: 1976.
Benjamin, W. *Charles Baudelaire*. London: NLB, 1973.
Illuminations. New York: Schocken, 1969.
Berger, P. *O Rio de Janeiro de ontem no cartão postal*. Rio de Janeiro: Rio de JaneiroArte, 1983.
Bergstresser, R. B. "The movement for the abolition of slavery in Rio de Janeiro, Brazil, 1880–1889," PhD diss., Stanford, 1973.
Bethell, L. *The Abolition of the Brazilian Slave Trade*. Cambridge: 1970.
Bittencourt, G. M. *A missão artística francesa de 1816*. Petrópolis: Ferreira da Cunha, 1967.
Boehrer, G. C. A. "The Brazilian Republican Revolution," *LBR*, 3, no.2 (December 1966).
Da Monarachia à República. Rio de Janeiro: MEC, 1954.
Borges, Dain E. "The family in Bahia, Brazil, 1870–1945" PhD diss., Stanford, 1986.
Bosi, A *História concisa da literatura brasileira*. São Paulo: Cultrix, 1970.
O pré-modernismo. São Paulo: Cultrix, n.d.
Boxer, C. R. *The Golden Age of Brazil*. Berkeley: California, 1969.
The Portuguese Seaborne Empire. New York: Knopf, 1969.
Brandão, P. J. P. "Dois bacharéis do Pedro II" in Colégio Pedro II, *Anuário do Colégio Pedro II*.
British Chamber of Commerce of São Paulo and Southern Brazil. *Personalidades no Brasil*. São Paulo: British Chamber of Commerce of São Paulo and Southern Brazil, 1932.

Broca, B. "Coelho Neto, Romancista" in B. Broca, *Ensaios de mão canhestra*.
"A literatura na biblioteca de Rui Barbosa" in Fundação Casa de Rui Barbosa, *Rui*.
Ensaios da mão canhestra. São Paulo: Polis, 1981.
Machado de Assis e a política. São Paulo: Polis, 1983.
Românticos, pré-românticos, ultra-românticos. São Paulo: Polis, 1979.
A vida literária no Brasil – 1900. Rio de Janeiro: José Olympio, 1975.
Burns, E. B. "The intellectuals as agents of change and the independence of Brazil, 1724–1822" in A. J. R. Russell-Wood (ed.), *From Colony to Nation*.
"The role of Azeredo Coutinho in the Enlightenment of Brazil," *HAHR*, 44, no.2 (May 1964).
Caffrey, K. *The 1900 Lady*. London: Cremonesi, 1976.
Calmon, P. *Historia social do Brasil*, 2 vols. São Paulo: Nacional, 1935.
O marquez de Abrantes. Rio de Janeiro: Guanabara, 1933.
Campos, C. L. "Symbolism and Mallarmé" in J. Cruickshank, *French Literatùre and its Background*, vol.5.
Cano, W. *Raízes da concentração industrial em São Paulo*. São Paulo: DIFEL, 1977.
Carassus, E. *Le snobisme et les lettres françaises*. Paris: Armand Colin, 1966.
Cardim, E. *Justiniano José da Rocha*. São Paulo: Nacional, 1964.
Cardoso, V. L. *À margem da história do Brasil*. São Paulo: Nacional, 1933.
Carlier, F. *Les deux prostitutions*. Paris: Dentu, 1889.
Carpeaux, O. M. *Pequena bibliografia crítica da literatura brasileira*. Rio de Janeiro: Artes e Letras, 1964.
Carvalho, J. M. de. "A composição social dos partidos políticos imperiais," *Cadernos do Departmento de Ciência Política*. Belo Horizonte: UFMG, no.2 (December 1974).
"As forças armadas na Primeira República" in B. Fausto (ed.), *História geral da civilização brasileira*, tomo 3, vol.2.
"Elite and state building in Imperial Brazil" (PhD diss., Stanford, 1974).
"Political elites and state building," *Comparative Studies in Society and History*, 24, no.3 (July 1982)
"A Revolta Contra Vacina." Preliminary draft. Semanário Rio Republicano, 4 October 1984.
A construção da ordem. Rio de Janeiro: Campus, 1980.
Cava, R. della, "Brazilian messianism and national institutions," *HAHR*, 48, no.3 (August 1968).
Chadbourne, R. M. *Ernest Renan as an Essayist*. Ithaca: Cornell, 1957.
Chafee, R. "The teaching of architecture at the Ecole des Beaux-Arts" in A. Drexler (ed.), *The Architecture of the Ecole des Beaux-Arts*.
Chapman J. M. and Chapman, B. *The Life and Times of Baron Haussmann*. London: 1957.
Charlton, D. G. "Positivism and its aftermath" in J. Cruickshank (ed.), *French Literature and its Background*, vol.5.
Positivist Thought in France During the Second Empire. Oxford: 1959.
Chevalier, H. M. *The Ironic Temper*. New York: Oxford, 1932.
Coaracy, V. *Memórias da cidade do Rio de Janeiro*. Rio de Janeiro: José Olympio, 1965.
Cobban, A. *A History of Modern France*, 3 vols. Baltimore: Penguin, 1965.
Colégio Pedro II. "Indice dos processos de matriculas de 1838 a 1930," 3 vols. (MS, Biblioteca do Colégio Pedro II in São Cristóvão). Rio de Janeiro: *c*. 1930.
Coleman, A., *Eça de Queirós and European Realism*. (New York: 1980).
Collegio Pedro II. Ministério da Justiça e Negócios Interiores (O. A. Pereira, comp.),

Almanack do pessoal docente e administrativo até 30 de Junho de 1924, no. 2. Rio de Janeiro: Revista dos Tribunaes, 1925.

Colson, F. "On expectations – perspectives on the crisis of 1889 in Brazil," *JLAS*, 13, no.2 (April 1982).

Conciencia y autenticidad histórica, Mexico: UNAM, 1968.

Connely, W. *The Reign of Beau Brummell*. London: Cassell, 1940.

Conrad, R. E. "Suggestions for further reading" in J. [A.B.] Nabuco [de Araújo], *Abolitionism*.

Children of God's Fire. Princeton: 1983.

The Destruction of Brazilian Slavery 1850–1888. Berkeley: California, 1972.

Slavery. Boston: G. K. Hall, 1977.

Corbin, A. *Les filles de noce*. Paris: Aubier Montaigne, 1978.

Costa, E. V. da, "José Bonifácio" in C. G. Mota, *1822*.

"The political emancipation of Brazil" in A. J. R. Russell-Wood, *From Colony to Nation*.

"A proclamação da República," *Anais do Museu Paulista*, no. 20 (1965).

"Sobre as origens da República," *Anais do Museu Paulista*, no. 19 (1964).

Da senzala à colônia. São Paulo: DIFEL, 1966.

Costa, J. C. *A History of Ideas in Brazil*. Berkeley: California, 1964.

Costa, N. do R. "Estado e políticas de saúde pública (1889–1930)," MA thesis, IUPRJ, 1983.

Coutinho, A. "Estudo crítico: Machado de Assis na Literatura Brasileira" in [J.M.] M. de Assis, *Obra completa*, vol. 1.

An Introduction to Literature in Brazil. New York: Columbia, 1969.

Cruickshank, J. (ed.) *French Literature and Its Background*, 6 vols. Oxford: 1969.

Cruls, G. *Aparência do Rio de Janeiro*, 2 vols. Rio de Janeiro: José Olympio, 1965.

Dantas, [F. C. de], S. T. *Dois momentos de Rui Barbosa*. Rio de Janeiro: Casa de Rui Barbosa, 1951.

Davidoff, L. *The Best Circles*. Totowa, New Jersey: Rowman and Littlefield, 1973.

Davis, D. *Fairs, Shops and Supermarkets*. Toronto: 1966.

Dean, W., *Rio Claro*. Stanford: 1976.

Delson, R. "Land and urban planning," LBR, 16, no. 2 (Winter 1979).

Dennis, R. D. "Brazilian literary nationalism among the critics, 1870–1900," PhD diss., Wisconsin, 1972.

Dias, D. de O. *O solar da marquesa de Santos*. Rio de Janeiro: C. Ribeiro, 1972.

Digeon, C. *La crise allemande de la pensée française (1870–1914)*. Paris: Presses Univ. de France, 1959.

Dimas, A. *Tempos eufóricos*. São Paulo: Ática, 1983.

Drexler, A. (ed.) *The Architecture of the Ecole des Beaux-Arts*. New York: MOMA, 1977.

Dunlop, I. *Degas*. New York: Harper & Row, 1979.

Elkington, M. E. *Les rélations de société entre l'Angleterre et la France sous la Réstauration*. Paris: Champion, 1929.

Enciclopédia brasileira mérito.

Enciclopédia delta universal.

Epple, J. A. "Aluisio Azevedo y el Naturalismo en Brasil," *Revista de Crítica Literaria Latinoamericana* (Lima), 6, no. 11 (1980).

Faoro, R. *Os donos do poder*. São Paulo: 1975.

Machado de Assis. São Paulo: Nacional, 1976.

Faria, G. L. de. "A recepção e a influência do Oscar Wilde na 'belle époque' literária brasileira," PhD diss., USP, 1979.
Fausto, B. "Expansão do café e política cafeeira" in B. Fausto (ed.), *História geral da civilização brasileira*, tomo 3, vol. 1.
(ed.) *História geral da civilização brasileira*, tomo 3, 2 vols. São Paulo: DIFEL, 1977.
Ferrez, G. "A Avenida Central e Seu Álbum" in M. Ferrez, *O álbum da Avenida Central*.
"A fotografia no Brasil" (separata da *Revista do Patrimônio Histórico e Artístico Nacional*, no. 10, 1953).
Aquarelas de Richard Bate. Rio de Janeiro: Galeria Brasiliana, 1965.
Fontoura, J. N. da, "Serzedello Correa: uma figura da República" in I. S. Correa, *Uma figura da República*.
Franco, A. A. de M. *Rodrigues Alves*, 2 vols. Rio de Janeiro: José Olympio, 1973.
Franco, J. *An Introduction to Spanish-American Literature*. Cambridge: 1969.
Freyre, G. *Um engenheiro francês no Brasil*, 2 vols. Rio de Janeiro: José Olympio, 1960.
Ingleses no Brasil. Rio de Janeiro: José Olympio, 1948.
The Mansions and the Shanties. New York: Knopf, 1963.
The Masters and the Slaves. New York: Knopf, 1971.
Order and Progress. New York: Knopf, 1970.
Perfil de Euclides e outros perfis. Rio de Janeiro: José Olympio, 1944.
Friedell, E. *A Cultural History of the Modern Age*, 3 vols. New York: Knopf, 1932.
Fundação Casa de Rui Barbosa. *Rui*. Rio de Janeiro: FCRB/MEC, 1980.
Furtado, C. *Economic Development of Latin America*. Cambridge: 1976.
The Economic Growth of Brazil. Berkeley: California, 1968.
Gabaglia [E. de B.] R. "O Collegio Pedro II" in Collegio Pedro II, *Annuario do Collegio Pedro II . . . 1° anno*.
Galvão, W. N. *No calor da hora*. São Paulo: Atica, 1977.
Gernsheim, A. *Fashion and Reality*. London: Faber & Faber, 1963.
Gerson, B. *História das ruas do Rio*. Rio de Janeiro: Brasiliana, 1964.
Godeschot, J. "Independência do Brasil e a Revolução do Occidente" in C. G. Mota (ed.), *1822*.
Gondim, E. R. *Vida e obra de Paula Brito*. Rio de Janeiro: Brasiliana, 1965.
Graham, R. "Brazilian slavery reexamined," *Journal of Social History*, 3, no. 4 (Summer 1970).
"Causes for the abolition of Negro slavery in Brazil," *HAHR*, 46, no. 2 (May 1966).
"Landowners and the overthrow of the Empire," *LBR*, (Winter 1970).
Britain and the Onset of Modernization in Brazil 1850–1914. Cambridge: 1972.
Graham, S. L. "The Vintem riot and political culture," *HAHR*, 60, no. 3 (August 1980).
Graña, C. *Bohemian Versus Bourgeois*. New York: Basic, 1964.
Guilleminault, G. (ed.) *La Belle Epoque*. Paris: Denoël, 1957.
Guimarães, A. *Diccionário bio-bibliographico brasileiro de diplomacia, politica externa e direito internacional*. Rio de Janeiro: Pongetti, 1937.
Haberly, D. T. *Three Sad Races*. Cambridge; 1983.
Hahner, J. E. "Feminism, women's rights, and the suffrage movement in Brazil, 1850–1932," *LAHR*, 15, no. 1 (1980).
"Jacobinos versus galegos," *JISWA*, 18, no. 2 (May 1976).
Civilian–Military Relations in Brazil, Columbia, SC: South Carolina, 1969.
Hall, M. M. "Reformadores de classe média no Império brasileiro" in *Revista de História*, 53, no. 103 (1976).

Halperín Donghi, T. *Historia contemporánea de América Latina*. Madrid: Alianza, 1972.
Hargreaves, A. G. *The Colonial Experience in French Fiction*. London: Macmillan, 1981.
Haring, C. H. *Empire in Brazil*. New York: Norton, 1968.
Hauser, A. *The Social History of Art*, 4 vols. New York: Vintage, n.d.
Hautecoeur, L. *Histoire de l'architecture classique en France*, vol. 6, Paris: Picard, 1955.
Hayes, C. J. H. *A Generation of Materialism*. New York: Harper, 1963.
Heuriot, G. *Les beaux meubles des collections privées*. Paris: Massin, n.d.
Hobsbawm, E. J. *The Age of Revolution*. New York: NAL, 1962.
Industry and Empire. Baltimore: Penguin, 1969.
Hollander, A. *Seeing Through Clothes*. New York: Viking, 1978.
Hughes, H. S. *Consciousness and Society*. New York: Vintage, 1961.
Hutt, M. G. and Campos, C. "Romanticism and history" in J. Cruickshank (ed.). *French Literature and its Background*, vol.4.
Hyams, E. *A History of Gardens and Gardening*. New York: Praeger, 1971.
Jefferson, C. *Anatole France*. New Brunswick, New Jersey: Rutgers, 1965.
Jenkins, C. "Realism and reality in the novel" in J. Cruickshank (ed.), *French Literature and its Background*, vol.5.
John, S. B. and Kedward, H. R. "Literature and ideology" in J. Cruickshank (ed.), *French Literature and its Background*, vol.5.
Julian, P. "Can-can and flappers" in E. Bairati *et al.*, *La Belle Epoque*.
Korn, F. *et al. Buenos Aires*. Buenos Aires: Sudamérica, 1974.
Kroeber, A. L. "On the principle of order in civilization as exemplified by change in fashion," *American Anthropologist*, N.S., 21 (1919).
Kurtz, H. *The Empress Eugénie*. Boston: Houghton-Mifflin, 1964.
Kuznesof, E. A. "The role of merchants in the economic development of São Paulo, 1765–1850," HAHR, 60, no. 4 (November 1980).
Lagarde, A. and Michard, L. *Les évolutions du XIXe siècle*. Paris: Bordas et Laffond, 1971.
Les métamorphoses du XXe siècle. Paris: Bordas et Laffond, 1971.
Latour, A. *Kings of Fashion*. New York: Coward McCann, 1958.
Laver, J. *The Concise History of Costume and Fashion*. New York: Abrams, 1969.
Taste and Fashion. London: Harrap, 1948.
Lavrin, A. "Women in Latin American history," *The History Teacher*, 14, no. 3 (May 1981).
(ed.) *Latin American Women*. Westport, Connecticut: Greenwood, 1978.
Leão, A. C. *et al. À margem da história da República*. Rio de Janeiro: Annuario do Brasil, 1924.
Lefol, G. (ed.) *Hôtels particuliers*. Paris: Massin, n.d.
Leite, M. L. M., Mott, M. L. de B., and Appenzeller, B. K. *A mulher no Rio de Janeiro no século XIX*. São Paulo: Chagas, 1982.
Lemos, C., Leite, J. R. T. and Gismonti, P. M. *The Art of Brazil*. New York: Harper and Row, 1983.
Levi, D. E. "The Prados of São Paulo," PhD diss., Yale, 1974.
A família Prado. São Paulo: Cultura 70, 1977.
Levine, R. M. *Pernambuco in the Brazilian Federation 1889–1937*. Stanford: 1978.
Lewin, L. "Politics and *parentela* in Paraíba," PhD diss., Columbia, 1975.
"Some historical implications of kinship organization for family-based politics in the Brazilian Northeast," *Comparative Studies in Society and History*, 21, no. 2 (April 1979).

Lima Sobrinho, B. *A língua portuguesa e a unidade do Brasil*. Rio de Janeiro: José Olympio, 1958.
Lima, H. F. *História do pensamento ecônomico no Brasil*. São Paulo: Nacional, 1978.
Lins, I. *História do positivismo no Brasil*. São Paulo: Nacional, 1967.
Lobo, E. M. L. *História do Rio de Janeiro*, 2 vols. Rio de Janeiro: IBMC, 1978.
Love, J. L. *Rio Grande do Sul and Brazilian Regionalism 1882–1930*. Stanford: 1971.
São Paulo in the Brazilian Federation, 1889–1937. Stanford: 1978.
and Barickman, B. J. "Rulers and owners," HAHR, 66, no. 4 (November 1986).
Lukács, G. *Studies in European Realism*. New York: Grosset and Dunlap, 1964.
Luz, N. V. *A luta pela industrialização do Brasil*. São Paulo: Alfa-Omega, 1975.
López-Morillas, J. *The Krausist Movement and Ideological Change in Spain, 1854–1874*. Cambridge: 1981.
Magalhães Júnior, R. *Rui, o homem e o mito*. Rio de Janeiro: Civilização Brasileira, 1965.
Vida e obra de Machado de Assis, 4 vols. Rio de Janeiro: Civilização Brasileira, 1981.
A vida vertiginosa de João do Rio. Rio de Janeiro: Civilizaação Brasileira, 1978.
Manchester, A. K. *British Preëminence in Brazil*. New York: Octagon, 1964.
Manson, A. "Quand les trois grandes régnaient sur Paris" in G. Guilleminault (ed.), *La Belle Epoque*.
Marchant, A. *Viscount Mauá and the Empire of Brazil*. Berkeley: California, 1965.
Marianno Filho, J. *Estudos de arte brasileiro*. Rio de Janeiro: n.p., 1942?.
Marrey, B. *Les grands magasins*. Paris: Picard, 1979.
Martin, G. "The literature, music and art of Latin America, 1870–1930" in L. Bethell (ed.), *Cambridge History of Latin America*, vol. 4.
Martínez Estrada, E. *X-Ray of the Pampa*. Austin: Texas, 1971.
Martins, L. D. *Presença de Paulo de Frontin*. Rio de Janeiro: Freitas Bastos, 1966.
Martins, L. "Introdução" in J. do Rio, *João do Rio*.
"O patriarcha e o bacharel," *Revista do Arquivo Municipal* São Paulo, no. 83 (May–June 1942).
Martins, W. *História da inteligência brasileira*, 5 vols. São Paulo: Cultrix, 1977.
Marx, K. "The fetishism of commodities and the secret thereof" in K. Marx and F. Engels, *The Marx–Engels Reader*. New York: Norton, 1972.
Mattoon, Jr., R. H. "The Companhia Paulista de Estradas de Ferro, 1868–1900," PhD diss., Yale, 1971.
Maxwell, K. R. *Conflicts and Conspiracies*. Cambridge: 1973.
Mendonça, C. S. de. *Salvador de Mendonça*. Rio de Janeiro: MEC, 1960.
Sílvio Romero. São Paulo: Nacional, 1938.
Menezes, R. de. *Dicionário literário brasileiro*, 5 vols. São Paulo: Saraiva, 1969.
Metcalf, A. C. "Families of planters, peasants, and slaves." PhD dissertation, Texas, 1982.
"Fathers and sons," HAHR, 66, no. 3 (August 1986)
Mignot, C. *Architecture of the 19th Century in Europe*. New York: Rizzoli, 1984.
Miguel-Pereira, L. *Machado de Assis*. São Paulo: Nacional, 1939.
Miller, M. B. *The Bon Marché*. Princeton: 1981.
Moacyr, P. *A instrução e o Império*, 3 vols. São Paulo: Nacional, 1936–8.
Moers, E. *The Dandy*. New York: Viking, 1960.
Montello, J. *O presidente Machado de Assis*. São Paulo: Martins, 1961.
Moody, J. N. *French Education Since Napoleon*. Syracuse: 1978.
Morse, R. M. *From Community to Metropolis*. Gainesville: Florida, 1958.

with Conniff, M. L. and Wibel, J. *The Urban Development of Latin America*. Stanford, Center for Latin American Studies: 1971.
Mota, C. G. (ed.) *1822*. São Paulo: Perspectiva, 1972.
Nordeste 1817. São Paulo: Perspectiva 1972.
"O processo de Independência no Nordeste" in C. G. Mota (comp.), *1822*.
Mulher brasileira. São Paulo: Chagas, 1979.
Nabuco, C. Notes to "Núpcias" in J. T. Nabuco, "Biography of the first Nabuco in Brazil" (MS). Rio de Janeiro: 1980, photocopy in author's possession.
A vida de Joaquim Nabuco. São Paulo?: Nacional, 1928.
Nabuco, J. T. "Biography of the first Nabuco in Brazil" (MS) Rio de Janeiro: *c.* 1980.
Nachman, R. G. "Positivism, modernization, and the middle class in Brazil" *HAHR* 57, no. 1 (February 1977).
Needell, J. D. "Making the Carioca *Belle Epoque* concrete," *Journal of Urban History*, 10, no. 4 (August 1984).
"The *Revolta Contra Vacina* of 1904," *HAHR*, 67, no. 2 (May 1987).
"Rio de Janeiro at the turn of the century," *JISWA*, 25, no. 1 (February 1983).
Neto, A. L. M. *Estrutura social da república das letras*. São Paulo: Grijalbo/USP, 1973.
Neto, N. de O. "A evolução dos transportes" in F. N. Silva, *Rio de Janeiro em seus cuatrocentos anos*.
Netto, P. C., "Imagem de uma Vida" in [H.M.] C. Netto, *Obra selecta*, vol.1.
Nicholas, B. L. "Poetry and pure art" in J. Cruickshank (ed.), *French Literature and its Background*, vol.5.
Nogueira, E. "Alguns aspectos da influência francesa em São Paulo na segunda metade do século XIX," *Revista de História*, 7, no. 16 (October–December 1953).
Nogueira, O. and Firmo, J. S. *Parlamentares do Império*. Brasília: Senado Federal, 1973.
Norris, H. and Curtis, O. *Costume and Fashion*, vol.6. London: Dent, 1933.
Nunes, M. L. *Lima Barreto*. Boston: G. K. Hall, 1979.
Orico, O. *O tigre da Abolição*. Rio de Janeiro: Civilização Brasileira, 1977.
Painter, G. *Marcel Proust*, 2 vols. (New York: Vintage, 1978.
Pevsner, N. *Academies of Art Past and Present*. New York: da Capo, 1973.
Phelan, J. L. "Pan-latinism, French intervention in Mexico (1861–1867) and the genesis of the idea of Latin America" in *Conciencia y autenticidad histórica*.
Pierrot, J. *The Decadent Imagination, 1880–1900*. Chicago: 1981.
Pinho, [J], W. [de A.] *Salões e damas do Segundo Reinado*. São Paulo: Martins, 1970.
Pinkney, D. H. *Napoleon III and the Rebuilding of Paris*. Princeton: 1958.
Poggioli, R. *The Theory of the Avant Garde*. Cambridge, Mass.: Belknap, 1968.
Pontes, E. *A vida exuberante de Olavo Bilac*, 2 vols. Rio de Janeiro: José Olympio, 1944.
Pouilliart, R. *Le romantisme*. Paris: Arthaud, 1968.
Prado Júnior, C. *The Colonial Background of Modern Brazil*. Berkeley: California, 1967.
História econômica do Brasil. São Paulo: Brasiliense, 1967.
Prévost, J. C. *Le dandysme en France*. Paris: Minard, 1957.
Rabello, S. *Euclides da Cunha*. Rio de Janeiro: Civilização Brasileira, 1966.
Ramos, A. "The Negro in Brazil" in T. L. Smith and A. Marchant (eds.), *Brazil*.
Reis Filho, N. G., *Quadro da arquitetura no Brasil*. São Paulo: Perspectiva, 1970.
Reis, O. "As administrações municipais e o desenvolvimento urbano" in F. N. Silva, *Rio de Janeiro em seus cuatrocentos anos*.
Renault, D. *O Rio antigo nos anúncios de jornais*. Rio de Janeiro: José Olympio, 1969.
Rio de Janeiro. Rio de Janeiro: Civilização Brasileira, 1978.

Richardson, J. *The Courtesans*. Cleveland: World, 1967.
La Vie Parisienne. New York: Viking, 1971.
Ridings, Jr., E. W. "Business, nationality and dependency in late nineteenth-century Brazil," JLAS, 14, no. 1 (May 1982).
"Class sector unity in an export economy," HAHR, 58, no. 3 (1978).
"Interest groups and development," JLAS, 9 (1978).
Rios Filho, A. M. de los "O Rio de Janeiro da Primeira Republica (1889–1930)," RIHGB, 272 (1966).
Adolfo Morales de los Rios. Rio de Janeiro: Borsoi, 1959.
Dois notáveis engenheiros. Rio de Janeiro: A Noite, 1951.
Grandjean de Montigny e a evolução da arte brasileira. Rio de Janeiro: A Noite, 1941?.
O Rio de Janeiro imperial. Rio de Janeiro: A Noite, 1946.
Robinson, J. (Notes to) "Julian Bream plays Villa-Lobos," LC 3231. New York: RCA, 1971.
Rocha, O. P. "A era das demolições," MA thesis, UFF, 1983.
Rosemburg, F. *et al*. "Suplemento bibliográfico . . . Levantamento preliminar sobre a situação da mulher brasileira" in *Cadernos de Pesquisa* (March 1976). São Paulo: Chagas, 1976.
Roxo, E.E. de A. and Ferreira, M. "O saneamento do meio físico" in F. N. Silva (ed.), *Rio de Janeiro em seus cuatrocentos anos*.
Russell-Wood, A. J. R. (ed.) *From Colony to Nation*. Baltimore: Johns Hopkins, 1975.
Saint-Saveur, H. *La décoration intérieure en France*. Paris: Massin, n.d.
Santos, J. M. dos. *A política geral do Brasil*. São Paulo: J. Magalhães, 1930.
Os republicanos paulistas e a abolição. Rio de Janeiro: Martins, 1942.
Santos, J. R. dos, *et al*. *Abolição*. São Paulo: Brasiliense, 1964.
Santos, P. F. "Arquitetura e urbanismo na Avenida Central" in M. Ferrez, *O álbum da Avenida Central*.
Saraiva, A. J. and Lopes, O. *História da literatura portuguesa*. Portos: n.d.
Saunders, E. *The Age of Worth*. London: Longmans, Green, 1954.
Scart, B. (ed.) *L'atelier Nadar et la mode*. Paris: Musées de France?, n.d.
Schorske, C. E. *Fin-de-Siècle Vienna*. New York: Vintage, 1981.
Schwartz, S. B. "Free labor in a slave economy" in D. Alden (ed.), *The Colonial Roots of Modern Brazil*. Berkeley: California, 1973.
Schwarz, R. *Ao vencedor as batatas*. São Paulo: Duas Cidades, 1977.
Scobie, J. R. *Buenos Aires*. New York: Oxford, 1974.
Secco, C. L. T. *Morte e prazer em João do Rio*. Rio de Janeiro: Francisco Alves, 1978.
Sevcenko, N. *Literatura como missão*. Rio de Janeiro: Brasiliense, 1983.
Shattuck, R. *The Banquet Years*. New York: Vintage, 1968.
Silva, F. N. (ed.) *Rio de Janeiro em seus cuatrocentos anos*. Rio de Janeiro: Distribuidora Record 65, 1965.
Silva, I. F. da. *Diccionario bibliographico portuguez*, 22 vols. Lisbon: Nacional, 1923.
Silva, M. B. N. da. *Cultura e sociedade no Rio de Janeiro*. São Paulo: Nacional, 1978.
Silva, R. M. de L. e. "Iluminação e gás" in F. N. Silva, *Rio de Janeiro em seus cuatrocentos anos*.
Skidmore, T. E. "The historiography of Brazil, 1889–1964: Part 1," *HAHR* 55, no. 4 (November 1975).
Black into White. New York: Oxford, 1974.
Smith, T. L. and Marchant, A. (eds.) *Brazil*. New York: Dryden, 1950.

Sodré, N. W. *História da imprensa no Brasil*. Rio de Janeiro: Civilização Brasileira, 1966.
Sousa, A. C. de M. e. "The Brazilian family" in T. L. Smith and A. Marchant, *Brazil*.
"O método crítico de Sílvo Romero" in *Teoria literária e literatura comparada* (São Paulo), 26, no. 1 (1963).
Formação da literatura brasileira, 2 vols. São Paulo: Martins, 1964.
Literatura e sociedade. São Paulo: Nacional, 1976.
Vários escritos. São Paulo: Duas Cidades, 1977.
Souza, H. A. de. "O Automóvel Club do Brasil e sua história" in "Suplemento" to *Revista Automóvel Club*, no. 10 (September 1972).
Souza, J. G. de. *O teatro no Brasil*, vol. 1. Rio de Janeiro: MEC, 1960.
Stein, S. J. "The historiography of Brazil 1808–1889", *HAHR*, 40, no. 2 (May 1960).
Vassouras. New York: Atheneum, 1970.
and Stein, B. H. *The Colonial Heritage of Latin America*. New York: Oxford, 1970.
Stepan, N. *The Beginnings of Brazilian Science*. New York: Science History, 1981.
Strowski, F. "O livro francês na biblioteca de Rui Barbosa" in Fundação Casa de Rui Barbosa, *Rui*.
Sweigart, J. E. "Financing and marketing Brazilian export agriculture," PhD diss., Texas, 1980.
Taunay, A. de E. *A Missão Artística de 1816*. Rio de Janeiro: MEC, 1956.
Tavares, A. L. de L. "A engenharia brasileira no segundo reinado," RIHGB, 338 (January-March 1983).
Thorlby, A. K. "The concept of Romanticism" in J. Cruickshank (ed.), *French Literature and its Background*, vol. 4.
Tinhorão, J. R. *Pequena história da música popular*. Petrópolis: Vozes, 1974.
Topik, S. "State interventionism in a liberal regime," *HAHR*, 60, no. 4 (November 1980).
Toplin, R. B. "From slavery to fettered freedom," *LBR*, 7, no. 1 (1970).
The Abolition of Slavery in Brazil. New York: Atheneum, 1972.
Trésor de la langue française. Paris: CNRS, 1977.
Trottenberg, A. (ed.) *A Vision of Paris*. New York: Macmillan, 1963.
Tuchman, B. *The Proud Tower*. New York: Bantam, 1966.
Valladão, A. *Vultos nacionais*. Rio de Janeiro: José Olympio, 1955.
Vargos Llosa, M. *La guerra del fin del mundo*. Madrid: Seix Barral, 1981.
Veblen, T. "The theory of the leisure class" in T. Veblen, *The Portable Veblen*. New York: Viking, 1948.
Viana Filho, L. *A vida do barão do Rio Branco*, Rio de Janeiro: José Olympio, 1959.
A vida de Joaquim Nabuco. São Paulo: Nacional, 1952.
A vida de Rui Barbosa. São Paulo: Nacional, 1943.
Vianna, H. *Vultos do Império*. São Paulo: Nacional, 1968.
Vianna, [F. J.] O. *O occaso do Imperio*. São Paulo: Melhoramentos, 1925.
Walzer, P.-O. *Le xxe siècle*. Paris: Arthaud, 1975.
Waugh, N. *The Cut of Men's Clothes*. London: Faber & Faber, 1964.
Wilson, E. *Axel's Castle*. New York: Charles Scribner's Sons, 1934.
Wirth, John D. *Minas Gerais in the Brazilian Federation 1880–1937*. Stanford: 1977.
Wright, G. *France in Modern Times*. New York: Norton, 1981.
Zanten, D. Van. "Architectural composition at the Ecole des Beaux-Arts from Charles

Percier to Charles Garnier" in A. Drexler, *The Architecture of the Ecole des Beaux-Arts*.

Zea, L. *The Latin American Mind*. Norman: Oklahoma, 1963.

Positivism in Mexico. Austin: Texas, 1974.

Zeldin, T. *France*. Oxford: 1977.

Index

People are listed by their last family name or by the family name by which they are generally known; brackets indicate names generally ignored by contemporaries. People given titles of nobility are listed by the name in the title; if the title employs more than one family name, the person is listed by the last of these names.